BUILD A
CO-PARENTING
TEAM

AFTER DIVORCE OR REMARRIAGE

PETER K. GERLACH, MSW

*VOLUME 6 IN THE
STEPFAMILY INFORMATION SERIES*

To order additional copies of this book, contact:
Xlibris Corporation
1-888-795-4274
www.Xlibris.com
Orders@Xlibris.com
15193

CONTENTS

This book is dedicated to the hundreds of clients
who shared their hearts and minds with me
and taught me about us all.

Acknowledgements

I'm grateful to *many* people for what you'll read here . . .
My parents, who gave their best despite profound inner wounds.

My former wife Liliana and stepdaughters Julie and Jennifer. They, and Susan Kerwin and her daughter Jessica, showed me the best and the worst of stepfamily life. Jeanne and Joe McLennan provide an inspiring example of a high-nurturance remarriage and stepfamily.

Frank McNair, who made it all possible despite his toxic heritage.

Devera Denker and Claudia Black, who turned the lights on for me.

Each of the dozens of lay and clinical authors, speakers, and teachers whose collective wisdom and insights have shown me the way since 1985. In particular, profound thanks to psychiatric pioneer Dr. Milton Erickson, and the colleagues and students who explored and applied his work. They taught the rest of us about the amazing potentials and dynamics of our several minds.

The knowledge and wisdom of psychologist-authors Hal and Sidra Stone; and Richard Schwartz, Ph.D. and the group of clinical colleagues and clients with whom I studied the "Internal Family Systems Model" were pivotal in this work.

Annette Hulefeld, LCSW; who led our inner-family recovery group with skill and compassion for eight years. Equal loving thanks to Jane, Jeff, Ronnee, Danna and her infant son Sam, and the others.

Hundreds of students, callers, Internet forum members, therapy clients, and their subselves and spirits. Special thanks to mentors Elizabeth Bormann and Dr. Robert Klien, who saw the potential.

The "Remarriage Team" mates who strove to prepare hundreds of unaware couples for stepfamily life—Steve and Jeanette Bell, Ralph and Shirley Hutson, Lou and Bill Scanlon, Sally and John Radka, and other dedicated couples. My appreciation also to Don and Lorrie Gramer, who included this vital work in their impactful Family Life ministry.

Warm appreciation to my unexpected virtual publishing colleague Gloria Lintermans, for her verve, spirit, wisdom, and encouragement; and . . .

Over all, I humbly acknowledge the patient, loving guidance of the One who provided the darkness, the light, the path, the teachers, the mission, and increasingly—the peace beyond all understanding.

Part 1) Foundations

Introduction

1) First Things First

2) Basic Premises: What Do You Believe Now?

3) What Are Your Key Attitudes and Expectations?

4) Overview: Co-parent Team-building

Introduction

I once moderated an Internet discussion group on "Stepfamily Issues." A message to forum participants from a stepmother cryptically labeled her husband's former wife as "his PBFH ex." Veteran group members decoded that abbreviation as "psycho bitch from hell." See Chapter 3 for the toxic family impacts of attitudes like this.

Do you know any divorced parents who are solid co-parenting *teammates*? If you're a divorced parent (or may be), do you feel your (ex) partner is a caregiving colleague, or an opponent? If you're dating or committed to a divorced parent, do you respect their kids' other caregivers as _ persons and _ *effective* nurturers?

Divorce is a destructive social epidemic that now affects far more millions of Americans than AIDS, yet rates few headlines or corrective legislation. Recent Census data estimates that about half of American first-marriers legally divorce. I've never seen an estimate of how many millions of cohabiting bioparents and their kids are enduring *psychological* divorce. The Stepfamily Association of America estimates that 60% of U.S. stepfamilies re/divorce legally, but doesn't guess at the rate of *psychological* re/divorce. The "/" notes that it may be a stepparent's first marriage.

Around 1900, most re/marrying parents were widow/ers. Thanks to advances in health care and women's "emancipation," most U.S. stepfamilies now form after the divorce of one or both new mates. The relationship between typical divorced moms and dads—and any new partners—ranges from cooperative to "indifferent" to intensely hostile and conflictual. In other stepfamilies, dead bioparents can powerfully affect the lives of their survivors and successors emotionally, financially, and genetically for decades. Stepparents can feel they're competing with an untouchable ghost or saint.

As a divorced stepfather and veteran family-systems therapist, I've specialized in working with prospective and troubled stepfamily co-parents (stepparents and divorced bioparents) since 1981. Much of their trouble came from strife between ex mates and their kids' "acting out." Their stress was often compounded by upset new mates, wounded kids, confused kin, and uninformed counselors, clergy, and attorneys.

The human and social prices we all pay for the roots and effects of our American divorce epidemic are beyond meaningful estimation. Statistics can't portray the mosaic of pain, guilt, shame, anxiety, rage, and regret that *millions* of parents, kids, and relatives experience for decades before, during, and after legal divorce. Never-divorced or once-divorced adults can't *really* empathize with the millions of men and women who have redivorced. In 23 years' research, I've seen no meaningful investigation of their or their kids' lives. Our multiply-divorced millions are as unseen and pervasive as the invisible legions of homeless Americans. Both have common childhood roots.

This book is one of a series which aims to _ reduce rampant U.S. re/divorce, and _ break the unseen toxic bequest of psychological wounds that cause and result from it. The series proposes five common re/marital hazards, and 12 concrete ways re/marriers can avoid and/or master them (p. 428).

Stepfamily Courtship (xlibris.com, 2001) suggests how courting co-parents can use the first seven of these ways (projects) to make three *right* re/marital choices. **The Re/marriage Book** (xlibris.com) proposes specific ways re/wedded mates can offset their five hazards, and nourish themselves and their relationship. **This volume** suggests specific ways divorced-family and stepfamily co-parents can reduce seven common factors that block effective caregiving teamwork. The next volume will offer suggestions on optimizing stepparent-stepchild relationships.

This rest of this chapter hilights _ who can benefit from this book, _ what's in it and _ why it's unique, _ why this series exists, and what it's based on; and _ how you can best use this book to fill your needs.

Should You Read This Book?

This series and the related Web site [http://sfhelp.org] aims to help divorced and stepfamily co-parents provide a high-nurturance family (p. 440), and protect dependents from inherited psychological wounding. This book is for . . .

Troubled mates who aren't getting their primary-relationship needs met well enough; and . . .

Separated or divorced bioparents who _ "aren't getting along," and/or _ whose kids are troubled; and . . .

Widowed parents who may remarry; and . . .

Childless adults who may marry a single parent; and . . .

Re/married co-parents (bioparents and stepparents) seeking to strengthen their caregiving harmony and effectiveness, and protect their descendents. This book is also for . . .

Supporters of such people, including relatives, caring friends, clergy, clinicians, family-law and law-enforcement pros, case workers, mediators, and those who train, fund, supervise, and certify them.

If you're in one of these groups, this book and series offers you effective options toward building lasting, high-nurturance family relationships.

What's in This Book?

Building on five prior books, this modular reference volume focuses on co-parent **Project 10** of 12: building an effective nurturing team after divorce and/or re/marriage. *These books and the related Web pages aim to augment, not replace, other qualified professional counsel.*

Part 1) presents four foundation chapters: _ this introduction, _ the knowledge you need to use this book well, _ and key relationship _ premises and _ attitudes. **Part 2)** provides chapters on resolving seven widespread post-divorce co-parenting barriers. **Part 3)** Describes 11 common *surface* barriers experienced by typical divorced-family and stepfamily co-parents, and relates them to the true barriers and suggestions in Part 2. **Part 4)** offers 14 worksheets, examples, and summaries to help you use the suggestions in Parts 2 and 3 effectively. These include recommended readings and a thorough index.

There are scores of books about divorce, co-parenting, stepfamilies, and "better relationships" available. Major Web booksellers now offer at least five books on effective co-parenting. None are like this one.

What's Unique About This Book?

Six important factors. First, this is the only one proposing that _ most co-parenting and (re)marital stress comes from a mix of **five interactive hazards**, which _ can be avoided or reduced by *informed* co-parents working together on **12 projects** over time (p. 429).

Another uniqueness is the core premise that the most toxic of these five hazards is a mix of **six psychological wounds** in one or more co-parents, and many kids and family-supporters. The primary wound is the dominance of a "false self," which evolved to survive a low-nurturance childhood. The group of personality *subselves* that form this false self cause a mix of five more inner wounds: excessive _ shame, guilts, and _ fears, and significant _ reality and _ trust distortions. Combined, these five can _ inhibit or block emotional *bonding* and exchanging genuine love and intimacy with other people. These six wounds amplify each other, until reduced by proactive **recovery**.

This core concept is based on my 12 years' clinical experience studying and practicing *inner* family therapy with a wide range of troubled adult clients. Many human-development and clinical pioneers have written about *moderate* personality fragmenting over the last century.

Related premises in this series are that if adults were too psychologically neglected as young kids, they *unconsciously* _ pick other wounded mates, and _ reproduce their low-nurturance childhood families, which wound their minor kids, just as their ancestors did.

Co-parent Project 1 of 12 helps you partners _ learn about family nurturance (p. 440), _ assess your adults and kids for these psychological wounds, and then _ intentionally heal them. This project is the foundation for all 11 other projects, and all the suggestions in this book. For detail on this, see the guidebook "Who's *Really* Running Your Life? [xlibris.com, 2000].

Thirdly, these unique books propose that most relationship problems adults and kids experience are *symptoms* of underlying needs. Based on over 30 years' study of effective thinking and communicating, **Project 2** offers seven learnable skills to help co-parents identify their *true* needs, and brainstorm effective solutions as mutually-respectful partners. Without doing this, most marital and parenting problems return and compound. Success at this vital project depends on co-parents progress at healing their inner wounds (Project 1)

Fourth, these unique divorce-prevention books are gateways to relevant resources on the Internet. Their pages are rich with pointers to hundreds of free articles, worksheets, quizzes, links, and a unique re/marriage-preparation course at the **Stepfamily inFormation Web site** at [http://sfhelp.org/..].

The fifth uniqueness here is my background, personality, vocabulary, and writing style. I'm the recovering son of two alcoholics, a (Stanford University) engineer, manager, trainer, and businessman for 17 years, and a Masters-level family therapist since 1981. I also have personal experience as a stepgrandson, stepson, stepfather, and stepbrother. Part of my professional uniqueness comes from studying clinical hypnosis, and doing *inner*-family therapy with clients for over a decade. I've consulted with over 1,000 typical co-parents and some of their kids since 1981. I've also worked with scores of women and men seeking to heal inner wounds. I'm an invited member of the Stepfamily Association of America's Board of Directors.

Sixth, in their modular design and layout these volumes differ from others in their genre. They're meant to be read and re-used over time by co-parents, professionals, and students as practical reference books. Modular chapters focus on individual co-parent projects and problems, and are studded with *Reality* and *Status* Checks to promote concept credibility and reader self-awareness. Page headers, cross-references, "Selected Resources," and thorough indices will help you find what you need. Several books in the series have unique glossaries to help you think and speak more clearly, and problem-solve more effectively.

Our somber American divorce statistics demonstrate that millions of divorced and stepfamily co-parents and their kids need *help!* There are many titles and programs offering earnest advice and encouragement. None of them offers the unique blend of experiential and conceptual knowledge, content, design, and style of the books in this divorce-prevention series. After absorbing this one, I encourage you to read and discuss several of the books in Resource [N] to broaden your awareness. I specially recommend "Becoming a Stepfamily," by Patricia Papernow; and "Stepfamily Realities," by Margaret Newman.

Why Does This Series Exist?

Our gloomy U.S. re/divorce statistics suggest that as the Christian Millennium dawns, most couples can't forge flourishing, high-nurturance relationships. The most tragic victims of this silent scourge are millions of bewildered, anxious, angry kids who must adapt to the low-nurturance environments their wounded co-parents unwittingly provide.

This series is a wake-up call to American parents and family-policy makers. Our living and future kids are vulnerable to a silent national epidemic far more devastating than cancer or heart disease: wounds + ignorance + denial + low-nurturance parenting. The inexorable effect of these is a widening fan of wounded kids growing into adulthood with a disabled true Self. Recent UCLA research confirms kids from low-nurturance families are at significant risk of major disease and shorter lives [http://sfhelp.org/01/research.htm].

What Is this Series Based On?

Several foundations:

1) My 23 years' study of divorced-family and stepfamily relationships, dynamics, and realities. That includes over 17,000 hours consultation with over 500 Midwestern couples and over 1,000 typical divorced and stepfamily co-parents. I have personal experience as a stepson, stepgrandson, and stepbrother, and later, the stepfather of two girls.

2) an integrated theory of personal, relationship, and family health. The components are . . .

. . . the premise that families exist to uniquely fill a set of identifiable core *needs* in kids' and adults. Families range from low to high nurturance (need satisfaction); and . . .

. . . a research-based proposal of 28 traits that indicate a *high-nurturance* family [Resource D]; and . . .

. . . the observable reality that normal human neurological systems ("brains") have an innate ability called *multiplicity*. This allows automatically (unconsciously) developing neuronal connections in response to childhood environmental stressors, in order to survive (vs. thrive).

This leads to the premise that young kids in low-nurturance family environments use multiplicity to survive. Their coalescing personality *fragments* (splits) into protective subselves, causing mixes of up to six interactive psycho-spiritual wounds (p. 448). They range from minor to extremely toxic. Unacknowledged and unhealed, they cripple personal health, relationships, and families. Usually low-nurturance parents suffer the same wounds, and don't know it. Chapters 5 and 6 are devoted to options for relating to a wounded co-parent.

A key element in this foundation theory is a framework of experience-based ideas on **how to recover** from these psychological wounds, once they're acknowledged. The framework synthesizes the work of dozens of other clinical researchers and professionals. I write after working to heal my own set of these inner wounds for 15 years. I'm recovering from a *very* low-nurturance (double alcoholic) family and wounded ancestry.

Other elements underlying this series of re/divorce-prevention books are:

3) Proven family-systems principles, applied to _ *inner* families of subselves (personalities), and _ physical families of adults and kids. My training and experience as an engineer has been an unexpected benefit in applying systemic ideas to understanding, preventing, and resolving internal and physical family-relationship problems.

These principles include a concept of what factors are needed for a high-nurturance relationship. The most basic factor is that each partner must enable their true Self (vs. a protective false self), if they came from a significantly low-nurturance childhood.

Chapters 2 and 3 use these principles to propose basic premises about resolving stepfamily relationship problems. These premises are the foundation of Parts 2 and 3 in this book.

Another framework contributing to these books is a practical set of . . .

4) Seven related communication skills that any co-parent can learn and use to resolve personal, marital, and family "problems." If you can't describe these skills and how to use them now, you're probably communicating at less than half of the effectiveness you could achieve. I've studied and taught these for over 30 years, and I'm *still* learning! Project 2 of 12 focuses on co-parents learning to use these skills internally and with each other, and teach them to their kids. Ineffective thinking and communication is a core cause of (re)divorce and barrier to co-parenting teamwork (Chapter 7). Another core concept here is . . .

5) A coherent concept of human **attachment, loss, and** (emotional + mental + spiritual) **grieving.** This series proposes that *blocked grief* helps to lower family nurturance levels, and is one of five roots of our U.S. divorce epidemic. Chapter 12 applies this concept to growing co-parental cooperation and effectiveness.

All five of these conceptual bases combine to yield . . .

6) A framework of five common re/marital hazards, and 12 projects (p. 428) co-parents can work patiently at together. Seven projects are best done during courtship, to make wise commitment decisions. Most of the hazards and projects apply to couples in first marriages also.

Bottom line: this book and series are unique in six major ways. In 45 years of study, including 21 years as a private-practice psychotherapist, I've never seen this integration of concepts in other family-support materials. This six-part mosaic needs to be validated by systematic research. I use the mosaic to propose co-parent options toward _ building high-nurturance relationships and families and _ reducing our unseen inner-wounding and (re)divorce epidemics.

Your co-parenting and re/marital decisions will affect many lives for years to come, including unborn descendents. Building your co-parenting team after divorce and/or re/marriage is (at least) as complex and challenging as gaining a four-year college diploma. As with entering college, your adults will need to know basic information to get the most from this book. The next chapter outlines what you need to know first.

How to Best Use This Book

Use the Internet. Bracketed items like [..nn/xxxxx.htm] in these pages point to Web articles and worksheets at the Stepfamily inFormation Web site [http://sfhelp.org/..]. Add any pointer to that base to access the referenced resource. The full address will look like [http://sfhelp.org/nn/xxxxx.htm], without the brackets.

Accept the reality that *you* are ultimately responsible for the quality and outcome of your life. You, and each co-parenting partner, have the option of developing your knowledge and daily awareness, and using them to live your life *on purpose.* Modeling this self-responsibility and teaching it to minor kids in your life is a priceless life-long gift. Did your early caregivers do this for you?

Note whether your true Self is in charge of your inner family as you read. If s/he is, you'll feel some mix of *calm, centered, energized, "light," focused, resilient, up, grounded, relaxed, alert, aware, serene, purposeful*, and *clear*—even in chaos or conflict. If your Self isn't leading you, a "false self" (other personality parts) are. These well-meaning, narrow-visioned subselves will probably hinder your benefiting from these pages. If this is a new idea, Chapter 5 and 6 and Resources [D and E] will give you initial perspective. These Webpage summaries can also expand your understanding: [..pop/personality.htm], [..pop/f+t_selves.htm], and [..01/innerfam1.htm].

Read Chapters 1—6 no matter what. If any of your co-parents _ are ruled by a false self, _ discount your stepfamily identity, and/or _ reject or exclude each other from full family membership, your odds of permanently removing the set of seven barriers to caregiving teamwork in Part 2 are nil.

Another way to get the most from reading this book is to . . .

Stay aware of your key attitudes as you read, mull, and discuss. They will unconsciously shape your relationships, needs, and reactions to the ideas in these pages. Study and apply Chapter 3, no matter how alien or disquieting! And as you read, . . .

Keep your long-term goals clear, and focus on the present. False selves tend to focus on the past or the future. Your ongoing goal is to build and keep a high-nurturance family (p. 440) for *all* your sakes—including your ex mate/s'! The seven core relationship problems in Part 2 are complex and concurrent. Resolving them requires knowledge, honesty, awareness, courage, experimenting, and effective communication. Shoot for *progress, not perfection*, and periodically affirm your progress as co-parenting teammates!

Keep a wide-angle perspective. In family uproars, it's inviting to focus only on dousing the biggest (relationship) brushfire, instead of patiently "fireproofing the forest." If your true Selves are guiding you, you co-parents will want to help each other stay aware of your hazards and all 11 active projects (p. 429) as you study and apply the ideas in this book. Note that Project 12 invites all your co-parents to keep your *balance* every day, as you fill your kaleidoscope of current needs.

Before (re)reading each chapter in Part 2, review these until they're familiar:

_ awareness "bubbles" in *Satisfactions* [xlibris.com, 2001] or [..02/a-bubble.htm] and . . .

_ digging down to your core unmet needs (p. 44): [*Satisfactions*] or [..02/dig-down.htm].

These will keep you balanced and clear on assessing _ what your *real* relationship problems are, _ who's *really* responsible for fixing them, and _ what your current options are.

Stay aware that the problems and options in these chapters are distorted, because they're described as stand-alone projects. Your family-relationship problems occur simultaneously with each other and other dynamic personal and social discomforts (needs). This series of books uses the idea that "the way to eat an elephant is a bite at a time." That is, you caregivers can progress together if you _ identify your current true needs (discomforts), _ rank-order them against your long-term goals, and _ *stay focused* on resolving a few problems at a time. False selves usually can't do that for long, or at all.

As you read, think, and discuss, **keep these resources in mind**. See the guidebook *Satisfactions*, or the other resource in brackets [ ]:

Communication basics, skills, blocks, and tips—Resources [H-K]

Your Bill of Personal Rights (p. 514);

How to give effective interpersonal feedback: [..02/evc-feedback.htm];

These examples of problem solving [..02/win-win.htm] and [..02/lose-lose.htm], and this reprint of "Couple Karate" [..02/karate.htm];

The difference between first order (superficial) change, and second-order (core attitude) change [..pop/changes1&2.htm]. For lasting resolution, each of the problems in Part 2 require you co-parents to *want to* make second-order changes.

The Serenity Prayer: *God grant me the Serenity to accept the things I cannot change, Courage to change the things I can, and Wisdom to know the difference.* (Reinhold Neibuhr, 1934).

The Gestalt Prayer: "*I do my thing, and you do your thing. I am not in this world to fill your expectations, and you are not in the world to fill mine. You are you, and I am me. If by chance we meet, then it's beautiful. If not, it can't be helped.*" (Fritz Perls, M.D.)

Option: read relevant chapters of this book **out loud** with other co-parents, and discuss as you go. You're apt to harvest far more than if you say "read this chapter (or book)." If you're reluctant to do this, your team-building barriers are at work!

Option: use *informed* professionals to help reduce your teamwork barriers. *Informed* means _ the person is qualified professionally, and _ can answer most of the items in Chapter 1. Stepfamily counselors who are familiar with some form of *inner* family therapy or Hal and Sidra Stone's "Voice Dialog" therapy can be specially helpful. See [..11/counsel.htm].

And to get the most from this book . . .

Keep Project 12 a daily priority: balance all your activities and co-parent projects, and enjoy the process often enough. If your wise true Selves (capital "S") are guiding your other subselves, you *can*! See *Build a High-nurturance Stepfamily* or [..12/links12.htm].

Pause now, and breathe fully. Note your thought-streams and emotions without judgment. See how you stand with the ideas you've just read:

 # Status Check: "T" = true, "F" = false, and "?" = "I'm unsure," or "It depends (on what?)"

Now I feel a mix of *calm, centered, energized, light, focused, resilient, up, grounded, relaxed, alert, aware, serene, purposeful,* and *clear,* so my true Self is probably answering these questions. (T F ?)

I feel no ambivalence about accepting my and/or my partner's ex mate as a full co-parenting partner in our multi-home family now. (T F ?)

I accept that to build co-parenting co-operation in and between our kids' homes, *I* must want to _ learn new information and attitudes, and _ change *my* behavior (T F ?)

I'm clear now on _ who belongs to our kids' nuclear (step)family, _ who leads it, and _ the key goals we're all striving for long-term. (T F ?)

I can tell another person clearly what I want to get from reading this book. (T F ?)

I _ feel true compassion for each of our divorced parents and stepparents, and see *each* of us as worthy, *wounded* adults with legitimate needs , feelings, and goals; *or* _ I want to learn what blocks me from having that "=/=" attitude. (T F ?)

Option: journal about what you're experiencing now . . .

The next chapter will help you assess whether you've learned enough from life and the prior books in this series to benefit from this one. If you ignore these prerequisites, you put all your kids and co-parents at risk of eventual psychological or legal re/divorce. There are no shortcuts here! Stabilizing after divorce or mate-death and building high-nurturance stepfamily relationships are *major* personal-growth opportunities. Long term, reducing your barriers to co-parent team-building is less important than what you learn about yourselves from the *process*!

Before continuing, bookmark the next page, get undistracted, and read Resources [A through F] in Part 4. They'll help you better understand the key ideas in the rest of the book.

About Terminology

As a communication, relationship, and recovery consultant, I've grown aware of how critical the choice of words can
be in achieving high-nurturance relationships and families.
Disagreement or fuzziness on key terms can cause conflicts
and block their resolution—specially in highly emotional and
alien situations. In this book and series . . .

Abuse is an incendiary (shaming) word and concept. It
happens when three conditions clearly exist/ed: (1) one person
has power over another, like a parent and child, or doctor and
invalid; (2) the power-person intentionally gratified their needs
in a way that significantly harms the dependent person emotionally, physically, or spiritually; and (3) the victim can't (vs.
won't) flee or defend themselves. If these three conditions don't
exist, the power person's behavior is *aggression.* "*You were
aggressive*" is less apt to inflame than "*You were* abusive!*"

A bioparent is a man or woman who contributes genes to a
new human. A *parent* or *caregiver* is someone who wants to,
or agrees to, nurture a dependent child. S/He may or may not
have genes and/or history in common, or live with the child
full time. In the context of these books, a *co-parent* is either
divorced bioparent, or a genetically unrelated stepparent, or
another person who provides significant nurturance to one or
more minor kids in your family.

Communication means "*any perceived behavior that causes
a significant emotional, spiritual, physical, or mental change
in another person.*" One implication of this is that it's impossible for people in relationship to "not communicate." I propose that all communication aims to fill one or more true current needs (p. 44).

Divorce means the complex psychological / relational /
financial / legal / spiritual / religious / social process that starts
well before a spouse moves out or calls a lawyer. Divorce "ends"
only when the last adult and child affected, including grandparents, has truly _ grieved (accepted) their losses and _ forgiven themselves and other family members. One view is that

a divorce really starts when either mate weds the wrong person, for the wrong reasons, at the wrong time [..07/project07.htm]. Reducing role and relationship problems among your co-parents can be hindered by assuming *divorce* just means the legal process or event that dissolves a marriage.

Need means "a significant spiritual, emotional, mental, or physical discomfort." Often needs have surface (conscious) symptoms, and underlying *true* discomforts.

Nurturance and nurturing mean "intentionally trying to fill the true current needs of an adult or child." Over time, any family can be judged as providing low to high nurturance to all grown and child members.

A post-divorce nuclear family means "all people regularly living in a child's custodial and non-custodial homes." One implication is that *both* divorced parents, and any new mates, are full members of a two-home nuclear stepfamily. Another: "**single-parent family**" is a misleading, divisive term, because it discounts the needs, feelings, and impact of another bioparent. There are *always* two (or more) bio and psychological parents causing and trying to fill a minor child's needs. I recommend "absent-parent family" as a more realistic, useful term.

An **inner or psychological *wound*** means a personality trait (like excessive shame, guilt, or fear) which significantly impedes a child's or adult's wholistic health in someone's opinion. See p. 448 for six inner wounds that seem to be common in divorced families and stepfamilies and their ancestors. I suggest that unawareness of these wounds is one of several core reasons for the current U.S. divorce epidemic. In this series, co-parent Project 1 is assessing co-parents and kids honestly for such wounds, and evolving effective recovery plans for any that you find. See Chapters 5 and 6.

An *effective* **co-parenting team is** _ two or more co-parents who want to provide _ a high-nurturance family [D] by _ learning the current normal and special needs of each minor resident or visiting child [F], _ agreeing on who should do what to help each child fill their needs well enough, _ learning to separate co-parenting conflicts from others, and _ learning how to lastingly resolve them. See Chapter 4.

See the Resource sections of *Satisfactions* and *Stepfamily Courtship* [xlibris.com, 2001] for glossaries of many more relevant communication, family, and relationship terms.

We've just reviewed _ who should read this book, _what's in it, _what's unique about it, _why this series exists, and _how to get the most from reading this. Now let's review what you need to know *before* you read it . . .

1) First Things First...

Are You Ready to Read This Book?

This book offers you options toward resolving seven core relationship problems between divorced parents or stepfamily co-parents. To understand and follow these options, **you co-parents need to know some concepts** from the prior volumes in this series (p. 555) or the Web pages at [http://sfhelp.org/]. Before testing your knowledge, do a . . .

Self Check

From my experience with over 1,000 typical co-parents and many human-service professionals, it's likely that a "false self" controls you *and you don't know it.* The value you get from each chapter in this book depends directly on who's reading it: your true Self (capital "S"), or other well-meaning personality subselves. If you haven't done co-parent Project 1 yet [A], you probably can't tell the difference. If this means nothing to you, I urge you to bookmark this page now, and spend undistracted time reading _ [http://sfhelp.org/01/project01.htm], [..01/innerfam1.htm], [..pop/f+t_selves.htm], and [..01/gwc-intro.htm]. Then use Resources [D and E], and return here.

If you _ had few of the high-nurturance traits in your childhood [D], and _ have many of the false-self traits in [E], your true Self is probably disabled—and that feels *normal*. If so, you're apt to _ be distracted, skeptical, numb, bored, and/or "confused" by what you read, and/or to _ "procrastinate" *using* (applying) these ideas to improve your situation. Caution: if a protective false self controls you, those well-meaning subselves may skew your perceptions of, or reactions to, Resources [D and E], and distort your results. False-self protections start with *denials* and repressions of scary thoughts, memories, and feelings.

Here's another way of judging: if you now feel some mix of *calm, centered, energized, light, focused, resilient, up, grounded, relaxed, alert, aware, serene, purposeful,* and *clear,* your Self is probably leading your inner family of subselves. If not, other subselves will urge you to ignore this.

If you're confused by this or you're unsure whether your Self is leading, I strongly recommend that you stop reading this book, and study "Who's *Really* Running Your Life?" [xlibris.com, 2000] or the Web articles and worksheets at [http://sfhelp.org/pop/assess.htm].

From 21 years' experience as a couples' and stepfamily therapist, I suspect you and your supporters don't know what you don't know about . . .

_ yourselves and your partners,

_ high-nurturance family relationships, and . . .

_ multi-home stepfamilies.

Most clergy, counselors, social workers, and legal pros I've met are just as unaware of your *and their* unawareness.

To test this premise, try answering each of the **48 questions** below clearly and in some detail. To minimize fooling yourself, answer out loud, as if you were teaching a class of young adults. Option: describe each answer to a trusted partner.

Get comfortable and undistracted, and reserve at least an hour to do this. Take notes on what you think and feel as you go, for your reactions are as useful as your answers. If you get boggled, numb, or distracted, take a break. Take comfort: the questions below would easily justify a full-semester college course!

Star or highlight any items that raise your energy. Check each question only if you can clearly answer all it's "_" parts. If you don't, you're cheating yourself and your descendents. Keep a long-range view!

If you're a divorced bioparent who's not currently dating or committed, try answering these anyway. They'll save you potential heartache if and when you date. If you *are* dating seriously, and either of you have living minor or adult kids, accept that you all form a psychological (vs. legal) stepfamily now. In other words, accept that these questions apply to you all, though you're not (yet) legally re/married.

Recall: this foundation chapter aims to help you by combating one of the five re/marital and co-parenting hazards: *unawareness*. The items are organized according to your 12 co-parenting projects. The links in [http://sfhelp.org/12-overvw.htm], and the first four books in this series [N], lead to answers for each of these:

Overall

___ **1) Describe** _ five hazards that typical stepfamily co-parents face, and _ at least two of their major implications.

___ **2) Highlight** _ each of the 12 projects that co-parents can work on together to overcome these hazards, and _ describe the main goal of each project.

Project 1: Empower Your True Self

___ **3) Describe** _ what a *family* is, _ why families exist in all human cultures and eras, _ what a *need* is, _ what *nurturance* means in a family context, and _ at least 15 of the 28 traits of a high-nurturance family.

___ **4) Describe** _ *multi-part personality* (*inner family*), _ *subself*, _ *false self*, and _ *true Self*.

__ **5) Describe** _ six psychological wounds common to co-parents and their kids, and _ how they relate to each other.

__ **6)** _ **Describe** at least 15 of the common behavioral symptoms of being ruled by a false self, *or* _ name where to find those traits.

__ **7) Describe** _ true and _ pseudo *recovery* from false-self wounding, and _ at least five of the common benefits that evolve from true personal recovery.

Project 2: Effective Communication Skills

__ **8) Describe** _ what *communication* is, _ two outcomes required for *effective* communication; _ the seven communication skills co-parents need to learn and teach their kids; and _ how the skills relate to each other.

__ **9) Describe** _ six needs all infants, kids, and adults try to fill by communicating, _ four types of messages we're always decoding from each other, _ what a R(espect)-message is, _ the three possible R-messages, and _ the single most important factor that determines whether communications are effective.

__ **10) Describe** _ the three parts of a typical "conflict" between two people, and _ the four common kinds of conflict that all adults and kids encounter.

__ **11) Describe** _ what an "awareness bubble" is, and _ why it's important in effective communication between two or more subselves or people.

__ **12) Describe** at least five of ~30 communication *process* factors that co-parents need to be aware of to problem-solve effectively.

To prepare for Chapter 7 and Part 2, read "*Satisfactions—7 Relationship Skills You Need to Know*" [xlibris.com, 2001], or all the articles at [..02/links02.htm]. To further test your communication knowledge, or invite another to test theirs, use [..02/evc-quiz.htm]. Most role and relationship problems (unmet needs), including those among your *inner* team of subselves, spring from ineffective communications!

Project 3: Accept Your Identity

__ **13) Describe** _ what "stepfamily identity" is; _ at least five specific signs that co-parents have *really* accepted their "step" identity; and _ why such acceptance is essential to build a high-nurturance stepfamily, over time.

__ **14) Describe** _ what a stepfamily "membership conflict" is, _ the two types of such conflicts, and _ why minor stepkids need their co-parents to develop a viable strategy to resolve each type.

__ **15) Describe** why it's *essential* for all stepfamily co-parents and supporters to accept that _ all three or four caregivers of each stepchild, and their kin, are full members of their new multi-generational stepfamily.

__ **16) Describe** _ what a family map or *genogram* is, and _ how co-parents can use one to identify and resolve divisive stepfamily *identity* and *membership* conflicts together.

Project 4: Form Realistic Expectations

__ **17) Describe** at least 10 of the ~30 concurrent stepfamily adjustment tasks that typical new co-parent couples need to work on together, over time.

__ **18) Describe** _ what *family structure* is, and _ at least 15 of the ~30 common structural differences between typical stepfamilies and intact bio(logical)families.

__ **19) Describe** at least 10 of the 15 new roles (e.g. like "step-cousin") that new-stepfamily adults and kids need to evolve, clarify, and stabilize over time.

__ **20) Describe** at least 10 of the ~ 60 common myths about stepfamilies, and their corresponding realities.

__ **21) Describe** and illustrate _ a "stepfamily loyalty conflict" and _ a "PVR relationship triangle;" and _ explain why it's essential for divorced or stepfamily co-parents to evolve a clear, effective strategy to resolve each of these unavoidable stressors.

__ **22) Describe** why legal battles between divorced

bioparents are *always* lose-lose-lose, and _ what they imply about _ false-self dominance and _ co-parents' communication skills.

Project 5: Build a Pro-Grief (Step)family

__ **23) Describe** _ interpersonal *bonding*, _ what *attachment* and *loss* are, _ the three levels of normal grief, _ the main phases of each level, and _ how to tell if grieving is "done" (enough).

__ **24) Explain** _ why blocked grief is common in divorced families and stepfamilies. _ Describe _ at least seven of the ~ 12 symptoms of blocked grief, _ the main reason it strangles stepfamily bonding and growth, and _ what a "grief policy" is.

__ **25) Describe** _ what inner and outer *permissions* to grieve are; _ at least four of the six factors that promote healthy grieving in persons and families; and how _ ignorance, _ false-self dominance, and _ ineffective communication skills combine to inhibit those factors.

For more awareness of what co-parenting teammates and supporters need to know about healthy grieving, see [..05/grief-quiz.htm] and [..05/links05.htm].

Project 6: Mission Statement and Job Descriptions

__ **26) Describe** _ **the key goals (purposes) of any family,** and _ at least five elements of a family *system*; and _ what a family *mission statement* is, _ who should make one and _ when; and _ why they're more vital in most stepfamilies than in typical biofamilies.

__ **27) Describe** _ the three or four sets of concurrent needs that typical minor stepkids must fill over time, and _ at least eight needs in each set.

__ **28) Describe** specifically what an *effective co-parent* is, in a divorced-family or stepfamily context.

__ **29) Describe** at least 15 of the ~40 common environmental differences between *stepparenting* and *bioparenting* roles; and _ why clear, shared knowledge of these differences is vital for average divorced and stepfamily adults and supporters, including co-grandparents and therapists.

___ **30) Describe** what a _ *co-parent job description* is, _ how it relates to a family mission statement, and _ why drafting job descriptions (ideally *before* deciding to re/wed) is essential for effective co-parenting.

Project 7: Make Three *Right* Re/marriage Choices

___ **31) Describe** at least five meanings of the terms _ *marriage* and _ *divorce.*

___ **32) Describe** _ at least five of the *right* reasons to commit to stepfamily re/marriage, and _ at least 10 of the common *wrong* reasons.

___ **33) Describe** at least 10 signs that it's the right *time* to re/wed.

___ **34) Describe** at least six traits each of the _ right *partner*, _ right *co-parents*, and _ right *stepkids* to re/wed.

___ **35) Describe** _ what the psychological condition of *co-dependence* is, _ how it relates to false-self dominance, _ common symptoms of it, and _ what's needed to recover from it.

___ **36) Describe** at least 10 common stepfamily-courtship danger signs.

___ **37) Explain** _ why more U.S. stepfamily re/marriages fail psychologically or legally than first marriages, and _ why millions of average co-parent couples re/marry anyway.

Projects 8 – 12

___ **38) Outline** _ at least five requisites for a stable, high-nurturance re/marriage.

___ **39) Describe** _ why it's harder for typical stepfamily co-parents to make quality couple-time than first-marriage mates, and _ why such time is more vital in average stepfamily unions than first unions.

___ **40) Describe** five specific reasons why typical U.S.

stepfamily couples divorce more often than first-marriers, despite love, commitment, and "more maturity."

___ **41) Describe** _ the main difference between *counseling* and *therapy*, and _ how to assess a competent stepfamily consultant or therapist.

___ **42) Name** _ at least 10 of the 16 groups of things that typical re/married co-parents and their relatives must merge over time to form a stable multi-generational stepfamily, and _ explain why it takes most stepfamilies four or more years after re/wedding to do this.

___ **43) Explain** what a _ *values* conflict, _ loyalty conflict, and _ PVR relationship triangle is, and _ key the steps co-parents need to take to resolve each of these as caregiving teammates.

___ **44) Describe** _ at least five requisites for an effective *team*, and at least six traits of effective *team leaders*.

___ **45)** _ **Name** at least four of the seven core barriers to co-parental teamwork, and _ identify a source of practical help for identifying and resolving common adult problems with stepkids' "other parent/s" (ex mates and new partners).

___ **46) Describe** what "successful child-visitation" is, and at least three things that can hinder that.

___ **47)** _ **Explain** why typical divorced and stepfamily co-parents need more support than most biofamily parents, and _ name four kinds (vs. sources) of co-parent support.

___ **48) Name** four things co-parents can *balance* as they do these 12 family-building projects every day, and _ describe how keeping their balance relates to who's running the adults' *inner* families.

Take a stretch, get back in touch with your body, and breathe well. Did these 48 items remind you of taking an exam for something important?

Trying to co-manage an average stepfamily *effectively* is one of the greatest relationship challenges you'll ever encounter. I hope the scope of this inventory makes that premise more credible to you. Does it make more sense now why well over half of typical U.S. re/wedded mates eventually give up? How many average co-parents do you think could do even 20 of these multi-part items? How many therapists, teachers, family-law attorneys, judges, and mediators, and clergy could?

We've just hit the highlights of 12 projects your co-parents will need to work at together for many years, to offset the five common re/marital hazards on p. 428. If this looks complex and daunting—it *is*! Take heart: you partners can help each other acquire the answers to these gradually. You don't have to learn them all at once! However . . .

If you can't clearly and confidently do at least 30 of these 48 items, *don't read this book yet.* Study all four of the prior volumes (p. 555), or all 12 projects linked from [http://sfhelp.org/12-overvw.htm]. If a false self rules you, and/or you're in a relationship crisis (have a short-term focus), you'll probably ignore this.

I see no quick way to learn how to co-manage a complex, dynamic stepfamily well. One of the best gifts you can give yourselves here is a patient *long-range* outlook. I agree with stepfamily researcher and therapist Patricia Papernow. In her helpful book *Becoming a Stepfamily*, she estimates that it takes even "fast" stepfamilies at least four years *after* nuptial vows and toasts to merge and stabilize (Project 9). Most take longer, and some never do.

For more awareness of what (I believe) you'll need to know about yourself, relationships, and families to solve your family team-building problems, see [..07/quiz.htm], [..02/evc-quiz.htm], and [..05/grief-quiz.htm]. Besides your love and commitment, a shared motivation to *learn* and *grow* is the greatest asset you co-parents have for protecting your living and future descendents from inner wounding.

To start learning the answers to these items or to alert someone else to them, see [http://sfhelp.org/Rx/prep.htm].

 # Status check: See where you stand with what you read in this chapter. T = true, F = false, and "?" means "I'm not sure."

I feel a mix of *calm, centered, energized, light, focused,* *resilient, up, grounded, relaxed, alert, aware, serene, purposeful,* and *clear,* so my true Self is probably answering these questions. (T F ?)

I _ was undistracted, and _ really took my time in responding to each of these 48 items (T F ?)

I can say clearly what needs I'm trying to fill by reading this book. (T F ?)

I'm clear on what the "next right thing" is for me to do now (T F ?)

I'm _ comfortable with and _ motivated to discuss this chapter with _ my partner and _ our other co-parent teammates and supporters now. (T F ?)

I feel confident I know enough now to really benefit from reading this book (T F ?)

Awarenesses . . .

This guidebook is about building an effective co-parenting team after divorce or re/marriage. A core premise here is that resolving *any* role or relationship conflict, including those among your subselves and with your kids, depends on your caregivers' _ knowledge, _ beliefs, and _ attitudes. The next chapter provides a way for you to learn what you *believe* now about people, relationships, and resolving conflicts . . .

2) Basic Premises

What Do You Believe Now?

M y divorced client was the thirty-something custodial mom of two pre-teen daughters. She sought help resolving a dynamic web of co-parenting problems with _ her kids' (two wounded) fathers, _ her live-in partner (a divorced father of two), _ her troubled older daughter, _ her judgmental (wounded) parents, and _ herself. Forming "an effective co-parenting team" to nurture her needy kids seemed like an impossible fantasy to her.

Is that true in *your* life now?

Think of your kids and their other co-parenting adults, including grandparents and any stepparent/s. Now reflect on one or several significant relationship *problems* or *conflicts* you have with any of them. (*"I'm frustrated that Jamie often interrupts me."*) A harder challenge: identify one or more relationship problems these people have with *you.* For extra credit, identify a relationship conflict between two of your personality subselves—e.g. your *Inner Critic* or *Perfectionist* and your *Self.* Use these people and problems as reality-checks as you read this chapter . . .

This chapter summarizes _ core premises (beliefs) about resolving *any* relationship problem, and _ related premises for single or re/married co-parents. What each of your co-parents

believe about these will affect how successful you are at nurturing your minor kids together, over time. Do you agree? Daily
distractions in your life probably obscure awareness of your
and your other co-parents' beliefs, and how they affect your
family relationships and caregiving success. Like my clients'
two girls, your kids are forming their own beliefs about _ people,
_ relationship problems, and _ co-parenting, as they watch you
adults interact. Do you know what you're teaching your custodial and visiting kids about these three things?

Bracketed numbers and letters below refer to chapters and
resources in this book—e.g. [B] means "see Resource B." Add
bracketed pointers like [..xx/xxx.htm] to [**http://sfhelp.org/**..]
and type the result [http://sfhelp.org/xx/xxx.htm] in your Web
browser to view one or more resource pages. Omit the brackets.

Options

Check each item below that you agree with, "x" those you
don't, or use "?" for any you want to consider more or discuss
with someone. Edit these items to fit you better.

Take your time, and take mind/body breaks as needed.
You don't have to do this whole inventory in one sitting . . .

Journal about your reactions and awarenesses as you go.
They're as valuable as your knowledge and beliefs!

Give copies of these premises to each of your other co-
parents, and discuss how your beliefs mesh (or don't). Where
they don't, discuss how you all adapt to that—e.g. argue,
blame, plead, avoid, manipulate, or compromise respectfully.
For copies, see [..10/premises-rln.htm] and [..Rx/mates/
basics.htm].

Use these 38 premises to design a discussion agenda for a
co-parent support group, course, or seminar—and/or for your
stepfamily members!

Reflect: if you feel some mix of *calm, centered, energized,
light, focused, resilient, up, grounded, relaxed, alert, aware,
serene, purposeful*, and *clear*, your true Self is probably lead-

ing your inner family of subselves now. If not, who *is* controlling them? See [..01/innerfam2.htm].

Overall . . .

Premise 1) The clearer you are on *your* set of core beliefs and attitudes, the more often you'll feel truly centered, clear, serene, calm, and productive in any life situation *if* your Self is leading your inner family. So _ develop your awareness, and _ empower your Self. Each of you co-parents can do this, with intent, practice, and patience. See co-parent Project 1 (p. 430) and [..02/awareness.htm].

Premise 2) Regardless of age, gender, and setting, mutually-satisfying (**nurturing**) **relationships usually have** most of **four groups of traits**: [..08/relationship.htm]. Once you co-parents are aware of them, you can help each other develop these traits, within your limits. Forming an effective team to nurture your kids and each other depends on your motivation to do this.

Premises About Persons

Premise 3) You co-parents (and kids) **each have** a unique blend of useful **talents and abilities** which you may or may not recognize, develop, and use. Doing these brings periods of fulfillment and satisfaction ("happiness"), over time. Other people have different (vs. better) gifts. You can't choose what talents you're born with. You *can* choose _ whether you develop them or not, and _ what you do with them. Effective nurturing and co-parenting teamwork are talents that each of you adults can develop. Your kids depend on you each to _ affirm, value, and nurture *their* gifts, and to _ motivate them to develop their talents on their own.

Premise 4) You all have inherent limitations (e.g. color blindness, tone deafness, or some personality traits), which you didn't cause, and can't change. You can _ calmly acknowledge and accept your limits and adapt to them; or you can _ feel guilty, ashamed, or angry about them, and _ minimize, project, and/or deny them. The Serenity Prayer (p. 24) can help you accept and adapt to your personal and situational limits.

Some limitations come from **psychological wounds** (p. 448) which affect _ who you choose to relate to, and _ *how* you relate. Most divorced and stepfamily co-parents and many minor and adult kids seem to be significantly wounded, and unaware of that. Once admitted, these wounds can be significantly healed, over time.

Premise 5) Each of you co-parents is a truly unique, *valuable* person. Each adult and child in your life was and is just as unique and worthy, in their own special way. Anyone who needs to see and label you as *worthless* or *bad* probably feels that about themselves, but can't accept and change that yet. If *you* feel that about another person, identify who leads your inner family.

Your inherent *worth* comes from your unique gifts and natural capacity to promote wholistic health and growth, peace, safety, and love in and among living things, starting with yourself and those who depend on you. *Your human worth does* not *depend on whether you please or make other people "happy,"* no matter what others say, demand, or imply.

More premises about *persons* . . .

Premise 6) All babies have the innate ability to feel and receive *love*. Part of "growing up" involves learning to feel and express genuine love for others. Depending on the nurturance-level of their earliest years, adults vary in their capacity to exchange genuine *love* with themselves, a Higher Power, and other living things. Because they didn't experience enough consistent genuine love as young children, wounded adults can unconsciously mistake *pity, duty, dependence (need), power, fear,* and/or *lust* for love, and not know it (reality distortion). This usually results in low-nurturance pseudo relationships, which usually decay or stay superficial.

Premises About Relationships and *Problems*

Premise 7) Your relationships with other people **range from awareness** to acquaintance to friendship to *close* to primary, **to spiritual**. Your ranking of each relationship is based on the degree of your exchanged respect, enjoyment, commonality, and caring (bonding)—i.e. *love*. Some badly neglected young children never develop the ability to form genuine emotional-spiritual bonds with others, (Reactive Attachment Disorder), and can only pretend to "relate." In marriage, this manifests as *pseudo* intimacy or mutuality. After divorce, a symptom of this wound is non-custodial parent "indifference" or "irresponsibility" (Chapter 17). The alternative is *genuineness* and *authenticity*.

Premise 8) Human **relationships evolve through stages**, as each partner ages, learns, and chooses whether to risk increasing honesty and intimacy. Each stage can either strengthen or weaken your relationship, or end it. Because the environments in and around each of you partners change constantly, your relationships with yourself and each other organically grow or die. This depends partly on if and how each person accepts change. Local change may be imperceptible.

Relationships and *Needs*

Premise 9) A *need* is a minor to major current physical, emotional, or spiritual discomfort. A *want* ("*I want a butterscotch sundae now.*") may or may not be a *need.* **All** adult and child **relationships and behaviors**, *including communication*, **are** unconscious and/or conscious **attempts to fill** current emotional, physical, mental, and spiritual **needs** well enough for now. The words *problem*, *conflict*, or "issue," mean "one or more unmet needs."

Premise 10) Adults' and kids' *needs* are . . .

neither good nor bad by themselves, like our eye color or fingerprints. The way we *act* to fill our needs can be judged *good* or *bad*, or *right* or *wrong*, if our perceived choices cause pain, or block health and growth in ourselves and/or others. Many of us were taught to shame ourselves or others for being "too needy." That's like scorning someone for breathing.

   interactive—e.g. my emotional, physical, and spiritual needs cause and affect yours, and vice versa; and our primal needs are . . .

   satisfied temporarily at best; and often recur. And they . . .

   come in complex clusters. At any moment, you and others have sets of minor to major emotional, physical, and spiritual *surface* and *true* needs that constantly shift and interact. They . . .

   follow a natural emotional ranking, or hierarchy: we semiconsciously rank some needs (discomforts) higher than others, which shapes our focus and behaviors. Some priorities never change, and others shift slowly or suddenly with age, wisdom, and circumstance. See [..02/needlevels.htm]. And your needs are . . .

   conscious, semi-conscious, and unconscious. Conscious needs are those we're first aware of (*"I need the car now"*). There are usually (always?) semi-conscious and unconscious *true* needs "underneath" them: i.e. lower in consciousness (*"I need the security of knowing now that I have a reliable way of getting to the bank and back, so I'll have cash to handle unexpected expenses."*)

   Recall: we're reviewing basic premises about your internal and social *relationships*.

True Needs

Premise 11) Common *true* needs are . . .
_ enough physical comfort.
_ Finding and keeping my daily personal serenity—inner-family harmony and security.
_ Getting enough nurturing (vs. toxic) physical touching and comforting.
_ Unconditional self love, vs. conditional love, indifference (neglect), shame, or self hatred.

_ Finding social acceptance, and reducing loneliness.

_ Maintaining my desire to keep growing and healing, despite obstacles.

_ Clarifying my personal identity: who *am* I?

_ Enjoying myself and my life enough.

More common *true* needs . . .

_ Developing my *spirituality*: finding my spiritual (Higher) self or Soul, and relating with a meaningful Higher Power.

_ Clarifying and pursuing the main meaning (purpose, goal, mission) of my life.

_ Identifying, overcoming and/or accepting my fears, confusions, and doubts.

_ Recognizing, developing, and using my talents.

_ Recognizing, accepting, and adapting to my limitations.

_ Valuing and _ maintaining my mental + emotional + spiritual + physical (wholistic) health.

_ Forgiving myself and others who disappoint or betray me (Chapter 11).

_ Mourning my stream of losses (broken emotional bonds)—Chapter 12.

_ Balancing my daily and long-term work, play, and rest.

_ Identifying, asserting, and enforcing my personal boundaries (Chapter 15).

_ Choosing and _ acting on my own short and long-term priorities.

Still more universal human true needs:

_ Evolve a set of personal rights like Resource [I] and _ act on them to maintain my integrity. *Integrity* comes from the Latin word *integer*, meaning "whole or complete." Have you ever defined your *integrity*? My definition is: "My *integrity* is _ knowing my core beliefs, values, rights, and true needs, and _ acting on them consistently *without undue shame or guilt*, despite resistance or criticism from others." Choosing to preserve your integrity is the source of self respect, a component of "happiness." Do you know what it feels like to act on your integrity? People who can are usually guided by their true Self, with some Higher Powered help. Mahatma Gandhi, Elizabeth

Cady Stanton, Billy Graham, Sandra Day O'Connor, Martin Luther King, and Eleanor Roosevelt provide high-profile examples . . .

_ Maintain my self respect and dignity (Chapter 8).

Can you think of other primal human needs like these? For perspective on how your and others' true needs rank in non-crisis situations, see [sfhelp.org/02/needlevels.htm].

Premise 12) Every adult is responsible for _ identifying and _ **filling their own true needs**. If you expect other adults and/or kids to fill your true (vs. surface) needs, you invite disappointment, frustration, hurt, anger, and resentment. This is specially true if the others accept the responsibility! Pause and identify who you hold responsible for filling your primary needs. Different subselves may have different beliefs . . .

We adults are the first generation to acknowledge the harmful relationship dynamic of **co-dependence**. If out of kindness, compassion, or misplaced guilt I feel over-responsible for *your* needs and feelings, *I block you from learning how to manage them.* Thus *enabling* is the opposite of *empowering*, which is what high-nurturance co-parents want to do for their dependent kids and each other.

A powerful implication is that co-parents (bioparents, stepparents, and other active caregivers) are responsible for helping dependent kids learn to _ take full responsibility for identifying and filling their own *true* needs, and _ asking for help in filling them, when needed, _ *without excessive guilt, shame, or anxiety.* Are you doing that now? Did your caregivers do that for you? Has anyone?

Premise 13) For order and harmony, **people in groups** (like a family) **evolve *roles*** (like "custodial parent") **and *rules*** (e.g. "We will not be naked when we eat together.") A *role* is a set of responsibilities (for filling needs) that a group-member is expected to accept. *Rules* are ways group leaders expect all members to perform their roles. Rules need meaningful consequences to be useful. In some inner and physical families, the key rule is *"we have few rules and/or consequences."*

Inner-family and interpersonal conflicts can occur in and between your kids' co-parenting homes about _ who belongs to the family, _ who determines the roles and rules, _ what these are, and _ what happens if members balk or fail at their roles, or _ break the rules. A key set of rules determines how your co-parents resolve significant conflicts about any of these. Do you know what these rules are?

For effective problem solving, it helps if all your adults are clear on the differences between _ a person, _ their roles (like "stepdad"), and _ the rules the group wants to live by.

Relationship "Problems"

Premise 14) *Problems* are opposing **needs**, preferences, perceptions, beliefs, or values. These **can conflict** concurrently _ **within us** (between our subselves) **and/or** _ **between people** (their ruling subselves).

One implication of false-self dominance is *inner* fights ("ambivalence"). One personality subself may want their host person to act (e.g. thought stream: *"Come on, come on, pick up the phone and* call*!"*), and other subselves may urge *"No! You'll probably get criticized, rejected, and* hurt*. Don't call!"* These inner disputes are so common most people aren't conscious of them. They distract and defocus us, and use up lots of energy (*"I don't know why I'm so tired all the time . . ."*) until we learn to intentionally resolve them.

When you choose to develop your *awareness*, you can start to recognize these semi-conscious inner struggles. In recovery from psychological wounds, you can learn to quiet and sort out all your inner voices (thought streams) and invoke the skill and wisdom of your true Self and other subselves to mediate and reach acceptable *inner* compromises. That promotes *outer* compromise.

Premise 15) Most significant **relationship "problems" have four parts**: Jack's surface and true needs, and Jill's surface and true needs. Unless Jack and Jill _ are clearly aware of all four, _ rank each other's (non-emergency) needs as important as their own, and _ agree to brainstorm filling their respective *true* needs cooperatively, effective *long-term* problem-solving (true-need fulfillment) is unlikely.

For example, if Jack says *"You never listen to me,"* and Jill dutifully or anxiously tries to improve her listening, Jack may remain dissatisfied because his unspoken *true* need is to feel more valued and respected. That would take spontaneous (vs. requested or demanded) new attitudes and behaviors from Jill. It also might take Jack healing his old *shame* wound, *which has nothing to do with Jill.*

Most partners (like you?) aren't used to assessing their and/ or their partner's current true needs like those above. This leaves them focused on _ surface needs, and/or _ attacking each other as persons, vs. teaming up to fill their respective needs.

The learnable Project-2 skills of *awareness*, *digging down*, and *metatalk* can help you co-parents discern your surface and true needs in important situations. See the guidebook *Satisfactions* or [..02/links02.htm].

Premise 16) Relationship problems often involve a vexing, stressful dynamic described by psychiatrist Dr. Murray Bowen and others as **relationship "triangles."** The basic idea is that "problems" between two people often involve a third person, in a way that keeps the problems going. Each person (i.e. their ruling subselves) *unconsciously* adopts one of three roles: Persecutor, Victim, and Rescuer. Solving such problems requires nonjudgmental awareness of who's needs create and maintain the PVR triangle, and filling their needs another way. People accepting any of these roles are rarely led by their true Self. See Chapter 16 (p. 303).

Premise 17) Adult relationships range between little bonding to over-bonding. (*"I'm* nothing *without you."*) An **interdependent** relationship is one in which both partners genuinely feel *"I choose to be with you, and I can live well enough without you if I have to."* Social surveys steadily report this feels best and lasts longest, compared to two alternatives:

A *dependent* or enmeshed relationship in which one or both people gives their power and personal responsibility to the other. *Enmeshed* and/or co-addictive (co-dependent) relationships occur when both partners are ruled by false selves. Symptoms of this are hazy identities, weak personal boundaries, and no clear life purpose. See [..01/co-dep.htm] and Chapters 15 and 20. The other end of the need/bonding spectrum is . . .

An *independent* relationship, where neither partner really needs much from the other, and has a weak or no psychological/spiritual bond with them. Their false self may pretend otherwise to themselves and/or other people. Co-parents with weak or pseudo bonds adapted to low-nurturance childhoods by learning to numb their emotions and not need or trust anyone. See [..01/bonding.htm] and Chapter 9.

Many divorced parents (i.e. their subselves) wish to have little or no relationship with their ex mate. Other subselves want a co-operative caregiving relationship for their kids' sakes. In stepfamilies, this challenge can be more complex because of the needs, attitudes, roles, and priorities of one or more stepparents.

Premise 18) *Need* **conflicts can be of three types**, which are resolved differently: _ communication needs (e.g. I need to vent, and you need to problem-solve); _ physical-resource needs (we each need the car or check book); and _ intangible needs (e.g. we each need to be *right*, to avoid shame and guilt). Identifying and resolving communication need-clashes requires both partners to be fluent in all seven Project-2 skills. Really resolving serious physical-need conflicts (i.e. the true needs "beneath" them) is more likely if you partners dig down to the true needs beneath them [..02/dig-down.htm].

Premise 19) A "problem" between co-parents usually (always?) involves the _ wounds, _ needs, and _ perceived behaviors of *all* involved caregivers, not just one. If any co-parent denies this and blames another for current surface problems, their *attitude* becomes a primary source of conflict (Chapter 3). Avoiding your half of family relationship problems indicates probable false-self control. Effective co-parent problem-resolution is a team sport!

Premise 20) Every relationship problem that you repeatedly disagree about or avoid is *secondary*. The overarching *true* problem is that you haven't found an effective way to solve concurrent _ innerpersonal and _ interpersonal relationship problems together. That's why Project 2 ranks second in priority among your 12 vital projects [A]. Part 3 describes 11 common secondary problems in typical divorced families and stepfamilies.

This is a lot of abstract ideas (which affect your lives). Put the book down, stretch and breathe well, and see if you need to take a mind/body break . . . When you're ready, compare what you believe to these . . .

Premises About Problem-solving

Premise 21) (Re)solving a problem means "_ identifying and _ filling your and my mixes of current *true* needs well enough, as judged by each of us." Trying to fill *surface* needs in serious conflicts will not work for long, until the true needs beneath them are satisfied. Problem-solving (conflict resolution) is an _ internal and _ interpersonal *process*, not an event.

Premise 22) Problem resolution *may* **happen** if all partners genuinely believe "*Your and my needs are equally important to me now, so let's seek to fill our needs co-operatively.*" In this series, this is called an equal/equal ("=/=") or win-win attitude. Most conflicts (and divorces) happen because partners' false selves aren't able to genuinely rank their needs or values as co-equal, over time. Is that your experience?

A key co-parent-team task is to patiently, lovingly guide minor inner and physical kids to change their natural "*My needs come first*" instincts to "*I rank your and my needs equally now.*" The latter value is one trait of true maturity and true-Self leadership.

Premise 23) Effective relationship problem-solving requires one or more people to *want to* **change** something: a belief, value, perception, knowledge, behavior, or limit. "First order" behavioral change is superficial, because the priorities and attitudes underneath the new behavior don't change. [*"OK, I'll listen to you more attentively (but my mind will still wander."*)]

Only second-order changes last, like quitting nicotine dependence without picking up a new addiction, because the changer's ruling subselves _ reorganize, and/or _ genuinely shift their core attitudes, priorities, and/or values. *Really* improving co-parental teamwork requires each of you to *want* to make second-order changes, because you see significant benefit to you and your kids, and are willing to let go of something familiar or comfortable.

Premise 24) When based on _ true-Self guidance and _ genuine (vs. pseudo) mutual (=/=) respect, the **seven** Project-2 **communication skills** on p. 512 can **empower any adult or child to resolve their** _ *inner*personal and _ interpersonal relationship and role **conflicts** well enough. I suspect that few parents or schools currently teach these skills, so you and your family members probably need to learn them together. Can you name the skills yet? Who's responsible in your homes and family for everyone learning *and using* these skills? See Chapter 7.

Premise 25) Becoming aware of *how* you co-parents _ think and _ problem-solve is as **vital** as identifying what needs you're trying to fill. The Project-2 skills of *awareness, digging down, metatalk* and *empathic listening* can help you do this, when based on genuine =/= mutual respect. The technique of communication *mapping* can help you identify communication–process problems. See *Satisfactions* or [..02/evc-maps.htm].

Premise 26) Without _ empowered Selves and _ *awareness* (communication skill #1), your kids and adults will try to fill your surface and true needs by ... .

fighting and arguing about _ what happened (or didn't), and/or _ who's to blame;

intellectualizing or repressing (ignoring or numbing emotional and spiritual needs);

threatening, controlling, and manipulating (*"My current needs outrank yours"*), and/or . . .

avoiding, postponing, defocusing, denying, and/or withdrawing _ emotionally and/or _ physically.

Each of these signals significant _ false-self dominance and unhealed psychological wounds (p. 448), and _ unawareness of the seven communication skills. That's why co-parent Project 1 (assessing for inner wounds and recovering from them) is essential to build effective problem-solving within and between your skins and homes.

None of these resolution alternatives fills all participants' current true needs well enough. People who use them are not bad, they're wounded and *unaware*!

Premise 27) Adults and kids who focus on resolving their *inner* need-conflicts first are best able to resolve current interpersonal problems. Is that what you partners usually do? Are you teaching your kids how do that?

Premise 28) Any day, you co-parents can decide to _ help each other **learn effective problem-solving**, and then _ model and teach it to your kids and others. Project 2 (p. 430) provides a framework and resources to help you do that.

Problem-solving Steps

Premise 29) based on these premises, a framework for resolving *any* relationship problem (need conflict) is . . .

Put your Self in charge of your inner family, and invite your partner do the same. This requires each co-parent to _ understand and accept your inner team of subselves [..01/innerfam1.htm], and to *want to* _ identify who leads them and _ harmonize them (i.e. to do Project 1). When you each steadily feel a mix of calm, centered, energized, light, focused, resilient, up, grounded, relaxed, alert, aware, serene, purposeful, compassionate, and clear, your Self is probably in charge. See Chapters 5 and 6.

Acknowledge that _ you have a problem (one or more unmet true needs), and that _ *you* are responsible for deciding what you need, and asserting respectfully and creatively to fill it.

Make (vs. "find") undistracted time to identify and fill your needs, alone and/or with others involved.

Promote yourself to equal (=/=). Accept that your current needs are just as legitimate and important as your partner's, no matter what others say, except in emergencies. Help each other accept that being "needy" is *normal*, healthy, and OK, not weak! It's also OK to need, request, and accept help, as long as you don't expect or demand someone else to fill your needs!

Create and use a Bill of Personal Rights (p. 514) to help, and affirm others' equal rights. Shame-based (wounded) people have major trouble with this, until in true (vs. pseudo) recovery. Many divorced and stepfamily co-parents appear to be shame based. Are you and/or your partner covertly controlled by shamed-activated subselves? See Chapters 5, 6, and 8.

Next . . .

Reality-check your expectations of yourself and each other. It may be that one or more of you _ can't fill another's needs, _ doesn't want to, or _ is afraid to. If so, switch your focus to brainstorming ways around this.

Focus on identifying your unmet true (vs. surface) needs (p. 44), vs. who's at fault (blaming and defending). Blaming agitates and evokes false selves, and usually *blocks* problem solving.

Help each other recall that innerpersonal and interpersonal conflict, and the emotions that go with them, are normal and healthy, not negative or bad!

Stay focused on your problem-solving *process*, and help each other learn and use all seven Project-2 communication skills (p. 512) with patience and mutual (=/=) respect. _ Identify your simultaneous need-conflicts, _ separate and rank them, and _ work on a few at a time. _ Identify and resolve *inner* conflicts first. The alternative is fruitlessly focusing on surface conflicts and "riding off in all directions."

Aim for good-enough compromises and solutions (need fulfillments), vs. perfection. People dominated by *Perfectionist* subselves have trouble doing this without high anxiety or guilt.

Help each other brainstorm creatively, vs. doing black/

white two-option thinking. True Selves know that there are *always* more than two possible short and long-term solutions!

Help each other stay centered on identifying and filling current true needs, vs. dwelling on the past or future too often.

Check to see if each person involved _ got their key current *true* needs filled well enough _ in a way that felt good enough. If someone didn't, help each other check for unseen communication blocks (p. 518), and review these tips (p. 528).

Enjoy growing the art and skill of praising and affirming _ yourself and _ each other. Learn how to assert "dodge-proof" compliments! [..02/assert.htm]

Learn what problem-solving techniques consistently work for you as individuals and co-parenting teammates. Then affirm and do more of them!

Pause and reflect: does this scheme seem practical? Could you omit any steps in resolving important conflicts? How does this framework compare to your present problem-solving strategy? What resolution framework are you teaching the youngsters in your life?

If you're in a stepfamily or you may be, premises like these will affect your problem-solving effectiveness . . .

Premises About Stepkids and Co-parenting

Premise 30) Legal divorce does not end a nuclear biofamily, it *reorganizes* it into two related homes. Minor and grown biokids still need intimate (vs. superficial) communication, undistracted time, informed guidance, protection, role-modeling, encouragement, affirmation, mirroring (feedback), and love from both parents, whether the adults re/marry or not. Without effective parental recovery from inner wounds, divorce will split a low-nurturance biofamily into two low-nurturance homes, with added stressors (Part 3). Minor kids remain at risk of psychological wounding and overwhelm from new concurrent adjustment needs (p. 464). Parental re/marriage and the five inexorable hazards (p. 428) *amplifies* this, vs. cures it!

Premise 31) Each living *or dead* psychological or biological parent of each minor or grown child in a divorced family or stepfamily **is a full member of the current multi-home family**. To build co-parental teamwork, family stabilization, and effective nurturing, all co-parent's needs, opinions, and values (or legacies) need to be equally respected by all other family adults. Committing to patiently healing the seven barriers in Part 2 can help you all achieve this family-membership goal. _ Adopting a long-range view, _ learning requisite information (Chapter 1), and clarifying your key _ premises (this chapter) and _ attitudes (Chapter 3) lay the foundation for the success you want to relish in old age. Typical insecure false-selves will blank this out or find ways of discounting it. See Project 3 in [A].

Premise 32) If any of you made one to three wrong re/marital decisions, these premises probably won't help, long term. From 21 years as a relationship therapist, I believe that typical divorced partners and new mates are usually _ wounded survivors of a low-nurturance childhood, _ unaware of significant false-self control. From neediness, unawareness, and reality distortions, typical co-parents (like *you?*) often choose the wrong people to re/wed, for the wrong reasons, at the wrong time. The horrific U.S. re/divorce epidemic documents this. The first seven co-parent projects [A] can help courting co-parents make three *right* choices for themselves and their descendents.

Protective false selves will focus on immediate gratification and "problem" co-parents, stepkids, and/or relatives, rather than face prior wrong re/marital decisions. To evaluate your re/marital decisions, see Project 7 in *Stepfamily Courtship* or [http://sfhelp.org/07/links07.htm].

Premise 33) Typical minor kids of divorce need *informed* co-parent help with _ healing early-childhood wounds, _ normal **developmental needs, and** _ two to five sets of overlapping **family-reorganization adjustments** (p. 464). If you co-parents can't form an effective team to _ learn these needs, _

communicate effectively, _ agree on how to nurture co-operatively, and _ monitor kids' progress (i.e. do Project 10), your
minor kids are at high risk of _ slowed or blocked development, _ amplified psychological wounds, and _ delayed self-
sufficiency. This promotes your kids _ leaving home too soon
(or *not* leaving), _ marrying and/or conceiving babies before
they can relate and/or parent adequately [D], and _ passing on
the ancestral bequest of low family nurturance and adaptive
false-self formation.

Kids' "acting out" often signals that _ their wounds and
web of unfilled needs are overwhelming them, _ they're not
getting adequate nurturing, and _ they need informed *help*. An
implication is that the nurturance level of their prior and current families has been too low. Kids "acting out" in a new
stepfamily can also mean _ normal or blocked grief, and _
healthy *testing* for security, and clarifying stepfamily membership, co-parental priorities, rules, and leadership.

Premise 34) If any re/married **co-parent _ rejects their
stepfamily identity** (Project 3), and/or doesn't proactively _
learn and _ *accept* stepfamily norms (Project 4), **they risk** up
to 60 **unrealistic expectations** [..04/myths.htm]. These will
hinder or block their _ forming a high-nurturance team and _
filling their and their minor stepkids' needs well enough. This
promotes low family nurturance [D] and eventual psychological or legal re/divorce.

Premise 35) Common personal stressors that inhibit co-
parent nurturance and team-building are **shame** (*I'm a bad
person and parent"*) **and divorce-related guilts** (*"I've broken
important shoulds, ought to's, and must-do's"*). These are specially likely in unrecovering survivors of low childhood
nurturance.

A common symptom of excessive shame and guilt in a
non-custodial bioparent is "ignoring" or "neglecting" their minor
or grown child/ren. This compounds itself—i.e. such wounded
moms and dads shame and guilt-trip themselves for being unable to admit or heal their shame and guilt. This is compounded
by unaware co-parents, kin, and professionals reviling them

for being an "uncaring" or "irresponsible" bioparent. See Chapter 17.

A related problem occurs if a wounded custodial parent denies or ignores divorce-related guilts. This often prevents their ruling subselves from giving a new primary relationship consistent genuine priority. It also inhibits essential grieving, and providing stable pro-grief home and family environments. *That* causes escalating secondary loyalty conflicts and relationship triangles among co-parents and kids. See Chapter 16.

Assessing for toxic shame and guilt, and learning how to heal each of them co-operatively promotes personal recovery and effective team-building. See Project 1 [A], [http://sfhelp.org/01/shame.htm], and Chapter 10.

Premise 36) Blocked grief in one or more family members can hinder building an effective co-parenting team. It signals _ significant psychological wounds, _ adult unawareness, and _ an unaware "anti-grief" ancestry and extended family. Divorce and co-parent re/marriage each cause major losses (broken psychological-spiritual attachments) in bonded adults and kids. If divorced mates or widow/ers haven't had time to grieve, and/or are psychologically blocked from doing so, co-parent relations will be conflictual, and true team-building difficult or impossible. Kids and/or grandparents who can't grieve will add stress. Moral: kids need their co-parents to *want to* help each other use Project 5 to build a "pro-grief" family environment, based on good progress on (at least) Projects 1-4. See *Stepfamily Courtship* or [..05/links05.htm].

Premise 37) If a stepparent _ feels their mate puts their kids' or ex mate's needs above her or his needs too often, and _ s/he doesn't assert for change, you all are at major risk of eventual psychological or legal re/divorce. If the stepparent *does* assert, and the bioparent is ambivalent (split) or resists usually putting their re/marriage ahead of their kids' short-term comforts, the same risk exists. This risk is higher if either mate is denying significant inner wounds. Two exceptions to this are _ the bioparent putting their own integrity and wholistic health before the stepparents' ongoing needs, and _ bioparent or stepchild emergencies. **Reality check:** After re/wedding, mates ask or tell each other at least monthly whether you're feeling valued enough by each other. Beware of assumptions and false-self distortions! See Chapters 7 and 16, Project 9b in *Build a High-nurturance Stepfamily*, or [..09/lc-intro.htm].

Premise 38) The effectiveness of your co-parenting team won't be known until your youngest child becomes fully independent and perhaps a parent. It depends directly on the degree of your shared, patient commitment to doing all 11 or 12 of the projects in [A] as partners with a shared goal: dependent kids' wholistic health and adult independence. *That* depends on each of you _ learning key things (Chapter 1), _ adopting a long range view, _ putting your Selves in charge, and _ working patiently to reduce any of your core barriers in Part 2, over time. Whew!

Before continuing, I encourage you to pause, breathe, stretch, and reflect. What are your subselves saying about _ what you just read, and _ what it *means* to you and those you care about?

Possibilities

Recall why you began reading this, and consider your choices now. You may . . .

Agree with much of what you've read here, and act on it "sometime" (vs. today); or . . .

Disagree with some or many of these premises, and stop there. Alternative: Disagree, and clarify for yourself and with your other co-parents what you *do* believe. Then use that to help in resolving your team-building problems.

Email or give printed copies of the Web versions of this chapter [..10/premises-rln.htm] to selected family members, professional supporters, and support-group participants. Use the copies to spur fruitful discussions together toward more effective relationship problem-solving.

Put a summary of your version of these premises where you adults can find it easily. Reread the premises out loud to each other when you feel stuck on some key co-parenting problem. And/or . . .

Reread this chapter periodically (e.g. at an anniversary or New year) and discuss your progress at _ building an effective co-parenting team together, and _ helping your kids satisfy their many concurrent needs (p. 464).

Periodically reread Project 2 together, and help each other improve your seven communication skills. See [H] and *Satisfactions* or [..02/links02.htm].

You have lots of choices here!

Recap

Boys and girls in divorced families and stepfamilies have a bewildering array of needs to fill to achieve stable adult independence. Kids need their custodial and non-custodial caregivers to _ know and agree on the kids' needs, and _ *want to* build a co-operative team to help fill them. Improving relations between co-parents also nurtures present and future re/marriages.

Building an effective co-parenting team after divorce or parental re/marriage is more likely if you adults are clear on, and act from, basic beliefs like those above. The purpose of this foundation chapter is not to tell you what to believe. It provides a way to discover what *you* caregivers believe now about _ people, _ relationships, and _ problem-solving. Premise 29 above (p. 52) offers steps to resolve *any* significant relationship problem, including those among your conflicted subselves.

The prior chapter proposed key knowledge you co-parents need to succeed, over time. This chapter adds a framework of useful beliefs. The next foundation chapter adds premises on how your co-parents' key *attitudes* will affect your team-building and family nurturance level, over time. Before considering them, take a . . .

 # Status check: see where you stand on what you just read: T = true, F = false, and "?" = "I'm not sure."

I feel a mix of calm, centered, energized, light, focused, resilient, up, grounded, relaxed, alert, aware, serene, purposeful, compassionate, and clear, so my Self is probably present now. (T F ?)

I believe we need to build an effective co-parenting team for our kids' sakes (T F ?)

I now accept that each of my kids' or stepkids' other parents as full, legitimate caregiving teammates. (T F ?)

Each of them accepts _ me and _ each other now as full caregiving partners in our multi-home family. (T F ?)

I see significant value in each of our co-parents _ discussing and _ becoming clear on beliefs like those above. (T F ?)

I can clearly define _ *problem*, _ *need*, and _ *conflict*, and _ I believe each other co-parent can too. (T F ?)

I believe that major conflicts between any of us co-parents are often concurrent problems _ inside each of us, and _ between us. (T F ?)

Each of our co-parents _ knows how to resolve *inner*-family conflicts effectively, *or* _ we know where to find out how to do that. (T F ?)

Each of us _ **can explain** the difference between a *surface* need and a *true* need, and _ can discern the difference. (T F ?)

I'm clear now on _ my version of each of the 38 premises in this chapter, and _ what each of our other co-parents believes. If not, _ I'm motivated now to learn this. (T F ?)

We co-parents _ now have an effective way of resolving most major family _ role and _ relationship conflicts, *or* _ we are each motivated to try out the problem-solving steps on p. 52 and edit them to fit us. (T F ?)

Awarenesses . . .

3) Key Attitudes and Expectations

Are Yours Assets or Barriers?

Working with hundreds of divorced and re/married couples since 1981, I've heard a rich medley of ex-mate descriptors like *Fang*, the *claw*, *psycho bitch*, *idiot*, *bastard*, *compulsive liar*, *irresponsible*, *crazy*, *uncaring*, *selfish*, *malicious*, *insensitive*, *abusive*, *stupid*, *ignorant*, *hopeless*, *wacko*, *heartless*, and *evil*. I've also heard ex mates described as "a really good parent, but a lousy mate." These are *attitudes* (good-bad judgments) about the ex mate's worth as a person and/or a co-parent.

Reflect: what adjectives do you usually choose to describe your and/or your partner's former spouse? Do your adjectives describe the kind of *person* s/he is, or how well s/he performs the complex role of *parent*?

What adjectives do you think s/he uses to describe *you*? How do you think these attitudes affect _ your co-parenting relationships, _ your kids' wholistic health, and _ the nurturance level of your multi-home family [D]?

Our U.S. divorce epidemic forces millions of parents and kids to live a stressful paradox, for years: one or both mates say "*I no longer like, respect, or trust you, and I choose not to live with you; but I have to interact with you because of my love and responsibility for our child/ren.*"

This chapter suggests key attitudes and expectations that can promote your co-parent team-building and long-term effectiveness. Use these pages to become aware of your caregivers' attitudes and expectations, and what they may *mean*, short and long term.

Premise: your current and long-term child-raising satisfaction depends on your _ inner-family leadership, _ awareness, _ knowledge (Chapter 1), and _ *attitudes* about key factors. Once you co-parents are aware of your attitudes, you may choose to discuss and "upgrade them" for long-term benefits.

What "key factors?"

- Are attitudes relevant or not?
- Are ex-mates bad or *wounded*?
- personal responsibility vs. blame
- Is *divorce* bad or wrong?
- Are re/marriages and stepfamilies inferior?
- Is marital and family conflict *bad?*
- Is *change* scary or comfortable?
- Is parenting mostly a joy or a stressor?
- Are losses and grieving good or bad?
- Is your glass half full or half empty?

Before exploring your attitudes about each of these and what they may *mean* to you and your loved ones, see what's true for you now . . .

 # Status Check: T=true, F=false, and "?"="I'm not sure, or "It depends on (what?)"

I feel a mix of calm, centered, energized, light, focused, resilient, up, grounded, relaxed, alert, aware, serene, purposeful, compassionate, and clear, so my Self is probably present now. (T F ?)

I see *both* bioparents of each child in my life, and any new partners (stepparents), as co-equal members of our multi-home nuclear family now. (T F ?)

I can clearly define what "an attitude" is. (T F ?)

I believe our co-parents' *attitudes* have a direct effect on the quality of our co-parenting, and how our dependent kids will "turn out," long-term. (T F ?)

I feel *attitudes* can be consciously _ chosen and _ changed, if there's reason to do so. (T F ?)

I'm responsible for the attitudes I hold. (T F ?)

When planning, making child-care decisions, and in family conflicts, I'm usually *aware* of _ my attitudes on the factors above and _ those of each other adult involved. (T F ?)

I'm comfortable discussing _ key attitudes and _ expectations with each of our co-parents now. (T F ?)

I feel my partner (if any) would answer "true" to each of these items now. (T F ?)

At this time, _ we co-parents have no serious "attitude problems" about family issues; *or* if we do, _ we have an effective way of resolving them now. (T F ?).

Pause and notice your thoughts and feelings. What do they mean?

With this fresh in mind, let's start our safari with your attitudes about . . .

Attitudes: Relevant or Not?

Have you co-parents ever discussed your "family attitude policy"? Do any of you have *biases* or *prejudices* about certain family attitudes, and the people who hold or promote them? If all your co-parents and supporters met together, see if you imagine anyone would disagree with these key attitudes:

Forming attitudes (good/bad, better/worse, or right/wrong judgments) is normal, human, and neither good or bad.

Certain attitudes are *better* than others in promoting personal healing, effective co-parenting teamwork, and high-nurturance relationships and families.

It's *good* for co-parents to help each other _ become aware of their key attitudes, and _ intentionally shift them toward those that are more helpful (below).

Co-parents ignoring or being unclear about family-related attitudes is *bad* because it risks hindering long-term success with their common goals. And . . .

Separating your attitudes from the people that hold them is *good*, because it reduces the chance of people feeling blamed, guilty, shamed, hurt, and defensive.

Pause and reflect: can you think of other attitudes about human, relationship, and family attitudes that you co-parents and kids would benefit from? How comfortable are you at discussing attitudes like these with your other co-parents and key supporters?

An overarching attitude question for each of you is . . .

Is Your Glass Half Full, or Half Empty?

How would you describe the key difference between a *pessimist or cynic*, an *optimist*, an *idealist*, and a *realist*? Which of these best describes you _ in general, and _ relative to your current family's status and future? Do you think life-attitudes like these can significantly affect your chances to build an effective co-parenting team over time? If so, do you think your co-parents can intentionally shift from one of these attitudes to another?

A pessimist would assume *"Divorced family and stepfamily relationships can never be as fulfilling as intact biofamily relationships. Working to build an effective co-parenting team will never work, and is a waste of time and energy."*

A realistic optimist would assume *"If co-parents are self responsible, patient, and resourceful, divorced-family and re/married-family relationships can be just as satisfying and fulfilling as intact-biofamily counterparts."*

An idealist or optimist would assume *"Love, faith, and God will heal all wounds, and conquer all obstacles. Families are stronger than any trauma or obstacle, if the adults try, and others don't interfere. Divorce or death will never overcome or block parents and kids core love for each other. We co-parents don't really need to be aware of our attitudes, or worry about building a co-parenting team. Stepfamilies are really not sig-*

nificantly different than biofamilies, no matter what so-called 'experts' say."

My experience is that the type of "glass" (life attitude) you have is a direct reflection of who is leading your inner team of subselves. Generally, wounded people are often led by critical, perfectionist, idealistic, scared, cynical, shamed, angry, or hopeless subselves much of the time. These usually promote glass-half-empty or unrealistically cheery, idealistic attitudes, in general, or in times of crisis and change.

People who are often led by their true Selves and Higher Power tend to be flexible, resilient, open "realistic optimists." Their glass is often half full spontaneously, not from duty, dogma, or need for approval.

This view implies that if you and any other family co-parents and key relatives are "half-empty" people, _ a false self often rules that person, and _ s/he *can* shift toward genuine half-full *if* s/he patently works toward recovery and freeing her or his Self to lead (wants to do some version of Project 1). It also implies that without attention, your "half-empty" co-parents' (subselves') will expect and focus on reasons why you *can't* build a co-parenting team, or why beneficial changes *won't work.* Half-empty people really distrust _ the competence of ruling subselves and key others, _ any Higher power, and _ "the universe" to be reliably *safe enough,* long term. See Chapter 9.

Part of shifting to a half-full (realistic optimism) attitude permanently and peacefully, is freeing any anxious, rigid subselves from old fears, guilts, or compulsions about having a different life-attitude than your dominant childhood caregivers. Did you grow up with genuinely "half-full" people and hero/ines? Would any key person/s censure or reject you if you shifted toward "realistic optimism"?

A key implication is that any "half empty" (wounded) co-parents probably can't be converted by threat, scorn, or "logic," but you *do* have impactful options. See Chapter 5.

If all your co-parents were steadily harmonious, you probably wouldn't be reading this. So what's your attitude: are . . .

Troublesome Co-parents: *Bad* or *Wounded*?

Do you believe some people are *better* than others? Do you feel some people are *bad* by choice or nature? If you judge an ex mate in your family as a *bad* person or *bad influence* on your kids (or vice versa), it will hinder every negotiation and interaction you have with them. Your kids lose.

One reason is this: you co-parents communicate to fill your current needs. A universal need is to feel *respected*, specially by your family members (right?). The effectiveness of your communication depends directly on the R(espect)-messages that you each perceive from each other (p. 510). If you or a co-parent decodes "*You don't respect me (as a person or a co-parent)*" from the other's behavior, _ hurt, resentful, defensive subselves will probably take over, causing _ your E(motion)-level to rise "above your ears," so _ your abilities to hear, empathize, and ability to problem-solve drop fast, and _ neither you nor the ex get your needs met. This is specially likely if either of you is a shame-based (wounded) person with low self esteem.

If you're not aware of this happening and what it means, you each will learn to expect that any time you and an ex mate interact, _ you and/or they will feel "badly" (disrespected and unheard), and that _ communications "won't work" (fill everyone's needs) This dooms important co-parenting negotiations before they start. Ex mates using lawyers or letters to negotiate, avoiding child-care contact, and repeated fights and phone hang-ups are clear signs this has happened. Everyone loses. See Chapter 18.

Your ex mates have a history of painful interactions and disagreements, ranging from minor to massive. New conflicts between your co-parents are inevitable as your multi-home family evolves. Because love has been replaced by some mix of the barriers on p. 109, ex mates often judge each other as *bad* people (unworthy, immoral, sick, selfish, uncooperative, spiteful, etc.)

For your kids' long-range welfare and your own old-age

satisfaction, I urge you to choose and promote the genuine attitude that a "difficult" co-parent is *wounded* and *unaware* (vs. stupid), not *bad* or *evil*. Read Chapters 5 and 6, and then use [D and E] to tentatively evaluate this wounding. Use Project 1 to confirm your findings. This doesn't mean you must accept or excuse toxic behavior from them. It means you can assert your needs, opinions, and limits *respectfully* (an =/= attitude), vs. sending provocative "1-up" R-messages that will raise the other adult's defensiveness, hostility, and antagonism. See Chapter 8.

When a child "acts out," do you see her or him as a *bad* (unworthy, inept) *person*, or do you focus on confronting the unpleasant impact of their actions? Your other co-parents need respect as much as your child/ren and you do. My experience is that "disrespect" and "hostility" from a co-parent is usually a combination of anger, distrust, guilt, shame, and anxiety. These are often seasoned with blocked grief, which is a sign of false-self wounds and unawareness. Would you agree that none of these merit moral censure or scorn?

A corollary: if experience and your values have taught you to view an ex mate or stepparent as *bad*, *sick*, or *evil*, that will usually determine what you expect of her or him. If you expect conflict, selfishness, aggression, or the like, your attitude will leak, and unconsciously *encourage* behaviors like that. Notice who's responsible for changing this . . .

What's your reaction to these ideas? If your inner voices are insisting that the co-parent is *bad* and that you shouldn't or can't view them as wounded and unaware, I'd bet Fort Knox that a false self rules you, at least relative to this co-parent. Have you done Project 1 yet—honestly?

Reality check: how do you feel now about each co-parent in your multi-home family? How does your partner (if any) feel? How do they others feel about *you*?

Beside your attitudes about attitudes and other co-parents, how do you feel about . . .

Personal Responsibility vs. Blame

If a storm causes a tree branch to break your window, would you growl "You're a *bad* storm (or branch)?" If someone intentionally withholds relevant information or lies, do you *blame* them—judge them as *wrong* or *bad?* How do you usually feel when someone blames *you* for causing them discomfort, or for not behaving the way they wish?

Thomas Gordon, the founder of Parent Effectiveness Training (PET), proposes that parents of an upset child get better long term results when they ask themselves "*Who's problem (unfilled need) is this, yours or mine?*" In family conflicts, change "child" to "co-parent," and ask that question.

A basic premise here is that each of your co-parents is ultimately responsible for filling their own needs. Do you agree? If an inner voice says "*Yes, but . . .*" suspect a false self is reacting. Implication: if a co-parent or someone else frustrates, hurts, attacks, or ignores _ you; _ your partner, if any; and/or _ a child you care for; s/he is responsible for her or his actions, and *you* are responsible for _ possibly *promoting* those actions, and _ reacting to them. The reverse holds true too.

As you know, our (perceived) behaviors affect other peoples' comfort (inner-family serenity), and vice versa. By indifference, accident, or intent, we frustrate, irritate, hurt, guilt-trip, scare, and shame each other. Human nature decrees that if you blame another for causing or prolonging your significant discomfort, s/he will feel hurt, frustrated, guilty, attacked, and/or angry *if* you are perceived as disrespectful.

In a co-parenting conflict, each time your attitude is "*It's (the other person's) fault, not* mine!" you're increasing the core barriers in Part 2, and decreasing your chance to build an effective co-parenting team. Your kids are the biggest losers, long term. Does this make sense to you?

Try this: in a recent or your next co-parenting conflict, ask yourself "*What have I done that promoted the other adult to act this way?*" Dishonesty begets dishonesty, insecurity, and distrust. Disrespect breeds disrespect. **In any problem with**

another co-parent, *you* are half of the problem! The good news: that means you can fix your half, if you choose to. You may promote the other co-parent fixing their half if you _ get clear on what you need, and _ assert that *respectfully* when s/he can hear you.

Incidentally, your dedicated *Inner Critic's* shaming and blaming *you* for a co-parenting problem breeds self-doubt, guilt, and shame. Lose-lose-lose.

Note: if a co-parent in your family survived a low-nurturance childhood, s/he probably is burdened with excessive shame and guilts. Those can manifest as "having a hair trigger," *over-defensiveness, hyper-sensitivity, selfishness, conceit, lying*, or *"never owning responsibility or apologizing."* If you blame a co-parent for these traits as being *bad*, you _ miss the underlying wound/s, _ invite increasing inner and family conflict, over time; _ reduce odds of co-parent team-building, which _ lowers your family's nurturance level, and _ unintentionally wounds your kids.

Bottom line: for long-term success building an effective co-parenting team and high-nurturance family, I encourage all your co-parents to _ choose the attitude *"I am responsible for my half of any family (or other) conflicts,"* and _ help each other replace toxic false-self *blaming* and *avoiding* with effective problem-solving (p. 52 and Chapter 7).

Is Divorce *Bad* or *Wrong*?

Over half of Americans who have tried marriage recently "fail," as judged by (re)divorce statistics and thousands of "Marriage and Family" clinics, consultants, and programs in every hamlet and city. Our Christian tradition decrees that we view _ sanctioned marriage as a sacred commitment to God, our mate, and ourself; and _ infidelity, desertion, and divorce as *sins*—disobeying God, and morally *weak* and *wrong*.

Were you taught as a child to not hurt other people—specially children? Do you still hold that value? Do you agree that *divorce* causes everyone affected, including minor and grown kids and grandparents, *pain*?

Premise: If any of your co-parents or key supporters views divorce or divorced people as significantly *wrong, bad, sinful* or *(shameful)* *"failures,"* it will hinder your forming an effective co-parenting team. It will do that via steady or situational shame and guilt (Chapter 10). These *always* breed _ false-self dominance (Chapters 5-6), _ ineffective communication (Chapter 7), divisive loyalty conflicts and relationship triangles (Chapter 16), anxiety, distraction, and blocked grief (Chapter 12). Does this proposal match your experience?

Do any members of your extended family believe that divorced families and/or stepfamilies are "not as good as" intact biofamilies? Does anyone believe "kids of divorce don't do as well," or "are likely to divorce too"? I suggest there's little constructive value in debating or "dis/proving" opinions like these. It's more useful to focus on the effects any such attitudes have on your co-parenting expectations, relationships, and team-building.

I recommend you co-parents help each other view any divorces as . . .

* sad and regrettable, not *bad*;
* clear evidence that one or both mates were/are unaware (Chapter 1) and significantly wounded (Chapters 5-6), not *bad* or *wrong*;
* a learning experience that has the potential to promote personal growth and healthy bonds; and . . .
* causing major losses that all family adults and kids need to grieve well, over several *years*.

I further propose the attitude that kids and adults in divorced families are *normal* people with *normal* human talents, limits, needs, and dreams, *and* _ an important set of personal and relationship adjustment needs to fill in addition to their normal developmental challenges. See Resource [F].

Re/marriage and Stepfamilies

From tradition, media influence, and unawareness, your co-parents and supporters may have harmful attitudes about re/married families and their members like these:

"Remarried people couldn't get it right the first time (there's something wrong with them)"

"Stepfamilies are alien, abnormal, and not as good as traditional (intact bio) families."

"Stepparents and stepkids are unnatural and second best compared to bioparents and their children."

"Stepkids don't turn out as well (as kids in intact biofamilies)."

Attitudes like these are toxic because _ they're vague generalities, _ they promote unawareness and bias, and _ they breed subtle or overt anxiety, pessimism, dishonesty, and *shame.* Most re/wedded adults seem to come from low-nurturance childhoods. They already wrestle with feeling unlovable, inept, and unworthy—specially if their *Inner Critic* was taught to view prior divorce as a shameful "failure."

A symptom of adults or kids holding attitudes like these is avoiding public acknowledgement of prior divorce, remarriage, and/or step-hood. (*"We're just a regular family . . ."*). See the Web worksheet [..03/identity-wks.htm] for more symptoms.

More nourishing attitudes are something like . . .

"Remarriage testifies to the power of love and hope over fear, and to the normal human longing to share the security, companionship, and joy of a committed primary relationship."

"Stepfamilies have the same potential for nurturance, security, pride, and fellowship as any other kind of family. They are different, *not better or worse."*

"'Stepparent' and 'stepchild' are roles, *not* people. *They are similar to, and* different *than, bioparent and biochild. There is nothing inherently* inferior (or superior) *about these common family roles.*

"Stepkids do *have higher odds of being psychologi-*

*cally wounded than kids in high-nurturance biofamilies.
With informed, consistent nurturing by healthy
caregivers, stepkids have just as much chance for happiness and productivity."*

If all your family members were together and undistracted,
and someone read these attitudes out loud, what might happen?"

Another important co-parent attitude to pay attention to has
to do with . . .

Is Marital and Family Conflict *Bad?*

What are your respective co-parents' attitudes about *fighting, arguing,* and *conflict* _ in general and _ in your homes
and family? Do you know anyone who sees conflict as a (potentially) good thing?

I recall a number of engaged co-parents saying proudly in
re/marriage-prep meetings, *"We* never *fight!"* That implied the
speakers _ believed conflict is *bad* or *wrong,* _ weren't confident about using disagreements to *build* their relationship/s,
and _ had probably never experienced most "fights" as constructive.

Divorce and later legal battles (Chapter 18) imply the ex
mates weren't able to problem-solve effectively. In typical divorced families and stepfamilies, disagreements _ inside people
and _ between members and homes are normal and inevitable,
not *bad!*

If you co-parents have usually experienced *fights* as stressful and unfulfilling in childhood and married life, your governing subselves will unconsciously expect them to be the same
after divorce. They'll probably _ avoid conflicts, and/or _ automatically react to family conflict with a combative (win-lose)
mind-set. If a false self rules any of you, your subselves may
enjoy the excitement of a good fight, and/or seek to punish
someone for hurting them. By definition, true Selves don't value
those.

Your terminology counts: *fighting* and *arguing* have the connotations of antagonism, aggression, disrespect, winning, and losing. *Problem-solving* and *conflict resolution* are associated with cooperation, mediation, willing compromise, and mutual respect. Note also the powerful difference between *aggression* (*"I want _____, and I don't care what you feel or want"*) and *assertion*: (*"I need _____ now. What do* you *need?"*) Review p. 26 in the context of what you just read . . .

Forming an effective co-parenting team over time *will* cause you all many major inner and shared conflicts over caregiving goals and values, styles, and preferences. If you all help each other learn that these disputes can often have positive win-win-win outcomes. See Chapter 7, [..02/win-win.htm], and [..02/lose-lose.htm].

Co-parents who . . .

are guided by their true Selves (Project 1), and choose to . . .

see each other as equals in dignity and worth (above); and . . .

are *aware* of what _ they and _ their family members really need [..02/dig-down.htm], and who . . .

are fluent in the seven Project 2 skills [H] . . .

. . . can view family conflicts as inevitable *opportunities* to build personal awareness, teamwork, and bonding together, not something to be avoided, denied, or criticized.

Your custodial and visiting kids and their descendents depend on you co-parents to *want* to do this for them. Do you, so far?

This is pretty dry (and important) stuff. Breathe, stretch, and see if you need a mind/body break . . . When you're ready, re-check: is your Self still leading your inner family? Let's continue strengthening your team-building foundation by exploring your co-parents' attitudes about . . .

Is *Change* Scary, or Comfortable?

Have you noticed the ceaseless wars inside you and around you? They're battles between avoiding the losses and uncertainties of changing the status quo, and the inevitability and *need* for change. Divorce or mate-death forces many changes on you and your kids. So does dating, re/marriage, and cohabiting. So does aging and the Earth spiraling through the cosmos. So does our relentless overpopulation. So do germs and evolution. Paradoxically, our need to accept and adapt to change never changes.

Your co-parents' (subselves') attitudes about *change* will greatly affect if and how well you all _ recover from inner wounds, _ grieve your many losses, _ resolve your many conflicts, _ form new (step)family bonds, and _ adjust to new living conditions. Do you agree?

Do you welcome change, and feel confident about your ability to adapt to it? Does each of your co-parents feel this way? Do your kids? Did your parents?

I suspect some of your subselves welcome change, others fear and oppose it, and still others may yawn and shrug it off. In other words, you may have different attitudes about change *within* you. "Conservatives" avoid change, and "liberals" promote it. **Reality**: you can't *force* insecure subselves to trust that environmental change won't cause too much pain or chaos (overwhelm). You can learn to demonstrate to them that change is safe enough *if* _ your subselves trust your Self to lead, and _ notice the outcomes objectively. See Project 1 and Chapter 5.

Some, vs. all, changes involve losses—broken psycho-spiritual bonds. Healthy grief is the emotional-spiritual-mental process that yields stable acceptance of significant losses *if it's allowed to*. My experience is that blocked grief is a major unseen stressor in typical divorced families and stepfamilies [A]. You co-parents can build pro-grief homes together (Chapter 12) *if* you all are _ aware of life-changes and accept their inevitability; _ see change as "usually safe enough;" _ evolve an effective change-management plan (Chapter 23), and _ view changes as "often beneficial, long term." Do these describe each of your co-parents, so far? What attitudes about *change* are you grownups teaching your kids?

Option: meditate or journal about what your subselves and your body are saying now . . .

Take heart: we're in the home stretch. While we're "in the (change) neighborhood," consider your attitudes about . . .

Losses and *Grieving*: Good or Bad?

Can you describe your personal, and your family's, "policies" on *grieving*? My bias is that our wounded pleasure-biased society places little value on understanding and promoting healthy personal and family mourning, yet normal life, and our U.S. divorce epidemic and family mobility make healthy grief a requisite in every person and home.

A *loss* is a broken psychological-spiritual attachment to something or someone. Life forces losses on all us adults and kids as we age, and we choose to break other bonds to ease discomfort or get a greater good. How well (our subselves) move through the phases of grief affects our wholistic health, our relationship harmonies, and when and if we can form new bonds.

Do you honestly feel *losses* are *good*, *bad*, or neither? Do you see *mourning* in _ yourself and _ your family members as useful, normal, and healthy ("good"), or something to fear and be repressed, avoided, and "gotten over fast"? Do you feel grieving *adds* to, or detracts from, the richness of family life and relationships? Note that "*I don't (want to) know*" and "*I don't care*" are *attitudes.*

Your childhood perceptions of what you saw your caregivers and hero/ines do with their losses, and how they reacted to yours, have shaped your subselves' attitudes about the value of grieving and how to "do it." Your crew of subselves' attitudes probably clash, so your dominant personality parts will determine your attitudes about losses and mourning.

Premises: _ Losses *hurt*! The pain of a loss is proportional to the strength and priority of the broken bond. Because most infants, kids, and adults automatically feel pleasure and attach to (care about) sources of it, losses are inevitable and *neither good nor bad.* _ Healthy three-level grief is *good*, because it promotes inner-family relief and harmony, wholistic health and long life, and (eventually) forming new bonds along the way. If our subselves perceive that grieving isn't safe enough, we slow or stop our journey toward acceptance, release, and re-building. Blocked grief _ promotes (secondary) health prob-lems, _ hinders ex mates' healing and childcare teamwork and forming new stepfamily bonds, and _ promote misinforming and wounding your kids. Do you believe this? *Does it apply to your family?*

Understanding and acknowledging losses, and valuing healthy three-level mourning, can help you all form an effec-tive nurturing team for your kids. Helping your youngsters learn to do "good grief" becomes one of your shared objectives, over time.

Pause and reflect: what do you believe each of your co-parents' attitudes are about _ losses and _ grieving? Is there any chance you and/or they are blocked in mourning key losses? See Chapter 12 and Project 5 [A].

Co-parenting is about nurturing minor and grown kids – respectfully filling their current true *needs.*

Is (Co)parenting a Joy or a Stressor?

Do you know adults who generally welcome the anxieties, doubts, and heartaches of child-rearing? Who see parenting as an exciting, rewarding long-term opportunity to co-create something (some*one*) of rare value? Did each of your parents and grandparents feel something like that? Do *you*? Do you know any foster, adoptive, or stepparents who feel some ver-sion of that about nurturing someone else's offspring?

Check to see if your Self is "leading your inner orchestra" (of subselves) now. Then try saying this out loud, and notice what you feel and think:

"*I _ often genuinely* enjoy *co-parenting, and I _ want the responsibility and rewards of nurturing the younger people in my life.*"

Does that ring true, or do you feel resistance and ambiva-lence? Do any inner voices (subselves) say "*Yes, but . . .*", or " . . .

except for . . ." Imagine each of your other co-parents saying that out loud, or ask them to. What would their reactions be?

Co-parents who . . .

- were unwanted conceptions themselves, and/or . . .
- had wounded, unavailable, overwhelmed parents,
- are too wounded,
- married prematurely or unwisely,
- had unplanned conceptions,
- have unrealistic visions of parenting,
- are environmentally overwhelmed, and/or . . .
- fear conflict and asserting their needs, and/or . . .
- think that having kids will bring social acceptance and/or fill the emptiness within them . . .

. . . often feel ambivalent, dutiful, guilty, or resentful about filling kids' needs. This is specially likely if they have too little healthy child-raising knowledge, confidence in their and their mate's capabilities, and social and spiritual supports.

Divorce and parent/mate death each cause special adjustment needs in surviving kids and adults. So do parental dating, re/wedding, and cohabiting [F]. Adequate *bioparenting* knowledge, confidence, satisfactions, and goals may be overwhelmed by these mosaics of new needs and environmental changes.

Most stepparents with or without kids of their own are stunned and disoriented by the complexity, conflict, and challenge of co-nurturing their mate's custodial or visiting kids. After courtship idealism and optimism inevitably wane, stepdads and moms can feel their nurturing role yields more stress than satisfaction and joy—specially if they and/or their mate are ruled by a false self, and their re/marriage is significantly troubled.

Premise: your co-parents' combined attitudes about their child-care responsibilities will help or hinder your forming an effective nurturing team. Do you each know what your (true) attitude about co-parenting is? Do you need anyone to *change* their attitude? What would they need for that to happen? Start by evaluating whether they're wounded and often ruled by a false self [E]. Then assess whether they have clear, realistic long-range images of how they want your dependent kids to turn out, or are focused only on resolving current conflicts. Note: all of this applies to typical co-grandparents and involved other relatives too . . .

We've just toured a set of nine *attitudes* about key aspects of you and your family relationships. The real value of meditating and discussing topics like these is in intentionally reducing one of five stepfamily hazards: *unawareness.*

Recap

Your multi-home family's co-parents can choose nourishing or toxic *attitudes* about key aspects of their lives and relationships. If each co-parent takes responsibility for growing nourishing, realistically-optimistic attitudes like those above, then building an effective co-parent team and a high-nurturance multi-home environment for you all is more likely. Your family situation is unique, so you may have other attitudes as primal as the nine above. Your adults' mix of attitudes have as much impact on resolving the team-building blocks in Part 2 as _ your inner-family harmonies (Project 1), _ your knowledge (Chapter 1), and _ your shared communication effectiveness (Chapter 7).

As you clarify, compare, evaluate, and harmonize your attitudes enough, your co-parents can better help each other reduce the team-building barriers on p. 109. Your attitudes, knowledge, goals, and barriers all interact together—and react to environmental changes—in a dynamic flux. With knowledge, awareness, and =/= discussion, you all can control some of the flux. You can use the Serenity Prayer (p. 24) to accept and adapt to the rest.

Now you've reviewed _ what you need to know to get the most from this book, _ an array of key premises about relationships and problems, and _ some core attitudes that will affect your co-parenting harmony. The last foundation chapter provides context and an overview of your whole vital team-building effort—co-parent Project 10.

4) Overview: Co-parent Team-building

Typical Goals, Barriers, and Options

Compared to peers in intact biofamilies, adults and kids in typical divorced families and stepfamilies have _ *many* concurrent special needs, and _ more barriers to filling them. Average multi-home stepfamilies have _ more kids than biofamilies, and _ three or more co-parents (bioparents and stepparents) who are often _ wounded and antagonistic; and _ unaware of stepchild needs; stepfamily norms, tasks, and hazards; and key relationship and caregiving skills.

Together, these factors _ create a high need for co-parent awareness and teamwork, and _ make it very hard to achieve these together. Without proactive adult effort at learning and team-building, existing and new kids are at risk of growing up in a low-nurturance environment, and inheriting major psychological wounds. This book illuminates seven core barriers to co-parental teamwork, and proposes effective ways to reduce them, over time.

This chapter hilights half of co-parent Project 10: build an effective co-parenting team, and nurture your dependent kids. It proposes three steps to effective teambuilding, and summarizes key factors that can hinder these steps. The other half of Project 10 is your caregiving team evolving effective child discipline: see *Build a High-nurturance Stepfamily* [xlibris.com, 2001], or [..10/discipline1.htm].

To *nurture* **is to fill someone's needs** and promote their welfare and growth. Families exist (partly) to nurture kids' needs to become independent, wholistically healthy adults who can raise kids effectively themselves. Caregiving adults have their *own* needs which need nurturing. Depending on many factors, families with and without kids range from low to high nurturance. Do you agree?

Who Needs What?

To raise your awareness for the rest of this chapter, bookmark this page. Imagine all the people in your kids' several homes, and thoughtfully read three things about you all. Notice your thoughts and emotions as you do . . .

- What most (all?) humans need: p. 44;
- What your minor kids probably need: p. 464; and . . .
- What typical stepfamily co-parents need: p. 493.

High-nurturance families consistently fill most or *all* of these (!), and grow specific traits like those on p. 440. Would each of your co-parents like to co-create such a family over time? Have you ever discussed this together? You may have, if you men and women have begun to evolve a multi-home family mission statement (p. 438).

Status Check: get a sense of where your co-parents stand now. Identify each adult you include as "one of our co-parents." Imagine all of you together in a comfortable place, and thoughtfully respond to these statements . . .

Right now, I feel some mix of *calm, centered, energized, light, focused, resilient, up, grounded, relaxed, alert, aware, serene, purposeful,* and *clear*—so my true Self is probably leading my other subselves. (T F ?)

Each of our co-parents can name most of the three sets of needs above now (T F ?)

I _ can clearly name the attributes of an "*effective* team," and _ I have belonged to one. (T F ?)

I believe I have an *"inner* family" or team of personality subselves, which regulate my thoughts, emotions, body, and behaviors (T F ?). See [..01/innerfam1.htm].

On a scale of 1 (very chaotic) **to 10** (very harmonious), I would rank my *inner* team of subselves as a __ in the past six months.

On the same scale, I'd rank the *inner*-team harmony of each of my other co-parents as: __ __ __ __ __

I'm _ clearly aware of the needs that each of our minor kids is trying to master, and I _ can describe each child's current status with each of their needs now. (T F ?)

Each of our other co-parents would confidently answer "T(rue)" to the items above now. (T F ?)

On a scale of 1 (completely uncooperative and ineffective) **to 10** (consistently harmonious and effective), I'd rate our group of co-parents as a __ now. Option: one at a time, imagine how each other co-parent would rank your group's recent effectiveness, 1 to 10: __ __ __ __ __

From 1 (impossible, not worth trying) **to 10** (achievable and well worth working at), I'd rank the likelihood of us all becoming a stable, *effective* co-parenting team in the next five to 10 years as a __.

From 1 (totally unmotivated) **to 10** (strongly motivated), my current interest in building an effective co-parenting team is a __.

One at a time, imagine the reaction of each of your co-parents to the last two items: __ __ __ __ __ and __ __ __ __ __

Put the book down, breathe well, and notice what your subselves are saying and feeling now . . . Option: journal about your reaction to this status check, and what your responses means to you, your kids, and your family's potential nurturance level.

Your co-parents have various caregiving goals now. They range from fuzzy and conflicted to clear and compatible. You all also have many resources, and some limitations and barriers. How can you optimize _ your caregiving teamwork and _ the nurturance-level of your family together, for your and your descendents' sakes? Consider these . . .

Three Project-10 Steps

If your co-parents are already working on Projects 1 through 6, this first team-building step uses them—specially the "job descriptions" you (may have) drafted [..10/job1.htm]. The following assumes you all are progressing on healing significant psychological wounds and building _ mutual-respect attitudes (Project 1), and _ effective communication skills (Project 2). It also assumes you all are motivated to learn and apply the key topics in Chapter 1.

Keep your perspective: these three steps span *many* years, and occur as your environment constantly changes. As you read this, mull who's responsible for seeing that steps like these occur in your multi-home family, over time? What might you feel in your old age if no one takes that responsibility?

Step 1) Form a stable co-parenting team. In most stepfamilies, this requires _ ex mates intentionally working to reduce their mix of the stressors on p. 109; _ all caregivers *wanting to* accepting your stepfamily identity and membership (Project 3), _ learning what that means (Project 4), and _ working to resolve up to seven concurrent core barriers via Project 2 skills. It also requires you all to *want to* learn how to resolve a stream of _ values and _ loyalty conflicts, and _ relationship triangles (Chapter 16). Progress on these sub-tasks may require _ one or more of your co-parents to *want to* free up blocked grief (Chapter 12, and Project 5).

As your caregivers and key supporters progress on these subtasks . . .

Step 2) Prepare to nurture. All your co-parents and supporters _ get clear on what *effective* parenting is *in a divorced family or stepfamily context* [..01/co-p-goals.htm]. Then _ agree on which kids you're responsible for nurturing as a team. _

Identify those kids' normal developmental needs, and _ learn the several sets of unique adjustment needs that typical stepkids must fill (p.464). Then _ assess each child for their progress and status with each of their developmental and adjustment needs, and _ agree on what kind of help each child needs to progress toward wholistically-healthy independence. Then . . .

Step 3) _ **Negotiate** which adults are responsible for what with each child, **and** _ *enjoy* **helping each other nurture your kids** *and each other*, over time.

I've rarely met stepfamily co-parents who could describe _ some version of these three multi-part teambuilding steps, and _ a viable plan for doing them. I believe y*ou all* can, if all your co-parents are clear on _ specifically what you want to achieve as responsible caregivers long-term [C]; _ what each of your kids and adults need now (above); and _ what your adults' true priorities are [..08/priority.htm]. Are your co-parents and supporters clear enough on these now?

The rest of this chapter explores these three steps. *Build a High-nurturance Stepfamily* includes this and a related chapter on evolving effective child discipline in your co-parenting homes [..10/discipline1.htm].

1) Form An Effective Co-parenting Team

Most stepkids like Patty McLean [..example.htm] have three or four co-parents in two homes: their biomom and biodad, and one or two part-time or full-time stepparents. If one or both of their *step*parents has biokids and a living ex mate, a stepchild may have five or six caregivers influencing their lives:

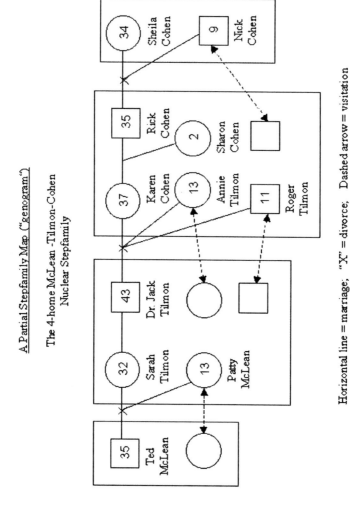

A Partial Stepfamily Map ("genogram")

The 4-home McLean-Tilmon-Cohen Nuclear Stepfamily

Horizontal line = marriage; "X" = divorce; Dashed arrow = visitation

In a small minority of U.S. stepfamilies, a stepchild's other bioparent is dead and their stepparent is childless, so they have only two active co-parents. From a child's point of view, having three or more co-parents can be anything between a wonderful asset to daily stress. What makes the difference, and what choices do well-meaning co-parents like you have?

Let's start by defining an *effective team*, and comparing the definition to your co-parents' current relationships. Then we'll look at barriers to your team building, and options for overcoming them.

What's an Effective Team?

Have you ever felt part of a team? (Option: consider your marriage/s.) Do you feel a *team* differs from a *committee*, a *club*, a *gang*, a *class*, a *crew*, or a *clan*? If so, how? How would you reply if a touring space alien asked, "What is this thing you humans call a *team?*" How about . . .

"*A team is two or more people who want to use their talents and resources cooperatively to achieve common goals, over time.*"

Would you agree that some teams are more effective at goal-achievement than others? If so, why? Go deeper than "because they're better." Better at what? Have you belonged to a team that "worked well," and another one that didn't? If you co-parents want to provide the most effective nurturance team you can for your family members, what criteria are you using to build your team? See if you agree that any *effective* team needs these **seven core elements:**

< Several people who _ share **clear high-priority goals**, and _ are motivated to work steadily toward them while balancing other life needs.

< **A talented**, committed, confident, far-seeing *leader* whom other teammates consistently respect, trust, and want to follow through challenges and conflicts.

< All teammates genuinely **prizing the team's welfare and success** as much or more than their own individual needs, except in personal emergencies.

< **An evolving, realistic *plan*** that guides teammates to use their resources toward their group goals;

And an *effective* team has . . .

< Flexibly-firm **team _ roles, _ rules, and _ consequences** that are _ clear and _ consistent enough for all teammates. Each

role (set of responsibilities) is harmonious enough with _ the abilities, motives, limitations, and current needs of the person filling the role; and with _ the team's major goals. And . . .

< **An effective way to resolve** conflicts between _ teammates, and _ between the team and its environment; and finally . . .

< **Supportive _ Natural and _ human environments** that allow the team to function, vs. creating major obstacles.

Can you think of other factors needed for an effective team? I encourage you all to evolve *your* definition. Long-term success is more likely if all your co-parents agree on specifically what you're trying to co-create for your kids and you. Jack and Sarah Tilmon [..example.htm] had never discussed this, let alone agreed on it. I suspect their parents hadn't either. Did yours?

Option: use this framework to build a practical definition of an effective *co-parenting* team. Some key elements are all your adults . . .

_ agreeing on the relevance and importance of the 12 co-parent projects [A], and sharing a long-term commitment to them;

_ desiring to _ learn the normal and special needs of family kids and adults (above), and _ help each other fill these short and long-term needs cooperatively, vs. combatively, for all your sakes; and . . .

_ committing to help each other reduce the teamwork barriers in Part 2, over time to progress toward the goals in your mission statement [C].

Your unique situation may merit adding other factors to your definition. The key is evolve a consensual definition, and *use* it and your mission statement!

 # Status check: Pause and take stock again. Take your time, and ignore items that don't apply (yet). Distorted or superficial answers risk hurting your kids and old-age remorse . . .

I believe my true Self is guiding my inner family now. (T F ?)

I agree that _ we are a *step*family (vs. "just a regular (bio)family"); and that _ all our kids' living bioparents and any new mates are each full members of our stepfamily, despite our differences or conflicts. (T F ?) If you don't really accept your stepfamily identity yet, review Project 3 in *Stepfamily Courtship* or [..03/project03.htm] now. Ignoring this will probably minimize any value from your reading further.

I can _ clearly define what *nurture* means in a family context; and _ I'm able to provide some nurturing to kids and adults now. *Some co-parents from very low-nurturance childhoods can't bond or nurture themselves, kids, or adults, without personal recovery.* (T F ?)

I can _ name at least 10 of the 28 traits of high-nurturance families now, and I _ know where to find the others. (T F ?)

I genuinely want to (vs. *have* to) help nurture each minor and grown child in our stepfamily now, within my limits. (T F ?)

I believe our kids have the best chance for developing healthy independence if our co-parents work as a cooperative team to promote that, over time. (T F ?)

I can _ name the factors needed for an effective team now; *or* _ I'm actively working to identify these factors, because I want to (vs. *have* to). (T F ?)

I'm genuinely willing to _ negotiate with our other co-parents and _ compromise some of my caregiving values and habits, to build an effective team for our kids' and descendents' sakes. (T F ?)

I'm confident that _ **my partner** (if any) and _ each other co-parent would respond "true" to each of these items now. (T F ?)

What do you notice about your answers? How do your subselves feel? What do they need now?

Barriers to Team-building

Every divorced family and stepfamily like yours is unique in composition, history, and circumstance. Yet over two clinical decades, I've seen common reasons that co-parents couldn't forge an effective caregiving team for their kids and themselves. See if any of these factors apply to your stepfamily:

1) Wounds: One or more co-parents have major psychological wounds (Chapter 5), and don't know it. If you've done Project 1 honestly, you'll know if this applies to any of you. *This common factor promotes all the other barriers below.*

2) Ineffective communications: Your three or more co-parents don't yet know how to resolve _ *inner*personal and _ interpersonal conflicts effectively. In six decades, I've never met one family where all co-parents helped each other learn the seven skills in Project 2, and taught them to their kids. This and unseen inner wounds make team-building unlikely or impossible, despite classes, books (like this one), therapy, and prayer.

3) Denials: one or more co-parents deny they're in a stepfamily like Jack Tilmon did [..example.htm], and c/overtly reject or discount one or several other co-parents. They're burdened with unrealistic expectations and an "us vs. them" attitude, and dependent kids are caught in the middle. The adults rationalize and tolerate this dis-unity over time, rather than seeing it as harming their kids and working to resolve it. Have you used Project 3 to assess whether this is true in your stepfamily?

4) Ignorance: All co-parents can't name or agree on what each of their dependent and grown kids need, so they don't have a clear, common team goal. None of the McLean-Tilmon-Cohen adults could name the needs in Resource [F]. Can your co-parents? Also see these Web resources: [..10/kids-want.htm] and [..10/kid-memo.htm]. Many co-parents are also ignorant of the realities in *Stepfamily Courtship* or [..03/facts.htm], and the differences in [..03/compare.htm]. That leaves them vulnerable to unrealistic role and relationship expectations [..04/myths.htm], which promote escalating conflicts and frustrations.

More factors that prevent co-parental team-building:

5) Blocked grief in one or several adults and/or kids. All stepfamilies are founded on two major sets of losses (divorce or death, and re/marriage and cohabiting). Inner wounds and ineffective communication combine to block stepfamily members from moving through the three levels of healthy grief (can you name them?), so they can't free up energy to form new (family) bonds. Project 5 is devoted to helping you all spot and free up blocked grief.

6) Relationship stressors: Divorced partners aren't _ motivated or _ able to resolve their toxic mix of old distrust, disrespect, hurts, and animosity for their kids' sakes. Stepparents, kids' testing, and biased relatives can amplify these conflicts. Verbal and legal battles over child custody, money, and visitations are major symptoms. So is little or no child-related communication. So is "Parent Alienation Syndrome" (PAS). Parts 2 and 3 suggest specific options for your adults' correcting this, over time. Other team-building barriers are . . .

7) No focus or merger plan: Co-parents aren't clear and agreed on their personal, marital, and stepfamily _ goals and _ priorities, so their merger and caregiving efforts are fragmented, uncoordinated, and conflicting. Few co-parents I've met care enough about themselves and their kids to evolve and *use* a stepfamily mission statement [C] to guide them. Have you all? Project 9 offers a framework to help you all cooperatively merge your co-parents' biofamilies.

8) Disabled adult leaders: a willful, "sick," or "acting out" (i.e. wounded and/or testing) child or other relative dominates one or more co-parental homes, and the resident co-parents don't know how to take appropriate leadership. Sometimes this occurs because a wounded custodial parent is enmeshed with a child. Another version is a child having been covertly encouraged to feel responsible for nurturing a wounded, needy parent. These are *always* symptoms of _ inner wounding (#1 above); _ personal overloads; and sometimes _ blocked grief (Project 5). Option: Use this series on "structural maps" to assess who's in charge of each of your kids' homes: [http://sfhelp.org/09/map-str1.htm].

9) Toxic advice: If troubled co-parents seek counseling or therapy for stepfamily problems, they often don't know how to evaluate whether the consultant is qualified. Typical clergy, therapists, mediators, teachers, case workers, attorneys, and judges have no training in assessing and resolving stepfamily problems. That promotes their using biofamily-based interventions, which often don't work or *increase* stepfamily stress. This sours co-parents on professional help, and raises their anxiety and self doubts. For suggestions on picking qualified clinical help, see [..11/counsel.htm].

Another version of this team-building barrier is co-parents **heeding** well meant but **inappropriate** (biofamily-based) **advice** from friends or relatives ["Your kids' needs really should come first, and (childless stepparent) Pat should accept that."].

A final common team-building barrier is . . .

10) Overwhelm: a mix of these factors combine to paralyze one or several of your co-parents. This usually indicates significant false-self dominance and unawareness. Some symptoms are continual values and loyalty conflicts and relationship triangles (Chapter 16), kids' "acting out," self-amplifying blame < > counterblame spirals, addictions, "illnesses" and "depressions," marital affairs, and (some) prescription medications.

Here's what these barriers look like all together:

- Co-parents' unseen inner wounds
- Ineffective communications
- Stepfamily-identity denials and rejections
- Blocked grief in one or more people
- Co-parent relationship stressors (Part 2)

- No team-building focus or plan
- Disabled household leaders
- Inappropriate (uninformed) help,
- Adult ignorances of all these, and . . .
- Co-parent overwhelm

In my experience, typical stepfamilies like yours are burdened with several or all of these barriers *at once*. Does the high U.S. re/divorce rate make more sense to you now? Notice a sobering paradox: if co-parents must work together to resolve these team-building barriers, the barriers prevent them. This is one reason that doing the first seven projects well *before* re/wedding is so helpful, long term.

Could you name these ten team-building blocks before you read them? Do you think the other co-parents and involved relatives in your stepfamily can? Can any clergy, clinicians, and/or attorneys? Your first step toward dissolving your set of these barriers is learning to name and describe them. If this seems like a major challenge, it *is*! So is re/divorce. I suspect your fierce wish to give your kids their best shot at adult success and happiness can empower you to patiently reduce these barriers, within your limits.

Take a breather. Relax, and note how you're feeling and what your subselves are thinking. I want to reassure you: the books in this series and the related Web resources at [http://sfhelp.org/] offer practical ways to help you all understand and master every one of these hindrances, with one exception: if one or more of you re/married the wrong people, for the wrong reasons, at the wrong time (Project 7), you can't undo that. You *can* learn from it and make the best of it, unless your dependent kids are getting harmed . . .

I've mediated with hundreds of antagonistic ex mates and new stepparent partners since 1981. The pattern is clear and consistent: the two core factors that cause ongoing mixes of the stressors above are _ unseen false-self dominance (Chapter 5), and _ unawareness of the seven communication skills in Project 2 (Chapter 7).

Premise: *If* wounded bioparents admit and want to heal their inner wounds, the quenchless love for their kids can empower them to improve relations with their other co-parents over time. That helps the adults to build an effective co-parenting team to nurture their kids after _ divorce and _ re/marriage.

Jack Tilmon and his ex wife Karen [..example.htm] seemed to have a truce as they co-parented after divorcing. They were polite, superficial, and wary. Though they didn't seem to argue excessively after each remarried, my impression was that they never resolved (assessed, admitted, grieved, and forgave) the hurts and disappointments that caused their divorce. Jack's shame-based false self continued to block him from seeing clearly *why* his first marriage and family had come apart. Karen had a clearer idea.

The psychological wounds and unawarenesses that burdened Jack, his new wife Sarah, and her former husband Ted totally blocked their ability to team up to help young Patty McLean with her daunting mix of needs. One result was that their combined wounds were destroying Jack and Sarah's re-marriage. Another was that their low-nurturance stepfamily continued to cause Patty to adapt by developing a protective false self, and the related wounds of excessive shame, guilt, fear, confusion, and distrust. These had begun in her early years, well before Ted and Sarah separated.

The bottom line: many divorced parents and new mates *can't* form a co-parenting team for a mix of the interactive reasons above. This inevitably stresses them, their children, and their re/marriages. Courting couples that work at Projects 1 through 7 may be able to see this before co-committing. If they (you?) don't, each new day is another chance for a wounded ex mate to break personal denials, start Project 1 (inner-family harmonizing), and commit to learning the seven powerful communication skills in Project 2. These empower you to do the other vital projects your kids need you to tackle [A], as you all grow a day at a time.

Whew!

Recall: this chapter overviews three steps your co-parents can take together to build a high-nurturance co-parenting team. We just reviewed seven factors needed for an *effective* team, and 10 common barriers your co-parents may have to over-come to build one. If team-building seems unlikely or impossible in your situation, what are the effects, and what are your options?

Implications

One probable effect is that you and your kids will experience fluctuating personal and relationship **stresses** in and between your homes for years after re/wedding. These **hinder _** personal **recoveries and growth, and _** stepfamily **bonding**. A common reaction to this is to blame "someone else." For shame-based survivors of low childhood nurturance, self-criticism and/

or blaming others are routine. So are defending, avoiding, explaining (justifying), ignoring, denying, and counterblaming.

A win-win alternative for you partners is to work steadily at developing your communication skills (Chapter 7), and replace finger-pointing with real empathy. This depends you helping each other to break false-self denials and free your true Selves to harmonize your *inner* families, over time.

Secondly, if you aren't forming an effective co-parenting team **your dependent kids will have a harder time** filling their simultaneous developmental and adjustment needs [F]. To seed possible team-building, consider giving a copy of this book to each of your other co-parents and other concerned relatives. This may help motivate them to work with you for the sake of the kids you all care about. It may also help if you alert any school or family counselors you work with to the ideas here, or to Project 10 on the Web at [..10/links10.htm]. If you do this, avoid sending the message: "*This book will show you how messed up you are.*" A better alternative is "*This book offers all of our family adults ways of helping our minor kids to heal and grow.*"

A third implication is that without a co-parenting team, **your re/marriage/s will be battered** by a stream of inner-personal and interpersonal conflicts over co-parenting values, decisions, and actions. Many of the hundreds of couples I've consulted with have said spontaneously "*When the kids aren't around, we rarely fight!*"

The ultimate implications of co-parental dis-harmony are that you're at significant risk of _ **eventual psychological separation and legal re/divorce**, and _ old-age remorse and regret over missed opportunities and troubled adult kids and grandkids.

Once again, we've covered a *lot* of ground. Before exploring options for resolving any team-building obstacles in your stepfamily, take another thoughtful . . .

Status check: where do you stand on these?

I feel a mix of calm, centered, energized, light, focused, resilient, up, grounded, relaxed, alert, aware, serene, purposeful, compassionate, and clear, so my Self is probably present now. (T F ?)

I've _ reviewed Resource [F], and _ am now convinced that our kids need us co-parents to act together to better help them fill their mix of developmental and adjustment needs. (T F ?)

I agree that our building a co-parenting team is _ related to Project 9 (merging your biofamilies), and _ will take us all some years of learning, experimenting, and changing to accomplish. (T F ?)

I _ feel clear enough on each of the team-building barriers now, *or* _ I'm genuinely motivated to get clearer on them by studying and discussing the books and Web resources in this series. (T F ?)

I _ believe our co-parenting team is effective enough now, *or* _ I can name which of the barriers above (or others) reduce our effectiveness. (T F ?)

If we have barriers, I'm clear on _ specifically what to do about them, and _ who is responsible for resolving them. (T F ?)

I believe _ my partner, and _ each of our other co-parents would confidently check the items above as "true." (T F ?)

Option: journal about your thoughts and feelings now, and/ or discuss them with a trusted supporter.

As you partners patiently _ heal, _ merge your biofamilies, and _ work at your other ongoing projects, the second team-building step is . . .

2) Prepare To Nurture Well Together

How? All three or more of your related co-parents . . .

_ **Clarify and _ agree on** what *effective* co-parenting after divorce and re/marriage is. Then . . .

_ **Agree on** your kids' normal developmental needs, and _ learn the sets of unique adjustment needs that typical stepkids must fill [F]. Then . . .

Assess each minor child for their status with each of these developmental and adjustment needs, and . . .

Agree together on _ what kind of help each child needs to progress toward wholistically-healthy independence, _ who among you should provide that help, and _ how. Option: use qualified professional help to do this.

Before reading further, interview yourself. How would you partners define a *successful, competent,* or *effective* parent? Do you know any? Compare your idea to this:

What's an *Effective* Co-parent?

Co-parent is the role (set of responsibilities) held by an adult who chooses to spend significant time and energy nurturing a live-in or visiting minor or grown child. The related family roles are biochild and stepchild (or co-child). Co-parents like you can be part-time or full-time bioparents or stepparents, or have both roles at once: they can care for bio and/or step kids. A live-in adult relative, an au pair, or a hired childcare professional can be a stepfamily co-parent too. Ideally, each such caregiver *wants* to _ identify and _ fill the current and long-range needs of each minor child in their care.

What needs?

Kids of parental divorce and re/marriage like Roger and Annie Cohen and Patty McLean [..example.htm] have *many* family-adjustment needs to fill, while mastering their developmental needs [F]. All these needs together make nurturing the kids effectively much harder than bio-kids. Think of your kids and their interactive needs as you consider this:

I propose that the **two basic goals of *effective* co-parents are**:

< **To lovingly help each boy and girl** in their care fill their basic developmental and any special needs over many years, toward becoming self-sufficient, healthy, productive young adults who can spontaneously provide most of the traits of high-nurturance families in [D]. And . . .

< As they do this, the **adults nurture *themselves* and each other** by _ healing any inner wounds, and _ learning, _ developing, and _ manifesting their talents and unique life purposes; and _ working at their complex merger and adjustment projects [A and G], a day at a time.

This definition implies that your co-parenting effectiveness can't be meaningfully judged until some years after each child leaves home. Before that, you teammates can monitor each child's progress with their mix of the tasks. We'll explore that below. Note that [..10/co-p-goals.htm] suggests 20 more specific goals of effective co-parents.

Our society requires legal licensing to be a plumber, beautician, pilot, angler, or accountant, but not a parent. We don't insist that adults need to demonstrate wholistic health and competence before raising a child, though our societal functioning depends on how well we all do at that. Most don't do very well, in my opinion. Can you imagine anxiously applying for the responsibilities and rewards of *co-parent* as you would any other important job? What qualifications would you need? After decades of mulling and professional study, and 15 years of personal recovery from childhood-nurturance deprivations, I believe these are core requisites of an *effective* co-parent.

Six Co-parental Qualifications

To succeed long-term, I believe a truly effective co-parent needs to have (at least) each of these attributes. How many of these related traits do _ you and _ each of your kids' other caregivers have?

Self-nurturing and balance: An effective co-parent _ is rarely controlled by a false self, even in confusion, conflicts, and crises. S/He _ values self-care highly, as a win-win way of nurturing other family members. S/he _ is steadily aware of his or her personal and co-parental priorities [..08/priority.htm] and can _ balance them despite uncontrollable life events. Restated: effective co-parents want to help each other do Projects 1 and 12: harmonize their *inner* families, stay balanced enough every day, and enjoy their unfolding adventure. Typical adults from low-nurturance childhoods like Sarah and Jack Tilmon have great difficulty maintaining their personal, re/marital, household, and nuclear-stepfamily balances, because of false-self dominance, denials, and unawarenesses.

Bonding, love, and *respect***:** S/He can _ form deep emotional-spiritual bonds with kids and adults over time, or can at
least deeply *respect* the inherent dignity and worth of each child
in her or his care. S/He has an equal capacity to _ form a loving
bond with a mate, and to _ maintain a steady respect and empathic compassion for the dignity, feelings, and needs of other
active co-parenting partners, *despite significant conflicts with
them.* Most survivors of too little early nurturance I've met can't
do that. Some can't bond with anyone, including themselves
and/or a benign Higher Power. See *Stepfamily Courtship* or [..01/
bonding.htm].

Motivation to nurture: An effective co-parent consistently
_ *wants* to guide each of their dependent children toward leaving home safely; and becoming a self-responsible, self-nurturing, productive adult member of society. S/He _ often *enjoys*
the overall challenge and process, despite local heartaches and
setbacks. Alternatives are to regard ongoing co-parenting responsibilities as _ an unfulfilling burden to be endured (i.e. a
duty), or to often feel _ ambivalent (conflicted) about the responsibilities, pleasures, and rewards of caregiving.

Typical stepdads and stepmoms may have less desire to co-
parent their mate's child/ren than their own, specially if their
stepkids are non-custodial, indifferent, hostile, adolescent, and/
or troubled. Other wounded stepparents can become obsessed
with trying to *save* troubled or neglected stepkids, and/or to
become the ideal parent that they never had.

Clear parenting, family, and life goals: An effective co-
parent can _ name explicitly how s/he wants each dependent
child to "turn out" (beyond *happy* and *healthy*), and _ is striving for a version of that in her/his own life. Restated: an effective co-parent is **living life** *on purpose*, and is "walking their
talk" rather than reacting randomly to daily events without a
meaningful long-range aim and plan. A symptom of having
this requisite is motivation to evolve and *use* a family mission
or vision statement [C]. How many parents do you know who
fit this description? Did your childhood caregivers *live on pur-*

pose? Did they know what they were trying to do with their lives and your family?

A desire to learn: Living on purpose motivates a Self-led co-parent to understand the specific factors promoting . . .

_ wholistic (spiritual + emotional + physical + emotional) personal recovery and health;

> _ healthy (vs. toxic) relationships [..10/premises-rln.htm];
> _ normal and special child-development needs, and . . .
> _ traits of a high-nurturance family [D].

Like Jack and Sarah Tilmon, most troubled, distracted, unaware stepfamily co-parents I've met, are content with superficial understandings of these, as their ancestors and media models were. Others *want* to learn more, but false-self defocusing and distractions make it hard.

These five traits naturally encourage . . .

Developing relationship skills: An effective co-parent prizes and steadily works to develop _ effective communication and problem solving skills (Project 2), and _ healthy three-level "good grief" skills (Project 5). This helps in developing _ the ability to *discipline* (assert) effectively: i.e. to declare clear behavioral limits and consequences with minor kids and other co-parents, and to enforce them *respectfully* and *consistently*. Project 2 (assertion skill), Project 10b in *Build a High-nurturance Stepfamily* or at [..10/discipline1.htm] propose options for learning effective discipline skills together.

How do you feel about these six proposed traits of effective co-parents? Would you change them somehow? Would your other co-parents agree with them (or care about them)? Would your own parents? Your kids' other co-parents? Seeing these key requisites together suggests why most family-life experts believe that *effective* parenting is among the toughest, most important, and most rewarding of all human endeavors. This importance is magnified because every child grows up to impact a great fan of people in their own and future generations.

My relative Harry McNair was an amateur genealogist. He wrote: "the collective offspring of William the Conqueror since 1000 A.D. could populate the island nation of Britain." This is just as true of every serf in William's domain, and *you co-parents*. Food for thought, eh?

The goal here is you and your co-parenting partners' *wanting* to clarify and agree on your own definition of effective co-parenting. By the way, do you see anything in the above (or your) definition that distinguishes between an effective *step*parent and an effective *bio*parent? Though both usually want the same thing (to raise healthy independent kids and earn self and others' respect), their personal, family, and social *environments* can differ in up to 40 ways! (p. 546).

There are other traits that will enhance your co-parents' shared effectiveness, like commitment, humor, patience, creativity, courage, empathy, and resilience. Those are wonderful "extras" to the six essentials above. Note your option to **identify and celebrate your co-parents'** *strengths* via this Web worksheet: [..07/strnx3-co-p.htm].

Option: if you haven't drafted a meaningful mission statement for your stepfamily together, (re)read [C] and Project 6 in *Stepfamily Courtship* and consider doing that now. It will serve as a foundation for all your family and team-building projects, guiding you all in times of relationship and role confusion and conflict.

We've just reviewed the first two of these three Project-10 steps, as context for the rest of this book:

* form a harmonious co-parenting team,
* prepare to nurture well together, and . . .
* nurture your kids effectively, over time.

Build a High-nurturance Stepfamily [xlibris.com, 2001] explores the last step, including a chapter on providing effective child discipline in and between your kids' homes. The next volume in this series explores effective stepparent-stepchild relationships.

Team-building Options

As you good people work patiently to evolve an effective nurturing team, you have lots of choices like . . .

Keep a long-range, wide angle perspective. Stay focused on long-range nurturing and family goals like [C] and [..10/cop-goals.htm], while local problems keep erupting. Your stepfamily merger (Project 9) is dauntingly complex [G]. It will take four or more seasons of holidays, special and routine occasions, mistakes and corrections, and much learning along the way to stabilize—*if* your adults' *inner* families are often harmonious.

Each time one or more of your co-parents re/weds, adjust your consensual biofamily *merger* plan—i.e. help each other to integrate the new adults and kids, and adjust and progress at Project 9 together. Your shared success at this will interactively affect and depend on your ability to develop a co-parenting team.

When confused or conflicted, **reaffirm your basic priorities**. For best long–term results, I suggest putting _ individual personal integrity and inner-family harmony (recovery) first, _ your re/marriage second, and _ all else third, except in emergencies. People who don't understand or believe the high risk of re/divorce, and/or who are ruled by false selves, may disagree with this.

I propose that courageously _ healing your inner wounds and _ ending the unconscious ancestral bequests of ignorance and psycho-spiritual neglect, are the greatest lifetime gifts you can give each of your minor kids. *Nurture yourselves and each other, as you nurture your kids*. Were you taught to do this as a child?

Another vital option you co-parents have is to **strengthen your key attitudes** that . . .

. . . mastering "co-parenting" is a priceless adventure and opportunity (glass half full), vs. an onerous duty.

. . . your kids' and co-parents' needs are of equal worth, and your welfares are interdependent; and . . .

. . . you each are students and colleagues in a challenging, alien, *normal* multi-home family environment.

Option: periodically, reread and discuss Chapter 2 together.

Stay clear and united on "what is *'effective'* co-parenting' in our situation?" Part of the answer depends on you all agreeing what each child needs. Use [F] or equivalent to assess that, and individual kids' progress.

Increase your fluency with the seven communication skills among your subselves and family members (Project 2). Harvesting the major benefits from this depends on _ your Selves being in charge, and _ genuinely respecting the basic dignity of other co-parents, *despite major disagreements*. Use Resources [H through K] to help along the way. Focus in particular on _ digging down to your true needs [..02/dig-down.htm], and _ identifying and resolving *values* and *loyalty* conflicts, and related relationship triangles (Chapter 16). Teach your kids about resolving these, to empower them as future adults.

Help each other build and *use* Personal Bill of Rights (p. 514). *Living intentionally* from your set of rights is the foundation of effective assertion and problem solving. Identifying and validating your personal rights helps recover from inner wounds. If you're a shame-based person, convincing your subselves you have such rights will be a second-order (core belief) change.

Yet another option you adults have is to . . .

Evolve a common definition of *effective* child discipline, and proactively discuss and merge your co-parents' styles and values. Work to resolve values conflicts and relationship triangles as you do (Chapter 16). Keep your priorities clear: I propose that aiming to grow and keep a high family nurturance level, and nourishing your re/marriage/s, are more important in the long run than converting another co-parent to accept your values about kids' table manners, grooming, home chores, school activities, hygiene, or gum chewing. Learn and adapt to the major differences between biofamily and stepfamily child discipline: see Project 10b in *Build a High-nurturance Stepfamily,* or [http://sfhelp.org/10/discipline1.htm].

If one or more other co-parents or relatives are indifferent, critical, unavailable, or hostile about child-related issues, work to see them as *wounded*, uninformed, and needy, not *bad*. If you don't, your behavior will imply that you feel superior ("1-up"). That will promote escalating hurts, resentments, distrusts, and arguments. Consider _ forgiving yourself and _ apologizing to them honestly, (vs. explaining and justifying) for past behaviors that have hurt them (Chapter 11). Reluctance to do that suggests you're controlled by a false self.

See "bad relationships" as webs of individual problems like those on p. 109. Keep a long-term outlook, and help each other patiently sort out concurrent problems, and proactively focus on improving one or two of these at a time. Small steps add up!

Appeal to resistant or indifferent co-parents to try counseling with you and a stepfamily-informed professional. The goal is to increase caregiving co-operation to help your kids fill their many simultaneous needs, not to prove someone is incompetent or inferior, or gain control. See [..11/counsel.htm].

Keep the Serenity Prayer visible in your minds and homes, and *use* it together:

> *God grant me the serenity*
> *to accept the things I cannot change,*
> *Courage to change the things I can,*
> *and Wisdom to know the difference*
> (Reinhold Neibuhr, 1934)

Before recovery, our false selves stress us and others by trying to control things we can't affect. Model and teach this prayer to your kids, and avoid using it as an excuse for evading tough confrontations (*"I just can't help it if . . ."*)

Refine your co-parenting role descriptions, over time and *use* them! See the sample stepfather role description at [..10/job1.htm] for ideas. _ Inform other extended-stepfamily members of your decisions, and _ invite their constructive input. _ Help key adults and older kids to stay aware of the ~40 environmental differences between traditional bioparenting and typical stepparenting [M].

And you adults can choose to . . .

Acknowledge without guilt that divorced-family or stepfamily co-parenting is new ground for you all. _ Keep the open "mind of a student," and expect to improve at co-nurturing as you experiment and learn, over time. _ Give yourselves and each other empathic permission to not be perfect co-parents, *often*! _ Intentionally seek veteran co-parents to commune with and learn from (Project 11). _ Seek and discuss available materials on post-divorce and stepfamily co-parenting (p. 555).

If a divorced bioparent seems disinterested in a biochild before or after divorce, study and discuss Chapter 17. S/He is probably _ wounded, _ overwhelmed with pain, guilt, shame, and anger, and _ unable to find a safe way to resolve these. Try standing in your "indifferent" co-parent's shoes . . .

Empathizing genuinely with such human agony is far more likely to help the wounded co-parent eventually heal and cooperate than sarcastic blame, ridicule, or angry black/white judgmental declarations. ("*If you were any kind of real father, you'd . . .*") If s/he needs to deny major inner wounds for now, you can *accept* that, but not affect it.

Trust your inner voices, and learn to compromise without excessive anxiety. Work to make "good enough for now" bulwark against your well-meaning, relentless *Perfectionist* and *Critic* subselves.

Get help along the way, and _ keep your balances—i.e. help each other do projects 11 and 12 together. Post-divorce and stepfamily co-parenting is *complex*! Remind each other you're working on up to 11 concurrent stepfamily-building tasks together, while you each attend other life priorities every day.

A final key team-building option is . . .

Affirm yourself, _ each other, and _ other family members periodically, for the co-parenting successes you achieve along the way. One way of doing that is to review and celebrate your individual and stepfamily strengths periodically, e.g. at anniversaries. Use the worksheets at [..07/strnx-intro.htm] for ideas and inspiration.

+ + +

Reality: each of your co-parents have personal and situational limitations. You can accept and adapt to them, and work toward the best co-parenting team you can forge together. I hope the options above illustrate how many ways you can help each other raise the nurturance level of your kids' homes, and guide them on their *many* concurrent developmental and adjustment needs!

Status check: Before we sum up, review where you stand on Project 10:

I now feel a mix of *calm, centered, energized, light, focused, resilient, up, grounded, relaxed, alert, aware, serene, purposeful,* and *clear,* so my true Self is probably answering these questions. (T F ?)

I can clearly define *effective co-parenting* in a divorced-family or stepfamily context now. (T F ?)

I can clearly describe the common barriers to forming a co-parenting team, and _ identify which of them apply to us now. (T F ?)

I can _ name the 16 sets of things that typical re/married co-parents and their relatives must help each other merge, over many years, *or* I know where to find a description of them. (T F ?)

I feel reasonably confident our co-parents can form an effective caregiving team over time. (T F ?)

I can name _ the three sets of major needs our kids must satisfy and _ at least eight of the needs in each set; and _ I know where to find the others. (T F ?)

I can _ name the three main steps in building an effective co-parenting team, and _ describe how to do each one. (T F ?)

I'm confident I know the main steps and resources needed to assess each of our kids for what they need from us adults now. (T F ?)

I know clearly where this team-building project ranks in our current general life priorities (T F ?)

I'm sure each of our other co-parents would answer "true" to these statements now. (T F ?)

Without judgment, notice your self-talk (thought streams) now. What are your subselves feeling and saying?

Recap

Over their first two decades, each of your minor kids must satisfy over a score of developmental needs to become independent, self-actualized, productive young adults. Typical kids in divorced families and stepfamilies need informed, patient adult help to fill sets of concurrent adjustment needs [F] on top of their developmental needs, that peers in intact, high-nurturance biofamilies don't face.

In this context, an *effective* stepfamily co-parent is one who _ proactively helps dependent kids fill these needs in a healty way, _ promotes many of the traits of a high-nurturance nuclear stepfamily [D], and _ nurtures themselves and other co-parents well in the process. To help each of your children fill their needs, you ex mates and stepparents need to do three things together, while working on your other concurrent tasks:

Accept your *stepfamily* identity (Project 3), _ learn what it means (Project 4), and _ overcome up to 10 barriers to forming an effective co-parenting team dedicated to building a high-nurturance multi-home family. All of you get clear on what effective parenting is, and what you all are trying to do long-term in your roles as caregiving partners. Then . . .

Together, learn _ the normal developmental needs **and** _ the other sets of family adjustment needs that your stepkids must fill. Then _ **assess each child's status** with each of their needs, and agree on what kind of help each child needs to progress toward healthy independence. Negotiate who should provide what help for which child, via evolving and using meaningful co-parental "job descriptions" [..10/job1.htm]. Ideally these will be based on a stepfamily mission statement [C]. Then . . .

Nurture yourselves and *each other* as you all work to fill your and your kids' needs while juggling many other responsibilities and goals. Your steady, patient work on all 10 other projects [A] will help you all master these three steps while you merge your biofamilies over many years. Though typical co-parents often have trouble forming a truly effective team, there are *many* things couples and supporters can do to help their minor and grown kids fill their *many* concurrent needs. The value and satisfaction of doing this over years of patient, compassionate effort is priceless. It reaches far into the future, affecting many unborn people you'll never know.

Your co-parents' overarching opportunity here is to intentionally end the ancestral bequest of low family nurturance (neglect) and resulting psychological wounds. Helping each other heal your *own* inner wounds (Project 1), and evolve *enough of* the nurturing traits in Resource [D] for all of you, is do-able over time—and an Olympic-Gold achievement!

This chapter overviews your whole long-term team-building project. A helpful, interesting resource for expanding your awareness and motivation here is Dr. Scott Peck's inspiring book "The Different Drum—Community Making and Peace."

Now we've built our foundation. First Things First (Chapter 1) outlined key *knowledge* you co-parents need to resolve the relationship problems (team barriers) in Part 2. Chapters 2 and 3 invited you to get clear on some key *beliefs* and *attitudes* about people (including any ex mates), relationship problems, and conflict resolution. Chapter 4 overviewed half of your whole long-term, multi-step co-parent team-building effort: Project 10. The other half is about effective child discipline.

The next group of chapters invites you to build on these basics to help you all provide a high-nurturance environment for your family members. Part 2 focuses on identifying and working to reduce seven common obstacles to achieving this.

Check in with your organs and subselves: do they need a break? Options: before continuing, _ recall what you want to get from reading this book, and _ review your options, starting on p. 21.

Part 2) *Real* Teamwork Barriers

This divorce-prevention series proposes that adults and kids need high-nurturance families to foster wholistic health and growth. A major nurturance factor is the degree of teamwork among divorced and stepfamily co-parents. Based on the foundations in Part 1, the next eight chapters explore ways you can reduce seven core barriers to building an effective co-parenting team:

5 and 6) Adapt to Psychological Wounds

7) Grow *Effective* Communications

8) Re/build Co-parental Respect

9) Re/grow Trust and Honesty

10) Reduce Excessive Guilt

11) Forgive Yourself and Your Ex, and . . .

12) Release Blocked Grief

These core hindrances, plus _ co-parent unawareness and _ lack of *informed* supports, underlie every one of the common *surface* teamwork-barriers in Part 3. Education and pa-

tient work on your version of these seven blocks can significantly raise your re/marital harmony and co-parenting effectiveness, over time.

If you've read the five prior volumes in this series, you've
gained much of the education you need. If you haven't read
them yet, follow the links in these Web pages for an overview
of what you need to learn: [http://sfhelp.org/07/quiz.htm], [..02/
evc-quiz.htm]. and [..05/grief-quiz.htm]. To begin learning,
follow the links in the "unawareness" section of [..5reasons.htm].

Each of these seven core stressors affects the others. They're
all affected by your co-parents' mixes of inner wounds: false-
self dominance; excessive shame, guilts, and fears; trust and
reality distortions; and difficulty bonding (loving).

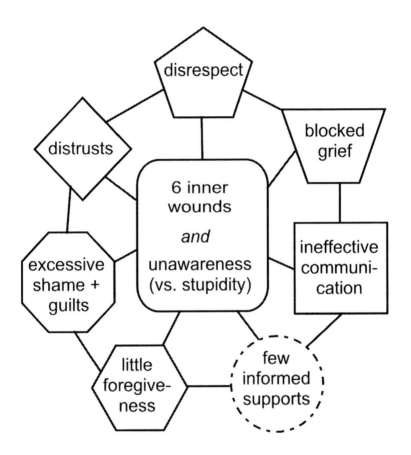

Barriers to co-parent team-building in divorced families and stepfamilies

The key to dissolving this web is co-parents learning about, assessing for, and healing, any significant inner wounds— Project 1. The next two chapters explore your options if one or more of your co-parents is significantly wounded, and denies it. The following chapters explore each of the other core barriers. Part 3 explores typical *surface* problems these barriers cause.

5) Adapt to Psychological Wounds—I

Grow Compassion and Assertion as *You* Heal

In my experience, the most powerful, least known hindrance to high family nurturance is significant psychological wounds in one or more co-parents. This chapter outlines six common wounds, and offers 19 option for dealing with them. The next chapter illustrates these options, and answers common questions. Assessing and reducing your co-parents' and kids' inner wounds is the theme of co-parent Project 1 (p. 430).

As a family-relations therapist, I've spent thousands of hours listening to hundreds of divorced parents and stepparents revile, scorn, blame, demean, and attack each other. Their *surface* disputes are usually about child visitation, custody, financial support, education, socializing, religion, and health. Many co-parents vented about stressful child-related lawsuits, lawyer aggressions, judicial unfairness, legal expenses, and lose-lose court rulings. Another theme has been ex mates' rehashing past marital and post-divorce hurts, traumas, and betrayals by former mates.

None **of these** are the real problems.

One universal *real* problem is that co-parents, specially divorced parents, don't know how to think, communicate, and problem-solve effectively (Chapter 7). Yet mysteriously, when they're offered seven skills that will correct that (p. 512), many try the skills superficially, or stick to their ineffective ways. **The deepest *real* problem is** usually that one or more of the battling or detached co-parents carries up to six major psychological wounds from a low-nurturance childhood, and protectively denies that. More accurately, dominant parts of their personality (their false self) denies their wounding, and blames their ex.

If you struggle with the co-parent team-building barriers in this book, I propose that you really can reduce them over time, *if* you commit major effort to Project 1 (assess for inner wounds and reduce them), and Project 2 (improve your communication skills).

Problem: what if you and any partner commit to these vital tasks, but other family co-parents resist or refuse? By the end of the next chapter, you'll be aware of over a dozen options you have to adapt to this while *you* heal.

To lay a foundation, let's review some basic premises about . . .

Inner Families and Wounds

From 23 years' clinical training and experience, I propose: if you're struggling with a "difficult" ex mate or stepparent, s/he probably has a mix of these psycho-spiritual injuries *and doesn't know it*:

_ frequent or constant dominance of a well-meaning "false self." This causes . . .

_ excessive shame, _ guilts, and _ fears; and . . .

_ excessive reality distortions (like denials) and _ distrusts, including spiritual. These wounds may combine to cause . . .

_ an inability to form stable emotional-spiritual bonds with some or all living things. This prevents feeling and receiving love, and exchanging true intimacy. (*"Nina's unempathic and self-centered. She only cares about herself."*)

My experience is that significantly-wounded people *unconsciously* pick each other over and over, despite painful results like divorce. *You and any new partner may have mixes of these early-childhood wounds too.* If so, they will feel *normal*, just as they do to your other co-parents. Combined with ineffective communication, the compound effects of these wounds on your life will promote significant relationship, financial, legal, occupational, and physical-health problems. Until you co-parents assess for these wounds and commit to heal any you find, you risk unintentionally re-creating a low-nurturance environment for your kids and wounding them, just as your wounded, unaware ancestors did. Unless you've broken your protective reality distortions, your false self will deny "being wounded." Your kids' other parent/s probably will too.

    Let's look more closely at these at these inner wounds and what they mean, starting with "significant false-self dominance".

True and False Selves

From birth, we're all taught by society and our own perceptions to believe "I am one person, and I have one personality." Recent advances in medical technology suggest that the latter is *wrong.*

By thermally imaging living brains via Positron Emission Tomography (PET), researchers have recently seen that our minds are modular. For example, many different regions of a normal brain activate concurrently to produce the single sensory experience "I see my child." Some of these regions are our *unconscious* mind. The natural ability of our brain to adapt to environmental stress by developing these semi-autonomous regions is called *multiplicity* by a growing number of mindscape researchers.

Premise: we each have one body and one (modular) brain, and our personality is formed of a group of semi-independent "parts," or subselves. For example, *"Part of me believes in UFOs, and another part says 'That's ridiculous!'"* We say routinely "I'm *torn* about talking to Ann"; "Ben has a musical *side*"; "I changed (or can't 'make up') my mind;" "I'm in a *blue mood*;" and "Nora has a *mean (or yellow) streak.*" We ask "How *are* you?", not "How *is* you?"

I now believe when young kids get too little emotional/ spiritual nurturance (p. 440), their brain automatically uses multiplicity to *fragment* or *split* moderately to excessively. They (we) develop protective, semi-autonomous subselves to survive our toxic local environment. Functionally, Each subself (neural region) has its own perceptions, values, goals, and talents. Each wants us to survive (avoid pain and injury), but may have different ideas about how to achieve that. All our personality parts together form what may be called an ***inner* family** or team. Like groups of people, your team ranges between harmonious to chaotic (conflictual) in various situations. Key question: *who leads your team?*

Every child appears to be born with an innately skilled inner-leader subself, called (here) our **true Self** (capital "S"). When developed, trusted, and *allowed* to lead your other subselves, this part is like the coach of a fine athletic team, a skilled orchestra conductor, or an expert business CEO. Part of "growing up" is the development of our Self's knowledge and ability to coordinate other subselves to get our needs met. When one or more other subselves rule your perceptions and behaviors, they become your **false self**. For more on your inner family of subselves, see [..01/innerfam1.htm] or *Who's* Really *Running Your Life?* (xlibris.com).

True-Self Traits

When their Self was trusted by their other subselves and free to lead, scores of my adult clients have spontaneously described feeling combinations of *calm, centered, energized, "light," focused, resilient, "up," grounded, relaxed, alert, aware, peaceful, serene, purposeful, compassionate, confident,* and *clear.* This seems to be true regardless of age, race, gender, sexual preference, or circumstance. *Some people deprived of too much early-childhood nurturance* (p. 440) *have never felt these.* The concept of an inner team of subselves and a wise, reliable Self is as alien and incomprehensible to them as advanced nuclear physics.

When false selves are making our decisions and behaviors, most of us _ are unaware of it (*"I don't know what got into me!"*), and _ may act in impulsive ways that hurt ourselves and other people *against our (Self's) better* judgment ("common sense"). False-self dominance is so common that, like air, most people don't "see" it. Social psychologists estimate that only about 5% of Americans have the *extreme* psychological condition psychiatrists called Multiple Personality Disorder (MPD), now dubbed Dissociative Identity Disorder.

As a recovering wounded man and a professional therapist, I've studied and experienced divorce and stepfamily life since 1974. I've also studied and experienced *inner*-family therapy for over a decade. I now believe moderate to major inner wounding is one core reason why over half of U.S. first-marriage couples _ pick each other, and _ divorce psychologically or legally, and _ even *more* couples re/divorce. Again: the "/" means that it may be a stepparent's first union.

Recall that we're building a foundation for practical ways to adapt to a "difficult" (wounded) ex mate or stepparent. To do this, you'll need to know some . . .

Effects of Inner Wounds

Significantly wounded adults and teens seem to choose each other *unconsciously*, over and over again, and eventually break up or live in misery. Implication: if you and/or your current partner are divorced, the odds are high that you and your (ex) mate/s are governed by a false self to some degree *and don't know it*. Reality-check this via Resource [E]. The guidebook *Who's* Really *Running Your Life?* and web pages for co-parent Project 1 [..pop/assess.htm] provide 11 more wound-assessment checklists, and recovery options and resources.

Significant inner wounding (false-self control) in one or more of your co-parents also means . . .

You'll probably have trouble really resolving _ inner-family and _ mutual conflicts together, specially those around your co-parenting roles. There are at least three reasons:

_ People ruled by false selves are often distracted by *inner* conflicts (among their subselves). They give confusing double messages (*"I want to cooperate with you / You're a lousy parent."*). Their false selves typically deny these messages (*"You're not* listening *to me!"*), and/or don't know what to do about them;

_ Wounded or not, conflicted co-parents are usually unaware of the seven communication skills needed for effective win-win problem-solving (p. 512). Can you name and describe these skills now? And . . .

_ Shame-based (wounded) people are unaware of often giving and perceive "1-up" R(espect)-messages (p. 510), which *always* degrade communication effectiveness.

Significant false-self control also means . . .

You bioparents are each at high risk of *unconsciously* making up to three wrong choices about re/marrying and forming a stepfamily (Project 7). This puts you and your kids at risk of a(nother) sequence of stressful years and potentially a(nother) family breakup; and . . .

If these realities *do* pertain to your co-parents and kids, you (i.e. your false self) will try creative, protective ways of denying them: e.g. you'll "forget," disregard, dispute, not understand, or ignore these ideas and implications. Like a tormented, self-medicating addict, you and/or a troubled co-parent will continue stressful (protective) behaviors until you or s/he "hits bottom" (commits to new priorities) or loses the will to heal.

I write this with compassion, after witnessing unseen inner wounds robbing hundreds of average co-parents of the joy, love, security, and harmony they and their kids long for. I believe they're typical of America's millions of troubled co-parents. My ex-wife and I, and her two daughters and their biofather, stepmother, and stepsisters, *lived* the four conditions above for seven years, until we divorced. None of us knew what you're reading here, nor did the several therapists we hired. I now see that all four of our co-parents survived low-nurturance childhoods, and were significantly wounded and ruled by false selves.

Reality Check: So far, these are just abstract ideas. Try putting them to work in real life, if you haven't so far. To form a tentative opinion whether another co-parent in your life is "significantly wounded," decide if your Self is currently leading your inner family (p. 114).

If so, get undistracted, bookmark this page, and invest time with Resource [D] to guesstimate the nurturance level (low to high) of _ your and _ any "difficult" co-parent's early childhoods. Then thoughtfully fill out Resource [E] with _ you and then _ an ex mate or stepparent in mind. For a more thorough assessment, use the 10 other checklists in [..pop/assess.htm] or *Who's* Really *Running Your Life*? When you're done, return here.

If your wise Self is distrusted and disabled by other protective subselves, you're apt to _ not know it, and _ get skewed results from these exercises; and/or _ to distort what the results mean. Your false self is specially apt to minimize or deny *your* wounds (protective reality distortion). Postponing or ignoring these exercises probably means your Self is disabled and held in "protective custody."

The more false-self behavioral traits in p. 451 your other co-parent/s have, the more likely that the rest of this chapter and book pertains to you and your kids. **Note:** half of the Project-1 guidebook W*ho's* Really *Running Your Life*? is devoted to options for *healing* these six psychological wounds [..01/recovery1.htm].

Pause, breathe comfortably, and notice your thoughts and feelings (self talk) right now. What are your inner-family members saying? Is an ex mate and/or stepparent making your lives miserable now? Is it likely they're ruled by a false self, and don't know it? If so, here are some powerful options toward reducing your stress and protecting your kids from inner wounding, over time. To be effective, each option needs your true Self to lead your inner crew . . .

Options for Adapting to Others' Wounds

<u>Prepare</u>

Do a *Self* check (p. 114): if s/he's not clearly leading your inner family, **focus on your own recovery** from false-self control and related inner wounds. Next . . .

Do a *power* check: do you agree that communication between two or more related people is sequential and often circular? That is, person A's perceived actions cause person B to react, so A reacts, then B reacts, then . . . etc. If you accept that this has been happening between you co-parents, then note the implication: if you change the way *you* act, person B (the "troublesome" co-parent) *may* react differently. That gives you some power, rather than feeling like a frustrated, helpless victim. Next . . .

Check your *goal*. Are your subselves primarily intent on finding a way to punish, change, or thwart a vexing co-parent? I propose that your best option for promoting desired change, over time, is wanting to shift something about the way *you* _ regard and _ communicate with this wounded person. If your ruling subselves need to *hurt* (punish, pay back, attack) the other co-parent, the rest of this book will probably be of little practical use. Recall: your main long-range goal is to provide the highest nurturance-level you can for your kids and adults. Next . . .

Check your *attitudes* (Chapter 3). Do you honestly believe that by changing something about yourself, you and any partner can significantly improve relations with your wounded co-parent? If not, lower your hopes for positive family change. Next . . .

Check your *priorities* and *patience*. Can you honestly say something like "*Improving my/our relations with this wounded co-parent over time is worth investing 10 to 20 hours of study among my other current responsibilities and goals*"? If so, read on. Harvesting true improvements from the options below will require at least that amount of undistracted time, effort, and patience.

A final vital preparation is . . .

Check your focus and time frame. If you conflicted co-parents are mostly focused on "child visitations this spring", "summer vacation," "getting the child support check," "the coming holiday," or "winning this court battle," you risk putting out endless brushfires and not "fireproofing the forest"—patiently building an effective co-parenting team.

Narrow-visioned false selves often want to dwell on *the past*, trying to _ justify your own actions, nobleness, and "rightness", and/or _ force your ex mate to (publicly) admit their horrible faults, failures, sins, and mistakes. Many people also have a protective *Catastrophizer* subself who wants you to focus mainly on the future. These can hinder healing and team-building if they're your subselves' primary focus. Things will improve if you partners focus on identifying and filling current and long-term family-relationship needs.

Your odds of gradually improving your multi-home family's nurturance level rise if you adults can help each other objectively deliberate the *long-term* effects (e.g. over the next 15 years) of your current actions. Can you do that now?

When you and any partner have these preparations in place, then choose the "mind of a student," . . .

Learn, and Act

You have many options. To optimize your learning, I recommend reading these sources out loud to each other, and discussing as you do . . .

Read this vivid excerpt about the inner "tribes" in an eloquent stepfather and his wife and stepson: [..01/ventura.htm]. then . . .

Read this brief introduction to your inner family by master therapist Virginia Satir: *Your Many Faces—the First Step to Being Loved* (Celestial Arts, 2000). Then . . .

Study and discuss *Embracing Each Other—Relationship*

as Teacher, Healer, & Guide; by Hal Stone, Ph.D., and Sidra Winkelman, Ph.D. (1992; New World Library, San Rafael, CA). This is an intriguing, useful introduction to how *your* inner family reacts to the troubled co-parent's inner family. The *inner voices* these insightful authors describe are your personality subselves "talking." Next . . .

Read *"Discover Your Subpersonalities,"* by clinical researcher John Rowan. This interesting book is about *you*, your child(ren), and all your other family adults. There are many more titles about inner wounds and recovery at [..11/books-gwc.htm]. Use what you learn from discussing these readings to . . .

Study this [..example.htm] of how unhealed co-parental inner wounds affected a real stepfamily couple and a helpless custodial daughter. Notice your feelings and thoughts as you read. Option: if you have a partner, read this vignette out loud to each other, and discuss how it relates to your situation. Option: offer a copy to any wounded co-parent and key others— for information, not vindication or blame!

Recall—we're reviewing options you have for adapting to one or more wounded co-parents. Next . . .

Review the premises in Chapter 2. See how those ideas about solving relationship problems compare to your beliefs. If your true Self leads your inner family, I'd be surprised if s/he doesn't agree with many or most of those premises. If s/he does, are you consistently *applying* them to changing your relationship with your wounded co-parent/s?

Strengthen your awareness of the seven communication skills available to you to resolve _ inner and _ interpersonal conflicts with and about the ex mate. **Read** the Project-2 guidebook *Satisfactions* [xlibris.com, 2001], or the resources at [..02/links02.htm]. When you can say confidently that you and any partner are _ consistently using these skills with your wounded co-parent/s and _ have few of the blocks on p. 518, you're well under way!

Pay special attention to the concept of **R**(espect) **messages**. If the ex mate or stepparent perceives anything but genuine "=/

=" (mutual respect) R-messages from you other co-parents, her or his ruling subselves will react with hostility, resentment, jealousy, suspicion, distrust, withdrawal, and/or anger. Reality: "1-up" and "1-down" R-messages promote false-self dominance and ineffective communication with the receiver, unless their Self is in charge.

Communication is anything you or your partner do (or don't do) that causes some conscious or unconscious reaction in another person. Therefore, actions like phone hang-ups, not returning messages, disparaging the co-parent to kids and others, hiring private investigators and/or aggressive lawyers, and filing court suits *all* send the wounded person inflammatory "1-up" R-messages. That inexorably *encourages* conflict, resentment, and distrust, which blocks the team-building your kids depend on you all for!

Also, pay attention to your typical **"awareness bubbles"** [..02/a-bubble.htm]. If you and any co-parent each focus only on filling your own needs (a sign of false self control), effective teamwork and problem solving aren't likely.

If your communication with the wounded co-parent is ineffective (doesn't fill your and their needs), **review the common blocks** on p. 518. If your false self is in charge when you do, s/he will probably skew the results to make the ex mate a villain, and you a saint. Unless you're aware of who's guiding your inner family, you won't be aware this is happening. See Chapter 7.

Use the seven skills to try and correct your half of these blocks with the ex mate, over time. Try out the tips on p. 528. Doing these will *only* improve communication outcomes if _ you see the other co-parent as a person of equal dignity and human worth, _ with whom you have some mix of the blocks on p. 109. Also **try mapping** typical recent communication sequences with them, with an open mind [*Satisfactions*] or [..02/evc-maps.htm]. Beware the natural tendency to delight in criticizing the ex mate, and see what you discover about *yourself* . . .

More options toward adapting to co-parents' wounds . . .

Learn about loyalty conflicts and relationship triangles (Chapter 16) and co-dependence [..01/co-dep.htm]. Then get a competent clinician or objective supporter to help you decide if _ you, the "problem co-parent," and a child or someone else are in one or more conflicts and triangles. Then _ use objective help to see if you or your partner have many co-dependent traits relative to the wounded co-parent. *If one or both of these are significantly true, that strongly suggests that* **you** *are wounded and ruled by a false self, at least in relating to the wounded co-parent.*

Mastering your loyalty conflicts and relationship triangles requires you co-parents to *want to* _ put your Self in charge [..01/ifs1-intro.htm], and _ get clear on your true long-term priorities. My bias is that for best long-term resolution of major impasses, each co-parent must *want to* usually put their integrity first, their re/marriages second, and all else third, except in emergencies. This scheme protects all of you from the trauma and wounds of (another) psychological or legal divorce.

Meditate on the Personal Bill of Rights on Page 514, and edit it to fit you. Then see how it feels to apply each relevant item to *you*. Here's the hard part: despite her or his recent attitudes and actions, try applying your Bill to the wounded co-parent, (or anyone else stressing you). Is your (ruling subselves') motto with the other co-parent *"An eye for an eye!"* or the Golden Rule (*"Do unto others . . ."*)? As you know, human nature decrees *"What goes around (e.g. dis/respect) comes around,"* and *"As Ye sow, so shall Ye reap."* Is that your experience? You can also choose to . . .

Sharpen your "dig down" and clear-thinking skills [..02/dig-down.htm, and ..02/fuzzy1-wks.htm]. Then use this book and your skills to identify which Part-2 team-building barriers you have with your wounded ex or stepparent. Rank order the barriers you'd most like to change over time, and (re)read the related chapters for effective action options.

Apply the Serenity Prayer to your situation (p. 102). When your Self is disabled, dominant subselves often obsess or argue about things beyond your control, or try to control them.

The guaranteed result is disappointment, frustration, and these Part-2 relationship problems. A final option is to . . .

Watch for chances to **invite your wounded co-parent to learn** what you're becoming aware of. Talking about your own wounds and recovery is a safe way of planting some seeds, if your subselves have no hidden agenda. Another option is to appeal to the other co-parent's love for their kids, and ask them to consider the ideas in Project 1 for their sakes. I suggest you think and speak of harmonizing your inner families (recovering) as a family-building team project, not one that the wounded adult "has to" do alone (implication: "you're 1-down").

Option: at an appropriate time, you or your partner _ describe to the wounded person what you're learning here, and _ ask (vs. demand) them to read [http://sfhelp.org/5reasons.htm], [..12-overvw.htm], [..01/project01.htm], and [..10/kid-needs.htm]. Your Self will sense the right time and way to do this. This may require preliminary work on other Part-2 core problems for some time, to raise your odds of being *heard*. If you do this, try to avoid any expectations. You're planting a seed, and can't control if or when it will sprout . . .

You can't make a wounded co-parent *want* to recover. You *can* _ empower your true Self, and _ **choose to see the other adult as *wounded***, not *bad*. You can also stay clear that the wounded co-parent's *actions* may be stressful, vs. thinking s/he is a despicable person.

Reasoning, pleading, explaining, scorning, rehashing, and threatening will *not* cause your wounded co-parent to "see", repent, change, apologize, and empower her or his true Self. Most often, those behaviors will *increase* distrust (insecurity), disrespect, and antagonism, and lower your family's chances for co-parenting teamwork and a high-nurturance environment.

If you feel the injured co-parent's false self is significantly harming a minor child, your attempts to show or prove that to the adult will probably make things *worse*. S/He will probably perceive your attempt as a 1-up insult which says *"You are an incompetent (bad) parent."* A more helpful option is to use respectful "I"-message assertions (p. 535).

You also need to act on what you believe is right. Your vulnerable kids depend on all you adults to protect them from abuse and neglect. As you discern what's right for each of you, including unborn kids, help each other keep a long-term view. Accept that your co-parental decisions are going to cast psychological ripples across future decades and generations, and will affect more people than just your current family members . . .

Blaming family and/or re/marital troubles on a villainous ex mate or stepparent and/or ancestor is a tempting way to avoid looking at yourself. If your governing subselves adopt that righteous 1-up attitude, they'll inexorably sabotage building an effective co-parenting team. You'll surely experience recurring loyalty conflicts and relationship triangles (Chapter 16) that will stress you all, and lower your multi-home family's nurturance level. That puts your kids' wholistic health and any re/marriages at significant risk.

I propose that you *can* change your attitude about the dignity of your wounded co-parent, *if* your true Self leads your inner team. This doesn't mean you have to be a doormat or wimp. Studying clinical hypnosis taught me that we all "leak" our true opinions and attitudes nonverbally. If you genuinely value the wounded co-parent's dignity and human worth as much as your own, your voice tone, body language, and actions will broadcast that—and vice versa!

If one or more of your other co-parents is significantly wounded and often controlled by a (protective) false self, you face **a harsh reality**. Despite your will, your heart, your lawyer, your determination, and the law, *you may not be able to protect a child you cherish from inheriting the co-parent's (and your) psychological wounds.* Kids growing up amidst co-parental unawareness and strife probably won't get *enough* of the vital emotional/spiritual nurturances they need (p. 440).

Because you can't control or fix a significantly-wounded

co-parent, their (false self's) attitudes and behaviors will probably promote *unintended psychological wounds* in custodial or visiting dependents. **You** *can* . . .

_ follow your conscience and integrity, with minimum guilt, shame, and anxiety;

_ heal yourself, and _ nourish your primary adult relationship, over time;

_ study and patiently tailor and apply this series of books and related resources to your situation;

_ intentionally treat any wounded ex mates in your lives with *compassion*, vs. disdain and disrespect; as you would if they had cancer or AIDS.

_ give as much love and nurturance to your minor kids in your lives as circumstances allow, and . . .

_ protect them against going through another family breakup (re/divorce) by choosing "realistic optimism," and working patiently on the 12 projects in [A] with your partners and supporters. Then . . .

_ ***Let go*** *of trying to control that which you didn't cause, and can't fix (the co-parent's wounds), without guilt, shame, or anxiety.*

Moral: you can do a *lot*—and you can't do it all!

Recap

After 23 years' study and experience, I propose that a major unseen cause of our U.S. divorce epidemic is mates' significant psychological wounds from low-nurturance childhoods: _ the dominance of reactive, protective personality subselves (a false self) who distrust and disable the wise true Self. This promotes _ excessive shame, guilts, and fears; _ significant trust and reality distortions, including denials of these wounds; and _ difficulty forming true, stable bonds with (caring for) some or all other people.

Project 1 offers your co-parents a way to assess for these wounds, and help each other recover from them over time. Doing this and the other projects in [A] promotes high family nurturance levels [D], which guards your vulnerable descendents from inheriting these toxic inner wounds.

Your odds of forming an effective co-parenting team over time depend on _ how wounded you parents are, _ your awareness of that, and _ whether you choose to help each other recover from them. This is compounded by (1) unawarenesses of healthy grieving and relationship basics, communication skills, and stepfamily realities (Chapter 1); and (2) little informed co-parenting help available locally or in the media.

This chapter _ reviews key ideas about inner wounds and their effects, and _ proposes over a dozen ways you can prepare, assess, and *compassionately* adapt to (vs. fix) a significantly-wounded ex mate or stepparent. These action options presume that you and any partner have honestly assessed *yourselves* for significant wounding, and are proactively healing any you find.

If you want to inform or discuss this chapter with someone, invite them to read the Web version at [http://sfhelp.org/Rx/ex/split.htm].

Some of the action-options above are complex and abstract. To make them more real and strengthen your belief that these options really can raise *your* serenity over time, the next chapter illustrates these options at work with a typical multi-home family like yours.

6) Adapt to Psychological Wounds—II

How Your Options Look in Action

This chapter describes inner-wound symptoms, illustrates the options from Chapter 5 in action, and offers answers to common questions about wounded co-parents.

Common Symptoms

Premise: unawareness, psychological wounds from low-nurturance childhoods, and the other barriers here *will* cause stress in and between your co-parenting homes, for years. Though details differ, there are common symptoms in typical divorced families and stepfamilies. For example: a custodial divorced dad or mom seems rigidly intent on . . .

limiting or preventing their kids' physical or telephone contact with their other bioparent, and/or . . .

demeaning, blaming, and attacking their former mate (and possibly a new stepparent) to children, relatives, and any professionals; and . . .

righteously justifying these actions, or vehemently denying them, despite clear evidence.

Our divorce subculture has recently labeled the extreme form of these behaviors as "Parental Alienation Syndrome" (PAS). The current (1994) edition of the American Psychiatric

Association's Diagnostic and Statistical Manual (DSM) doesn't include this as an "official" mental disorder.

Other common themes are a wounded bioparent or stepparent . . .

Having few of the birthfamily traits in [D]; and . . .

displaying many of the behaviors in Resource [E]; and . . .

causing "endless" disputes over child visitations, financial support, a legal parenting agreement, discipline, education, health, or similar matters; and/or . . .

initiating a series of draining, expensive legal fights with their former mate over these, or alleged neglect or abuse, and/or moving out of state; and/or . . .

a bioparent forbidding their kids to _ mention their non-custodial stepparent by name or title, or to _ obey the stepparent. Or the Mom or Dad _ threatens that if the stepparent tries to discipline his or her child/ren, something really awful will happen (*"I'll take the kids away, and you'll never find us!"*).

When behaviors like these occur, the other bioparent can _ seethe and endure, _ assert their needs firmly and *respectfully*, or _ try to persuade, threaten, plead, manipulate, or legally force the "offensive" co-parent to *change*, and maybe admit their flaws and offenses. Over time, the **common results** of the first and last of these three options **are** . . .

_ growing disrespect, distrust, avoidance, impatience, intolerance, frustration, hurt, guilts, and resentment in and between both co-parenting homes, so . . .

_ wounded co-parents' ineffective attempts to communicate (problem solve) *add* stress; which . . .

_ embroils adults and kids in confusing relationship triangles and loyalty conflicts (Chapter 16) they can't understand or control. These *raise* the level of conflict between ex mates and any new partners, with opposing camps blaming, arguing, or avoiding each other, vs. problem-solving. Then often . . .

_ minor kids feel overwhelmed and unsafe, and "get depressed," or "act out" (plead for help) at home and/or school. This *increases* co-parents' anxiety, guilt, finger-pointing, and bitterness, and deflects everyone (including involved professionals) from the **four well-disguised *real* problems**:

_ co-parents' unseen inner wounds, and . . .

_ unrealistic expectations (specially of the "offensive" co-parent/s); and . . .

_ ineffective (undeveloped) communication skills. These three are usually compounded by . . .

_ unawarenesses in co-parents and supporters—e.g. Chapter 1, [..07/quiz.htm], [..02/evc-quiz.htm], and [..05/grief-quiz.htm]; and . . .

_ little effective help available to overcome these combined stressors.

Bottom line: co-parents who don't _ assess for inner wounds, _ admit and heal their own, and _ adapt to (vs. fight against) wounds in their kids' "other co-parent/s; are *sure* to experience mounting relationship stresses and disharmonies. Unattended, these stresses corrode self esteems, re/marriages, and the family's nurturance level; which wounds everyone, specially vulnerable kids.

Once you understand these factors and your options, you can choose among action-options like those in the last chapter to protect against family stressors like these. Let's see this in action . . .

Example

Beth (38) is the divorced, custodial mother of Sean (8), and Mary (12). Two years ago, the kids' father Louis (44), remarried Sharon (33), who had never married or parented. Beth and Louis blame each other for their divorce. Each feels unheard, attacked, and misjudged by the other, and secretly guilty for various choices and actions. Sharon believes that Lou's ex wife caused the split-up by "being self-centered, controlling, and rigid." She feels Beth "won't step up to (admit) that." Sharon acknowledges Lou had some responsibility for their divorce, but far less than Beth.

The parents' divorce settlement took 31 months, and (legally) ended four years ago. It was bitter, contentious, and costly in many ways. Louis and Beth were court-ordered to hire a mediator because they couldn't agree on custody and a parenting agreement. They righteously defended themselves, and blamed each other for this expensive, demeaning imposition. The first professional mediator quit because one or the other of the antagonistic co-parents "kept missing and rescheduling appointments." Beth won legal custody, despite Lou's allegations that she was "a poor excuse for a mother."

Specially since Louis and Sharon married two years ago, Beth has been defying the legal parenting agreement she had signed. She has erratically refused to allow the kids to receive phone calls from their Dad, and makes a variety of "wild, irrational excuses" (per Louis) to avoid allowing the kids' regular weekend visitations with him and their stepmom. When he "complains" about this (verbally attacks Beth), she explodes and refuses to talk.

No matter how diplomatic Louis is, Beth seems to categorically oppose anything he proposes for the kids, like a summer camp, a math tutor for Mary, or special school programs. When Louis is "a few days late" with child support checks, Beth calls and "screams obscenities at him" (per Louis) until he hangs up. Beth shakes her head and says "Lou just can't take being confronted with his constant irresponsibility and procrastination. If I get direct and assertive, he pouts or whines or runs away like a little boy."

Despite his requests and then *demands*, Beth unpredictably "forgets" to tell Louis of important school events. She hotly denies this in the face of school-substantiated "proof." Beth threatens court action to prevent Sharon from taking part in school conferences for the kids, though the new stepmom has been cautious and respectful about asserting her new role.

Sharon and her stepkids seem to like and trust each other. Louis's brother and sister-in-law, and his father, praise her as having "a warm, natural touch" with Mary and Sean. This gets back to Beth, and seems to enrage her. Beth's mother, divorced long ago, appears to "coldly" side with her daughter against Louis and "that other young woman."

After two years of strife, Sharon and Louis have begun to tell their supporters that Beth is "a sad (mental) case" and is maliciously subjecting them and the kids to "Parent Alienation Syndrome." They believe that Beth is obsessed by old resentments, has a pathological desire to "brainwash" the kids against their father, and wants to relentlessly punish him for "something" by depriving Louis, Sharon, and the kids of regular visitations and calls. Several people who know the stepfamily feel that "the only life Beth has is her children."

Beth's parents divorced when she was five, and she had seen or heard little of her father as she grew up. Her (wounded) mother often publicly reviled him as "a deadbeat boozer," "lousy father," and "a perennial failure." Unlike her older brother Marty, Beth had been a "surprise baby."

Sharon increasingly feels impatient, frustrated, and weary that so much of her new marriage seems focused on "the Beth problem." She feels . . .

- blindsided ("I never expected this");
- "second best" with Lou too often, compared to his kids, ex mate, and work; and . . .
- confused on what her rights, role, and limits are.

Sharon's attempts to discuss these with Lou (vent) often wind up in a fight, because he feels unconsciously that he must "fix" his wife's discomfort, and he doesn't know how. Both feel confused, anxious, and frustrated. He says *So what do you want me to do, hire a hit man? Disown my kids?"* Torn, Sharon says *"Of course not, but . . . , I just don't know."* Neither one has identified what they *really* need yet.

A counselor friend of Sharon asks *"Do you think Lou accepts that you're a* stepfamily*, and that Beth will always be part of it?"* The stepmom shakes her head and grimaces. *"I have trouble with that last part, though I know I'm a stepmother. Lou gets irritated if I talk about 'my stepkids.' I think he wants* *to believe we're just a 'regular family,' which shouldn't have to include Beth. We don't talk about it."*

None of these three co-parents or their key supporters have read much about stepfamilies. There is much more to their story, but this sketch gives us enough to work with.

Do *you* and any partner and kids have some kind of "Beth problem"? If so, have you begun thinking about applying your version of the options in the last Chapter? Here's how Sharon, Lou, and *you* can use them to reduce mounting co-parenting stress . . .

Needed: Second-order Changes

These typical co-parents aren't aware of three things that are intensifying their mutual hurt + guilt + anxiety + resentment + confusion + anger. The first is that Beth, Louis, and to a lesser extent Sharon, _ are **psychologically wounded** and _ don't know it. Since their early years, they've been unconsciously controlled by protective false selves. These reactive, short-sighted subselves strongly influenced _ who they chose as mates, why and when they did, and _ later, why and how they divorced. Their false selves still control their perceptions, decisions, and behaviors, specially in values and responsibility conflicts over young Mary and Sean. Each adult regards this as *normal*, and righteously blames one or both others for disputes, flaws, and "bad attitudes."

Secondly, because they're unaware of their and Beth's inner wounds, Louis and Sharon have significantly **unrealistic expectations** of her. Without real personal recovery, Beth *cannot* (vs. will not) meet their co-parenting expectations. Their expecting her to "act civilly," "grow up," and "stop hurting the kids" is like expecting diamonds to rain from the sky. They must fully accept that _ *all three of them* are "the Beth problem," _ they can't *make* Beth change, and _ without healing, she *can't* be a "rational," sensitive, cooperative teammate. Lou and Sharon have to accept that while Sean and Mary live, the couple is chained to an extremely wounded co-parent with whom they may never be able to reason or negotiate as team-mates.

Third, Lou and Sharon must leave the comforting shelter of blaming Beth for past and current offenses and problems, and courageously accept that their (1-up) attitudes and judgmental, disrespectful behaviors are fully half of "the Beth problem." As long as they're ruled by guilty, shamed, and fearful subselves, the couple will be unable to do this.

Have you and any partner done versions of these yet? If not, who's subselves are in the way?

Doing these might motivate this couple to read and discuss this book or the equivalent Web pages, and then brainstorm ways to reduce their *three-way* "Beth problem."

If they did, Sharon and Lou would each ideally *want* to _ adopt a patient, long-term outlook, and _ evaluate all three adults for significant inner wounds, despite anxiety and resistance from their false selves. In the real world, wounded, un-aware co-parents will procrastinate or avoid assessing, because it requires you each to take full responsibility for your past and present discomforts, and resolving the current ones. See [..02/dig-down.htm].

How do you and any partner now feel—honestly—about assessing each of your kids' co-parents for inner wounds via [E] and the other Project-1 checklists [..pop/assess.htm]? If you haven't done so, will you in the next week? Notice your inner voices now . . .

If Sharon and Lou were motivated to tailor and act on relevant suggestions in the prior five chapters, they'd agree to invest, say, at least an hour a week discussing and practicing the seven Project-2 communication skills on p. 512. Early learning targets would be to try _ *mapping* recent verbal conversations between Beth and either of them [..02/evc-maps.htm], and _ using Resources [I, J, and K] to rough out how their communication attitudes (e.g. 1-up) and habits were contributing to "the Beth" problem."

As they better understood that *all three* of them were wounded and often ruled by reactive false selves, this couple would probably want to talk about "our co-parenting (or team) problem," rather than the inflammatory (1-up, blaming) "the Beth problem." They would remind each other for all their sakes to see beyond Beth's frustrating, disrespectful behaviors, to her inherent dignity as a worthy person, burdened by wounds she was unaware of and didn't cause.

To change their half of this normal, stressful situation, Louis and Sharon must *want to* make several second-order (core attitude) changes, as teammates. All their attempted solutions to date have been first-order (superficial) changes, like trying to "reason," with Beth, accusing and arguing with her, hanging up the phone, sending registered letters, and appealing to Beth's (false-self dominated) Mother to "do something with the kids' Mom."

None of these actions have gotten Beth to *want to* cooperate more about Louis' contact with young Sean and Mary, and to accept and value Sharon as a helpful co-parent. That's because the couple hasn't changed _ their basic attitudes of superiority, blame, and criticism of Beth and her actions; and _ their unrealistically expecting her to behave like a "normal" (non-wounded) divorced mother.

Lou's and Sharon's unawareness of _ these harmful attitudes and expectations, _ the vital difference between first-order and second order human changes, and _ how to communicate *effectively* about and with Beth, are relentlessly fuelling the stressful cycle they're trying to stop. They each blame Beth for this, because it's safer, and they see no viable alternatives. She *feels* blamed by them and *her own Inner Critic*, and reacts defensively, without awareness.

Louis, Sharon, and *you*, have some powerful options for adapting to, rather than fighting or *fixing*, an ex mate or stepparent unconsciously dominated by a "false-self" group of personality parts like those sketched below. Use this example to reality-check your life experience, and expand the ideas in the prior Chapter . . .

False selves at Work

Like most survivors of low childhood nurturance, Louis and Beth are burdened with deeply-buried toxic shame. They were each unintentionally raised to feel they're not good, worthy, lovable people. Because this illusion *hurts*, their false selves keep this searing belief well below their conscious awareness (reality distortion).

As wounded adults in protective denial, Louis and Sharon rarely look at *their* half of relationship problems with Beth, because doing so brings up excessive guilt ("*I did a bad thing*") and toxic shame ("*I* <u>am</u> *a bad thing*"). When conflicted, subselves soothe each of them by insisting persuasively "It's not *my* fault!" This means conflicts must be "someone else's" fault, and the most convenient target is—their "terrible" ex mate. This has nothing to do with logic!

Most relationship and parenting actions Louis takes, including divorcing Beth, are interpreted by her ruling subselves as direct or implied accusations that "*Our main family problems are your fault. You are an incompetent, bad woman, person, and mother!*" This activates a Vulnerable personality part we'll call **Shamed Beth**, who has the feelings, perceptions, needs, and values of about a four year old. *Shamed Beth* learned to believe early that she is *bad* and unlovable, which is unbearably painful.

When some (perceived) behavior by Louis activates *Shamed Beth* (triggers her feelings of self-disgust and worthlessness), a group of Guardian subselves instantly activates. All these parts together comprise her false self:

Beth's **Skeptic** subself declares "*You know you can't trust Lou and Sharon. They want to persuade the kids to live with them and leave you, and you know what that would mean . . .*"

Her protective **Catastrophizer** subself shrilly screams "*Aaiieeee . . . They'll find a way take your kids away from you and you'll die early, a lonely, broken, sick, unloved, homeless old woman!*"

This activates another young subself; **Terrified Beth**, who

developed when the physical Beth often felt emotionally abandoned, alone, and scared, as a young girl. The intensity of this
overwhelming *feeling* is close to the primal mindless hysteria
"*I'm going to* die *right now!*" This terror isn't logical, and cannot be soothed with words.

Beth's **Inner Judge**, righteously thunders (like her father
always did), "*Bad people deserve to be punished, for their own
good.*" Shamed Beth hears this and says "*Then I must be punished, because I am bad. I don't deserve to be happy, even if it
hurts Sean and Mary.*"

Beth's **Magician** subself immediately soothes *Shamed Beth*
by misdirection and distortion: "*Oh, no honey,* Lou *is the bad
one. If anyone deserves punishing, it's* him! *After all, he left
you and the kids for a (sarcasm) younger woman . . .*" Inner
Judge: "*Yeah, that immature, weaseling bastard!*"

This causes a Guardian part we'll dub Beth's **Rager** to activate, flooding Beth with hormones and angry feelings, amplified by her protective **Amazon** subself, who says with fierce
determination "*OK, we'll get that louse. No visitations for him.
Maybe if he hurts enough, he'll stop attacking and threatening
us with abandonment.*"

Good Mom says "*But wait—WAIT! You all know the kids
need time and attention from their Dad. He really* does *love
them, and they need him. It's wrong to . . .*"

Common Sense (Beth's *Adult* subself) says evenly "*She's
right. You know, if we overdo this, it's more likely that Lou could
get the courts to agree that we're not being fair to him and the
kids. That might mean . . .*"

Beth's **Inner Critic** says icily: "*You're wrong to put your
wimpy fear and neediness before the kids' healthy need to have
two loving parents!*" Shamed Beth moans and wails. *Terrified
Beth* is overwhelmed, so the **Anesthetist** devotedly numbs out
("represses") her intense emotions.

Magician quickly says "*No, no! You're seeing this wrong!
By protecting the kids from Lou and this Sharon . . .*"

Judge interrupts: "*She's never raised kids, so she won't know
what to do. And you know what they say about stepmothers . . .*"

Magician continues *" . . . you're giving Mary and Sean the loving mother they need. That's the right thing to do, don't you (Good Mom and Common Sense) see?"*

Beth's *Catastrophizer* moans *"No one will ever understand why we have to do this. It's hopeless. There's no way out!"*

Magician adds protective denial: *"Come on! We're not trying to punish Lou by prevent the kids from seeing him, we're protecting them and us!"* Judge adds firmly *"And you know Lou won't admit that he's exaggerating / lying / punishing / manipulating us. He's too spineless and wimpy."*

Skeptic: "They care more about their own needs than mine or the kids. Lou just wants to control us, like always. And he'll never openly admit that he wants to take the kids away from us . . ."

Terrified Beth "Noooo-o-o-o-o . . ." Then the woman's **Victim** subself pipes up: *"They (Louis and Sharon) are always picking on me and falsely accusing me. I'm helpless. This isn't my fault!"*

and so on . . .

These semi-independent parts of Beth's personality are real and normal. **We *all* have subselves like these**, who give us thoughts, ideas, images, and feelings, all the time. So do Louis and Sharon. So do the kids Mary and Sean, and Beth's "cold" mother. So do *you* and any ex mates you're struggling with. Do you ever have inner hubbubs like this example? We've all experience them daily since early childhood, and regard them as *normal.* Note that **Beth's Self** was absent from the dialog, because the other subselves distrusted, overwhelmed, and paralyzed her.

This inner-family sequence took under ten seconds. As it evolved, the mom felt "confused" and "upset" – common signs of current false-self control. Because her Self is disabled, Beth will react impulsively and unconsciously, rather than with the wide-angle, long-term wisdom her Self could provide. That drives Sharon's and Lou's ruling subselves *nuts!*

Like their ancestors and probably yours, these three well-meaning adults have never been encouraged to be aware of their subselves and inner tumults. They can describe "what I think," and "what I feel," but they don't know who's causing these reactions or why. This is one of the *unawarenesses* that contribute to family and marital stress, and (re)divorce.

As an *inner*-family therapist, I've experienced scores of average clients becoming aware of their various subselves in my office since 1988. I know of dozens of other therapists who have the same experience.

For more perspective, bookmark this page and read another stepfamily inner-family example at [http://sfhelp.org/example.htm]. Also read a vivid excerpt from "Shadow Dancing in the USA" by stepfather Michael Ventura [..01/ventura.htm]. He writes intuitively and poetically of the group of subselves interacting in and among himself, his wife, and his stepson.

If a Co-parent isn't Aware of Their False Self . . .

If Louis and Sharon are each to change scorn to compassion, their true Selves must be solidly in charge of their own inner families. Recall your reaction to reading the inner dialog above. Did you think about your own inner crew and who leads it?

When our *Inner Critic* is in charge, we over-focus on our *own* failings and faults, specially if we have an active *Perfectionist* subself insisting that we *must* do the impossible. This is specially powerful for those of us who have a reactive *Shamed Child*, like Beth's. When our true Self leads our inner tribe, we can say without excessive guilt, anxiety, or shame, *"Yes, (something un-thrilling) is true about me and my actions, and I am responsible for it."*

What might happen if Sharon and Louis read these six Chapters, and self-assess for false-self dominance and inner wounds? They each use the 12 self-exam checklists in *Who's Really Running Your Life?* or [..pop/assess.htm], and conclude (uncomfortably) that *they* each have significant inner wounds, though not as severe as Beth's. The couple admits that when either of them has doubted the safety of young Sean and/or Mary, and/or felt disrespected by Beth's false self, *their* unempathic false selves took over, and sent Beth disrespectful and threatening messages. Their "awareness bubbles" didn't include her [http://sfhelp.org/02/a-bubble.htm].

They begin to see Beth as the *wounded survivor of childhood neglect,* rather than bad, *selfish, malicious, vengeful, and sick. That could foster compassion, rather than scorn. That would improve their communication with her, which could promote real co-parental problem-solving, vs. the escalating hostility and disrespect they all experience now.*

Louis says *"It's like her false self is a sorcerer strapped to her back, constantly altering her vision, and whispering distortions to her. If we say 'Beth, you have a sorcerer on your back! For your and the kids' sakes, get rid of it!', she turns around, and sees—nothing. The sorcerer (false self) whispers persuasively 'See, they're blaming you, and trying to make you think you're crazy! They're not safe—they're the crazy ones. Never trust them You don't need to change anything!"*

If Sharon and Louis don't decide to self-assess for significant inner wounds, their false selves will probably ignore or discount their five re/marital hazards. They would see little need to do the 12 projects in [A] for their kids' sakes. *Neither co-parent would be aware this was happening.* Implication: if *you* don't check to see who's running your inner family, you'll probably miss some real chances to improve your version of "the Beth problem" . . .

Questions and Answers

To shift from antagonism toward "your Beth" to compassionate assertion, you'll need answers to questions like these . . .

"Why doesn't Beth *(or any significantly-wounded person) see that she's ruled by a false self and do something about it?"*

Because she has no reason to examine *and change* her inherited belief that all normal people have a single personality. Western society teaches her and the rest of us "people with multiple personalities are *weird, dangerous, unpredictable, and crazy*!" Who wants to risk being judged "mentally ill," and discovering *"I've had a fragmented, chaotic set of subselves running my life, in general, and trying to parent my kids"?* Not the millions of Beth's in Millennium America! And Sharon and Lou might wonder . . .

"OK, but why can't we reason with her—even show her these chapters and Web articles, so she can see like we have?"

Because her distrustful subselves will doubt or mis-read your motives and genuineness. Normal false-self symptoms are cynical suspicion, excessive fear, and reality distortions. Until true recovery, dominant Guardian and Vulnerable personality parts usually interpret well-intentioned behaviors as threatening, demeaning, and disparaging (*"Oh, so you think I'm 'wounded,' weak, sick, and crazy, huh? And just what cosmic authority appointed you as my psychoanalyst, personal judge, and life director?"*)

"So does this mean we have to give up, and let Beth disrespect me/us, and hurt Sean and Mary *even if she doesn't see that she is?"*

I vote *no*. You can choose as many of the options in Chapter 5 (and others) as fit your situation, including grieving the lost dream that you can protect the kids *perfectly*. You can't. If your Selves are leading and you feel Beth is truly abusing or neglecting either child, you're obliged to invoke the legal and child-welfare systems on their behalf—*compassionately* expecting Beth's false self to react impulsively and defensively.

Once co-parents like Sharon and Louis (and *you*) find credible answers to questions like these, and grieve the lost dream that they can control the uncontrollable, then they're ready to make . . .

Another Second-order Change . . .

As our couple begins to view Mary and Sean's Mom as *hurt* and *unable*, vs. unwilling, to make cooperative (true Self) co-parenting decisions, some expectations of Beth spontaneously change. Instead of fruitlessly expecting and demanding her to fit *their* idea of a "responsible" divorced mother, they relaxed somewhat *without guilt*.

Instead of expecting Beth to *want* to tell them of school events involving either of the kids, Lou and Sharon proactively ask the kids, and arrange with key teachers and counselors to inform them. They found the school had a Web site from which they often could learn what they needed, and plan from it. This shift reduces the number of arguments with Beth, and lowers her feeling attacked and threatened—specially since the couple didn't blame her for "making" them adopt this new way of filling their needs.

Instead of expecting Beth to flex and not "over-react" if Louis's child-support check was a few days late, they understood that as long as her true Self is paralyzed, she can't prevent her false self from "overreacting." So instead of continuing to try *logic* and *arguments*, Lou works to keep his Self in charge, and use empathic listening skill when she calls to berate him. To his surprise, he finds that when he stops *disagreeing, explaining, defending, and counterattacking,* Beth's E(motion)-level falls "below her ears" and she can actually hear him.

Instead of expecting Beth to accept Sharon's co-parenting help, Sharon and Louis struggle to validate that Beth's false self is *scared* to do that, for a variety of distorted reasons. When the kids show their confusion about "obeying" their stepmom during visitations, Lou explains "*I know this is hard for you. Your Mom has a different way of seeing and doing things than we do. We need you to help us when you're here by cooperating when Sharon asks you to do something.*"

They help Sean and Mary understand how stepfamilies work, and that "stepmother" is an important family *job*, not a person. Lou and Sharon consistently avoid the temptation to imply to the kids that their Mom is *bad, screwy,* or *wrong.*

Accepting Beth's wounds and their own, the couple stops arguing over each short-term visitation or telephone conflict with Beth. They start to think about how each child-related dispute with Beth relates to "the next 15 years."

They decide to invite Beth to change *gradually* by steadily treating her with respect and firmness, as they all encounter values and loyalty conflicts over the kids. Sharon and Lou realize they had *not* respected his ex mate's dignity as a worthy, troubled person, which activated her shame, hurt, and resentment, and fueled their spiral of animosity and distrust.

New Knowledge + New *Attitudes* = New Outcomes

Sharon and Louis decide that they needed a new *way* of communicating with Beth's shame-based false self. They begin to study and experiment with the seven communication skills in Project 2.

They read and discuss the basics in resource [H], and the common communication blocks and tips in [J and K]. To their discomfort, Sharon and Lou discover their typical communications with Beth have been *riddled* with these blocks, and that *they caused half* of each one! With their new 15-year timeframe in mind, they set out to patiently evolve new ways to assert, listen, and problem-solve with Beth. To gain more perspective on *how* they've been communicating, the couple . . .

reviews and discusses [..02/lose-lose.htm], [..02/win-win.htm], and [..02/prblmslv.htm];

maps some recent communication sequences with Beth [..02/evc-maps.htm]. They discover that Lou consistently gets hooked into *arguing, explaining, disagreeing, blaming, defending, and bringing up the past,* instead of *listening* to (vs. agreeing with) Beth. They discover that each parent had grown to unconsciously expect demeaning "1-up" R-messages (p. 510) from the other, before anyone spoke. The partners agree that when they assert or confront Beth, intentionally using *respectful* (=/=) empathic listening will help lower her E(motion)-level "below her ears," and raise the odds of effective two-way communication.

They also decide to try . . .

"digging down" [..02/dig-down.htm] to discern their and Beth's true (vs. surface) needs, vs. focusing on Beth's aggravating behaviors ("she was so *rude!*") and traits ("I can't believe how *malicious* she is") Applying the chapters in Part 3 of this book, the couple begins to see that the roster of "Beth problems" they had resented and scorned were symptoms of the *three-person* problems on p. 109.

And they decide to . . .

help each other stay focused. They become aware that in typical conflicts with Beth, all three would get tangled in a web of _ inner-family and _ interpersonal need-conflicts, and _ rehash old unfinished disputes and traumas, and lose sight of their concurrent *present real* needs. The couple agrees to help each other concentrate on one set of true needs at a time, *no matter how Beth's false self reacts.* And Lou and Sharon agree to . . .

plan key communications with Beth. They commit to discussing *"What do I/we really need from her now?"* before calling. The hard part was trying to use this awareness to guesstimate *" . . . and what does she need from us?"* A difficult attitude shift was to accept that Beth's dignity, feelings, and needs were just as worthy as their own, though their *values* and priorities were *very* different. Lou and his wife constantly remind themselves of this by referring to their version of the Bill of Personal Rights (p. 514).

The couple acknowledges that they had unconsciously joined Beth's anxious false self in reducing typical complex stepfamily situations into **black/white two-choice scenarios**: our (right) way vs. Beth's (wrong) way. Black/white thinking excludes *lots* of good-enough compromises. They begin brainstorming different ways of getting their co-parenting needs met, and discover there are usually more options than they realize.

Lou and Sharon accept that *each member* of Beth's inner family, like their own, needs to feel heard and respected, and *hadn't* felt those with Lou before or since their divorce. Each parent had grown to unconsciously expect demeaning "1-up" messages from the other, before anyone spoke. Lou takes responsibility for changing his R(espect) message to "=/=", regardless of how Beth's false self spoke.

What did these new awarenesses and attitudes mean? Lou's half of their communication process changed like this:

Old way: Lou would say to Beth "*I can't believe you have the gall to go against our parenting agreement and block my rightful visitation with Sean and Mary!*" (implied messages: "*I righteously pronounce that you're wrong and bad, and I'm right and good.*")

New way: "*Beth, when your needs make it hard for me to get time with our kids, I get really frustrated.*"

Old way: "*Beth, I am sick and tired of your selfish, vindictive attempts to alienate the kids from me and Sharon. What kind of so-called mother are you?!*"

This kind of 1-up (blaming) statement, and the hand-grenade (emotionally explosive) term "Parent Alienation Syndrome," are implicitly insulting, accusatory, and disrespectful. Choosing to think and speak like this will *increase* inner and interpersonal conflicts with shame-based co-parents who aren't aware of their reactive false-self. Does this make sense to you? Are *you* thinking, writing, or speaking any hand-grenade terms with your "Beth"?

New way: Lou says "*Beth, I worry that unless you and I do something to improve our mutual respect and trust, the kids are going to get hurt worse than they already are. I fear we'll regret not trying when we're old. Will you work with me to find out what's really blocking you and me and Sharon from co-parenting better, for Mary and Sean's sakes?*"

Lou's true Self would nonjudgmentally expect Beth's distrustful false self to respond with acrid blame, distortion, skepticism, and criticism. He'd be ready with _ compassionate =/= empathic listening, and _ clear, respectful re-assertion of his need to problem-solve their barriers as co-equals.

Old way: Lou would say angrily "*How come you didn't tell me Sean had a parent-teacher conference next Wednesday night?*" (Lou's words and voice tone imply "*you're bad,*" which triggers shame, guilt, and resentment in Beth's subselves.)

New way: "*I understand from Ms. McKendrick that we have a parent-teacher night for Sean next week, Beth. I want to let you know that Sharon and I will be there.*"

Beth: *"How many times do I have to tell you that woman (Sharon) has no business coming to these meetings about our kids? I won't allow it!"*

Old way: Louis (i.e. his false self): *"You can't dictate what we will or won't do. Sharon is my wife, and the kids' stepmother. She has a perfect right to come to these meetings!"* (*Implied 1-up message: "I don't care what you feel or need. I'm right, and you're wrong."*)

New way: Calmly, vs. sarcastically: *"Mmm. So you feel strongly that there's no value in Sharon's meeting with Sean's teacher and me. (silence)"*; or . . .

"Well, I guess we have a major values conflict on this, Beth. What is it about Sharon's meeting with the teachers that bothers you?"; or . . .

"Ok, I understand you're very uncomfortable with Sharon coming next Wednesday. I really value her help with the kids, so I think what we'll do then is meet with Ms. McKendrick another time next week"; or . . .

"On our kids' behalf, I'm really sad and frustrated that you feel that way, Beth. (silence)"

Beth says on the phone to Lou a week later: *"My Mom's been asking for time with the kids, so I'm taking them to her house this weekend (instead of the normal visitation schedule). You pick them up in two weeks."* The implied false-self message is: *"My (and my mother's) needs are more important than yours. I expect you to adapt to my needs, without arguing or complaining."*

Lou—Old way: *"What? You can't just tell me how visitation's going to be! The court order which you signed says that I get every other weekend! This is my weekend, so find another time for the kids to be with Martha!"* Implied message: *"No, my needs come first here, and yours and your mother's come second. You will do visitation my way. The court says you have to."* This is a 1-up power response, *guaranteed* to cause Sharon's false self to erupt. Each co-parent's awareness bubble excluded the other person's feelings and needs, and neither false-self was willing to admit this and it's impacts.

New way: "*Yeah, I agree with you that it's good for the kids and Martha to have times together.*" Pause . . .

Beth (sarcastically): "*Well, amazing! Do you have a fever? You've decided to be reasonable for a change!*"

Lou's true Self (calmly deciding not to get hooked into a lose-lose fight with Beth's false self, and staying focused): "*You know, I feel frustrated when you wait until the day before to tell me of a visitation change you want, because then our weekend plans get messed up.* (Pause, to collect and sort thoughts.)

"*I, uh, have three needs now. First, I need to discuss whether there are other times Martha and the kids could get together in the next week or two. Second, I need to ask your help in giving me more notice on visitation changes you need. Third, I need to say that when you make decisions about us and the kids without consulting me, I feel ignored, disrespected, and resentful. That makes it harder for me to want to cooperate with you, Beth. Are you in a place to talk about optional times with Martha now?*"

Beth's distrustful, protective *Amazon* subself, replies with righteous sarcasm: "*Lou, I am so sick of your stupid control games. You are not going to decree when the kids see my mother, just because of your precious 'plans'.*" (false-self invitation to battle!)

Lou's true Self is aware of their process, and suppresses *his* combative Warrior part: "*So you feel I'm trying to control you.*" (empathic listening, not *agreeing*).

Beth (startled, suspicious, and feeling *heard*): "*Huh? You've never said that before . . .*"

Right! That kind of response affirms that something (Lou's attitude and way of communicating) really *is* changing!

These brief samples illustrate a whole class of new communication sequences open to these three co-parents. These sequences will (eventually) have different outcomes than their old (unaware, antagonistic) exchanges. The new outcomes will be in proportion to how much Lou and Sharon *want to . . .*

help each other _ empower their true Selves, and _ shift from seeing Beth as *bad, wrong,* and *the enemy* to *wounded, unaware,* and *dominated by a shame-based false self;* and . . .

keep a long-term outlook (vs. "next weekend"), and . . .

stay focused on _ the present, and _ one current *true* need-clash ("problem") at a time, and how much Sharon and Lou want to . . .

stay objectively aware of their three-way communication *process,* specially R-messages, E-levels, awareness bubbles, surface vs. true needs, effective assertion and *listening*, and their favorite blocks [J]; and . . .

accept what they can and cannot change about Beth and their complex stepfamily situation; then . . .

If these co-parents help each other work patiently at factors like these and other barriers, new co-parenting teamwork *may* gradually grow between the three adults. Lou and Sharon can control their half of co-parenting communications with Beth. If she doesn't "see" that she's being controlled by a reactive, chaotic false self, then there are limits to the benefits from these core-attitude and communication shifts.

With a mutual respect (=/=) attitude, the seven Project-2 skills are also effective in resolving disputes between your subselves. For example, when Lou's *Warrior* subself wants to counterattack Beth, his Self says "*No, not a good long-term idea. Let's try empathic listening and firm assertion instead. Trust me!*"

Pause and listen with interest to what your inner voices (thought streams, images, memories . . .) are saying now. How would you describe your *feelings*? Numb? Excited? Skeptical? Bored? Confused? Motivated? Who's leading your inner crew right now, your Self, or other subselves? How do you know?

Recap

This chapter illustrates some of the options in the last chapter for adapting to a wounded ex mate or stepparent. Your success depends on you and any new partner helping each other to . . .

- *Want* to _ make some second-order (core attitude) shifts, _ learn new ways of filling your co-parenting needs, and _ believe you *can*;
- Adopt a long-term outlook, vs. focusing on short-term relief;
- Admit and heal your *own* inner wounds, and empower your true Selves to lead your inner families, (Project 1); then help each other . . .
- Shift _ your scorn and blaming the wounded co-parent/s to genuine *compassion* for them, and _ see *all* of you as "the problem." That frees you to _ form more realistic expectations of the wounded person/s; and helping each other to . . .
- Dig down below surface co-parenting needs to the real ones "underneath" them (p. 44); and . . .
- Decide to _ reduce your current mix of the core team-building barriers in Part 2, starting with this one; and _ to learn to . . .
- *Respectfully* assert your true needs and boundaries with your wounded ex or stepparent, using the skills from Project 2; and then help each other . . .
- *Let go* of complaining about, and trying to change, that which you cannot change. If you're spiritual, *turn those over* to your Higher Power.

I hope you agree that you have *many* options toward adapting to a wounded co-parent, and improving teamwork with them over time for all your sakes, not just your kids.

Pause and reflect on the last two chapters. What are you feeling, and what have you learned? Notice your self-talk: can you say who's in charge of your team of subselves right now?

The next chapter explores a powerful set of options you have toward building co-parenting teamwork: intentionally improving the effectiveness of your thinking, communicating, and problem-solving together. Refresh your vision by glancing at the diagram on p. 109. Do you need a stretch or comfort break before continuing?

7) Grow Effective Communications

Turn Fighting Into Win-win Problem-solving

My client was a college-educated mother of two in her forties. Sally had been remarried for seven years to the divorced superintendent of a large urban school district. She and her second husband Ed had recently separated because of tensions between him and her resident 15-year old son Jason. Sally shook her head as she described a recent phone conversation with Ed: "*All he could do was rant about how rude my son is, and how unfair I am by siding with Jason when he (Ed) points out his rudeness. I finally hung up on him.*"

I asked "*What do you feel Ed needed from you in that conversation?*" She frowned and shrugged. "*Ed didn't want to problem solve, he wanted me to admit that I'm unfair, my son is ungrateful and bad, and he's a noble martyr.*" I had witnessed both of these veteran parents trying to express their feelings and needs to each other. When talking about co-parenting problems or Ed's excessive drinking, they were about a "2" on an effectiveness scale of 1 to 10—and their remarriage appeared to be psychologically dead. Both were *clearly* significantly-wounded survivors of low-nurturance childhoods, and neither realized it—so far.

This troubled couple typified the ~1,000 single and stepfamily co-parents I've consulted with since 1981: they *fought, argued, preached, explained, debated, blamed, hinted, threatened, demanded,* and/or *avoided*—and couldn't *problem-solve* as mutually respectful co-parents trying to help their bewildered, needy kids.

To see if this chapter is relevant to your situation, see if you see anything familiar here:

Symptoms of "Communication Problems"

Ineffective communication is not a stand-alone problem. It promotes, and is amplified by, all the interactive relationship problems on p. 109. To assess whether "serious communication problems" are a major team-building barrier among your co-parents, do two things: with all family adults who affect your kids in mind, scan the common communication blocks in Resource [J]. Then see how many of these symptoms fit any of your three or more co-parents recently: **I or we often** . . .

_ avoid contact whenever possible;
_ hang up the phone on each other; and/or . . .
_ leave messages or use email, vs. talk directly;
_ usually *argue, vs.* negotiate and brainstorm;
_ feel _ *unheard* and _ *misunderstood*;
_ defocus easily, and/or _ overfocus on the past;
_ feel *disrespected* and/or _ *blamed*;
_ get *interrupted* or _ *lectured*;
_ feel *frustrated*, and/or _ *confused*;
_ feel *controlled*, and/or _ used;
_ blow up or freeze up with each other;
_ use the kids or lawyers as messengers;
And two or more of our co-parents often . . .
_ write notes and letters instead of talking;
_ rehash "the same old problems" endlessly;
_ "bad mouth" the other co-parent to kids or others;
_ communicate through attorneys or relatives;
_ often say "*That's not what happened!,* or . . .
_ "*That's not what I said (or meant)*";
_ raise our voices with each other ("yell");

_ aren't aware of, or _ don't use the tips in [K];
_ avoid focusing on *how* we communicate;
_ expect our communications to not "work";
_ vow *"These (symptoms) are not my fault!"*

Bottom line: if you co-parents have _ many of the blocks in [J], and _ "too many" of these symptoms "too often," then ineffective communication *is* hindering the caregiving co-operation, and you definitely can profit from this chapter—*if* your Self is guiding your other subselves.

This chapter proposes two ways to reduce the second biggest problem between typical co-parents like you: *ineffective* (vs. "poor") communication. The biggest stressor—unseen psychological wounds (p. 448)—amplifies caregivers' inability to problem-solve: This chapter and resources [H—K] are taken from *Satisfactions—7 Relationship Skills You Need to Know* (xlibris.com, 2001). I draw on over 30 years' experience studying, practicing, and teaching communication skills for those and what follows.

If you're not already committed to _ harmonizing your inner family (Project 1) and to _ growing facile with the seven communication skills (Project 2), you probably don't know what you don't know about this vital topic. To see if that's true, I suggest you bookmark this page, reduce distractions, adopt "the mind of a student," and read . . .

the communication quiz at [..02/evc-quiz.htm];

these Web articles: [..02/lose-lose.htm], [..02/win-win.htm], [..02/gender.htm], [..02/prblmslv.htm], and [..02/karate.htm]; and . . .

resources [H—K] in Part 4 of this book; and . . .

the introduction to _ your and your kids' *inner* families at [..01/innerfam1.htm], and _ *inner*-family communications in W*ho's* Really Running Your Life? or [http://sfhelp.org/01/ifs8-innr_cnflct.htm].

These will give you a better understanding of what's possible among your busy subselves and co-parents. Not reading these implies that other things rank more highly with you than improving your communication effectiveness. Consider that you co-parents depend on your communication knowledge and skill to meet your daily needs. Would you be interested in learning seven skills (p. 512) which will probably *double* your success at filling your short and long-term needs? Would you like to teach your kids how to do that?

To begin reducing this core teamwork barrier, **confirm a key prerequisite**: do you genuinely feel that *both* bioparents of each of your minor kids are full members of your multi-home family, whether they're actively co-parenting or not? If you don't, I urge you to bookmark this page, and focus on Project 3 in *Stepfamily Courtship* or [..03/links03.htm]. If you and/or your mate reject a child's "other parent/s" from full family membership (ignore or discount their needs), you'll get much less from this chapter and book.

Premise: all subselves, adults, and kids *communicate* to fill two to six current *needs* (p. 508). Your communication is *effective* (vs. "open and honest") when _ each of you feels your needs got filled well enough, _ in a way you each feel good about. Can you name these needs yet?

Typical co-parents and kids have trouble filling their communication and other needs because of . . .

Two Core Problems

One or more of you are often ruled by a false self. This can be assessed and significantly healed over time via Project 1 or equivalent (p. 430); and . . .

Several or *all* of you are probably *unaware* of . . .

_ the topics in Chapter 1; and . . .

_ the communication basics in Resource [H] and blocks in [J]; and . . .

_ your *inner* families of subselves and _ who's been leading them (Chapter 5); and . . .

_ how your *inner-family* conflicts cause and shape your *interpersonal* conflicts (below). And you probably don't know . . .

_ the three kinds of conflicts (concrete resources, abstract topics like values and opinions, and communication needs), and _ how to identify and resolve each of them effectively; and . . .

_ the four sets of requisites for a healthy relationship (vs. "friendship")—[..08/relationship.htm]; and . . .

_ how to dig down below your *surface* needs to discern your *true* needs (p. 44).

And your conflicted co-parents are probably often unaware of . . .

_ why denied shame will *always* hinder effective communication until you choose to identify it, own it, and replace it with self-love. Many co-parents are significantly shame-based and aren't aware of it. And you (all) may be unaware of . . .

_ the difference between *fighting* or *arguing* and win-win *problem solving*; and . . .

_ how typical "male brains" and "female brains" like yours perceive the world, and automatically process information, *very* differently. See the helpful books by Moir and Jessel (p. 557) and Deborah Tannen (p. 561); and also . . .

_ the communication processes occurring *in* and *between* any two people all the time, and _ how to *talk* together about your internal and interpersonal processes, as "=/=" co-parenting partners [..02/metatalk.htm].

Are you boggled? The good news: *motivation* to learn about these barriers can reduce each of them. A powerful motivation is your wish to teach your kids how to communicate effectively.

Status Check: Take a moment to assess where you stand now:

I feel a mix of *calm, centered, energized, light, focused, resilient, up, grounded, relaxed, alert, aware, serene, purposeful,* and *clear,* so my Self is probably leading my inner team of subselves now. (T F ?)

On a scale of 1 (consistently *in*effective) **to 10** (consistently effective), I feel the recent communications between co-parents in our family is about a ___. (Option: use a range, like "4 to 6")

I can clearly describe _ what a true Self and false self are, _ the six inner wounds that most co-parents are burdened with, _ how they hinder effective communication, and _ what they main steps are in Project 1. (T F ?)

I can clearly describe _ co-parent Project 2, _ the seven communication skills, and _ how the skills relate to each other now. (T F ?)

Each ex mate and other co-parent in our family can describe these clearly now. (T F ?)

On a scale of 1 (totally indifferent) **to 10** (strongly motivated), my drive to do Project 2 now with or without my co-parenting partners is a ___.

On the same scale, I'd rate the Project-2 motivation of each (other) ex mate in our family as a ___, ___, and ___.

My current motivation to become aware of each "awareness" item on p. 152 is about a ___ now.

I can describe clearly what I hope to get from reading this chapter. (T F ?)

I agree that building an effective co-parenting team for our kids depends directly on how well we adults can communicate and problem-solve with each other and each child. (T F ?)

If there's something blocking me and/or any of our co-parents from working to improve our communication, I know clearly _ what it is, and _ how to reduce it. (T F ?)

I believe we co-parents can significantly improve our communication effectiveness over time if we _ *want* to, and _ can agree on a viable plan to do so, like Project 2. (T F ?)

I'm teaching the young people in my life how to communicate effectively now. (T F ?)

Reflect for a moment . . . What did you just learn?

You *can* intentionally improve your communication effectiveness (get more mutual needs met more often) **by** helping each other do _ Project 1 (healing your inner wounds) and _ Project 2 (learning seven skills) together, over time. Yes, this is a *big*, long, complex project! The alternative is daily life full of fights, hurts, and frustrations (unmet needs), and a low family nurturance level which will wound your kids.

As long as you defer, or "sort of" commit to these two vital projects, your family communications and relationships will be stressful. If you *are* motivated to do Projects 1 and 2 now, stop reading this and study the guidebooks for each of them on p. 555. First things first!

As you ex mates and any stepparents progress on these two foundation projects together, you'll find _ the other 10 co-parent projects in [A], and _ resolving your mix of the barriers on p. 107 *significantly* easier!

Unless you're an inner-family or "personality parts-work" veteran, I suspect no one has showed you the powerful connection between your subselves and your co-parenting conflicts. Adopt the open "mind of a student," and get interested in . . .

How Inner Wounds Block Communication

In their mid-thirties, Gina and Tom divorced conflictually several years ago. They have joint custody of their nine-year-old son Harry, and need to talk together about him several times a week. Both acknowledge that "poor communications" was one reason that they separated, after seven years of marriage. They have a number of the problems on p. 150, and have never discussed them cooperatively.

Their expensive work with a marriage counselor and a di-vorce mediator didn't focus meaningfully on the two *real* prob-lems hindering their communication and strangling their mar-riage: false-self control and unawarenesses. Both Gina and Tom came from low-nurturance childhoods [D], and are *used to* being ruled by reactive false selves, specially in relationship con-flicts. Neither knows this, and each believes "something's very wrong" with their ex mate.

Each co-parent is also largely unaware of _ the topics on p. 152 and in Chapter 1. Like the great majority of their divorced and stepfamily peers and ancestors, these parents don't know what they don't know about these things. They feel their (inner and mutual) conflicts are aggravating and *normal.* Young Harry's parents are resigned to their ineffective communication, and have no idea how, or motivation to, improve it for their son's sake and their own.

Here's a glimpse of the *three* **concurrent dramas** that unfold when Tom calls Gina to discuss Harry's alarming report card: _ Tom's and _ Gina's *inner*-family dialogs, and _ the spoken exchange between them. Versions of these dramas have happened *many* times before, despite both parents feeling dissatisfied with the outcomes. They each care deeply for their son, and feel sadness and piercing guilt about Harry's sufferings from their divorce (Chapter 10).

The titles in italics are active subselves. The sentences and phrases are their (inner) "voices," and form the adults' *thoughts.* Pause and reflect: do *you* have "inner voices"? Do they ever argue? Which voices are the most persuasive and compelling with any ex mates in your family?

TOM thinks, before calling . . .

Catastrophizer: "*Four D's on Harry's report card! Oh, man; he's gonna flunk! He'll never make college, and will have to struggle for money his whole life! We'll have to support him forever, and that means . . .*"

Good Dad: "*Oh shut up, Gloom King. We have to help Harry now!*"

Inner Critic (acidly): "*Really nice job, Tom. What drug were you on when you thought you could be a competent father? Now Harry's failing because you messed up.*"

Shamed Boy: "*See? I AM no good!*"

Distracter: "*Hey, a beer would taste great now. Why don't you . . .*"

 # True Self: "*Not a good idea: we've already had two. We should call Gina and talk this report card over.*"

Good Dad: "*Yes, good. Let's do that.*"

Historian: "*Remember the last couple of times we talked about Harry's school problems, Gina got real sarcastic, blamed us (as usual), and blew up.*"

Skeptic: "*Yeah, we can call, but you'd better brace yourself for the usual hysteria, accusations, and no constructive ideas. Don't get your hopes up, pal.*"

Inner Judge: "*What a lousy excuse for a woman and mother she is. How did you ever get involved with her?*"

Practical One: "*You'd better balance the check book before you go to bed. You bounced two checks last month, and that cost us.*"

True Self—"*Stay focused on Harry; he needs help from Gina and all of us. Call her now.*"

Tom dials his ex, and she answers: "Hello?"

TOM says: "Hi, it's me." **He thinks . . .**

Skeptic: "*Hear that voice tone? No way she's going to listen now! This is a waste of time.*"

Peacemaker: "*Easy does it, go easy, now . . .*"

Good Dad: "*Come on, we can do this . . .*"

GINA (weary from work, enduring a slight headache) **says**: "Hi." **She thinks . . .**

Worrier: "*Oh God, what kind of problem is he going to dump on me now?*"

Optimist: "*Wait a minute, will you? Maybe we can have a good conversation, for a change. Maybe this time . . .*"

TOM says: "I think we should talk about Harry's grades. I'm worried: his grades have been dropping this whole school year."

Analyzer: "*Could it be a problem with a teacher? Maybe Harry's glasses are too weak, or . . .*"

GINA thinks:

Good Mom: "*Yeah, Tom and I really do need to talk together about this . . .*"

GINA says: "I'm concerned too. I think he feels bad about it— he's holed up in his room now. We ought to set up a conference with his counselor, and maybe consider a tutor;"

TOM thinks . . .

Good Dad: "*Sounds like good ideas . . .*"

Practical One: "*Where's the money going to come from? We can't afford a tutor.*"

Judge: "*See, there she goes taking control again. Hell will freeze before she thinks about asking our opinion. She is so self-centered . . .*

Historian and Guilty One: "*Last time, the counselor im-

plied Harry's problems came from our split up. She talked about parents 'like us' needing post-divorce counseling. His low grades are really our fault . . ."

TOM says: "Well, I'm not real crazy about Ms. Richardson (the school counselor). She's got 40 kids to take care of, and I . . ."

GINA thinks:

> **Judge**: *"See, right away, it's the 'yes but' game. I make a constructive suggestion, and Tom shoots it down with no alternatives. Why did he call me, anyway? What a jerk!"*

GINA says (sarcastically): "Well Tom, what do *you* think we should do?"

TOM thinks:

> **Judge** and **Skeptic**: *"Uh huh, hear that sarcasm? Here we go again . . ."*

TOM says: "Gina, you know I feel he watches too much TV at your house. Why don't you cut that back, and pay closer attention to his homework?"

GINA thinks:

> **Guilty One**: *"He's right. I really should insist Harry do his homework first.'*
>
> **Weary One**: *"But he puts up such a stink, it's just easier just to let him watch . . ."*
>
> **Inner Critic**: *"No excuse. You chose to have Harry, and you're his mother. Stop whining, and do your job!"*
>
> **Shamed Girl**: *"Aagh—I am so BAD!"*
>
> **Good Mom**: *"I'm really trying, but it's so hard, because . . ."*
>
> **# True Self**: *"Wait, wait all of you! Calm down, so we can . . ."*
>
> **Chorus**: *"Ah, shut up, wimp!"*
>
> **Scared Girl**: *"Something bad is going to happen. I'm gonna get hurt again!"*
>
> **Amazon:** *(Guardian subself):* *"NO! We are not going to let him trash us again! Watch this!"*

GINA says: "Ah, so you think that I'm causing Harry's bad grades, because I'm a lousy Mother, huh? We're going to get into finger pointing and complaining again? Some things never change . . ."

TOM thinks:

Warrior and *Judge:* "You want to fight, Gina? Fine with me, you moron. I know just how to make you back off."

Good Dad: "But wait, this is about Harry . . ."

Scared Boy: "Oh no, no . . ."

Skeptic: "See, I told you so!"

Health Director: "Man, your tooth really hurts! You have to get to the dentist this week."

Catastrophizer: "This is bad. Gina and her shark lawyer will probably turn this into a tabloid court fiesta. That'll mean . . ."

Shamed Boy: "Dad was right. I'll never amount to anything."

Distracter: "Look, this is going nowhere. Tell her you'll call back, and get that delicious cold beer . . ."

Warrior: "Oh no you don't. We've had a lifetime of backing away from controllers like her. Time to stand up and draw the line!"

True Self: "Will you all be quiet so I can think? I can't make a good decision unless you all . . ."

Chorus: "Yeah sure; your 'good decisions' got us into this mess! Butt out!"

<<< inner chaos / mind babble / tooth pain >>>

Paralyzer (Guardian subself): "Alright, this is too much. I'm going to shut everyone down."

(Silence)

GINA says: "Are you still there?"

Notice what you're thinking and feeling. This three-way drama happened in *less than two minutes*. Similar versions had happened hundreds of times before, which conditioned Gina and Tom to expect to feel unheard, blamed, misunderstood, and frustrated. How would you guess the conversation turned out: would either parent get their needs met?

Recall: in *effective* **communication** _ each person's *true* (vs. surface) needs get filled well enough, _ in a way that both people feel good *enough* about.

In this brief example, notice several things:

Neither Tom's nor Gina's Self was trusted to coordinate the opinions and needs of their other subselves. The outcome was each parent got buffeted by the thoughts and feelings of the crowd of personality parts forming their "false self," and neither knew it. One result was that . . .

Neither co-parent had begun to get clear what _ their or _ their partner's *true* needs were. Tom could have clarified *"What do I need from Gina?"* before he picked up the phone. Conversely, she could have asked him what he needed from her when he called. Neither knew the six reasons they communicate (p. 508). From long habit, . . .

Neither Gina nor Tom were aware of what was happening inside themselves or between them, so they couldn't use *metatalk* skill to describe their inner and mutual processes, and what was hindering it. And . . .

Their conversation was beginning to polarize into a (familiar) mutual spiral of attack > defend > counterattack (1-up / 1-down R-messages). This polarity was powered by the strong *feelings* of their shamed and scared (Vulnerable) inner kids, and the Guardian subselves that activated to protect them.

And in this example . . .

Neither adult was feeling _ respected or _ trusted by the other (like *many* prior interactions), leaving a primal communication need unfilled. *That* caused their E(motion)-levels to rise "above their ears," which blocked their ability to hear each other—making brainstorming and problem-solving impossible. The net result: *ineffective communication, reducing the chance that both parents could act together to _ assess what their son needed, and _ provide it. Lose-lose-lose.*

The point: communications among your adults and kids are powerfully shaped by the members of your inner families, specially in conflicts. Your family members are almost surely unaware of this. Think of recent conversations between you and other family co-parents. Can you begin to see them in a new way?

To expand your awareness, read the description of a real stepfamily couple and their kids and ex mates at [http://sfhelp.org/example.htm].

A Better Way

If Tom and Gina had each progressed on Project 1, their true Selves would have been in charge of their inner-family processes. That's specially likely if both had become fluent with the seven mental/verbal skills (p. 512) by working at Project 2. Their Selves would have focused their other subselves on _ their unfolding communication *process* to keep it effective, and on _ trying to help their son Harry without _ getting into a toxic blame > defend > counterblame spiral, and/or _ defocusing on other past or recent conflicts.

If your co-parents often experience frustrating communication, you *can* make major improvements, over time. You probably have several interactive relationship problems like mutual distrust, disrespect, resentment, guilt, and related hostility. With commitment and patience, improved communications and more *inner*-family harmony can help you improve all of them. Use your shared love for your child/ren and your vision of later-life satisfactions to empower you.

To help each other do this, _ identify and separate your caregiving barriers into separate targets, and _ work on re/building self and mutual respect (and Self-leadership) *first*. Without those, you'll have difficulty sending the genuine =/= R-messages that you all need to enable the seven Project-2 skills fill your respective needs.

Resolving *Values* Conflicts

Which do you feel is a better color, orange or purple? Which is more useful, a watermelon or a banana? Do you favor the Republicans, Democrats, or another political party? Should your kids express disagreements to you adults, or repress them and obey you? Are Baptists better than Muslims? Are abortion, murder, and suicide ever justified? Whose needs are more important in a family conflict: the custodial parent's, their ex mate's, a stepparent's (if any), or their child's?

Among the disputes that vex your subselves, co-parents, and kids every day, probably the most common are abstract conflicts over *values, priorities, preferences*, and *opinions.* Divorced families and stepfamilies are riddled with these. Do your co-parents have a strategy to resolve values conflicts yet? For perspective, try defining the rules your parents used to govern their behavior when they had a major disagreement over *values.* How did your grandparents resolve theirs?

All partners and groups experience values conflicts, so you've experienced many different approaches to them. Your basic options are:

Pretend they don't exist (reality distortion).

Acknowledge they exist, but _ do nothing (i.e. silently suffer and seethe), or _ postpone confronting your partner/s (conflict avoidance).

Try to persuade each other to adopt your value or preference; (*"Catholic education is better because . . ."*).

Demand that your partner/s *want* to adopt your value, or at least defer to it (*"You* must *agree to send Martha to Catholic school."*);

Blame each other for not agreeing with your value [*"You just don't care about Martha's relationship with God. (You're a bad parent.)"*]. Favorite variations include preaching, lecturing, moralizing, worrying, and catastrophizing. Or you can . . .

Get into a power struggle over who's *right*, and lose sight of the original conflict. A symptom of this is invoking "authorities who *know*," including God, a Holy Book, and your favorite talk-show host or guest. Or you can ...

Focus as team-mates on *how* you're trying to resolve your values conflict, and what your usual outcomes are (*"I'd say we're increasingly avoiding talk about this school issue, and we each are feeling increasingly frustrated and distrustful that we can problem-solve together."*)

Respectfully agree to disagree, and seek a mutually-acceptable compromise (*"OK, How about if Martha goes to Catholic Middle School, and then our public High School?"*)

Pretend to agree, and (your subselves) secretly roil in criticism, anxiety, resentment, guilt, and self-pity.

Defocus on other past or present conflicts to avoid the discomfort of this one. (*"Before we talk about Martha's school, I need you to explain why you're late with the child support again."*) Or you can react to major values-conflicts by . . .

Using "dig down," metatalk, and empathic-listening skills to help each other explore what's underneath your surface need to have the other person agree with your value or preference. You'll usually find a false self needing security, immediate gratification (comfort), excitement, or to avoid anxiety, guilt, or shame. Or you can choose . . .

Some combination of these or other options.

<u>An Effective Strategy</u>

See if you think the steps below would help you reduce values conflicts, and raise the co-parenting teamwork in and between your kids' several homes . . .

Agree on _ a definition of "a values conflict," and that _ these disagreements are normal in any relationship and group, not *bad* or *wrong*.

Agree on your long-term co-parenting **priorities**: e.g. is protecting your child from (another) divorce more important than what school she goes to? See [..08/priority.htm].

Choose an =/= (mutual respect) **attitude**, and check to see if your true Selves are leading. If not, determine why, and work to fix that.

Work together to agree on long-range co-parenting goals, and keep focused on them in resolving local disputes.

Brainstorm your options. If you can't find a genuine mutually-satisfying compromise, agree to disagree for the sake of more important long-range goals. Option: adopt this . . .

Key to Mental Health

*"Settle for disorder in lesser things for the sake of order in
greater things; and therefore be content to be discontent in
many things."* (anonymous)

As teammates, help each other stay aware on *how* you're
resolving your values (and other) conflicts over time. Separate
concurrent problems (e.g. p. 150), and work to resolve them a
few at a time. Celebrate your successes, and improve strategies
that don't fill your key needs.

Stay aware that you'll also have daily conflicts over _ tangible things, and _ current communication needs (p. 508); and
help each other evolve effective strategies to spot and resolve
these disputes cooperatively.

Teach your kids and other key people what you're doing,
and why; and _ coach your kids to form their own values-
conflict strategy, over time.

At all costs, avoid using lawyers and judges to force your
values on another co-parent, unless someone's wholistic health
is clearly in danger. See Chapter 18.

Note that your home's and family's values-conflict strategies will affect how well you co-parents resolve your inevitable *loyalty* disputes and relationship triangles (Chapter 16).
Note also that "no strategy" *is* a strategy!

Pause and reflect: what are your subselves saying now?
Who's the most vocal, and who's leading them?

Chapters 5 and 13-17 build on this strategy. They outline
options for your confronting a combative (wounded) or disinterested co-parent, and asserting and enforcing boundaries (limits) *respectfully* using your seven communication skills. Other
chapters in Part 3 help you look below surface conflicts over
child visitation, money, addictions, excessive resentments, and
legal battles. Once you discern the needs under these. You can
apply the seven skills to fill them.

Recap

Adults and kids communicate to fill local and long-range *needs*—i.e. reduce discomforts. Your co-parents need effective inner and mutual communication to reduce each barrier to nurturing your kids as a team. Typical divorced parents and stepparents often have two major blocks to co-operative problem-solving as teammates with common goals: _ a disabled true Self and related inner wounds, and _ unawareness of the seven communication skills in [H], and when and how to use them.

This chapter offers _ a two-part definition of effective communication (can you name it?), _ describes common symptoms of ineffective communication between co-parents, and _ a brief illustration of how false-selves degrade well-meant co-parenting communication without your knowing it. The chapter ends with a summary of _ co-parenting *values* conflicts, and options for resolving them well together. Your strategy at doing this will affect your success at resolving a stream of inevitable loyalty conflicts and relationship triangles (Chapter 16).

There are *lots* of resources to help your co-parents improve your communication, even with hostile (wounded) ex mates and/or "defiant" (hurt, overwhelmed) kids. The most comprehensive resource is the Project-2 guidebook "Satisfactions—7 Relationship Skills You Need to Know" [xlibris.com, 2001]. See other useful books in Resource [N] and at [..11/books-evc.htm]. Resources [H—K] will help you get started. *Also see* [http://sfhelp.org/02/links02.htm] for further detail, and helpful worksheets, inventories, and practice exercises. Use [..02/evc-quiz.htm] to invite communication awareness and interest in your other family members. Share any of these resources with other co-parents and professional supporters along the way, including live or online support-groups.

What would happen if you gave a copy of this chapter [..Rx/ex/cx.htm] (or book) to any ex mates you struggle with? Is your Self answering that?

+ + +

A core requisite for effective communication is self and mutual *respect*. Typical divorced mates and stepfamily co-parents often don't respect themselves or each other, in general or as effective nurturers. The next chapter explores this major team-building barrier, and suggests practical options for re/ building mutual respect.

8) Re/build Co-parental Respect

Earn Respect, or Choose *Compassion*

Think of a child-nurturer you know, past or present, whom _ you strongly admire, and _ who is justifiably proud of their ability to co-parent effectively. Note whether you respect them as a *person*, a *parent*, or both. Did you include yourself as a candidate?

Marital separation and divorce usually follow a gradual shift in one or both partners. Courtship admiration and approval shifts into disrespect and contempt in _ one or several roles like *lover, provider, partner, wo/man, parent*, and *friend*, or in _ *all* these roles (*"I've lost all respect for Nina as a person."*) Can you think of a more potent barrier to co-parenting teamwork than *disrespect*?

Reread the opening paragraph on p. 61 and note your reaction. If one or both divorced parents disrespects _ the other, and/or _ themselves, they and their kids *will* have ongoing communication and relationship problems. These conflicts compound if a new (stepparent) partner disrespects an ex mate, or vice versa. The article at [http://sfhelp.org/Rx/spsc/disrespect.htm] suggests options for increasing respect between a (step)child and a co-parent.

Disrespect differs from *distrust, envy, indifference, frustration*, and *hostility*. Conflicted people who don't separate these feel *dislike*, which can seem immune to change ("*I just have bad chemistry with Louis.*") Note that at times, "disrespect" for another person blooms when you don't assert your own values, needs, and boundaries with them *respectfully*. Would you agree that disrespect promotes disrespect in return?

Does disrespect hinder co-parenting teamwork in your family now? There may be up to **four basic problems** to solve: _ One or _ both ex mates disrespect _ themselves, and/or _ each other. The principles are the same if a *stepparent* disrespects _ themselves and/or _ their partner's ex spouse, and vice versa. See the Project-1 guidebook *Who's* Really *Running Your Life?* or [..01/recovery1.htm] for options on converting shame (self disrespect) into self love.

This chapter focuses on your options for intentionally re/ growing *respect* and *compassion* for each of your kids' nurturers, despite major disputes, past hurts, and *dislike*. The more you all value and work at this together, the greater your combined abilities to help your kids with their challenging array of needs [F].

The chapter builds on Part 1 by exploring options for _ converting disdain for another co-parent into compassion while asserting firm limits with them; and _ intentionally earning the respect of another co-parent.

To begin, learn about yourselves:

Use a "Respect Map"

Use some undistracted time to draw a co-parent "respect map." As you do, note the difference between *liking* or *being attracted to* someone and *respecting* them:

I feel a mix of *calm, centered, energized, light, focused, resilient, up, grounded, relaxed, alert, aware, serene, purposeful,* and *clear,* so my Self is presiding now. (T F ?) If s/he isn't, I suggest focusing on re-empowering your Self before doing this exercise. See Project 1.

Your co-parenting team includes two or more adults who are nurturing your dependent kids part-time or full-time. To identify your team, draw your version of the nuclear-stepfamily "map" on p. 84. If you don't want to include any of your kids' bio and stepparents, see p. 33 and Project 3.

Mentally image the custodial, visiting, and/or grown children in all your lives to be standing in a line, gazing at all you co-parents in another line facing them. How would that feel?

On a piece of paper, write the first name or initials of each co-parent in your generation who now significantly affects the life of _ you, _ each minor or grown child, or _ your current partner. Include any that aren't yet remarried, *and any who have died.* Arrange the initials in a triangle several inches apart, or a circle, if you have more than three people. Now draw a line between each pair of people, representing the relationship between them. If you have five co-parents, you'll have [(5 x 4) / 2] = 10 lines.

Using a scale of 1 (total *dis*respect) **to 10** (steady high respect), thoughtfully put a number on each end of each line to represent your opinion of how much that person recently respects the other *as a co-parent.* If you're not sure, put a range (e.g. "3-5") or "?" Take your time, and notice how you feel, as you do this. This may or may not be the same as the respect-ranking you'd use for *person* or *wo/man.*

Now guess how each person recently respects *themselves* as a co-parent, and note that (1 to 10) next to each name or initials. Option: distinguish between respect as a bioparent vs. a stepparent, if they have both roles.

To identify problems worth working on together, use your map to ponder questions like these:

Who has the lowest and highest respect for _ themselves and _ another co-parent in your family?

Would I say the average respect among all of us is _ low, _ moderate, or _ high?

What does that *mean* for our dependent kids, long range? Option: review [F] before answering.

If I feel that one or more of us co-parents needs to raise our respect for another co-parent for our kids' sakes, **who**?

How do I feel about the liklihood of that happening now? (pessimistic to optimistic, 1 to 10)?

If raising co-parental respect seems unlikely, what are the main barriers? To what extent can I and/or my partner/s reduce them?

If none of us tries to improve our co-parenting respect for _ ourselves and _ each other, will I feel content or regretful in old age?

What might happen if I called us all together in person or by phone (conference call) to _ describe this exercise, _ ask other co-parents do their own version, and _ work together with the results, for our kids' sakes?

Take a moment to objectively notice your thoughts and feelings ("self talk") now. What are you aware of? Option: for balance and perspective, fill out this inventory of co-parent *strengths* now: [http://sfhelp.org/07/strnx3-co-p.htm].

Because this is a complex subject and space is limited, the rest of this chapter is in semi-outline form.

Premises About *Respect*

An early step in raising co-parental respect is to become aware of how it operates, and what you believe about it. Your co-parents' versions of the beliefs that follow will profoundly affect your family relationships, satisfactions, and nurturance level. Take your time, and note your honest reaction to each of these. "A" = "I agree," "D" = "I disagree," and "?" = "I'm not sure," or "it depends" (on what?).

Members of an *effective* team need to have steady high respect for _ themselves and _ each other *in their roles*, if not as persons. (A D ?)

Each member _ needs to be clear on their responsibilities to the team (their *role*), and _ is responsible for their own self respect in their role. (A D ?)

Respect must be *earned*, vs. demanded or expected. Disrespect automatically breeds hurt, anger, distrust, and disrespect. (A D ?)

It's hard to respect a person who disrespects and neglects themselves (A D ?). Many typical divorced and re/married co-parents are shame-based people from low-nurturance child-hoods. They (you) can intentionally change self-disrespect (shame and guilt) into genuine self esteem over time, via true recovery from inner wounds. See *Who's* Really *Running Your Life?* or [..01/recovery1.htm].

Many divorced parents disrespect themselves and/or each other as _ persons and _ caregivers, because they caused their kids pain and loss, and feel they "failed" at marriage and family-building. (A D ?) See Chapters 10 and 11.

It's hard to respect yourself in a role (like *bioparent, stepparent*, and *child of divorce*) that you _ don't want, _ don't understand, and/or _ feel overwhelmed by. (A D ?)

More premises about *respect* . . .

Divorced and re/wedded co-parents often disagree on their definition of "good (effective) parenting," and _ "who among us is 'supposed to' do what for our kids?" Your minor kids depend on all you co-parents to *want to* resolve serious family role confusions and conflicts, though they can't say so. (A D ?) See Project 6 in [A].

Anyone can raise their self respect in a role or as a person if _ they commit to that *and* _ *their Self is in charge of their inner family.* (A D ?) See Chapter 5 and Project 1.

True self respect depends on a person's governing subselves genuinely respecting the abilities, values, goals, intentions, and leadership of their true Self and each other subself. (A D ?)

Not confronting a disrespected co-parent lowers _ your *self* respect and _ your family's nurturance level; and _ may block the person from healing. (A D ?) The latter is called "enabling." Common examples are fearing to confront a co-parent about inner wounds, child abuse, law-breaking, self-neglect, or an addiction.

Deciding whether to respect a co-parent depends partly on understanding and accepting their personal limitations (e.g. psychological wounds, ignorances, and unawareness). (A D ?) See Chapter 5.

Respecting a co-parent's role performance will be affected by your and their basic (unconscious) attitudes. (A D ?) See Chapter 3.

Disrespect is different than *distrust* (Chapter 9), *hostility* (Chapter 13), and *resentment* (Chapter 14). Each of these is healed differently. They can combine into *dislike*. (A D ?)

Short and long term, *compassion* raises relationship and family nurturances. Unhealed disrespect lowers both. Genuine (vs. dutiful or pretended) compassion and empathy promote respectful (caring) confrontations and limit-settings (Chapters 14 and 15). *Empathy* and *compassion* are inherently respectful. *Pity* can feel insulting (1-up). (A D ?)

Disrespecting _ yourself and/or _ another co-parent will inevitably hinder effective communication and problem-solving among you all. Co-parents constantly evaluate each other's respect via the 1-up, =/=, or 1-down R(espect)-messages embedded in every perceived behavior. (A D ?) See Chapter 7 and [H].

A final premise . . .

Co-parents who don't genuinely respect _ themselves and/ or _ each other *unintentionally* promote anxiety, anger, and shame in their dependent kids every day. They can't tell you this directly until they're aware adults. (A D ?)

Have you ever considered the vital role that *respect* ("esteem") plays in your family (and other) relationships? Did your childhood caregivers respect _ themselves and _ each other as _ parents and _ persons? How each of your co-parents feels about premises like these forms your multi-home family's unspoken "**respect policy.**" It can nurture or wound.

Options for Converting Disrespect

Regard these alternatives as a buffet to select from, in any order. They're written assuming the person you're focusing on is your or your partner's ex mate. If not, change "the ex" to "the (disrespected) co-parent" and edit the item to fit better.

Option 1) Do a *Self* check. In my experience, people unaware of domination by a protective, narrow-minded false self have difficulty spontaneously feeling balanced respect, empathy, and compassion for _ themselves and _ other wounded co-parents. If you're unsure who's in charge of your *inner* family, use [E] to get a preliminary reading. For more clarity and options for Self-empowerment, use the guidebook *Who's* Really *Running Your Life?,* or the resources at [..pop/assess.htm].

2) Refresh your awareness: reread Chapters 1 and 2, if you haven't recently. Affirm that this second-order contempt-to-compassion change is a *long-term* project: you won't achieve it over a weekend!

3) Clarify your concepts and terms: write down your definitions of *compassion, empathy,* and *pity.* Be as specific as you can. Then write your thoughtful definition of *integrity* and *dignity.* Your concepts and vocabulary shape your thoughts, expectations, and behaviors, which will help or hinder your success here. Use a dictionary as a last resort, because *your* definitions will determine your success here. The clearer and firmer you are on them, the easier your path.

Option 4) Strengthen your motivation by defining specifically how converting contempt into compassion will benefit you and other family members. If you have an active *Skeptic* or *Inner Saboteur* subself, s/he will try to dissuade or discourage (i.e. protect) you via thoughts like *"Get* real—*this will never happen!"* and *"This is a waste of time and energy."* Respectfully acknowledge such thoughts, and ignore them.

I suspect your key benefits will include _ less fighting, and more cooperative compromising, _ better listening and problem-solving, _ less anxiety, guilt, and anger in kids and adults; _ freed up energy to enjoy each other, _ higher self-respect, and _ better bonding among you all. These all contribute to _ raising the nurturance level of your family [D], which has *major* long-term benefits for you all and your descendents!

Option: imagine the youngest of your children as middle-aged adults, and picture discussing how this compassion-building project affected them and their kids.

5) Reduce doubts and ambivalence: meditate and evolve a clear list of _ every reason you *shouldn't* try to convert your disrespect into compassion for an ex mate or other co-parent, and _ why your effort can't possibly work. Listen carefully and respectfully to each inner voice: they're trying to *protect you!* Your true Self is the one who's "listening." Your Vulnerable and Guardian subselves [..01/innerfam2.htm] are more apt to *want* to co-operate if they feel your Self genuinely values (respects) and wants to hear their ideas and worries. Hearing does not necessarily mean *agreeing!*

Option 6) Review your resources: who's available to help and encourage you to convert your scorn to real compassion (and limits)? What inspirations and non-human resources can strengthen and guide you? Inform key people of what you're setting out to do, and why. Stay clear on your goals, boundaries, Rights (p. 514), and *integrity*, because friends, kids, kin, and counselors will all have their own biases and agendas . . .

7) Choose a reference: Think of someone who's doing their best, despite some major physical, psychological, or mental handicap. The key is picking someone for whom you feel real empathy, respect, and compassion, not *pity*. Consciously identify *why* you feel those things for this person, and tell someone about this. You'll learn something about your values and perhaps your own burdens . . .

8) Assess the scorned co-parent for inner wounds. Read Chapters 3, 5, and 6—and ideally, *Who's* Really *Running Your Life?* or the articles at [..pop/assess.htm]. My 21-year clinical experience is that 80% or more of typical American divorced and stepfamily co-parents are significantly wounded and ruled by a false self and don't (want to) know it. This option is just as critical as your checking to see if your Self is leading. If you identify and accept *your* wounds, you're more apt to see and empathize with the other co-parent's wounds and behaviors [E]. Do you agree?

Option 9) Build a new image: If you conclude that your disrespected co-parent is probably or surely a significantly-wounded wo/man (p. 448):

Identify the adjectives you've been semi-consciously using to describe them recently. Favorites I've heard include lazy, irresponsible, untruthful, wimpy, stupid, undependable, self-ish, controlling, manipulating, crazy, lazy, hopeless, weak, un-trustworthy, unfeeling, macho, rigid, domineering, bitchy, child-ish, sick, . . .

Face the reality that thinking, speaking, and writing these adjectives nourishes your contempt. Which comes first: choosing new adjectives, or changing your attitude to compassion? Possible new adjectives: burdened, wounded, tormented, un-aware, hurt, scared, shamed, guilty, confused, overwhelmed, orphaned, disabled, misinformed, self-protective, neglected, stuck, distracted, self-doubting, isolated, . . . Notice the theme or feeling of all these.

Get very clear on the difference between the ex mate's past *actions* and *behaviors*, and their human dignity—*i.e. their potential high worth.* Their *actions* may have hurt, frustrated, disappointed, and betrayed you and/or beloved others. Their potential for good in the world, their worth, has been blocked by their wounds, *through no fault of theirs—or yours.*

Try the idea that your ex mate's hurtful actions were and are controlled by their false self, which s/he's not known, and couldn't help (so far). *Review the* typical Guardian subselves at [..01/innerfam2.htm], *and mull which of your ex mate's Guardian subselves caused her or his hurtful behaviors. Note that Guardian personality parts are intent on relieving current acute discomforts vs. "being nice,"* before you condemn the ex as bad . . .

Get undistracted and centered, and experience some visions. Notice your thoughts and feelings as you do, without judgment. Option: have someone neutral read these out loud slowly, pausing for several minutes between each image . . .

Imagine an uncut diamond, encrusted with filth and buried in the dark earth. Reflect: is this a *bad* diamond? Picture the diamond being discovered, cleaned, expertly cut and lovingly polished, over time. Vividly see it's brilliant sparkle in the sunlight . . .

Imagine a hard-shelled seed buried deep underground. Sense the potential within the seed for vibrant shoots of new life. Imagine *being* the seed, waiting for the right conditions that will cause your shell to split, and the miracle of unique life within you to instinctively thrust up through the darkness toward the light and air . . .

Vividly imagine the ex mate you disrespect as a child— bewildered, needy, scared, and alone. Imagine her or him trying to survive (vs. thrive) with too few of the nourishments s/he needed [D].

Imagine this young person splitting physically into a group of related children: one terrified, one shamed, one confused, one guilty, one *angry*, one very lonely, and perhaps one feeling *lost* and *hopeless*. Image the young true Self, trying to coordinate and lead all of these related kids without enough wise adult guidance. All of these kids (just like *yours*) longed for love, safety, comfort, hugs, and encouragement. Their wounded, distracted, unaware adults couldn't supply enough.

Picture the group dressed in rags, gaunt, filthy, with festering sores, banding together *alone* in a menacing, unpredictable world. Picture the ex mate's real-life childhood caregivers being unable to see this invisible band of young ones they were living with.

Now image a crowd of protective Guardian subselves [..01/ innerfam2.htm] emerging and surrounding this group of anxious young kids. Imagine the Guardians seeing that the ex's young true Self wasn't yet wise enough to be trusted with the little band's comfort or safety. Picture the Guardians paralyzing or overwhelming the inept Self, and perhaps the child's Spiritual part—maybe even entombing them for *more* safety.

Imagine the real child becoming used to seeing the world through the distorted lenses of these Guardian parts, and relying on their emotions and biased judgments to survive.

Now see this band of vulnerable kids and Guardians evolving over the years, as the ex's body matured. Some of these Vulnerable and Guardian subselves weren't aware of the years passing. New Guardians developed to handle new social situations and adult responsibilities. The Guardians became used to controlling (protecting) their group of kids, believing no other leadership could safely protect them from more pain, loss, and death. The disrespected ex mate's Self and Spirit languished in their prison.

If you disrespect your ex mate, remember falling in love with the seductive, charming, appealing mask that these Guardians had cleverly fashioned to protect their band of shamed, guilty, sad, lonely, confused, angry kids. Understand that much your lives together after your vows were probably *unconsciously governed* by the perceptions and interactions of your and your ex mate's Vulnerable and Guardian parts—*not your true Selves.*

Image the ex mate's true Self imprisoned deep within them, waiting to be set free. *Perhaps yours is too.* Recall that true (vs. pseudo) Project-1 recovery [..01/recovery1.htm] can set your true Selves free to lead and harmonize your inner crew, over time, once the person commits to personal healing. If your *Skeptic* subself declares something like *"That will* never *happen in this lifetime!"* – don't buy it! Consider: Typical 12-step meetings are full of people who were once thought "hopelessly" out of control and "sick" (wounded).

Now review the sample Bill of personal rights (p. 514) and see if your ruling subselves feel that the ex mate has the same personal rights that you (they) do. If not, your Self is probably disabled.

A final step in building a new image of the ex . . .

Apply Chapters 10 and 11 if they're relevant. This can help you stay in the present, and not obsess about past traumas and hurts.

Pause now and experience your thoughts and feelings fully, without judgment. Have you ever thought of this ex mate and/ or your Self this way before? *Now* what adjectives seem appropriate to describe the ex as a person and a caregiver? Do you think you can learn to convert disrespect for him or her (or someone else) into genuine compassion and empathy? *"No,"* probably indicates a distrustful false self leads your "inner orchestra" now . . .

Option 10) When you next talk with the ex mate, vividly imagine their voice and appearance to be a disguise that has been forced on her or him by their well-meaning Guardian subselves. Keep a vision clear of their true Self waiting to be freed to lead their whole inner family. If you choose, share some or all of these steps with the ex, when s/he's receptive and you're both undistracted. See what happens, over time.

11) Study the other chapters in Parts 2 and 3 with this person in mind. Working on each of these relationship and surface problems can help you grow genuine compassion for a disrespectful ex mate. Pay special attention to Chapters 10-12 and 15.

12) If these options don't shift disrespect toward compassion, re-do option 1. One or more of your subselves don't yet feel it's *safe* and/or *right* ("fair"), to feel real compassion for the ex spouse. If so, this suggests you have more personal work to do on harmonizing your inner crew via *inner* family therapy or equivalent. Options:

Read [..01/innerfam1.htm] and the series of articles at [..01/ifs1-intro.htm] for context and background.

Meditate and invite the subselves who don't *want* to feel compassion for the ex to identify themselves, via an image, a "voice," (thought stream), or a physical or emotional feeling. It may be paired Vulnerable and Guardian subselves.

(Your Self) invite each such personality part it to tell you (via thoughts, images, memories, "senses," . . .) why compassion seems an unsafe or unfair choice now.

Assess whether the (or each) scared part is living in the past or the present. Ask it *"What year is it now?"* and trust the first answer that occurs to you. Convene all inner family members, and brainstorm a solution, with your Self leading the process. See [..01/ifs7-rescuing.htm] for ideas.

Be alert for the possibility that one or more subselves still don't trust _ your Self and _ other Regular subselves and _ outer people to keep you safe from some imagined harm the ex mate might inflict. If so, educate the distrustful part/s on how you're going to . . .

Option 12) Learn how to assert your boundaries (limits) *respectfully* with the other co-parent: see Chapters 7 and 15.

Note the implication: feeling compassion for this wounded co-parent does not mean condoning harmful parenting behavior or disrespecting *you* or other family members! Use your Bill of Personal Rights (p. 514) as a foundation for your *respectful* assertions

Finally, consider your option to . . .

13) Invite the disrespected ex-spouse to join you in this attitude-conversion project, for all your sakes. This is specially relevant if they don't respect *you* as a child-nurturer or a person. That brings us to the other possible disrespect barrier: you truly respect your other co-parents enough, but one or more of them scorns *you* as a person and/or nurturer. What are your options?

Earning a Co-parent's Respect

Have you ever intentionally tried to earn someone's respect (vs. "being liked")? Do you know anyone who has succeeded at this? If not, you may feel ambivalent or skeptical. Consider Henry Ford's blunt opinion: *"Whether you believe you can or you can't, you're right."*

If your subselves are skeptical, consider starting with something like *"I don't know what may happen here, and I'll give it my best shot."* A firmer attitude is *"I* can *improve my ex mate's respect for me. I will find a way."* Reread Chapters 1 and 2, and clarify your attitudes. Then note with interest to see if they help you get your needs filled via options like these . . .

Requisites

I propose that you *may* upgrade your ex mate's (or anyone's) respect for you if you _ meet some key conditions, and then _ act patiently on some options. To avoid feeling overwhelmed, coach your subselves to see that each of these is an individual task that you *can* master, over time. Keep your future self and your kids' long-term welfare in mind as you consider these requisites one at a time.

To re/build your ex mate's (or anyone's) respect for you, these need to be true *enough* . . .

Your _ Self is solidly in charge of your subselves, and _ your subselves are learning to genuinely trust and respect her or him and themselves as a worthy group—i.e. you're progressing well on your version of Project-1 recovery.

You truly accept that you must *earn* your ex mate's respect as a competent co-parent, vs. demanding or expecting it.

Your subselves accept that *you* are probably half the relationship problem—i.e. some things you did or are now doing are promoting your ex mate's disrespect. This is not about blame or badness, it's about what's *real.*

You _ understand and _ are working to apply the ideas in Part 1 to your situation because you *want to*, vs. *have* to. This happens naturally if your Self is leading.

You're making an honest effort to change major scorn and/or pity for your ex mate into compassion. If you *pretend* compassion, your body, voice, and behaviors will surely leak the truth. That will probably harvest resentment, distrust, and disrespect in return.

You clearly _ understand the concepts of _ values and loyalty conflicts, and _ relationship triangles (Chapter 16), and _ you and any new partner are intentionally evolving a thoughtful strategy to manage each of them. Notice the difference between *"My ex mate disagrees with my parenting* values" and *"My ex mate doesn't respect me as a competent co-parent."*

Another requisite you need is . . .

You're making progress healing any significant . . .

* guilts about your past actions with the ex,
* distrust of her or him,
* resentments about your ex's behaviors, and . . .
* learning whether either of you is blocked in grieving major losses.

Use Chapters 9-12 and 14, and related Web resources.

Once you feel you have enough of these respect-building factors in place, then choose among your . . .

Action Options

Name your target. Get clear on various labels which all imply disrespect: *scornful, contemptuous, sneering, jeering, disparaging, reviling, libeling, discounting, ignoring, interrupting, sarcastic, rude, aggressive (vs. abusive), selfish, demanding,* and so on. Unaware (preoccupied, distracted, wounded) people often focus more on some of these than *disrespect.* The distinction is important because *respect* (feeling personally worthy and valuable) is a fundamental need we seek to fill by communicating and "relating."

Review Resources [H—K]. Then assess whether you've been unaware of sending "1-up" or "1-down" R(espect)-messages to the ex by behaviors like these:

_ anger and attacking (blaming)
_ explaining and defending endlessly
_ cowering and apologizing
_ numbing, repressing, and/or feeling paralyzed
_ withdrawing emotionally or physically
_ complaining to others (including your kids)
_ avoiding (what?)
_ revenge (punishing)
_ triangling (Chapter 16)
_ lying or pretending
_ sending double messages (a false-self symptom)
_ yelling or exploding
_ using the kids to manipulate or control the ex
_ hiring a lawyer to force co-operation or "victory"

A better (=/=) alternative to all of these is _ clarifying your true needs [..02/dig-down.htm], _ asserting them respectfully [..02/assert.htm] and [..02/I-msg-wks.htm], and calmly handling the ex's responses with _ empathic listening [..02/listen.htm]. These can lead to win-win problem solving *if* you respect your ex as a person of equal human dignity.

Study and practice your seven mental/verbal skills, specially assertion and empathic listening; and _ and affirm your Personal Rights (p. 514). See the guidebook *Satisfactions.*

Notice the "awareness bubble" you share when communicating with your other co-parent [..02/a-bubble.htm], and work to *want to* include both of you in it. Then . . .

Try *mapping* a typical communication sequence between you and the other co-parent, and see what you learn [..02/evc-maps.htm]. Assess who got their true needs met (p. 44) by the end of the sequence.

Evolve a strategy for responding to disrespectful behavior from the ex mate. That may include talking directly with her or him about your wish to merit their co-parenting respect (without losing your dignity). See Chapters 10 and 11.

Questions

Meditate or discuss questions like these to clarify and broaden your perspective:

"On a scale of 1 to 10, how strong is my real need to feel respected by my ex mate now?" Your results on this team-building project will clearly reflect your truth here, over time.

"Who do I feel solidly respected by (vs. "liked by") now? Why? What's different about my relationship with them vs. with my ex mate?" What does that mean?

"1 to 10, how important is it for our kids' long-term welfare that my ex and I respect (or at least feel empathy and compassion for) each other?" Note your option to discuss this honestly with your ex and each of your kids. Are you and they comfortable with doing that?

"What evidence do I have that my ex mate clearly sees the difference between 'bad behavior' (hurtful or ineffective actions) and 'a bad person' (me)? If s/he's not clear yet, can I influence him or her respectfully to get clearer?"

"Is my ex mate's disrespect for me significantly influenced by one or more other people? If so, who, and what can I do about that?" Resource: the Serenity Prayer (p. 102). Beware

an impulsive or conflict-avoiding answer of *"Nothing."* Imagine the effect on your *self* respect if you thoughtfully designed and gave a clear, firm *"=/="* assertion to the person/s promoting your ex mate's disrespect . . .

"Are **my** *responses to my ex's disrespect significantly shaped by someone else? How do I know? If they are, who?"* Hint: start with each of your parents and kids, and include God, the church, and close mutual friends. What's at stake for them? Mull: *"How would my attitude and behaviors change if I weren't influenced by them?"*

"When I'm an old wise wo/man reviewing my life, what will I think about my ex mate's disrespect and how I responded to it? What do I want my Older Self to think?"

"If I need help in clarifying how I want to respond to my ex's disrespect, _ who would I trust, and _ what help do I need?"

Let yourself become physically comfortable, and calm, and *still*. Relax without anxiety. Breathe fully and steadily for some moments. The respectfully ask any voices in your mind to quiet for a while. When you feel *centered*, focus inside on a question like this:

"What should do next about my feeling disrespected by my ex mate?" Trust the first response that comes to you. Try not to edit your response, analyze it, or worry about someone else's reaction to it. Note that "nothing" (numbness or blankness) *is* a response . . .

As you evolve and work your plan to respond to your ex mate's disrespect, experiment with this last question and grow a version that works best for you. It will be a steadfast guide to the "next right thing" you should do. Incidentally, this quieting, questioning, listening, and *trusting* works with *any* life confusion or challenge! The part of you who "answers" is probably your true Self, your (guardian) Spirit, your Wise One, or all of them. Notice your reaction . . .

Allow any other questions and awarenesses that these spark to surface, now and later. Honor each one, one at a time. Consider journaling about them and your emotional and mental reactions without judgment. Awareness, patience, and acceptance are priceless assets here!

Pause again. Notice with interest where your thoughts and feelings are going . . . What are your inner voices (subselves) saying? Who are they? Is your true Self present? How do you know? If you're a significantly wounded wo/man, your Guardian personality parts will urge you to . . .

think of other things now, and/or . . .

numb your feelings, or make you mysteriously *tired or apathetic*; and/or . . .

"blank out" on what you just read; or . . .

catastrophize, and feel anxious, overwhelmed, depressed, and hopeless; or . . .

review the sacred (comforting) litany of your ex's wonderful failings *again*; or . . .

consume or do something to comfort yourself; or your subselves may . . .

give you physical discomfort like a headache, "heartburn," "upset stomach," tight muscles, diarrhea; and/or urge you to . . .

play *"Yes, but . . ."* – i.e. generate convincing "practical" reasons why you couldn't possibly take any options like those above); etc.

Are any of those occurring? If not, what *is*?

Reflect: before you read this, were you aware of how many possible responses you have to a co-parent's (or anyone's) disrespect?

Recap

Disrespect is a common block to building an effective co-parenting team after divorce and/or re/marriage. It is usually a symptom of false-self dominance, and often well-hidden *shame*. If ignored, chronic disrespect will cripple your co-parents' child-related and marital communications and satisfactions. Major disrespect combines with distrust, resentments, hurts, frustrations, guilts, values disputes, and anxieties to cause reciprocal *dislike* and *hostility*. If your co-parents _ assess for significant disrespect among any of you, and _ take responsibility for converting it into (at least) *compassion*, you'll probably raise your multi-home family's nurturance level. That lowers the chance that your minor kids will inherit significant inner wounds and a disabled true Self. *That* improves their chances for successfully filling their mix of the needs in [F], with your co-parents' informed, cooperative help.

This chapter _ invites you to assess for this barrier by making a "respect map" of your three or more living and dead co-parents. The rest of the chapter explores your options for _ changing *your* disrespect for another co-parent into genuine compassion, and/or _ intentionally seeking to raise the respect of another co-parent for *you*. A prerequisite to both of these is each of your adults attaining genuine *self* respect, by empowering your Selves to harmonize your inner family of subselves— i.e. working at Project-1 recovery.

If someone else might benefit from this chapter, refer them to [http://sfhelp.org/Rx/ex/disrespect.htm].

Keep your long-range goal in view: raising the nurturance level of your family to protect your descendents from inner wounds and major misery. Healing inner wounds, improving your communications, and raising the respect and compassion levels among your co-parents reduce three big barriers to that goal. Now let's explore a fourth step: you co-parents choosing to re/build mutual *trusts*.

9) Re/grow Trust and Honesty

Learn to Trust *Your Self* First

My clients were the divorcing parents of four year old Nathan. They were referred to me by family court to resolve an impasse: the father wanted overnight visitations with his son, and the mother refused. He had left his wife shortly after their son's unplanned conception, and was now living with a divorced mother and her two children. His ex-wife said flatly "You were totally irresponsible in abandoning me, and you showed no interest in Nathan when he was born. You show poor moral judgment by living with another woman before we're even divorced. You drink too much, and you deny it. "You've lied to me repeatedly, and I don't feel Nathan is safe with you and *her* overnight."

Young Nathan's three wounded co-parents were struggling with all nine caregiving barriers on p. 109. One was significant distrust: the biomom distrusted her ex to be honest, "responsible," or a competent father. From painful experience, he had lost any faith that she would ever accept _ his paternal interest as genuine, _ his new partner's dignity and legitimacy as a stepfamily co-parent, _ respect his needs as a person and a man, or _ be willing to compromise. When I first met this combative couple, neither believed that the other wanted to rebuild trust, respect, empathy, or a cooperative co-parenting relationship for Nathan's sake. They seemed to be right.

Is *distrust* a significant hindrance to your caregiving teamwork? If so, it will combine with your other teamwork barriers to lower your family's nurturance level. To clarify the extent of this barrier, try this . . .

Status Check: think of a man or woman in whom you have complete trust now—including yourself. Option: reflect on the feeling of *faith* (trust) in your Higher Power. Using these as a basis, check to see that your Self is leading, and invest undistracted time in drawing a 1-to-10 *trust* map of your co-parents like the respect-map exercise on p. 168. As you do, notice your thoughts and emotions without judgment. They'll probably teach you something important . . .

This chapter proposes that under the right circumstances, co-parents can intentionally re/build their trusts in each other as teammates. Do you believe that? These pages offer _ a perspective on trust, _ the benefits of re/building it, and _ requisites and _ options for doing so over time.

Do you remember when and how you learned to dis/ trust other people? Imagine answering a child who asks *"What is* trust, *and where do I get it?"* Adopt the curiosity and open mind of a student, and explore this . . .

Perspective: Trust 101

To build a foundation for some action-options, let's review what trust *is*, where it comes from, and what you co-parents need to trust about yourselves and each other, for all your sakes.

What *Is* Trust?

Compare your definition to this:
"Trust is the primal feeling *that results from evaluating current or long-term safety from major spiritual, emotional, and/or physical discomfort."*
Your adults and kids each instinctively seek reassurance that _ you're safe enough from surprise, injury, or loss (dis-

comfort), and _ that unavoidable discomforts will be *tolerable*. For example, do you *trust* the sun will rise tomorrow? Answering "Yes" means you avoid the terror (discomfort) of living in a freezing, lightless world.

Your trust state comes from un/conscious confidence that you can predict the amount of pain or pleasure related to something or someone. Trusts determine the degree of *risk* (vulnerability) your subselves will tolerate within and between you. That determines your semi-conscious tolerance for the emotional intensities of conflict, passion, and intimacy.

Signs of distrust are feeling *anxious* ("worried"); *fearful, apprehensive, uncertain, doubtful, or ambivalent*; *or general "unease." Disrespect* is feeling "I don't value you as a worthy person," which can cause *disinterest. Distrust* is "I don't feel safe with you." *Dislike* is "I'm uncomfortable when I relate to you." Making these distinctions helps identify and reduce each of these stressors.

Where Trust Comes From—or Doesn't

We acquire the state of trust from _ repeated experience ["*I know (trust) the mail will come tomorrow.*"] or _ on faith— trust with little or no experience. The protective reflex to distrust blooms from our being too *uncomfortable* (scared, hungry, tired, sick, hurting, lonely, angry, confused, overwhelmed, disoriented . . .) as an infant and young child. Do you think most newborn animals and people naturally trust most aspects of their world, until physical and emotional *discomfort* teaches us caution?

Our pain-pleasure reactions to repeated experiences are the seed and soil for growing trust in relationships and situations. We unconsciously come to trust how we'll feel and "be" with each other child and adult. "*I always have a good time with Angel, and get bored with Marvin.*"

Besides painful personal experiences, another root of unconscious dis/trust can come from our early caregivers, hero/ines, and teachers. If our impressionable young minds constantly receive messages like *"Don't trust anyone / females / Asians / people in uniforms / lawyers and politicians / college grads / addicts / divorced men . . . ,"* we absorb selective or global distrusts that become second nature: reflexive *unconscious* judgments uncritically adopted from someone else's experiences, biases, or ancestries.

The core distrust too many of us learn within months of our birth is *"I don't feel good here [with these huge gods (parents)]. I can't expect (trust) that anyone will really care about me or fill my needs."* To survive, young kids deprived of key nurturances [D] automatically grow Guardian personality parts who insist *"Don't trust anyone. Do it (Life) yourself!"* That defensive, skeptical attitude and related behaviors are self-nourishing, and—without awareness and motivation to change—usually arrive intact in adulthood.

So: your mosaic of trusts or distrusts cause a mental/emotional state that you grow selectively from _ early instruction, and _ a lifetime of general and special experiences. "Experiences" include your relationships in general, with your *Self*, with your ex mate and key supporters and authorities, and with your Higher Self and Power.

Trust is a primitive natural survival instinct. It's function is to forecast with certain life forms and situations, "Am I *safe enough* from pain or harm here?" *Safe* measures our quenchless need to fill a hierarchy of true (vs. surface) needs (p. 44). You and I feel safe when our immediate true needs are met well enough, including our need to feel they'll still be met well enough in the near future.

Trust *What?*

From infancy, we learn that many things can cause us predictable or unexpected emotional and physical pain. We automatically grow to trust or mistrust . . .

- our own perceptions, judgments, worth, and competences;
- the behaviors, motivations, and abilities of other people and groups,
- human and environmental situations, and . . .
- Higher Selves, Guides, and Powers.

You caregiving teammates need to evolve trust in *many* things about each other for group harmony. If you have an ex mate in your life now, note the extent of your trust in her or him about these primary attributes:

Honesty and genuineness: *"I trust Martha to not keep key information from me, or to shade the truth."*

Reliability: *"If Jerry says he'll be here at 6:00, I can count on him to be on time."*

Responsibility and motivation: *"My experience is that Max steadily wants to be the best dad he can be. I admire the way he admits his mistakes without whining or blaming other people."*

Good judgment: *"I usually feel Rena's decisions are wise and good for the kids and us."*

Cooperation: *"I really appreciate that Jose is a team player. He rarely puts his own needs ahead of all of ours."*

Stability and resilience: *"I've never seen Cheryl lose her cool under fire."*

Moral, ethical, and spiritual values: *"Noriko really lives by the Golden Rule. She's an inspiration!"*

Genuine caring, empathy, and respect: *"I can't think of a time that Jason hasn't wanted to know what I need and feel."*

Asking for, and accepting, help: *"Jenny promptly says when she's overwhelmed, so I know when she's OK."*

Acceptance and safety: *"I feel real comfortable around Louise. I always feel safe with her that I can be the real me."*

Motivation to compromise: *"Sharon and I have our disagreements, but she's usually willing to meet me half way without grousing."*

Self motivation and respect: *"Nick's never been a parent before. He decided to learn about it, and has been going to a weekly class at Mills Center."*

Role clarity: *"I admire how Luwanda makes it a point to be clear on what she's responsible for."*

Can you think of other things teammates need trust about each other? Could you have defined all these before you read them? Can your other co-parents describe these? Taking the time to notice specific trust factors like these can help you clarify and resolve vague or general distrusts in *yourself* and with other co-parents. It also can help you teach your kids about *trust.*

For more perspective, use this checklist to evaluate your trust in _ yourself; _ your partner, if any; _ each parent (past or present); and _ your best or oldest friend. What do you notice?

<u>Realities About Trust</u>

See if you agree with these observations:

Trust in someone or something ("x") ranges from *none* to *total*, _ now and _ over time. A useful awareness is whether you trust "x" *enough* for now. If not, you'll probably live in stress, or act impulsively or thoughtfully to regain your comfort level.

The degree of trust or *faith* you feel in "x" will vary depending on which subselves control your inner family. To survive low-nurturance (painful) childhoods, kids automatically develop several Guardian subselves like the *Cynic or Skeptic, Pessimist, Controller, Conservative, Catastrophizer, Magician, Doubter, Idealist, and Optimist.* Fear-based people tend to trust too little. People dominated by a *Good Child* or *People Pleaser* subself often trust too easily, or unwisely. One of six wounds that most of us survivors need to heal in adulthood is learning to discern who and what is safe to trust, and learning to trust our own trusting. Do you now?

Trust that has built over years can be lost gradually or in a heartbeat. If that happens between people like ex mates (or a parent and their child) . . .

Trust can be intentionally re/grown between two people who _ value themselves and their relationship enough, and _ proactively decide to do that; *if* their true Selves are solidly in charge (Chapter 5), and they can communicate effectively (Chapter 7). Do you agree?

Because trust relates directly to primal security and often personal worth, many of the terms we use to think and speak about dis/trust are "hand-grenade" words: i.e. they can evoke emotional "explosions." Recall your reaction if someone you respect said *"You're a liar," "You* betrayed *me," "You distort things all the time,"* or *"You're never on time, or do what you say; you're* irresponsible." Unaware people automatically equate *"I don't trust you about (something)"* to *"You're BAD (shameful, unlovable)."*

Chronic false-self dominance breeds double messages (*"I love you; go away."*) These breed semi-conscious confusion and mistrust, over time. Therefore major *distrust* in yourself or another may be a symptom of a deeper problem: *unawareness* of inner-family disharmony and a disabled true Self.

Dishonesty means that a child's or adult's ruling subselves don't trust that it's *safe* to tell the truth. Denials and repressions (self-dishonesty) exist because subselves feel admitting the truth will cause too much pain or emotional overwhelm (*"I'm not obese and addicted to food, I'm just big-boned."*) If people in your family tell "lies" or avoid disclosing their truth, it suggests they don't trust that _ their own reactions and/or _ yours will feel safe (comfortable) enough. Shame, guilt, anxiety, rejection (loss), and conflict are major reasons we fear telling the truth (right?). Do you have any "dishonest" (i.e. distrustful, scared) kids or grownups in your family? For more perspective, see [..Rx/mates/honesty.htm].

A final reality . . .

Most dis/trusting is unconscious and reflexive, until you intentionally choose to focus your conscious awareness on it. Such focusing is necessary to intentionally raise your trust in someone or something, including your own perceptions and judgments. Do you believe (trust) you can focus your awareness?

Keeping factors like these in mind can help you re/grow missing trusts among your co-parents. It also helps to know . . .

We've just assembled our "trust rebuilding tools:" _ what trust *is*, _ where it comes from, _ how it "works," about it and _ what we need to trust in important people. What do all these abstract concepts mean in your life and home? If you did the "trust map" at the start of the chapter, you should have no trouble doing this brief . . .

 # Status check:

I feel a mix of *calm, centered, energized, light, focused, resilient, up, grounded, relaxed, alert, aware, serene, purposeful, compassionate,* and *clear*, so my true Self is probably leading my *inner* family of subselves now. (T F ?)

I'm very clear on the difference between *disrespect, distrust, resentment,* and *dislike* (T F ?)

I fully accept that each bioparent and stepparent of each of our minor or grown kids is a full member of our multi-home family now: i.e. their needs, feelings, and opinions as valid and important as my own. (T F ?) *If you don't, you have a* membership conflict. *Apply Chapter 5, and do co-parent Project 3 (p.431).*

I _ understand the idea of family nurturance [D], and I _ agree that our kids need us adults to build an effective co-parenting team for them. (T F ?)

I _ see long-term value for all of us in raising my trust in one or more of our co-parents now, and _ I want to work at that with an open mind. (T F ?)

My partner (if any) would thoughtfully answer each of these as "True" (T F ?)

If you distrust your *partner* as a competent co-parent,

see Chapter 5, and [..Rx/mates/trust.htm]. The rest of this chapter refers to "the ex" as your target person. Substitute "the stepparent" or their name, if that's whom you distrust.

Re/building Trusts

If co-parental distrust is a major barrier now, you have at least two sets of options: _ change *yourself*, and _ invite (vs. demand) change in the unsafe caregiver. Get undistracted, take a good breath, get curious, and examine . . .

Are *You* Half of the Problem?

If so, the good news is: you control at least half of the solution! There are at least three things you can change.

Imagine that you're a psychologist or news reporter researching the person with your name, body, personality, and history. You want to understand this important person, not to judge if s/he's *good* or *bad*, or *right* or *wrong*. To prepare for your research, review Chapters 2 and 3. Then let your objective inner *Observer* take over, and see if s/he thinks any of these apply to you . . .

Use worksheet [E] to learn if **you may be controlled by a false self** when thinking about, discussing, or interacting with the ex mate (or in general). If so, your false self is probably a mix of subselves like your *Inner Critic, Historian* ("memory"), *Skeptic* or *Doubter*; *Worrier* or *Catastrophizer; Analyzer; Warrior or Amazon*; *Controller, and Magician* (reality distorter). These Guardian subselves diligently work to comfort and protect your *Shamed, Guilty, Fearful*, and *Enraged* inner kids, relative to the ex mate. If this idea is alien or alarming, study [..01/innerfam1.htm] or the Project 1 guidebook *Who's* Really *Running Your Life?*

Subselves like these may rule you because *they don't trust your Self* to consistently provide enough safety for your inner kids (Vulnerables). To avoid painful shame and guilts, your governing subselves may vehemently insist that you focus on the ex mate's despicable failings, *and not* your *half of the relationship*. This guarantees the ex will feel attacked, discounted, and disrespected by you (1-down). That promotes her or his defending and counterattacking, or avoiding you. *Your physical kids are caught helplessly in the crossfire.*

If you're ruled by a well-meaning, biased false self, your subselves will probably be indignant and defensive on reading this: your *Magician* will give you thoughts like *"That's absurd!"; "No way!"; "The author's a crackpot, and this false-self idea is weird psychobabble!"*; or the like. (Notice your thoughts . . .) Your protective *Distracter* subself may cause you to "blank out" or defocus (*"Oh my God, I forgot to floss . . ."*)

Until your subselves trust your Self to lead them, they'll try to block your awareness of _ their control, and _ your circular communication process with the distrusted ex mate. *Until you and the other co-parent "see" your inner and mutual processes, you'll probably keep repeating the same* act > react *cycles, and get the same (dissatisfying) outcomes.* Reflect on this observation from Steve and Carol Lankton: *If you always do what you've always done, you'll always get what you always got."*

If your ex mate's behavior causes anxious subselves to paralyze your inner leader (Self), one of many probable implications is . . .

Your protective, myopic subselves may vehemently oppose feeling compassion for the ex despite her or his behaviors (Chapters 2, 3, and 5). This guarantees your behaviors will send "1-up" or "1-down" R(espect)-messages (p. 510) to and about the ex, which dooms effective communication and problem-solving. Restated: your governing subselves probably have low or no empathy, compassion, or respect for the distrusted ex mate as a co-parent or a wounded, tormented person. If so, two options are . . .

take responsibility for your (subselves') attitude, and

read, tailor, and apply Chapters 3, 5, and 7, working toward growing a genuine "=/=" attitude towards the ex. Or you may . . .

listen to your false-self's (or someone else's) insistence that converting disrespect for your ex is unjustified and/or impossible. If you choose this, the ideas below won't help you or your kids.

Whether you're dominated by a false self or not, I'd bet that a second component of your *distrust* barrier is . . .

Neither **you nor the ex mate** know or use the effective communication skills in Project 2 (p. 512). If so, this means that both of you . . .

_ are prone to defocusing and fuzzy thinking (ineffective *inner* communication and problem-solving among your subselves); and . . .

_ you've probably grown an unconscious ritual of *fighting, arguing,* and/or *avoiding*, rather than helping each other _ identify your underlying true needs (p. 44), and brainstorming win-win solutions together. This probably means neither of you *trust* that you to communicate effectively. Most conflicted co-parents I've met don't know what they don't know about how to resolve family relationship and role conflicts effectively (Chapter 7). Among other things, this means your kids aren't learning how to _ think clearly and _ communicate effectively from you. Re-read that out loud, and notice your reaction . . .

Your distrust may be amplified by **someone else's distrust or disapproval of the ex mate.** If your parent, sibling, new partner, close friend, or a lawyer, teacher, or counselor have their own loyalties to you and your child/ren, they may label the ex mate *untrustworthy* and expect you to agree. (*"We can always count on Wendy to avoid responsibility, can't we?"*)

Such people may *mean* well, but their biased attitude and unawareness of inner wounds nourishes your mistrust. That hurts your kids by lowering your family's nurturance level. If such allies accept the concepts of inner wounding and recovery, they'd be more apt to feel that the ex merits *compassion*, not scorn.

Reality check: identify each of your key personal and family supporters, and ask *"What is her or his attitude about the distrusted ex mate, and how does that affect* my *attitude?"*

So how likely is it, *honestly*, that at least half of the distrust you feel for your other co-parent is due to _ your biased (1-up) false self, _ your unawareness of effective communications and inner wounds, and _ the influence of biased supporters? Listen with interest to what your subselves (inner voices) say now . . .

Let's build on the ideas above, and explore your trust-rebuilding options. Do you need a mind or body break?

Recall: your overall goal here is to intentionally grow the most effective co-parenting team you all can, for all your sakes. We're exploring options to reduce a common post-divorce barrier to that: *distrust* among ex mates and step-parents.

Two targets here are: _ improve your trust in the ex mate, and _ improve his or her trust in *you*. Let's look at your options to . . .

Improve Your Trust in Another Co-parent

Use the following options as a buffet of choices, and an inspiration for other possibilities:

You may have already taken the first step: assessing whether you're led by a wise, resilient true Self. If not, make inner-family harmonizing (Project 1) your highest priority. Among other benefits, this will raise your subselves' trust in *yourself* as a competent adult, fe/male, or co-parent.

If you have a partner, invite him or her to join you in trust-(re)building options like these. The odds of this working rise sharply if your partner's Self is in charge. Reflect on the potential benefits to him or her, and the skills and assets s/he can add.

Review your attitudes (Chapter 3). They'll silently shape how successful you'll be in trust re/building, specially if a false-self controls you.

Define your goals. Assess your (subselves') levels of trust with the ex in categories like those on p. 189. Thoughtfully clarify *specifically* how each significant distrust (or all of them) effects _ you (e.g. anxiety, frustration, hurt, anger, despair, weariness . . .); _ your re/marriage, if any; and _ each of your resident or visiting kids. What will probably happen long-term if you don't find some way to increase your trust for the other co-parent/s? If you have a new partner, what does s/he think?

Adopt a long-range view. Learn from the past, and focus on the future. In your experience, how long does it take to rebuild lost trust? Have you ever experienced that?

Help each other separate your *distrust* from *disrespect, dislike, disinterest, guilt,* and *resentment.* These interact, and merit separate solutions. Your odds of improving them rise if you focus on one or two at a time.

Decide if improving your trust for the ex is a shared *ours* problem, or is *his* or *her* problem. The latter view risks you defeating yourself and hurting your dependent kids by causing your ex to feel blamed and disrespected. If your subselves can accept the *ours* view, are they willing to make the first move?

Review the concept of surface and underlying *true* needs on p. 44 and at [..02/dig-down.htm]. Then clarify which of your *true* needs the ex mate's behaviors are blocking. For balance, reverse your roles and imagine how *your* behavior affects the ex's true needs. Option: discuss this with your ex mate, if s/he's willing.

Invite all your other co-parents to join you in working to **upgrade your communication skills** (Project 2). Invest time and energy mapping your typical communication sequences with your ex honestly [..02/evc-maps.htm] to *learn* and improve, not to blame and shame! Review Resources [H—L] for helpful ideas and tools. Commit to listening empathically to your ex mate [..02/listen.htm and ..02/listen-lynch.htm], and using *hearing checks* to reduce misunderstandings. Recall: *listening is* not (necessarily) *agreeing or giving up your needs and values!*

More options for your trust-rebuilding . . .

Research the chance that you, your ex, and a third person (like a child or new partner) are unconsciously caught in a major loyalty conflict, and co-creating a stressful lose-lose-lose relationship triangle. If so, see Chapter 16 for options. Expect *vigorous* internal and external resistances!

Research whether some other persons are unconsciously urging you to distrust the ex mate. Separate their needs from yours (and your kids'), and stay focused on long-term co-parental team-building. If useful, confront the other distrusters respectfully. Explain what you're trying to do, and assert what you need them to change (*"For the kids' sake, join me seeing Jocelyn as* wounded, *not a sly, conniving bitch."*)

Stay aware that *dishonesty* implies the person doesn't feel safe to tell the truth. If you distrust a co-parent's honesty, explore whether _ *you're* doing something to promote their anxiety, and/or _ their false self is too scared. Choose *wounded* and *frightened* rather than self-defeating judgments like *liar* and *dishonest.* See Chapter 5.

Decide whether distrust without compassion and assertion breeds reciprocal distrust and disrespect. If your ex distrusts *you,* brainstorm (ideally with them, for your kids' sakes) how you can *both* raise at least co-parenting trust in each other.

When your Self is in charge and it feels "right," **tell the ex mate and key others** that you want to improve your trust in the ex, for everyone's benefit. Describe your conclusions and ideas from the above options, and *listen* to their reactions. Option: do this as part of a common family-building task: e.g. invite all other co-parents to do their version of the trust map at the start of this chapter. Can you imagine all of you calmly discussing how to *help each other* strengthen your mutual trusts and respect for each other to help the kids who rely on you? What (not *who*) prevents that?

Face this reality: if you and the ex don't accept responsibility for _ improving your co-parental relationship, then _ rebuilding trusts and mutual compassion and respect will be hard or impossible. *Imagine explaining that to your kids when they're middle aged, perhaps with kids of their own.*

As you select from these and your own trust-re/building options, keep _ your partner (if any), _ minor and grown biokids, and _ any key relatives and/or professionals informed of what you're doing, and why. Keep your responsibilities and boundaries clear: this is *your* work to do, not theirs. They can surely support you as you do it, so tell them what you need!

If you have a new partner, s/he may distrust an ex mate. S/He may also distrust one or more of your kids. These premises and options apply to those situations as well! Rebuilding those is your partner's work, and you can support it.

As you all re/build trust over several *years*, help each other **keep your daily balances** (Project 12), and give yourself some nourishing affirmations and guidelines like "*progress*, not perfection!" along the way . . .

A more challenging team-building project is . . .

Improve a Co-parent's Trust in *You*

Choose from options like these:

Confirm that your Self is leading your inner family.

Review the trust categories on p. 189, and make an honest guess as to how well the other co-parent trusts *you* in each of them. Define any you want to improve.

Perhaps with an unbiased partner, **evaluate whether** anything prevents you from discussing and confirming these distrusts co-operatively with the ex. If there are blocks, do what you can to reduce them toward improving long-range family teamwork.

If the other co-parent is willing, review the options

above with her or him, and apply them together toward re/ growing their trusts in you. Help each other stay _ focused on long-term payoffs, and _ aware of any other barriers like disrespect, disinterest, unawareness, guilts, and values conflicts. Work on them separately, a few at a time.

Note that these groups of options apply to relatives, kids, and other special people too.

Recap

Trust is an instinctive human strategy to avoid pain. From infancy, we automatically grow an inventory of people, things, and situations we believe will and won't cause us too much discomfort or harm.

Each child and adult in your multi-home family has an array of trusts and distrusts about themselves and each other. (*"I know that Nancy will get hyper if I want to talk about sex."*) These beliefs unconsciously shape your relationships with each other. Recall that "telling the truth" depends on trusting that it is *safe* to do so. People from divorced families often have grown to *unconsciously* distrust key things about each other which inhibit cooperation and cause conflicts.

Kids and grownups in typical new stepfamilies face complex, alien situations, roles, and relationships. They have little prior experience to base self and mutual trusts on (*"I've never been a stepfather before."*), and build them via successes and mistakes. If co-parents work together to _ heal childhood trust-distortions, and re/grow _ post-divorce and _ new-stepfamily trusts in each other, they (you) are more likely to form an effective nurturing team over time. Does this make sense?

Part of co-parent Project 1 focuses on correcting childhood *trust* distortions by re-learning who and what to trust— starting with your Self and a nurturing (vs. punishing, vengeful) Higher Power.

This chapter uses that ability to help you to intention-

ally improve your trusts with your kids' "other parents."
Doing this promotes co-parenting teamwork and raising the
nurturance level of your kids' several homes. The chapter
first offers ideas on _ what trust *is*, _ where it comes from;
and _ typical things that co-parents need to trust about each
other. The second half uses these to suggest options for your
intentionally re/growing appropriate trusts among your co-
parents, over time. Trust (re)building is usually most needed
between _ divorced parents, _ and bioparents and new stepparents; specially if a stepparent has never parented before.
Improving trusts between Stepparents and stepkids is covered in the next volume of this series.

Re/building co-parent trusts is most likely if you adults
want to help each other _ build *inner*-family trusts (Chapter
5), _ raise your communication effectiveness (Chapter 7),
and convert disrespect into compassion and respectful assertion (Chapters 8 and 15).

If you want to share or discuss these ideas with someone, refer them to [http://sfhelp.org/Rx/ex/distrust.htm].

Take a breath, stretch and say hello to your body. Reflect on your reactions to what you just read. Do you need
to take a break?

10) Reduce Excessive Guilt

What's the *Real* Problem?

Have you felt *guilty* today? That's what Westerners call our reflexive emotional response to breaking some behavioral rule. Our word comes from the old English root *gylt*, which meant *crime* or *offense.*

For many reasons, typical divorced parents and stepparents are burdened by moderate to obsessive guilts. Often their parents are too. Unhealed parental and ex-mate toxic (vs. normal) guilts can promote family stress, re/divorce, and some health problems like depression and addiction. These all hinder forming an effective co-parenting team. Your kids probably need guidance in understanding, describing, and managing their guilts, too.

Reflect for a moment. Starting with you, are any of your co-parents *guilt-ridden* or *guilt-trippers*? Have you ever devised a strategy to manage or reduce excessive guilts? Do you know anyone who has?

This chapter offers perspective on _ what *guilt* is, _ where it comes from, _ how it can affect your family relationships, and _ options for reducing *excessive* co-parental guilts to normal. Do you believe the latter is possible? The next chapter adds to this one by focusing on *forgiveness.*

These pages may be more impactful if you can see photos of _ yourself as a child, and _ each minor or grown child in your life now. Let's build a base by exploring . . .

Where Guilt Comes From

Guilt is a normal emotional response that regulates our solo and social behaviors. Like all emotions, it's a helpful signal, and neither good nor bad. Too much guilt too often *can* have bad effects (below). How does guilt develop, and how can it become *too much, too often*? See if some version of the vignette below is familiar . . .

If you haven't recently, (re)read Chapter 5 and [..01/innerfam1.htm]. These will refresh your understanding of how growing up in a low-nurturance family usually causes a child's personality to form a protective "false self" of subselves.

As a young girl, Sharon was taught a powerful **rule** by many people and media characters, in different ways *"You should always be nice."* There were many variations: Mom said "Nice *girls are* never *rude."* Grampa Larry often said *"Your brother Nick is always so thoughtful and polite."* The minister praised Bible characters and congregational members for being *courteous, respectful, obedient, humble,* and *charitable.* Girlfriends scathingly criticized peers for being "*stuck up, gross,* and *self-ish."*

From parental scoldings, praises, and other behaviors, young Sharon began the life-long process of accumulating *rules* for living among other people: *shoulds, oughts, musts, can'ts, and have to's,* Among her personality subselves, her budding *Historian* collected and stored these perceptions. Her tireless *Librarian* subself indexed what became thousands of behavioral rules to cover "how Sharon *should* or *must* act" in all kinds of solitary and social situations.

To win daily approval and acceptance at home and school, she developed an *Inner Critic* subself. This zealous inner-family Guardian (her "conscience") assumed the protective responsibility of comparing Sharon's daily and past thoughts, decisions, feelings and actions to these rules. To prevent painful disapproval and possible rejection, *Critic* studied Sharon's parents, and copied their words and voice dynamics to chide and scorn the girl whenever she broke any rules.

The adults' voice dynamics and body language were often sarcastic, angry, pitying, scornful, exasperated, and disapproving. Like Sharon's (wounded) parents, her *Inner Critic* didn't praise her for following the rules. *Critic* learned to preach *"That's just what's expected, and merits no praise."* *Critic* heard the minister say *"Pride is a sin, (and sin is BAD),"* and sternly rebuked Sharon for feeling self-satisfaction for "being nice."

As we all do, young Sharon grew a *Guilty Child* personality part. When aroused, this forever-young subself infused Sharon with the *feeling* of guilt and related *thoughts*. This happened every time an adult or her *Critic* said or implied that the girl had broken some rule. (like not being "nice"). At the same time, another young subself was learning to feel and store her *shame.* In her early years, Sharon didn't know many family and social rules, so she broke them often. Her siblings, relatives, and caregivers told her that, often, "for your own good" (and their comfort). Fueled by her need to be "good" (liked and accepted), Her "law-library" of behavioral rules grew and grew.

As Sharon decoded thousands of perceived criticisms and praises from her outer and inner Critics during her childhood, her *Shamed Girl* grew the conviction *"I'm* real *bad. I always break the rules. I am SO stupid and dumb. No one could ever love me!"* When *Critic* delivered scathing lectures on how she'd broken another rule *again*, her *Shamed Girl* and *Guilty Girl* infused her with agony.

They would merge with Sharon's young true Self, giving her thoughts like _ *"I did a bad thing (broke a rule)"* and guilt *feelings*; and/or she thought _ *"I am a BAD girl,"* and felt *ashamed.* When she thought people around her knew she did and felt these things, she felt *embarrassed.*

Soon all it took was certain people *looking* at her, rolling their eyes and sighing, or just saying "Sharon . . ." and her inner *Guilty* and *Shamed Girls* spasmed. The guilt and shame thoughts and feelings tended to merge and feel the same. Like each parent as a child, no one helped her be aware of all of this.

Because these feelings *hurt,* Sharon automatically developed a *Hurt Girl* subself. Her inner-family job was to bring Sharon the useful emotion of *discomfort.* Some related Guardian members of her inner family (personality) developed too. They included a *Perfectionist, an Idealist,* a crafty *Liar,* a persuasive *Postponer,* a *Magician,* an hysterical *Catastrophizer,* a *Sneak,* a shrill *Worrier,* a powerful *People Pleaser,* a glib, insincere *Politician,* and a *Loner.*

Their specialized 24-hour jobs all aimed to guard the *Guilty, Shamed, and Hurt Girls* from perceived sources of inner and outer pain. Sharon grew an *Angry* subself, too, who developed over time into an adolescent *Rebel.* But that one impulsively broke too many rules in the social world, so the Guardian subselves tried to lock the *Angry Kid* up, at least in public.

All these Guardians worked tirelessly with *Librarian* and *Historian* subselves to decide what actions might produce significant pain. Sometimes they'd invoke *Critic* to sternly rebuke and lecture Sharon like her parents, hoping she would avoid painful experiences.

Based on their inherited (unconscious) libraries of *parenting rules,* Sharon's Mom and Dad believed they were raising their daughter well enough. They weren't aware of the protective band of subselves their daughter was developing, or how often she was tormented by her vigilant *Inner Critic* because of their well-meant or reactive criticisms.

As she grew, Sharon's increasingly knowledgeable, wise, far-seeing true Self was often overpowered or unheard by her reactive inner kids and their Guardian subselves. That resulted in her *Self* doubting her own wisdom and inner-family leadership ability (which was her real talent). Most other subselves ignored and distrusted her Self.

Sharon wasn't aware of these inner-family members and their dynamics. No one ever talked about people having complex, dynamic "inner families," or encouraged her to pay attention to how hers operated and what resulted. She *was* aware of "feeling crazy" at times, when various agitated subselves took her Self over, giving her conflicting thoughts and feelings.

Sharon grew up, left home, got a degree and a job, and married. Her Vulnerable inner kids and Guardian personality parts (her false self) agreed that "everyone" expected her to marry at least by 22. They all decided that Richard was a safe, fun, attractive young man. Richard's outer and inner families, including his *Lusty* part, agreed that Sharon seemed like a "really great girl" to marry and start a family with. Richard's inner family had been run for over 20 years by his false self, which he, Sharon, and others didn't realize.

They married, against the advice of each person's true Self. Years later, Sharon recalled thinking as she walked down the aisle *"Don't do this!"* A raucous chorus of other inner voices (thoughts) quickly overruled that counsel.

Seven years later, after having a son and a daughter, Sharon told Richard to leave. An expensive, painful, bitter divorce unfolded, with relatives and friends polarizing or pulling away. As this awful process evolved, Sharon's *Critic*, and *Shamed, Guilty, Hurt, and Angry-Girl* subselves often dominated her inner family.

A gifted Guardian subself, the *Shrew*, helped by constantly focusing Sharon's thoughts and memories on all Richard's *many* faults. The *Magician* contributed by distorting Sharon's perceptions of what had really happened in their relationship, which helped her periodically avoid painful *guilt* and *shame* about her own part. Other times, her *Critic* scathingly berated her for stupidly picking the wrong mate, and causing her parents and bewildered kids so much pain. Her powerful *Skeptic* and *Good Mom* subselves distrusted Richard with their kids, and fought fiercely against his bid for custody.

Some years later, her second husband increasingly complained that she cared more for her kids than him. Her *Magician* and *Politician* subselves hotly denied this. Sharon's *Guilty Girl* and *Critic* saw nothing wrong with preferring the kids. Her Self saw this could lead to *another* divorce if Sharon couldn't compromise, but was usually overruled.

This is a skeletal sketch of where (I think) excessive guilt and shame come from. Does it seem credible? The keys are:

From _ **primal needs** to be loved and accepted, and _ parent's (perceived) behaviors, young kids quickly evolve a complex array of good-bad, right-wrong *rules* on how they're "supposed to" think, believe, and behave. This starts well before a vocabulary and *thinking* start to form.

To avoid the agony of possible parental (and later, social) rejection and abandonment (i.e. *death*), kids develop *Guilty* and *Shamed* inner kids, a tireless *Inner Critic*, and an array of other protective subselves. These normal personality parts distrust and overwhelm the child's immature true Self.

Depending on many factors, a child may grow up to be often dominated by their guilty, shamed, and self-critical subselves. Toxic guilt and shame can self-amplify if the child was taught rules like "*I* shouldn't *feel so guilty*," and "*I should love myself*!" Until psychological healing occurs, self-doubt and self-rejection also bloom.

Typical shame-based adults unconsciously choose each other, develop relationship and parenting problems, and divorce psychologically or legally. From cultural, ancestral, religious, and parental training, their *Inner Critic* or *Blamer* insists the divorced parent is *bad* (shameful) for breaking fundamental rules—shoulds, musts, and have-to's.

How can excessive guilt and shame affect typical divorced families and stepfamilies like yours? For clarity, we'll focus on guilt here. Shame Is healed differently.

Five Effects of Toxic Guilt

Like other emotions, guilt ranges between "minor" to "occasional normal" to "chronic massive." We'll say that *toxic* guilt is frequent and intense enough to cause health or relationship problems that any of your family adults feel is "significant." Typical divorced dads and moms who deny they're over-dominated by guilt-driven subselves or don't know how to change that, risk . . .

over-indulging an insecure or demanding child who needs firm limits, to "make up" for family-breakup losses and pain. Parents can think "*I've already caused my kids so much pain, I* *can't bear to cause them more.*" This can be amplified by custodial parents working two jobs (paycheck and parenting), and having little stamina to discipline wounded, needy kids [F].

Non-custodial guilty parents with limited visitation time can also feel ambivalent about disciplining their kids. Overfocusing on "having a good time" (being a playmate vs. a parent) can contribute to co-parental values and loyalty conflicts (*"You're way too easy on Jenny."*), specially if courting or legal stepparents are a factor. This is more likely if the parent was over-disciplined (shamed) as a child.

Guilt-driven divorced parents also risk . . .

often "caving in to," or avoiding confrontations with, an aggressive (wounded) ex mate. This promotes escalating resentments, self-criticism, anxieties, and ineffective communications. These hamper effective two-home co-parenting, which raises minor kids' anxieties and promotes "acting out" (protesting) and (more) inner wounding. Such parents also risk . . .

absorbing shame-based childcare criticisms from their (wounded, unaware) relatives, vs. healthy disagreement. This can deepen guilt and shame, and grow Self-distrust, confusion, and anxieties among the adult's subselves and households. Over-guilty divorced parents are also vulnerable to . . .

avoiding thoughts and talk about their divorce, its results, and their part in causing and conducting it. This risks blocking healthy mourning of their many losses (p. 247). Blocked grief promotes many secondary personal and relationship problems, including addictions, illness, skewed relationships, and kids who can't feel or bond. A final harmful impact is . . .

unintentionally modeling to minor kids that adults don't acknowledge excessive guilt and it's effects, or take proactive steps to reduce it. This raises the odds your kids will create a low-nurturance family if they have kids.

These five common effects of excessive guilt combine to stress relations with kids and other co-parents. Without awareness and proactive healing, they promote webs of values and loyalty conflicts and relationship triangles (Chapter 16). Note that these problems are usually caused by all five co-parental hazards (p. 428) and other teamwork barriers (p. 109), not toxic guilt alone.

We've just explored what guilt is, where it comes from, and five effects of toxic guilt. What are your options for reducing its impacts in your multi-home family? Let's look first at action-options for . . .

Reducing *Your* Excessive Guilt

Whether you're a custodial or noncustodial divorced parent, a stepparent, or both, there are *many* reasons you may feel significant situational or chronic guilt. This is specially likely if you survived a low-nurturance childhood.

<u>Prepare</u> . . .

Reducing toxic guilt is more likely if you start with some or all of these . . .

Assess yourself for false-self dominance via [E] and other Project-1 checklists in *Who's* Really *Running Your Life?* or [..pop/assess.htm]. If your Self is disabled, commit to a personal high-priority recovery program while balancing other projects [A] and the rest of your life (Project 12). Get to know who comprises your inner family. *Excessive guilt and shame are major symptoms of being ruled by a false self.*

Commit to improving your thinking, communicating, and problem solving skills by applying Chapter 7, Resources [H—L], and Project 2 [*Satisfactions*]. This will help you harmonize your inner family (above), and reduce all of the co-parent barriers in this book! If you're unsure whether you need to do this, invest time in this [..02/evc-quiz.htm].

Tailor the above ideas on guilt and shame to fit your values and experience to date. Then assess yourself for *excessive* (toxic) guilt, relative to kids, your ex, or your parents. If *you* feel excessive guilt, then . . .

Note the difference between first-order (behavioral, false self) and second-order (core attitude, true Self) changes. Reducing guilt from excessive to normal is a second-order change, like permanently deciding to end an addiction without relapsing or starting a new one. See [..pop/changes1&2.htm].

Read the action-options below, and then **review your attitudes and expectations** about this team-building project. (Chapter 3). Do they include *"I can and will reduce the excessive guilt that burdens me, starting now,"* or something else? If "something else," reflect:

Have I changed at least one other core aspect of my personality before? (e.g. *"I used to: laugh when I hurt / lie, at times / never say 'no' / never call the doctor / fear sex / . . ."*)

If so, how did I make that change? (e.g. consciously, or *"It just happened"*? With help, or alone? Gradually, or suddenly? Because of a painful trauma, or just *"It was time to change"*? With tools like affirmations, prayers, reminders, images, or not?; etc.

Another helpful attitude to re/affirm is *"My guilt is a normal emotion which, in moderation, helps me to make healthy life decisions. I am not trying to become guiltless, I'm going to reduce excessive guilt to a moderate (non-obsessive) level."*

Seek and use a "guilt hero/ine." Do you know anyone who has really freed themselves from (vs. denied, ignored, or repressed) excessive guilt? If so, learn from them. If you don't know anyone, ask other people if they do. Clergy and counselors are good potential heroes and referral sources.

Review your rights as a dignified, worthy human being. Evolve your version of the ones on p. 514, and use them to validate the rules someone feels you've broken. See if you agree: *"As a child, I was taught "You* must *obey me/us. Do not break our (adult) rules."* Potential new rule: *"As an independent adult, I'm responsible to devise and live by my rules, and accept the consequences."*

A final preparation option is . . .

Review the benefits. Meditate, journal, or tell a receptive friend in detail, the *specific* payoffs you envision that will occur when you succeed in reducing your toxic guilt about divorce, re/marriage, and/or other things. How, *specifically*, will your and others' lives be better? If you're not clear yet, try identifying the specific personal or relationship discomforts that your obsessive guilt causes you. Ask others who know you for caring feedback. Then vividly imagine your life to be free of those. Keep this vision, or a written description or symbol of it, where you can remind yourself along the way of *why* you're making this vital second-order personal and team-building change.

Now you can choose to _ reduce your old guilts to normal, and _ intentionally minimize new guilts. The former has three steps: _ identify and validate the rules you've broken, _ make appropriate amends, and _ work with your *Inner Critic* and *Guilty Child(ren)*. Let's briefly explore them.

Reduce Old Guilts

Pick a familiar guilt, and imagine applying these ideas to it as you read. Three common guilts are "*I feel so badly that by divorcing, _ I've disappointed and saddened my parents, _ broken my commitment vows, and _ hurt my kids.*"

Identify and validate your broken rules. Recall: guilty thoughts and feelings erupt when your subselves feel you've "made a mistake," or "done something wrong" – i.e. broken an important *rule*. Start healing by identifying the key divorce-related *rules* that someone feels you've broken. Then decide whether each rule is *yours* or implied or imposed by someone else.

Across your years, you unconsciously absorbed scores of rules (shoulds, oughts, musts, supposed to's) about "good" marriage, divorce, and parenting. Your caregivers and hero/ines taught you some; books, movies, music, and TV taught others; and your religion, if any, proclaimed God's rules. Some of these rules or values about marriage and divorce feel authentic and right to you. You may have followed others from old habit or to avoid conflicts. (*Rule: "Honor your Father and*

Mother, and don't challenge their beliefs about marriage and divorce!")

Consider this scheme *when your Self is in charge*:

Identify each adult and child in your life who has been significantly hurt or hindered by your divorce process and what caused it. Start with yourself, continue with the person you fell in love with, and add key others.

Inventory your guilts. Reflect on statements like these, and collect as many answers as you can:

* "Relative to my courtship, marriage, and divorce, I feel badly that I _____"; or . . .
* "I really regret that I ___"; or . . .
* "I shouldn't have _____," or . . .
* "I was wrong to ____."

Write a sentence or two about any "wrong" attitudes or values you had ("*I often thought mostly about myself.*"), and any major "mistakes" you made ("*I should have agreed to counseling.*")

Describe each "mistake" as specifically as you can: "*I made a bad marriage choice*" is vague, compared to "*I let lust over-rule over good sense, got Sylvia pregnant, and I married her out of shame, guilt, fear, and duty instead of from a free choice of balanced and mutual love and respect.*"

If you are or were "religious," meditate on what your minister/s, church members, and sacred book/s have taught you about marriage, love, honor, parenting, divorce, and "sin." Identify each important religious *rule* you think you've broken or violated by your marriage and divorce actions. Watch for overt or implied *should (not)s, must (not)s, have to's*, or other decrees like . . .

"*Marriage is a Holy sacrament, and divorce is a mortal sin, so I'm a (shameful) sinner who broke my commitment to God.*" Possible rule: "*I must always obey God's laws, as decreed by the Bible and church authorities.*"

Decide if you believe that "*I have the right to decide my own* shoulds, oughts, *and* musts. *I don't have to agree with or* *please others who have different rules. I'm responsible for the effects of this on myself and others."*

Take each rule "violation" that causes you excessive guilt, and thoughtfully decide where you got it. Is it *your* rule, or someone else's? The key question to confront is *"Why should I feel badly if I've broken a rule that I, as a self-responsible, experienced, unique adult, don't agree with?"*

As you do this rule-review, watch for black/white (absolute) thinking. For instance, is lying to another person *always* "wrong"? Many personal and social rules are relative, depending on our local inner and outer contexts for "rightness." Some philosophers observe *"There are no 'rights and wrongs' (rules), only consequences."*

In defining *your* rules, it can help to ask *"Do I always gain self respect when I act on this* should, ought, *or* must, *or am I seeking the approval of someone else?"* If you have a zealous *People Pleaser* like Sharon (and most of us), that tireless subself focuses on following *other* people's rules, to avoid the agonies of (childhood) criticism and possible abandonment.

If you discover a guilt-promoting broken rule that someone else originated, thoughtfully decide what *your* rule is. For example:

"Others have told me to believe that _ marriage must be a life-long commitment, and that _ mates who break that commitment are wrong, weak, and (bad)." What now feels more realistic to me is *"When marriage produces steady pain. emptiness, and disappointment for both partners and stresses their kids, and they've tried everything they can to heal this, then respectful divorce may be the best choice for everyone's wholistic health and chances for long-term happiness."*

From childhood, your *Inner Critic* may still insist that putting your rules ahead of other "authorities" is *selfish, arrogant, disrespectful, and self-centered.* Validating your life and relationship rules *is* beneficially *Self*-ish: that's learning to respect your Self and your needs and values as much as (vs. more than) other peoples,' without *guilt, shame, or anxiety*!

Your priceless **integrity** grows from your knowing and acting on *your* rules, values, and priorities, in the face of scorn and criticism. For most of us, disagreeing with or defying the adults who raised us brought pain, so we often chose to follow their rules. Violating your integrity breeds shame, guilt, and self-doubt. These increase life stress and strengthen your false self's control. How do you feel about this?

Incidentally, are you teaching your kids to question and authenticate your rules, or to blindly obey you because you're "the adult or parent" (have power), and "know better than they do"? Long term, do you want your kids' to learn how to responsibly form their own rules, or to follow other people's rules? What did your early caregivers teach you about this?

When you've validated the main broken rules that cause you excessive divorce and re/marriage guilts, the second option you can choose is to decide if you want to . . .

Make selected genuine apologies. The 12-step philosophy helps many people manage addictions and compulsions. One reason is that it encourages people to become self-responsible, overcome embarrassment, guilt, and anxiety, and make sincere amends (reparations) to people they've hurt. After preparing well, this usually helps *both* people reduce hostility, resentment, and guilt. Where it doesn't, look for _ dominant false selves and _ other problems that need resolution (p. 109).

Are you able to teach kids the **ingredients of an *effective* apology**? I suggest that they include . . .

- empowering your Self to lead your inner family;
- seeing your worth, needs, and integrity as fully equal to the other person's (an =/= attitude); so you don't shame yourself by apologizing;
- taking genuine (vs. pretend or strategic) responsibility for your thoughts, values, and actions;
- identifying (or asking) specifically how your actions have significantly hurt or hindered other people;
- allowing your true feelings to emerge about each such incident, without editing or justifying;
- (ideally) describing your feelings to the hurt person, with good eye contact, in a way they can hear you, and . . .

- *listening* respectfully to any feedback that may cause, without explanation, defense, excuses, or arguing.

How does this compare to your definition? Have you ever apologized *successfully* to another person? Remember how that felt to both of you?

Over many years, the three phases of psychological and legal divorce [..pop/divorce.htm] *hurt* you, kin, and kids in many ways. Do you agree that you and your partner share responsibility for these hurts equally?

Option: for each person significantly affected by your past family actions, design a genuine apology for each major hurt, and deliver it when they can hear you. Ideally, do this in person. Start with *yourself,* and then focus on your ex mate (Chapter 11). Your Project-2 communication skills will be a major help here!

When you do this, consider an attitude of *"I am apologizing to grow harmony in my inner and our physical families, not to debase myself or to fill your need."* If saying *"I'm so sorry that I . . ."* feels like losing a battle or *giving in*, refocus on empowering your Self. Recall: our context here is building a co-parenting team for your kids' and your long-term welfares.

_ Validating your broken rules and _ making selected amends work best if you also work to . . .

Adjust your *inner* family. The following assumes you're familiar with the idea that we all have an inner family or team of personality *parts* or subselves. If this is new to you, (re)read Chapter 5 and return. If you feel "endless major " guilts about divorce (or anything), your inner family is out of harmony, and your Self is probably disabled. You can choose to improve that by doing some kind of "parts work": retraining and reorganizing your subselves [..01/ifs1-intro.htm].

Here's a skeletal outline of how to do that: Begin by respecting and affirming every subself's dignity, good intentions, and unique talents and limitations. *Listen* to them, remind them of your common goals, and brainstorm win-win small changes that everyone feels are safe enough.

Each of your inner family members has it's own set of perceptions, goals, and emotions. This is why you can feel confused or "torn," or bored and excited, and love and "hate" at the same time. Reflect, and trust your *intuition* vs. your intellect: *"Is it my* Self *that feels the excessive guilt about my divorce, or is it some other personality part/s?"* If you're not sure yet, that's OK.

All your subselves want to _ have an important job to do, _ be appreciated, and _ protect you from pain and harm, *as they* perceive it. There are no bad or evil parts, though some may cause you or others harm because of unawareness and/or distorted perceptions.

Usually, excessive guilt and shame involves subselves like these:

Your true Self; who's natural talent is to lead your subselves, and make wise wide-angle, long-range decisions. When you *feel* excessive guilt and *think* related obsessive thoughts, your Self is overwhelmed by other skeptical, anxious subselves. This is like an orchestra conductor being deposed by several disgruntled musicians, only your Self can't fire them! Other key "players" (personality subselves) include . . .

Your *Historian*, who helps by storing and recalling relevant experiences to guide your *Self* and your *Critic*;

Your *Librarian* (or *Law Clerk*), who stores and organizes (vs. *makes*) your rules;

Your *Spiritual One*, who steadily offers real compassion, empathy, and forgiveness to all your inner members and other people;

Your *Inner Critic*, whose job is usually to keep you safe from egotism and social abandonment by making right/wrong judgments and *applying* the rules *without caring who originated them*. S/He may not (yet) trust your Self to _ apply the rules effectively, or _ make safe new rules in first-time situations. You probably also have a . . .

Nurturer *or Good Parent / Mom / Dad*, who's innate talent and motivation is to protect, guide, and care for needy subselves and people, including . . .

Several *Inner Children*, usually including a *Guilty Child*, a *Shamed Child*, and perhaps a *Fearful Child.* When they're upset, one or more of these blend with (take over) your Self, so you experience their emotions; and . . .

One or more Guardian subselves, like a *People Pleaser*, a *Nurturer*, *Distorter (Magician) Perfectionist,* and a *Catastrophizer* who are dedicated to protecting each of these inner kids from upset and hurt. They exist because they haven't learned to trust that your Self, *Nurturer/s*, and *Spiritual One* will protect the vulnerable kids.

Typical Project-1 parts-work (recovery) goals here are, over time . . .

Grow your interest in, and clear, calm (objective) awareness of, your inner family's dynamics, specially noting *who's in charge* now? Answer that any time you're (subselves are) significantly upset. Recall: when you feel a mix of calm, centered, energized, light, focused, resilient, up, grounded, relaxed, alert, aware, serene, purposeful, compassionate, and clear, your Self is probably guiding your team.

When your Self is in charge . . .

. . . **invite** each involved subself to meet with you alone and in groups. Review and clarify everyone's goals, jobs, and fears, and ask them to _ trust in your wisdom and innate good judgment, over time, _ stop blending or overruling you, and to _ give you a chance to demonstrate you're far wiser and more reliable than when you all were young.

. . . **validate** your behavioral rules per the above. Firmly encourage your *Critic* to use these new rules in re-evaluating your past and present marital and divorce decisions. Note that this is not asking your *Critic* to stop judging. Moderate, non-obsessive guilt is useful!

. . . **with** your *Nurturer*, coach your *Critic* on how to pronounce judgments respectfully, vs. with impatience, scorn, cynicism, and sarcasm. This is just like learning to value expressing discipline *respectfully* to a physical child. Your *Critic* may not have observed your childhood adults doing that.

. . . **connect** your Guilty, Shamed, and Scared inner kids with your *Nurturer* and your *Spiritual* subselves. The latter subselves *want to* provide them comfort, security, and reassurance. Develop and experience guided images of your subselves interacting that help make this real. Then . . .

. . . **revise** key Guardian-subselves roles as needed, so they don't accidentally increase your *Critic's* self-accusations, and activate your Shamed and Guilty inner kids. For example, renegotiate your *Pleaser's* values and inner-family role, so that s/he's less anxious about you disagreeing with or disobeying certain other people's rules. And (your Self and inner advisors) have . . .

. . . **all of** your adult subselves objectively evaluate the people around you who may be covertly or openly critical of your marriage and divorce choices and actions. Identify those who promote unreasonable guilt, and either _ confront them and ask for more constructive feedback, or _ if they won't, choose to distance from them *without guilt*! They're probably ruled by a false self, and don't know it.

False selves often have blurry or no boundaries (Chapter 15). They can be oversensitive to, and feel responsible for, someone else's divorce guilt—e.g. your parent's or a child's. Practice differentiating *your* guilt from other people's guilt, and encourage your inner team to respectfully give other adults and kids responsibility to reduce theirs while you work on yours.

Often, inner kids and their Guardians are living in the past. Not only do they think your Self is still as incompetent (undeveloped) as in your childhood, but they may fear against all logic that the people who hurt or shamed you will magically appear today, and do that again unless the subselves are constantly alert to that. See the "rescuing" option in *Who's Really Running Your Life?* or at [01/ifs7-rescuing.htm] to see ways of bringing all your subselves into the present.

Option: over time, become an expert on how guilt is intentionally reduced. When you feel guilty, build the reflex of wondering *"What am I to learn from this feeling? Have I already learned it?"* Tell your *Critic* what you've learned, and ask that important subself too stop reminding you of your rule-breakings, and re/activating (tormenting) your *Guilty Child*!

Tailor and apply relevant ideas and options from Chapter 11 to forgive yourself and your ex. Your Self needs to lead your other subselves to succeed. Do you agree that genuine forgiveness and reducing guilt go hand in hand? Finally . . .

. . . *after* taking steps like these, if your Self feels it's the right thing to do, use your Project-2 communication skills to assert a sincere apology to each person you feel was hurt or stressed by your marriage, divorce, and perhaps re/marriage. Ideally, do this when their Self is in charge, and they can *hear* you clearly.

Please treat this parts-work outline as suggestive, not absolute or definitive. As you see, it's long-term work, not a weekend project. Use the Project-1 guidebook *Who's* Really *Running Your Life?* or the series of Web pages at [http://sfhelp.org/01/ifs1-intro.htm] to help you expand and implement steps like these. Versions of this basic inner-family framework can help you with every other relationship problem in Part 2. Recall the big picture: Project 1 aims to help you co-parents _ harmonize your inner family, _ protect your kids, and _ reduce your odds for re/divorcing and/or dying prematurely.

Reminder: converting the common inner wound of excessive shame to genuine self-love is a separate, vital part of Project 1. Each of your wounded co-parents doing such a conversion will help you build a high-nurturance team together, and relish old-age satisfaction and pride.

Besides reducing old guilts, your second option is to . . .

Minimize New Guilts

As your subselves increasingly trust your Self to lead and s/he becomes more clear on the rules you want to live by, you can consciously avoid new toxic guilts. Can you imagine that?
Options:

Periodically review and amend your version of the key attitudes in Chapter 3 They're one foundation of building an effective co-parenting team. See *moderate* guilt as a helpful alert that something needs attention.

Stay clear on who's rules you live by (or break), and evolve and use a Personal Bill of Rights as a foundation (p. 514).

Monitor and coach your *Inner Critic* to render opinions *respectfully*, vs. shaming you. See [..02/evc-feedback.htm] for ideas. Use parts work to ensure that your *Critic* is living in the present, vs. some time in your childhood. See *Who's* Really *Running Your Life?* or [..01/ifs7-rescuing.htm].

Develop your Project-2 communication skills, specially awareness, assertion, and empathic listening. Use them with your subselves, important adults and kids, and everyone else.

Patiently work toward reducing the old childhood wounds of excessive fears and distrusts [..01/recovery1.htm]. Mixed with excessive shame, they promote conflict-avoidance among your subselves, and with other people. That promotes dishonesty, timidity, and procrastination, which encourage guilt and shame.

Consider writing down the main principles you wish to live by—i.e. define your integrity values. Choose to consciously use them to guide you in confusing and conflictual times. When you stray, look for inner-family imbalances and use parts work to rebalance.

Stay clear on your responsibilities, specially as a co-parent and perhaps as a new mate. Define and enforce your boundaries (Chapter 15), and respectfully give other people responsibility for themselves. Compassionately expect their false selves to resist, and to (try to) blame and guilt-trip you. Decline—don't accept their rules over yours. If they're open to it, invite them to evaluate whether they're ruled by a false self, avoiding the need to rescue them.

Read at least one book on the false-self symptom of *co-dependence* (e.g. "Codependent No More," by Melodie Beatty), to expand your awareness and compassion. Co-dependence promotes over-concern with another person's welfare *and rules*.

If you have co-dependent traits [..01/co-dep.htm], that's a sign of false-self dominance. Factor that into your Project-1 recovery decisions and goals.

Overall: _ empower your Self, _ work to convert shame, _ stay alert for new guilt feelings, _ validate who's rule/s you broke, _ apologize and/or forgive (including yourself—Chapter 11), and *let go.*

Let's build on the above, and briefly explore a related co-parental team-building barrier: what are your options . . .

If Another Co-parent is Too Guilty

Excessive shame and divorce-related guilts in any of your co-parents will stunt or block _ effective communication and _ healthy grieving, and inhibit _ team-building and _ stepfamily bonding. A over-guilty (wounded) ex mate may be "too lax" in disciplining visiting or residential kids. That promotes _ kids' feeling unsafe, and too powerful and acting out; _ and divisive values and loyalty conflicts and relationship triangles, in and between your homes. All these lower your family's nurturance level.

If another of your co-parents is excessively guilty over divorce-related behaviors, you have choices like these:

- clarify your priorities and attitudes (Chapter 3) act on them;
- evolve effective loyalty-conflict strategies together;
- reduce your own wounds and guilts, and *trust your Self* to know what to do;
- improve your communications (Chapter 7);
- empathize with this wounded co-parent, vs. blame her or him, and . . .
- ask if s/he's open to reading this chapter and discussing how his or her guilt may be affecting the kids.

The overarching issue is whether s/he is willing to work

with you on building a co-parenting team for the kids' long-term welfare.

It's unlikely you can persuade the other person to reduce their guilt if s/he feels you're *blaming* or *attacking* them for it. This is specially true for shame-based co-parents whose subselves feel guilty about their guilt. If the co-parent resists learning about guilt or owning it (and the related inner wounds), see Chapter 5 for options.

Recap

Guilt is a normal human response to believing we've broken one or more significant *rules*—shoulds, musts, supposed to's, and have to's. Moderate guilt helps to promote harmonious social behavior, if inner families are Self-led. *Toxic* (excessive, unwarranted) guilt springs from the childhood myth that behavioral mistakes mean you're a bad, worthless, unlovable person. Divorce and what causes it, and forming a stepfamily offer *many* chances for parents (and kids) to feel they've broken major personal and social rules. This can yield *excessive* guilt, which hurts health and relationships, and may hinder healthy grieving. Guilt ("*I did a bad thing*") feels like shame ("*I AM a bad thing.*"), but heals differently.

This chapter proposes that you co-parents can intentionally reduce excessive guilt to normal, once it's identified and owned. We explored where guilt comes from, why it can cause major problems in divorced and remarried families, and options for _ reducing your excessive guilt to *normal*, and _ avoiding new toxic guilts. You can encourage another co-parent to use the ideas here to admit and reduce her or his toxic guilts.

Key options here are _ empower your Self to lead your other subselves; retrain your overzealous *Inner Critic*, and re-educate your *Guilty Child*; _ raise your family's awareness of guilt and it's impacts in your lives; and _ encourage all of you to evolve and live serenely from a new set of personal attitudes (Chapter 3) and rules (p. 514). As with all the teamwork barriers on p. 109, patient guilt-reduction can help you all raise the nurturance level of your unique multi-home family.

The next chapter complements this one. It explores your options for *forgiving* yourself and other co-parents vs. holding on to divorce-related blame, bitterness, and resentments. Before continuing, mentally summarize what you learned here, how it applies to you and your family relationships and nurturance level, and key points you want to remember or act on . . .

11) Forgive Yourself and Your Ex

Release Crippling Regrets and Resentments

Have you ever belonged to a group where members had major bitterness or resentments toward each other? If so, how did that affect the group's ability to function effectively? How did the group deal with that? How did *you*?

Think of any divorced parents you know well. Do they hold major grudges about their ex mate's behaviors or traits? Do they torment themselves with major guilts and regrets? If so, how do you feel this affects their _ personal serenity, and _ ability to nurture their kids? American family courts are jammed with co-parents who seethe with resentments and bitterness toward each other. Aggressive lawyers and the legal process usually *amplify* this (Chapter 18). Millions of other rancorous divorced parents never enter a courtroom.

This chapter focuses on a key aspect of recovering from family divorce trauma and building co-parent teamwork: ex mates *letting go* of *blaming* themselves and/or each other for "what happened." If you're progressing on reducing excessive co-parental guilts (Chapter 10), this chapter can help you forgive yourself, your ex mate, and/or other family members. As you know, guilt-reduction, shame conversion, and forgiveness work together.

I write this from personal experience and clinical consultations with over 1,000 typical co-parents since 1981.

Here we'll explore . . .

* What is forgiveness?
* Forgive *what*, relative to typical divorce and re/marriage?
* Why is selective forgiveness vital for most divorced and stepfamily co-parents?;
* What's needed for true (vs. pseudo) forgiveness?; and . . .
* Your options: forgive, hang on, or . . .

To begin, take a . . .

Status Check:

I feel a mix of calm, centered, energized, light, focused, resilient, up, grounded, relaxed, alert, aware, serene, purposeful, compassionate, and clear, so my Self is probably present now. (T F ?)

I _ have a clear idea now of what _ pseudo and _ genuine forgiveness is, and _ what each of these *feels* like. (T F ?)

I can name several common alternatives to genuine forgiveness. (T F ?)

I have truly forgiven (some) people who have significantly hurt, betrayed, or disappointed me. (T F ?)

I know what it feels like to be genuinely forgiven by someone I have offended or hurt. (T F ?)

I can name at least three things that can block divorced parents from forgiving themselves and each other. (T F ?)

I believe people can intentionally choose to forgive, when they want to. (T F ?)

I understand the connection between inner (psychological) wounds and the ability to forgive myself or other people. (T F ?)

At least one of the co-parents in our multi-home family is having major problems forgiving themselves or an ex mate. (T F ?)

All our co-parents now agree on _ why and _ how to help

each other reduce major family bitterness and resentment related to divorce and/or re/marriage. (T F ?)

Pause, and tune in on your "self-talk" (thoughts and feelings) now . . . What did you just learn?

What is *Forgiveness*?

Microsoft's Bookshelf 96-97 says: " . . . Synonyms (for "forgive") are *pardon, excuse,* (and) *condone.* These verbs mean "to refrain from imposing punishment on an offender or demanding satisfaction for an offense."

This suggests that *forgiveness* has at least five surface elements:

_ A person who causes . . .

_ some (perceived) event or action, which . . .

_ offends (hurts, betrays, injures, deprives) another person, who . . .

_ decides whether or not to require "satisfaction" (fill their need to *punish* the offender) before . . .

_ pardoning (releasing hurt, resentment, bitterness, and anger at) them.

A sixth vital *forgiveness* factor is . . .

_ the "offender's" reaction to the event. If s/he feels significant guilt, shame, and/or remorse, s/he faces the same choices as the "victim:" _ if, when, and how to punish themselves (atone) adequately, or _ to forgive *themselves* without that "satisfaction."

Relative to divorce, adult *forgiveness* nets out to each ex mate eventually reaching one of two stable emotional/mental decisions: "*Shall I spend ongoing emotional energy _ blaming and resenting myself and/or my ex mate for our breakup (and enduring the consequences); or _ shall I let go of blame and move on?*" The choice between these depends on _ which subselves are ruling, _ the post-relationship values and behaviors of each parent, and _ the stability and welfare of minor kids.

Blame is deciding "*Who's the bad (insensitive, thoughtless, selfish, abusive, inept, . . .) person here, me or you?"* Beneath this early-childhood compulsion is the primal need to believe without doubt *"I merit my own respect and approval here: In this situation (marriage and divorce), I behaved well enough. I am a* good *(worthy, respectable, lovable) person."*

Survivors of low-nurturance childhoods often deny or minimize their false-self's fierce need to blame others to protect against the (familiar) agony of *shame* and *guilt*. In my experience, most U.S. divorced parents (like you?) are such wounded survivors.

So *forgiveness* is an emotional-mental-spiritual process of _ intentional or accidental offense, _ significant pain or deprivation, and _ *both* people releasing residual feelings of guilt, shame, resentment, and perhaps the need to cause reciprocal pain in the offender (punish). How does this compare to your definition? Your ex mate's? Your new partner's? Your parents?

Let's build a base for your *forgiveness* options . . .

Premises

See how you feel about these key ideas:

Young kids accidentally deprived of too many nurturances (p. 440) survive (vs. thrive) by developing a protective false self. This promotes up to five other psycho-spiritual wounds:

_ excessive shame (*I am an unworthy, unlovable person*) and _ excessive guilt (*I often break important rules. I behave badly*);

_ excessive fears and _ reality distortions, including denial (*I'm* not *excessively shamed or guilty, and I'm* not *denying those*); and _ *repression* (emotional numbing or blocking). These serve to mute and camouflage inner wounds, to survive (vs. thrive) in relationships and our society, as they did in childhood. All five wounds may cause . . .

_ an inability to *bond, love, empathize,* and exchange intimacy.

Legal and psychological divorce suggests that *both* partners, their parents, and their kids have sets of these wounds.

Most co-parents (i.e. their ruling subselves) don't want to assess themselves for false-self dominance, and are quick focus on their ex mate as wounded and "needing help."

Common symptoms of co-parents' excessive shame and guilt are . . .

_ resistance to admitting their half of interpersonal offenses and conflicts;

_ unwillingness to apologize genuinely, or apologizing falsely, excessively, or unnecessarily;

_ reflexively blaming _ other people (e.g. parents, ex mates, authorities . . .) and/or _ uncontrollable factors (fate, genes, God, nature . . .), for hurting other people—specially kids and a former mate;

_ difficulty communicating and problem-solving;

_ self-sabotage and/or self neglect;

_ being obsessed with *winning* and being *the best*;

_ being excessively concerned with appearances, and other peoples' opinions;

_ avoiding introspection and true intimacy;

_ habitually distorting the truth; and . . .

_ denying or defending these traits.

For symptoms of all six inner wounds, see *Who's* Really *Running Your Life?* or [..pop/assess.htm].

More foundation premises about forgiveness . . .

Until choosing true (vs. pseudo) recovery, most wounded adults *unconsciously* pick each other for partners, despite painful consequences. This relentlessly increases their shame, guilt, reality distortion, true Self disability, until they "hit bottom," and choose to heal. *So . . .*

Many co-parents (i.e. their dominant false selves), have great difficulty *genuinely* forgiving themselves and each other for pre-divorce and recent "offenses" until they intentionally choose to _ empower their true Selves, _ let go of bitterness and blame, and _ reduce other key relationship stressors (Chapters 1-12).

Holding on to blame, resentment, and guilt blocks co-parenting teamwork, stepfamily bonding, and forming a high-nurturance family environment, so . . .

Your kids are at high risk of forming protective false selves and denials, growing up, marrying wounded partners, and repeating and spreading the ancestral cycle of unintentional neglect.

Key signs of true forgiveness are _ your Self is clearly in charge, and _ you can think about and discuss a prior "offense" or "mistake" without feeling excessively uncomfortable (guilty, shamed, remorseful, angry, "depressed," or anxious).

Finally, **forgiveness may be *pseudo* or true.** Have you ever met a person who said "I forgive (someone)," or "(some offense) is no problem;" but whose body and actions said otherwise? That's a classic false-self double message: one subself spoke (and meant) the words, and other subselves aren't willing to let go yet.

People who exhibit pseudo forgiveness are not cowardly, deceptive, insincere, or dishonest (*bad*); they're significantly *wounded*, and their true Self is currently disabled. See Chapter 5.

Authentic, true forgiveness happens when _ *all* active subselves agree to pardon the "offender" without ambivalence, and _ the forgiver's behavior is consistently guided by their true Self. When that occurs, _ words and actions usually match (no double messages), _ healthy grieving can proceed (Chapter 12), _ new relationship-bonds can grow (Project 9), and _ mutual co-parenting trust and respect can rebuild and stabilize over time (Project 10). Nice, huh?

If you have different ideas than these, how do you explain that many divorced parents have major trouble forgiving themselves and each other? "I don't know" is a protective avoidance.

With these premises in mind, lets explore what typical "offenses" ex mates blame each other for, and the true needs beneath them.

Blame vs. Unmet Needs

True forgiving is usually easier if you can consciously identify (and therefore meditate, discuss, and learn from) specifically what causes your bitterness and resentment. Use the examples below to help you identify how you and/or your ex offended or blame each other.

Most divorce and re/marriage-related "offenses" have _ *surface* traits or behaviors, and _ underlying unmet needs [in brackets below]. See if you've experienced and/or been accused of things like these . . .

"**S/He** (the ex) was wild and irresponsible with our money, despite my protests." [The real injury: "I felt disrespected, unheard, ignored, and *unsafe* too often."]

"**S/He** never wanted to *do* anything together." ["I felt unwanted, unimportant, and bored."]

"**S/He** wouldn't stop controlling and manipulating." ["I didn't assert my boundaries and values, and lost my *self respect*."]

"**S/He** was selfish, arrogant, and *abusive*! " ["I felt disrespected, unappreciated, ignored, powerless, unsafe, and *unloved*."]

"**S/He** was addicted to (something), and wouldn't admit it or do anything about it." ["I felt too much pain, anxiety, guilt, and anger, and I finally lost *hope*."]

"**S/He** never really cared about my sexual needs or satisfaction." ["I was too sexually unfulfilled and dissatisfied."]

"**S/He** was sexually unfaithful." ["I felt humiliated, rejected, disrespected, and betrayed, and I couldn't trust or respect my mate."]

"**S/He** refused to go to church with me, or participate in church activities." ["I needed a companion to share my spiritual journey and community."]

"**S/He** was away from home all the time, and wouldn't change that." ["I felt too unimportant, unloved, bored, anxious, lonely, and undesirable."]

"**S/He** didn't want (or enjoy) children." ["I really need to co-create new life, and enjoy nurturing kids with my mate."]

"**S/He** was way too involved with her/his parents (relatives / siblings), and wouldn't change." ["I felt too unimportant, unconsidered, unloved, disrespected, unheard, and powerless."]

"**S/He** wouldn't pitch in, despite my requests. I had to do all the work." ["I felt *used*: taken for granted, unpartnered, unheard, unappreciated, unloved, and *weary*."]

"**S/He** didn't show me who s/he *really* was until we married. I feel *deceived*." [I was needy, lusty, and unaware of the signs of inner wounding, and I made a wrong marital choice."]

Any of these sound familiar?" Notice that the surface "offenses" blame the ex mate. The bracketed true needs (dissatisfactions) focus on "I", without blame. *Option*: collect reasons from divorced friends on "why it didn't work out." See if you notice any themes or trends about who blames whom.

A second group of powerful "offenses" occur during or after the legal divorce process. Mates already weary of conflict and frustration have lower tolerance for the confrontations and decisions that legal divorce forces on them. The scope and degree of these offenses are proportional to _ adults' inner wounds, _ ineffective communications, _ co-parental values conflicts, and _ degree and nature of attorney aggression. A mix of these can amplify pre-divorce resentments, and/or cause new ones around child custody, visitation, and financial support disputes (Part 3).

Note that co-parents may forgive themselves and their mates for marital and divorce offenses, and may not forgive bad, abusive, neglectful, or irresponsible *parenting*, by their standards.

Typical divorced parents (like you?) fall into one of four groups: they . . .

blame their partner for vague or specific reasons their marriage died; or they . . .

accept half of the responsibility ("*We* just couldn't make it work."), or they . . .

fault themselves ("*I just felt too inadequate, guilty, inept, dumb, and ashamed, too often. I couldn't fill my partner's rela-*

tionship needs well enough, often enough.") A fourth group of divorcees . . .

avoid any blamings ("*I really don't know what went wrong. We just sort of drifted apart . . .*")

Relatives and key friends attitudes and behaviors can hinder or help true ex-mate forgiveness. Typical grandparents also have choices to forgive or blame themselves and/or their kids for divorcing.

A third impactful level of "offenses" are those experienced by the kids of divorce. Co-parents' abilities to *really* forgive are shaped by their perceptions about _ how injured each child was and is, _ how well they're adapting, and _ how empathic and cooperative the other parent is in filling their kids' developmental and divorce-adjustment needs.

The point, so far: Most U.S. re/marriages follow the divorce of one or both new spouses. The divorce process and it's causes breed a variety of *hurts* which each partner must choose to _ forgive (let go of related resentment, guilt, shame, and anger at) themselves and their ex mate, or to _ stay emotionally reactive to (blame and resent) either of them.

Blaming and forgiveness have different long-term impacts on the people in your kids' several homes, including any new partners and stepsibs. What are the most important effects?

Why Is Post-divorce *Forgiveness* Vital?

I'd understand if you think "*Well, duh—stupid question!*" Compare your answer with this:

The *choice* to truly forgive or keep blaming yourself and/or your ex mate for relationship and co-parenting offenses shapes your _ self esteem; _ inner-family harmony; _ communication effectiveness, and _ chance to identify your unique life-purpose, and develop it, over time.

All four of these in you and your ex combine to affect the level of emotional/spiritual nurturance that your minor (and any new) kids receive during and after your legal divorce process.

Premise: if one or both divorcing partners are unable to *really* forgive themselves and each other, their dependent kids are much more likely to develop or expand false-self dominance and inner wounds. Does this feel "right"?

This promotes a kaleidoscope of emotional, physical, and social stressors, which causes secondary relationship problems. Until co-parents become aware and take corrective action, a low family-nurturance level tends to be self-amplifying, which spreads the ancestral legacy of unhappiness, stress, and premature death.

These factors have a profound effect on whether you or your former mate re/marry, who you choose, why, when, and whether your new marriage and stepfamily are nourishing or stressful, long term.

I propose that these impacts justify the view that true post-divorce forgiveness of yourself and your ex mate are *essential*, and a moral obligation for every divorced dad and mom. What's your opinion? If you're controlled by a protective, reality-distorting false self, you'll probably ignore, intellectualize, defocus from, "get bored with," "not register," or disagree with these ideas. Note your reaction . . .

"It's ___ o'clock. Do you know where your *true* Self is?"

Options Toward True Forgiveness

Have you ever genuinely forgiven someone, including yourself, for a major hurt or offense? How can you tell if you've *really* forgiven, vs. some subselves' numbing or repressing old hurt, resentment, and bitterness? Can people (like you) intentionally *choose* true forgiveness in themselves and/or others?

Key options here include you forgiving _ yourself and/or _ your ex, and _ encouraging your ex (and kids and others) to forgive themselves and *you*. What's needed for each of these?

The framework that follows will appeal to people who like mental structure (*security*). Others sense instinctively how to forgive, and evolve it organically. Note that over-avoiding "logic" and "intellectual stuff" can be subselves' protection against imagined threat and horror of seeing *the truth.*

<u>Prepare</u>

Become aware of . . .

_ specifically what you mean by *forgive.* Note the difference between _ *denying* ("*I wasn't offended*"), _ *forgiving* (releasing judgment, guilt, and resentment) and _ *excusing* (rationalizing or ignoring judgments, hurts, and resentments);

_ how pseudo and true forgiveness differ;

_ the symptoms of true forgiveness;

_ the alternatives to forgiving _ yourself and _ others;

_ your beliefs and attitudes about forgiving (Chapter 3); and become aware of . . .

_ your current forgiveness state with _ yourself and _ your ex mate: blocked, progressing, or "OK."

To gain accurate awarenesses, you'll need . . .

Your Self to be consistently in charge of your other subselves. If you're not sure whether s/he is, use [E] for a preliminary reading. Better, study Project 1, and use all 12 self-assessment checklists. If warranted, _ read *Who's* Really *Running Your Life?* or the articles at [..pop/assess.htm], and _ evolve and work a personal recovery plan. If you're controlled too often by a well-meaning false self, keep a long-range outlook, and make personal recovery your highest discretionary priority *without guilt, shame, or anxiety.*

When you're confident your Self and Higher Power are guiding you often enough, then . . .

Get clear on the difference between *guilt* and *shame*, for they're healed differently. You and your ex mate will probably need to reduce both of them to exchange true forgivenesses. Feeling guilty is a normal reaction to believing we've broken a significant rule (*mustn't, shouldn't, can't, never ___, always ___, . . .*). *Shame* is the feeling related to believing "*I'm worthless, unlovable, and unimportant.*" Without awareness, guilt

("*I do bad things*") promotes shame ("*I* am *a bad thing*"). Your true Self knows this isn't true.

The prior chapter focused on options for reducing major divorce-related guilts. Project-1 work on harmonizing your inner family will lead you toward converting excessive shame to self love. *Inner* family therapy is one effective way to do that, over time: see *Who's* Really *Running Your Life?* or [..01/ifs1-intro.htm].

Another preparation you can choose is . . .

See forgiveness-building as a high-return, long-term investment in the quality of your and any kids' lives. Then authorize yourself to take your time as you would with, say, earning a college diploma!

Remind yourself of the difference between hurtful *actions* ("offenses"), and being a *worthy, valuable person.* Have you ever really thought about what your *dignity* is, and where it comes from? Are you *dignified*?

Another impactful preparation is to . . .

Review the Bill of Personal Rights on p. 514, and see how you feel applying it to *you.* Then evolve your own Bill, as a basis for _ owning responsibility for your actions, and _ forgiving (vs. excusing) yourself and others.

More forgiveness preparations . . .

Become aware of your ability to talk back firmly and respectfully to (set boundaries with) "inner voices" (subselves) that don't *want* you to forgive yourself or your ex. I suspect you wouldn't hesitate to do this with someone who righteously commanded you to adopt their religious or political beliefs. See Chapter 15.

Accept the realities that . . .

_ your ruling subselves make the best personal relationship decisions they can, with current knowledge and skills. Later wisdom and growth (and an empowered, wiser Self) can suggest you or your ex were "wrong" or "stupid" for your actions. Would you scorn a teen for not being able to fill out your income tax forms? Also accept that . . .

_ if you or your ex mate have been controlled by myopic,

reactive subselves who caused and conducted your divorce, you _ didn't choose that, _ couldn't control it, and _ are not *sick, crazy, wrong,* or *bad*! You *are* responsible for your subselves' choices and actions, to the extent that you had conscious choices about them at the time. If you need to blame someone, try faulting *all* our ancestors for being wounded and unaware.

Ask yourself *"Are mistakes* bad *(glass half empty), or are they chances to learn and improve?"* (glass half full). If you have active *Skeptic* or *Pessimist* subselves, you know which opinion they'll try to sell you on. Reflect: what are you learning so far from your divorce experience?

Assess whether you have an active *Perfectionist* subself who shapes your perceptions, judgments, and decisions. If your true Self is disabled, your *Perfectionist* will set impossibly high standards which your tireless *Inner Critic* uses to brand you a "failure" or "loser." That activates your *Guilty* and *Shamed* Inner Kids, which activates their Guardian subselves, which may disable your Self. Whew.

Insecure subselves often judge you and the environment as black or white, because shades of gray (uncertainties) are too confusing. This can manifest as your *Critic* assessing your divorce-related actions as either *perfect* or *bad.* Reflect: how often do your inner voices (thoughts) *praise* your decisions and behaviors? If so, do other voices immediately discount the praise (*"no big deal; I was just doing my job."*), and harp on your weaknesses, failings, and mistakes? (*"Yes, but . . ."*)

If you have overactive *Perfectionist* and *Inner Critic* subselves, _ acknowledge them respectfully, and _ do some job retraining. The goal here is to _ realistically identify your and your ex's divorce-related "offenses," and _ objectively assess who was hurt, and how badly.

Getting your *Critic, Perfectionist, Catastrophizer,* and *Realist* ("Common Sense") subselves to work together cooperatively under the leadership of your true Self is a worthy goal in doing Project-1 recovery "parts work" (*inner*-family therapy).

Recall: we're considering your options for preparing to forgive yourself and your ex mate. This is a lot of abstract ideas. Do you need to stretch and regroup?

Choose a "forgiveness time frame." Decide what span of your life you're including in this work: courtship, marriage, divorce, post-divorce, and possibly, re/marriage?

Reflect and list the specific "offenses" by _ you and _ your ex mate that you want your subselves to accept and release. There is no right or wrong here, only *feelings* of intense regret and/or remorse, anger, guilt, and blame.

Blocked grief can inhibit you from forgiving yourself and others, so use Chapter 12 as a springboard to raise your "grief IQ." Option: try this [..05/grief-quiz.htm] to learn what you need to know about healthy three-level mourning. Option: for each item on your "offense inventory," identify any important losses you experienced. Use the concepts in *Stepfamily Courtship* or [..05/abstract-loss-inv2.htm] to assess whether you're well along in grieving each one. *If not, defer seeking self-forgiveness, and refocus on freeing up your grief.* Patience is a great asset here!

When you feel prepared enough, focus on . . .

Forgiving Yourself

Your goal is to intentionally evolve an effective way to forgive yourself for each "divorce offense" in your time-frame. Doing this before pardoning your ex raises the odds you can communicate with him or her from an $=/=$ (mutual respect) position, vs. "I'm 1-down" (Chapter 7).

I know of no cook-book way to do this, for you and your situation are unique. Listen to and follow your Self's and Spirit's wisdom. Build on options like these . . .

Accept that other adults are responsible for filling their needs, and you are for yours. Evaluate whether each "offense" included trying to fill someone else's needs which you couldn't control ("*I should have made my mate happier.*") Expect inner and perhaps social resistance to this belief. Explore this further with [..02/dig-down.htm].

Accept that if your false self was responsible for past hurtful decisions or actions, your subselves *meant* well. They naturally put your welfare above other people's, directly *or* indirectly. *You have no "bad" subselves. Your Guardians and Vulnerable personality parts are often misinformed, narrow-visioned, impulsive, and perhaps living in the past.* Also . . .

Accept that you weren't and aren't responsible for being wounded and unaware. Neither are your ancestors and teachers. If your punitive subselves insist that *someone* must be blamed, mull *"Who's at fault for the AIDS epidemic?"*

Help your subselves accept that at any time, _ you (all) have too little information to make perfect ("right") long-range decisions. So you make the best local decisions you can. You can't undo ineffective, hurtful decisions. You *can* accept and learn from them, and calmly adapt to the outcomes *if* your Self usually guides your other subselves.

Evolve a meaningful way of measuring *"How do I tell if I have really forgiven someone?"* Recall past actions that have hurt people, *which you no longer cause you major remorse or guilt thoughts and feelings. Refresh your awareness of what "acceptance" feels like mentally and emotionally.*

Use a mirror to look yourself in the eye, and say something like *"I let go now of any need to judge you for (each offense you listed above). I forgive you _____ (your name)."* Try saying that out loud. I suggest doing one or two at a time, not the whole list. Breathe well, and invite your *Perfectionist* and *Inner Critic* to relax.

As you do this, notice your thoughts (inner voices) and feelings without judgment. If you feel resistant, anxious, phony, or "wrong," you probably have more work to do on that item. Reflect on *"What do I need to do to release blame, guilt, and bitterness here?"*

Consider asking a trusted lay or clinical supporter to listen (objectively) to you talk about key self-forgiveness targets. Having someone else hear us forgive ourselves out loud can reinforce the reality of our *letting go* of toxic guilt over a past offense or mistake.

Consider thoughtfully choosing a physical token that symbolizes your "offense" like a picture, card, letter, or receipt, and burning, burying, or giving it away with a suitable private or public ritual.

Think of someone you really love and admire, preferably of your gender. Imagine them offending you, and what it would sound and *feel* like to truly forgive them. Then picture that person as *yourself*, and see if you feel the same way. If you don't (yet), you have more work to do on one or more of the steps above.

Make the spirits and words of the Serenity and gestalt Prayers (p. 24) part of your "acceptance tools." Read and reflect on them, and other inspirations you collect, often. Note how they affect your patience, compassion, and serenity. Scan [..01/inspirations1.htm] and notice how you feel.

And . . .

As you evolve and progress through your version of these forgiveness options, call on your Higher Power to companion, encourage, focus, guide, and strengthen you. *Listen* to the still, small voice that's *always* there, and encourage your inner crew to really trust what it gently suggests. My experience is that "the voice," or a "sense", hunch, image, or intuition, is usually very brief and simple—like *"Call Margaret now."* Our many other inner voices are more wordy, raucous, and complex, and usually urge short-term comforts and pleasures. What's your experience? See [..01/insprations8.htm].

Now let's check out your options for . . .

Forgiving Your Ex, and Others

Once again, treat these ideas as a buffet of options and idea-provokers, rather than a guaranteed menu. Honor the uniqueness of you, each related person, and your situation; and evolve your own pace and way of pardoning. Your future self will bless you!

Identify and validate your forgiveness "rules." Over your years, you've probably evolved semi-conscious *attitudes* (good-bads, and right-wrongs); and inner *shoulds, oughts,* and *musts* (rules) about forgiving other people. Your attitudes and rules may differ for adults, vs. kids, and for spouses vs. relatives or other adults.

One way of starting this leg of your divorce-healing journey is to **write a short "essay"** describing your specific key beliefs and habits about forgiving other people. If you do, let some time pass, and then come back with "fresh eyes." As objectively as possible, for each belief or rule about forgiving people, meditate on *"Where did I get this? Is this* my *belief, or am I using someone else's rules?"*

Patiently trust your <u>S</u>elf's direction in evolving a set of authentic attitudes and guidelines, *whether other people agree with them or not.* Reaffirm and *use* your Bill of Personal Rights! (p. 514) Then . . .

Clarify who needs *who* to forgive *who*, for *what.* An alternative is your feeling responsible for someone else's forgiving or blaming (co-dependence).

Pick one person to forgive at a time, to protect against feeling overwhelmed and discouraged. If you have kids, I suggest starting with your ex mate. If you do . . .

Assess that person for a low-nurturance childhood, significant inner wounds (Chapter 5), and normal denials and unawareness. If you conclude s/he was or is being controlled by a protective false self, mull how that affects your need to blame her or him for divorce-related "offenses." Would you be bitter at someone with a brain tumor for causing you pain?

Build and keep your motivation. Picture yourself as old, and imagine clearly how you want each of your grown kids to feel about themselves, you, and their other parent. Angry? Numb? Depressed? Loving and compassionate? Resentful? Fully grieved and renewed? Trusting? Afraid? Disgusted? Distant? Then image clearly how you want any *grandkids* to feel about you and their other grandparent, and what kind of relationship you want to build with them. You, your ex, and your kids have *years* to co-create this vision . . .

Use these visions to help focus on the long-term goal of making the best possible future life for you all. Envision (eventually) making this a shared vision with your ex mate. Option: write your vision down, and refer to it periodically as you go . . .

Another way to keep your commitment to forgiveness is . . .

Protect your kids by learning what _ loyalty conflicts and _ (persecutor-victim-rescuer) relationship triangles are, and how to master them (Chapter 16). Be alert for unconsciously snaring you co-parents and kids in these stressors because of ruling false selves + blocked grief + residual divorce-blamings, guilts, and resentments. Your learning to avoid and resolve these common post-divorce and stepfamily stressors will help all your family members now, and strengthen your future relationships. Note that you can have loyalty conflicts and triangles among your *inner* family members too, specially if your Self isn't solidly in charge! *Resolve those first!*

More options . . .

Separate your *forgiveness* goals from other relevant post-divorce team-building barriers in Part 2. of this book. Stay aware that Project 1 (inner-wound recovery) and Project 2 (learn effective-communication skills) help you reduce *all* of them.

Stay aware of your *attitude*. If you (your ruling subselves) feel hopeless, overwhelmed, or confused in all these team-building tasks, see if the "eat an elephant a bite at a time" metaphor helps center and motivate you. If it doesn't, your false self may have higher local priorities than long-range team-building for your kids' welfare and your old-age satisfaction.

Each Part-2 topic is a potential block in evolving true forgiveness for you and your ex mate. Do you agree? Conversely, *forgiveness* may well help you heal each of them that apply in your situation. Your Self knows the best short and long-tem things to do here, so *listen, trust,* and *act!*

Stay aware of your *focuses*. Your odds for true forgiveness are best if your ruling subselves focus mainly on _ your *current* true needs (p. 44), vs. over-dwelling on _ your ex or a child, in _ the past or the future. Are you often able to be "in the present moment" now? If not, what's in the way?

Tailor versions of relevant "forgive yourself" options above to fit your list of ex-mate "offenses." before, during and

after your divorce process. I again recommend that you patiently work with each hurtful event separately, to raise your
chances of it not resurfacing months or years from now.

Tailor and use these 12 steps for Grown Wounded Children as a resource: [..01/12-steps.htm].

Decide if and when giving your ex or another a copy of
this book or chapter [..Rx/ex/forgive.htm] would help either or
both of you. Alternatively, let your ex know you're working on
self and mutual forgiveness, and ask if s/he's be interested in
joining you *for your kids' sakes.* Use the Serenity Prayer (p.
102) to guard you both from your false self trying to control
your ex mate's attitude or response.

If you feel your ex was or is burdened with an addiction,
read and apply Chapter 20. Pay special attention to learning
about "co-addicts" (codependents), *for you probably are one.*
Also consider the healing information and help available from
a local 12-step support group like Codependents Anonymous
(CoDA), Al Anon, or Alcoholics Anonymous (AA).

Evaluate whether qualified professional family or pastoral
counseling would be a useful investment in freeing you all from
the burden of divorce-related blame and resentments. Finally . . .

As you evolve your strategy to forgive people who co-
created your marriage and divorce impacts, take steady
strength, courage, inspiration, and comfort from your Higher
Power. If you don't have one so far, try not to fault yourself, or
others who believe in theirs. Pain inexorably nurtures spiritual
openness, growth, and awareness . . .

The last part of this co-parent team-building work is to . . .

Invite Selected Others to Forgive You

You can't *make* someone let go of their hurt, resentment,
and blame toward you. You *can* do things that encourage that,
over time. Review the options within your control, and accept
those that aren't. Periodically review the ideas on key attitudes
that shape the relationship quality between you ex mates (Chapter 3). The most powerful things within your control are . . .

_ patiently shifting inner-family control from your false self to your true Self, via real recovery (Project 1);

_ forgiving *yourself* for divorce-related actions, and then . . .

_ *genuinely* forgive the other person/s, for your and any kids' sakes, not the other adult's.

As you progress on these challenges over time, you're increasingly likely to accept the inherent dignity and potential for real good in you and your ex, despite past wounds, disappointments, betrayals, and "mistakes."

It's hard for people to maintain resentment towards someone who has the courage and humility to say directly, and *mean*, something like:

"(Name), I believe I hurt you, when I (name the specific event or cause). I am <u>truly</u> *sorry you suffered because of my need to (name your specific true, vs. surface, need/s) that motivated (the hurtful event)."*

It's also hard for another to stay in blame-and-attack mode if you make a point to learn and use effective communication skills (Project 2), *based on a genuine "=/=" attitude of mutual respect.* You probably can't *really* do this without _ empowering your Self, and _ truly forgiving yourself and the other person/s.

If you take steps like these over time, and another co-parent or family member continues to blame and revile you, consider that _ s/he may be reacting to an earlier (e.g. childhood) trauma s/he experienced and isn't yet aware of, and _ *you can't control that.*

Assert and enforce your boundaries with dignity (Chapter 15), trust your <u>S</u>elf and Higher Power, keep your daily balances (Project 12), and focus steadily on developing your inner family harmony and co-parenting teamwork.

Recap

This chapter focuses on your co-parents' needs for four related forgivenesses following a divorce and/or stepfamily formation. The chapter includes _ perspective on what forgiveness *is*, _ typical benefits of achieving it, _ why it's vital for post-divorce families and society, _ the difference between pseudo and *true* forgiveness, and _ minimum ingredients for it.

You read specific options for forgiving _ yourself and _ others causing divorce and re/marriage-related pain and losses. Option: use these ideas to forge pro-forgiveness inner and outer families, and teach them to your kids.

Pause, stretch, breathe well, and reflect: why did you read this chapter? Do your kids' parents have a significant need to *forgive* to build an effective co-parenting team? What do you want to remember and apply from what you read here? Is there anyone you want to discuss these ideas and options with now? How would each of your co-parents react to them? What do your kids need you to do with these ideas about forgiveness?

Can you name the six core barriers to co-operative caregiving that we've studied so far? There's one more. It affects every one of the people you care about, starting (hopefully) with *you.* Your co-parents have probably had little formal "training" in it, and aren't aware of what you all are teaching your kids about it. I believe it results from _ psychological wounds and _ unawareness, and is one of the five main reasons most Americans divorce or avoid commitment.

Take any break you need, resume the inquiring, open mind of a student, put your Self in charge, and explore options for helping your co-parents *grieve* your many losses well.

12) Release Blocked Grief

Build a Pro-Grief Team and Policy

My client "Myra" was an attractive red-headed custodial mom in her mid 30's. She and her former partner "Dennis" had been referred to me by their divorce-court judge to resolve a deadlock: he wanted overnight visitations, and she refused. He had left her shortly after their son was born, and was now living with another woman and her two children.

I first met each parent separately, and heard two very different stories of their history and current situation. Four years after separating, this mom and dad could barely speak to each other about parenting issues and finalizing their divorce without escalating into bitter mutual accusations. They each agreed that their conflict was hurting their son, and vehemently blamed the other.

Our initial meetings confirmed for me that this couple was snarled in a tangle of all nine core barriers to cooperative caregiving. They couldn't articulate this, and had no clue about how to untangle their barriers for their son's sake. *Both appeared significantly controlled by a false self.*

It quickly became apparent that part of their impasse was Myra's endlessly re-wounding herself by obsessively recounting a litany of things Dennis had done to her and their son. She perceived herself as the tragic victim of an insensitive, childish, alcoholic, selfish man who had betrayed her; wasn't capable of caring for their boy, and was "living in sin" with another woman. Dennis saw her as controlling, selfish, domineering, "totally unreasonable," and "unwilling to acknowledge her part" in their separation. They (their ruling false selves) were stuck. Neither was willing to accept half the responsibility for their divorce, and compromise for their son's sake.

Myra had not dated anyone in four years, saying she had no time for that between caring for their boy and running her cosmetics business. She repeatedly described her agony over losing a wonderful courtship relationship and bright new-marriage dreams of their happy family future. She saw this as all Dennis's fault, saying "I had absolutely no idea he was unhappy with me and (overwhelmed by) becoming a father." My assessment was (partly) that this tormented woman was psychologically wounded, and stuck in the rage-phase of grieving her major divorce-related losses.

My clinical experience since 1981 is that blocked grief is often one of the (unseen) core barriers to post-divorce co-parental teamwork. It also burdens kids and relatives in many divorced families and stepfamilies. Could it be reducing the nurturance level of your multi-home family now? How can you assess that? If so, what can you caregivers do to free up healthy three-level mourning?

This chapter _ reviews "good grief" basics, _ summarizes behavioral signs of blocked grief, _ illustrates a sample family "Good grief" policy, and _ offers specific options toward reducing this barrier. Before reading these, learn what you know (and don't know) about *good* grief: take this [http://sfhelp.org/05/grief-quiz.htm]. Then review Project 5 in *Stepfamily Courtship* or [http://sfhelp.org/05/project05.htm] and return here.

Let's review some basics:

About Losses and Grieving

Grieving is the primal (reflexive) human response to forced or chosen *losses*. A *loss* is any broken emotional-spiritual attachment, or bond. Your lives are full of physical and abstract losses: prized relationships, freedoms, youth, hopes, dreams, power, status, and many more. Your adults and kids need to grieve *many* more things than death. To raise your awareness of common things people lose from divorce or death *and re/ marriage*, see the two-page inventory starting at [..05/physical-loss-inv.htm].

Healthy grief leads to acceptance of key losses, and frees up motivation and energy to form new bonds. "Good grief" happens at it's own pace on two or three levels, in several phases:

Mental grief moves through confusion, to trial questions and answers, to clear, credible answers, to full understanding of current losses and their impacts, and conscious acceptance of them. Typical questions include . . .

"What have I lost, and why?"
"Why now? *Can I get it back? How?"*
"Did I cause this loss? Could I have prevented it?
"What does this loss mean *to me and key others?"*
"What do I need now?"

Emotional grief moves back and forth among these phases: _ shock (disorientation), _ magic (distorted) thinking, _ anger or rage, _ sadness and despair (often mistaken for depression), and _ stable acceptance (emotional peace).

Spiritual grief occurs in people who have true faith in (a bond with) a Higher Power. If allowed to, it moves from _ initial faith and communion to _ shock, confusion, questioning, and disbelief, to _ resentment, anger, and rejection, to _ gradual rebuilding new stable faith. Losses can cause unaware or *religious* people to experience their first *real* spiritual awareness, comfort, and faith.

So "good (healthy) grief" happens when an adult or child is allowed to move through all three of these levels at their own pace, in their own way. To do that, I propose that they (you) need . . .

_ Progress healing significant childhood wounds; and
_ *Awareness* of the three grief levels; and . . .
_ Confidence in this natural healing process, and . . .

_ Commitment to it; and . . .

_ Inner and _ outer encouragements ("support"), and . . .

_ Enough solitudes to meditate and release, and . . .

_ Time and _ patience to move through the process.

When an adult or child doesn't get consistent, geniune inner and outer permissions to grieve on all three levels [..05/grief-permits.htm], their progress toward full acceptance of their losses gets hindered or blocked. My sense was this had happened to Myra, and she didn't know it. One implication was that she was at risk of unconsciously inhibiting her young son's ability to mourn *his* losses.

How can you tell if one or more of your co-parents is stuck in some phase of their mourning?

Symptoms of Blocked Grief

Lacking some of these seven requisites, losers may not start their mourning process, or can get stuck in one of the three levels. Use the following list to check for frozen grief in yourself or one you care about. Look for repeated patterns over time.

Some or many of the behavioral symptoms of _ false-self dominance [E] and/or _ co-dependence [..01/co-dep.htm].

Seeming "forever" sad, angry, or depressed, or often feeling numb or "nothing"—in general, or about a loss (broken bond). People who always seem very intellectual or "unemotional" may be frozen grievers with disabled true Selves.

Repressed anger. Signs include repeated: procrastination; lateness; sadistic or sarcastic humor; cynicism; excessive sighing; inappropriate cheerfulness; over-controlled monotone voice; insomnia or excessive sleep, waking up tired, tiring easily, or inappropriate drowsiness; irritability; clenched jaws ("TMJ") or teeth grinding (specially at night); back pain; muscle spasms, tics, or twitches; and fist clenching, or other automatic actions. Some of these may have medical causes, though our mind-body connection is a relevant mystery here.

Minimizings and/or denials. Consistently downplaying either the loss itself (*"Oh _____ wasn't that important to me."*), or feelings about the loss (*"No, I'm not sad; just tired again, is all."*). The ultimate denial is of one's own denial. (Recall: denial is a common form of false-self reality distortion.)

Chronic weariness, depression, or apathy. It takes a lot of personal energy to steadily repress frightening emotions and awarenesses. Recovery pioneer John Bradshaw likens this to trying to swim while holding a big beach ball under water. Therapist Virginia Satir suggested it's like constantly holding a door closed against a basement full of starving dogs . . .

A probable sign of significant inner wounds and blocked mourning are . . .

Addictions to . . .

_ *activities* (e.g. work; hobbies or sports; worship; committees; socializing, TV, or personal computers; fitness and health; sex; cleaning and organizing; shopping or gambling; hoarding; reading or "endless" education);

_ *substances* (nicotine, caffeine, fats and/or sugar, alcohol or other hard drugs, or medications);

_ *"causes"* (abortion, gun control, ecology, feminism, save the world's hungry, homeless, repressed, . . .);

_ *emotional states* (e.g. "rageaholics" or an addiction to sensual or other excitement); or to . . .

_ *toxic relationships* which consistently produce notable shame, fear, rage, pain, guilt, anxiety, stress, and/or unhealthy dependence.

Often, people using addictions or obsessions to medicate their grief pain have several of the above ("cross addiction"). True addicts will deny, minimize, or rationalize their compulsive dependencies, until real (vs. pseudo) personal recovery begins. Usually, their partners or relatives, who may be addicted to their addict's feelings and welfare (co-dependence), will join them in such denial ("enabling"). Others may acknowledge their partner's addiction, and fiercely deny their own. See Chapter 20.

More common symptoms of blocked grief . . .

Repeated avoidances. These can be verbal, mental, and/or physical. If the loss (or something associated with it or similar to it) comes under discussion, a blocked mourner will often become silent or irritable, tune out, try to change the subject, or leave. They may also reflexively shun certain . . .

_ *places* (like former dwellings, neighborhoods, cemeteries, churches . . .);

_ *people* (who remind the loser of what's gone, or how it got gone);

_ *activities* or rituals (holidays, vacations, births, deaths, graduations . . .); or . . .

_ *painful mementos* (photo albums, movies or videos, music, old letters, holiday ornaments, special clothing . . .) that remind them of that which is gone.

Blocked mourners will often protectively deny, rationalize (intellectually explain, without feelings) or minimize such avoidances. Absent-parent and stepfamilies abound with such painful reminders of sets of real and intangible losses! Are there such mementos in your life now? Your kids' lives?

_ **(Some) chronic pain or illness/es,** specially ones without clear biological cause. A growing number of professional healers feel that recurrent asthma, migraine or other headaches, digestive or colon problems, back pain, shoulder and neck stiffness or soreness, breathing or swallowing troubles, panic attacks, nightmares, allergies, and the like are body signals that emotions are being unhealthily repressed. Unconsciously-fearful mourners will often scoff at this, or get angry (i.e. scared) if it's proposed.

Obesity and (some) eating disorders. It's been said of some obese people that "every fat cell is an unshed tear." Adults or kids can numb the pain of unresolved loss by compulsive overeating. Others are metabolically unbalanced. Griefwork can be far more helpful for the former than endless dieting/regaining cycles, which typically build guilt, shame, and eventual depression and hopelessness.

Other eating problems like anorexia (self-starvation) or bulimia (compulsive binge-purge cycles) may signal blocked mourning and underlying inner wounds. Obesity may be a symptom of childhood sexual abuse. This shattering personal violation forces the massive losses of innocence, trust, security, and Self respect in a child too young and dependent to understand and protect themselves.

Repeated anniversary "depressions." Significant apathy, sadness, sluggishness, sickness, sleep disorders, irritability, or feeling gloomy "for no reason" may recur annually around the time or season a major loss happened. This can appear to be (or be increased by) "seasonal affective disorder (SAD)," where people explain recurring depression by short, dark Winter days.

Enshrining or purging mementos. People who obsessively display, revere, discuss, or protect, special real or abstract reminders long after an agonizing ending can be blocked mourners. Such mementos can include foods, music, clothes, pictures, rituals, furniture, letters, jewelry, perfume, gardens, and many more.

Perpetually revering or reacting to such reminders *excessively* is the symptom here. The opposite may also signal blocked grief: i.e. compulsively throwing away every reminder of the lost person or thing can help avoid an intolerably painful loss.

A final symptom of blocked grief is . . .

having intense emotional reactions to the losses or traumas of strangers, acquaintances, animals, or fictional characters. Such reactions include uncontrollable sobbing, lasting depression, intense rages, insomnia, obsessions, and over-identifications ("becoming" the hurt one).

Emotionally-stuck mourners may have one or more of these symptoms, and hide or disguise them out of repressed shame, guilt, and anxiety. This is specially likely when the key people around them disapprove. Having one or several of these symptoms doesn't *prove* an adult or child is blocking major grief, but does justify assessing for it.

Bottom-line question: is it likely that any co-parent in your multi-home family is significantly blocked from accepting the

loss of something they hold dear? Who? What are their symptoms? How does their blockage affect them and you all? Take a
few moments to breathe, and notice where your thoughts and
feelings go. Think about the present relationships among all
your co-parents, and take this . . .

Status Check: again, "T" = true, "F" = false, and "?" =
"*I'm not sure . . .*"

I feel a mix of calm, centered, energized, light, focused,
resilient, up, grounded, relaxed, alert, aware, serene, purposeful, compassionate, and clear, so my Self is probably present
now. (T F ?)

I can now clearly describe _ what "losses" are, _ the three
levels of healthy grief and _ their main phases; and _ the value
of healthy grieving. (T F ?)

I can name _ at least six common symptoms of blocked
grief, _ five or more requisites for healthy grief, and I _ can
describe what a "family grief policy" is. (T F ?)

I can describe _ what the current grief policy is in _ my
inner family, _ my home, and _ my multi-home family now. (T
F ?)

I am motivated now to _ assess myself and _ our other co-
parents for significant blocked grief, and _ I have a general
idea of our options if I find such symptoms. (T F ?)

I'm confidant that my partner (if any) and/or my ex (if
any) would answer "T" to all these items; *or* if not, _ I know
what to do about that now. (T F ?)

I have, or want to, take this "good-grief" quiz to gauge
my knowledge and attitudes: [..05/grief-quiz.htm]. (T F ?)

I'm satisfied that I'm doing everything I can to help the
children in my life learn to practice healthy three-level mourning now. (T F ?)

What did you just learn? If you feel blocked grief may be,
or *is* one of the significant barriers to co-parental cooperation,
here are some key . . .

Options

Don't _ discuss this chapter with other family adults and supporters, **and/or** _ don't **assess** yourself and other co-parents for symptoms of blocked grief now or after finishing this book. Doing this suggests a protective false-self controls you. Or . . .

Finish this book, and use Chapter 24 ("Summing Up"), to help evolve a team-building plan with your other co-parents. If you haven't yet, begin implementing your plan by assessing yourself and other co-parents honestly for false-self dominance and related wounds (Chapter 5 and 6). Ignoring or delaying this will significantly limit the value of what follows. And you can choose to . . .

Take this [..05/grief-quiz.htm], and study the Project 5 ideas and resources in *Stepfamily Courtship* or [http://sfhelp.org/05/links05.htm]. Then explain what you're doing and why (e.g. to help you adults team up to help your kids with their grieving), to each other co-parent and family supporters, and invite them to do the same. If a co-parent seems "resistant," ambivalent, or disinterested, tailor and apply Chapters 5, 6 and 16.

Starting with *you*, assess each co-parent in your multi-home family for symptoms of blocked grief. If you find any, tailor option like these to fit your situation:

Get more education on healthy grieving. Learn your own values about grieving to foster greater Self-awareness and empathy here: [..05/griefval.htm]. Encourage your other adults and kids to do the same.

Educate your family members on what losses, healthy grieving, and blocked-grief symptoms are, and why you all need to know about these. Options: _ give other co-parents and supporters copies of this book or *Satisfactions*; _ download, print, and pass out (free) copies of the Project-5 Web pages [..05/links05.htm] or the 44-page good-grief booklet from [..site/ftp/08-grief.exe]. Make good-grief education a family project! And you may choose to . . .

Invite all adults and older kids to fill out copies of the grief values worksheet [..05/griefval.htm], and discuss the results as a group. Think of the example you set for your kids.

Research your community for _ an effective grief-support group, like Rainbows; and _ qualified professional grief-counselors. Check local public and private mental-health agencies, and hospital outpatient services.

If another co-parent seems significantly blocked, get clear on how, specifically, their blockage affects your family relationships and roles. Check your respect-level. If you lack respect for them, see if Chapter 8 helps. If you feel respectful, assert your perceptions and needs [..02/assert.htm] and [..02/I-msg-wks.htm] (*"Laura, your frequent anger explosions have us all walking in eggshells, and inhibit our being spontaneous. Will you commit to investigating if you're _ wounded, and _ blocked in mourning some key losses?"*)

Review your rights (p. 514), and avoid taking responsibility for their response. Stay aware: blocked mourning is a protective false-self defense against perceived pain. It is *not* a "defect," "character flaw," or a sign of cowardice or weakness! If you avoid such caring confrontations, you're enabling false-self dominance and low family nurturance.

An overarching option is to . . .

Ask your co-parents and other members to join you in drafting and *using* a family-wide "Good Grief" policy. Here's an example:

Our Family's Good Grief Policy

Everyone in our multi-home family has experienced broken emotional bonds ("losses") from both divorce (and/or spouse death) and blending our several biofamilies. Losses *hurt*. Grieving is Nature's way of healing our hurts, sadnesses, and "holes" over time, so we each can bond with new people, ideas, and activities, and move on.

Mourning is a normal, healthy reaction when kids and adults attach to, and later lose, precious things. Some big losses take people years to mourn (accept) fully. This policy describes how we want to help each other mourn our losses.

1) We believe that the natural process of Good Grief happens on three levels:

A sequence of **emotions**: _ shock, _ pleading (maybe) and "magic thinking," _ anger or rage, _ deep sadness, and _ eventual acceptance (vs. *forgetting*); and . . .

Getting **mentally** focused and clear, over time, on the answers to some personal questions about _ our important losses, and _ what they mean to us, and . . .

Restabilizing or re-clarifying our **spiritual** beliefs, if they were upset by our loss-reactions.

2) We believe that adults and kids can get stuck in this grieving process, if they don't feel safe enough to move through any level. The adults in each of our co-parenting homes are in charge of _ grieving their own losses well; _ making each of our homes a safe place to mourn, and _ respectfully helping each other and our children to grieve well, over time.

3) We believe that it's good to . . .

_ **Accept** that emotional attachments and losses are a normal part of every life, and that the people and things we lose will never come again in the same special way;

_ **Get clear** on specifically _ what we each lost, _ why we lost it, _ why we miss it, and _ how we really feel about losing it. Losing special people (relationships), dreams, things, pets, customs, health, freedoms, places, securities, roles, identity, privacy, and opportunities all can hurt a *lot*!

_ **Get clear on** the kind of support we need (and don't need) from other people; and learn how to _ ask for and _ accept it _ without anxiety, guilt, or shame.

_ **Talk openly** about important things that are gone for good—over and over, if we need to—until the hurt and anger subside. The other half of talking is *listening* with our hearts, without judgment, to ourselves and each other. That really helps! And we believe it's good to . . .

_ **Use good-grief language**, without guilt or embarrassment. It sounds like:

"I hurt!" / "I feel . . ." / "If only . . ."
"I'm really sad!" / "Goodbye, _____ "

"I miss _____ so much!"
"I wish . . ." / "Not now . . ." / "I remember . . ."
"I'm not ready"../.."I am so angry that . . ."
"I've lost . . ."

_ **Cry**, alone and with each other, when we need to. This is true for each of our boys, girls, women, and men. People who *feel* their anger and pain, and cry it out are strong and healthy. It can hurt our health to block crying.

_ **Feel** *angry* about our losses, and express that, as long as we don't hurt ourselves or other living things (Chapter 13).

_ **Forgive** any person or Being who caused us to lose someone or something dear, when we're ready to. This is not a "should." Forgiving is a good way to set ourselves and others free from old anger, resentment, guilt, and stress. (Chapter 11)

_ **Remember** the people and things we've lost in our own ways, with deep love and appreciation. As our normal grief ends, some sorrow and sadness may stay.

_ **Ask for** help from God and each other when we need comfort, or some information about our losses or other people's related feelings or beliefs.

_ **Pray for help** or understanding or patience or strength or guidance, alone and together;

_ **Invite** people in and outside our family to tell us honestly if they feel burdened by our grieving, or if they can't listen to or support us at the moment. It's OK to not help a griever, if we feel really distracted or weary at the time!

_ **Say and** *mean* "I did," and "I'm sorry" when any of us causes a significant loss to another. Then work to understand and forgive ourselves for what we did.

_ **Act** to help ourselves and each other move through our mourning phases. Each of us can decide for ourselves what things and memories to keep, which to let go of, and when to do so. We can't decide these for someone else.

_ **Accept** that we can't "fix" or heal another person's hurt, or fill the holes in their life after important losses. We can love, support, and be with them, as they fill these holes themselves.

_ **Understand** that we really can't always know what our

Mourner is feeling and thinking, even if we've lost what they have. Saying *"I know just how you feel"* can be arrogant, insulting, and aggravating, not comforting. Asking gently *"What's this (loss) like for you now?"*, and really *listening* with our heart, can be more helpful.

_ **Write** in a special diary or make a scrapbook about what we lost, what we miss, how we feel, and anything else we need to do. If anyone does this, they can keep their writing private without guilt or shame, or show it to people they trust.

_ **Be alone** with our own thoughts and feelings, as long as we don't cut ourself off from nourishing comfort and support. It also helps our grief progress when we talk to trusted others about our losses and our feelings.

_ **Be unique**. No one has to mourn like anybody else: we each find our own way of saying goodbye and letting go (accepting), when we're ready.

_ **Affirm and encourage** anyone who's grieving, if we choose to. We don't *have* to. Affirming can sound like:

"I feel really good that you're able to feel _____ / . . . talk about _____ / . . . cry about _____ / . . . take your time with _____ / . . . face _____ (major discomforts), / . . .

"Good job!"

_ **Experiment and change** how we mourn, over time: there's no "perfect" way!

_ **Learn** from our losses to really appreciate and enjoy the special people and things in our lives while we have them.

_ **Enjoy life** as best we can, and care well for our Selves, both while we mourn and after the hurt and anger have faded away.

_ **Get** special (professional) **help**, if any of us gets really stuck in moving through their grief. The adults in each of our family homes are responsible for deciding if this should happen, and doing it.

_ **Support each other**. When any of us has an important loss, the others will try in their own ways to:

_ *Understand* and believe in our good grief process.

_ *Ask* our loser what they need from us, if we're not sure.

_ *Be empathic*, comforting, and available "enough."

_ *Really* listen from our hearts, often, without trying to "fix" our griever or be responsible for their healing [..02/listen.htm].

_ *Offer* patient, warm acceptance and encouragement, without rushing their process.

_ *Honestly* say when we've heard enough, or need to attend our own affairs, without guilt or anxiety.

_ *Be* as steady, realistic, honest, and optimistic as we can.

_ *Be* at ease with strong feelings in ourselves and our Mourner.

_ *Avoid* yanking our Loser out of their feelings by _ asking too many questions, or _ giving unrequested advice.

More good-grief support options . . .

_ *Hold and touch* our Griever when they need that, and respect their wish to avoid these at other times.

_ *Work towards* knowing how and when to smile, laugh, and share comfortable eye contact.

_ *Be comfortable* with shared silences, and trust in their healing value.

_ *Hold* no secret bad feelings (like resentment) about giving our time and energy to our Mourner.

_ *When* s/he's receptive, gently remind our Griever of (vs. preach about) the new choices that always appear from their losses.

_ *Make* our home a safe place for our family members and others to grieve well.

_ *Care for* and love ourselves just as we do for our Loser.

These statements form our family's policy on how we want to help each other mourn our life-losses and endings effectively, mentally, emotionally, and spiritually. *Using* this policy is important to each of us, because blocked grief can make people stressed, unhappy, or even sick.

+ + +

If you want to show this to someone, copy [..05/
griefpol.htm]. Let this sample inspire you to create your own
family good-grief policy, from your own unique values, terms,
customs, and language. Note your similar options to intentionally create family policies on anger, conflict, privacy, spirituality, loyalties, and individuality. These can augment your family
mission statement [..06/mission1.htm].

We've just reviewed ways your co-parents can help each
other _ identify and _ release any blocked-grief teamwork barriers. This is part of Project 5, which includes assessing your
kin and minor and grown kids for frozen mourning. Though
the principles are the same, your kids' losses can differ in ori-
gin and intensity from your adults'. See [..10/kid-needs.htm].

Recap

Kids and adults are blessed and burdened by the ability to
care: i.e. form significant emotional-spiritual attachments
(bonds) to relationships, places, rituals, dreams, freedoms, and
other special things. We periodically chose to, or have to, break
these bonds, causing painful *losses*. Our actions can cause others to break important attachments, and need to grieve.

We're also endowed with a natural *mourning* process, which
allows us to eventually accept our losses mentally, emotionally, and spiritually. That returns our energy and motivation to
move on with our lives, and form new bonds.

Most kids and adults in divorced families and new
stepfamilies, including grandparents, have all had mosaics of
many minor to major abstract and physical losses.

Because of too little childhood nurturance, some have been
psychologically wounded and can't form major attachments.
Others have learned to protectively _ repress normal grief anger and sadness, _ ignore their own needs to grieve, and _
unconsciously discourage each other from releasing them. Their
false selves impose an unspoken "anti-grief" policy in and

among family homes, which promotes many secondary problems.

Until intentionally identified and released, blocked grief hinders _ stabilizing family relationships after divorce or death, _ forming healthy new stepfamily relationships, and _ kids and adults filling growth and adjustment needs. It also promotes _ addictions and _ significant long-term health risks. These all contribute to blocking the co-parental teamwork that your minor kids need from you caregivers.

This chapter encourages all your co-parents to study and apply Project 5 help each other assess for blocked grief, and free it up. See *Stepfamily Courtship* or [..05/project05.htm]. We've summarized _ "good-grief" basics, _ seven requisites for "good grief," _ common behavioral symptoms of blocked grief, and _ a buffet of action options.

One of them is to evolve an informed "pro-grief" policy and environment in and between your linked homes, and help each other *use* it. Two vital prerequisites for doing this are _ assessing yourself and other co-parents for significant psychological wounds (Project 1 and Chapters 5 and 6), and _ learning and discussing "good grief" basics [..05/grief-intro.htm]. These and other options will help you _ build co-parental teamwork *and* _ enable you to model and teach your children (and others) how to grieve mentally, emotionally, and spiritually. Priceless!

Let's regain the big picture: you've now reviewed ways to identify and reduce seven of nine interactive barriers to co-parental teamwork after divorce and/or re/marriage:

* Six psychological wounds from low childhood nurturance (false-self dominance and five others);
* Ineffective thinking and communication;
* Significant _ disrespect, _ distrust, and _ guilts;
* Blocked _ self and _ mutual forgivenesses, and . . .
* Blocked three-level grief.

The eighth barrier is *unawareness*, which you're significantly reducing by reading and discussing this book and related resources. Intentionally reducing each one of these core
barriers over time protects all your kids and adults from three
of the five re/marital hazards on p. 428.

A basic premise throughout this series of books and Web
resources is that family role and relationship **"problems" have
surface symptoms and underlying *true* problems** (unmet true
needs—p. 44). Focusing on the former rarely fills your family
members' true needs for long. Part 3 outlines 11 common *surface* hindrances to co-parental teamwork after divorce and/or
re/marriage. Each of them is a symptom of the true barriers
you've just studied.

The bad news: mixed with "regular daily life (needs)," these
common concurrent surface problems can feel confusing, discouraging, and overwhelming. The good news: if you co-parents _ adopt a long-range view and commit together to _ break
your problem-mixes into individual targets, _ learn to dig down
to the true needs that need filling, and _ patiently use your
version of the 12 projects in [A] together, you *can* strengthen
your family's nurturance level! Do you believe that yet? Do
you know which of your subselves is answering?

Breathe well, stretch, and release all these details. When
you're ready, expect to see you all in some of these common
surface stressors in typical divorced and stepfamily co-parents.
Like inner wounds, these surface problems usually occur simultaneously, and amplify each other.

Part 3) Common *Surface* Barriers

Premise: every one of the stressful co-parental problems below is a <u>symptom</u> of the core team-building barriers in Part 2 (p. 109). Identifying your core barriers and working to reduce them together can significantly reduce these symptoms, and improve your co-parental teamwork, effectiveness, and satisfactions over time.

Conversely, avoiding or fighting over these stressors will probably *increase* your underlying core barriers That promotes psychological and legal re/divorce, and wounding your vulnerable kids. Your core barriers and surface stressors occur because each of your co-parents have surface and underlying *needs* you're trying to fill (p. 43).

Do your family's adults want to fill your local and long-term needs as opponents or caregiving teammates? The wholistic health of your descendents, and your longevity and old-age contentment depend on your collective choice. *That* depends on the leadership and harmony of your respective inner families (Project 1).

This section covers 11 surface problems . . .

13) Make Anger *Work* for Your Family

14) Tame Excessive Resentments

15) Assert and Enforce Your Boundaries

16) Loyalty Conflicts and Triangles

17) If a Co-parent is "Uninvolved"

18) Avoid or End Legal Battles

19) Resolve "Money" Disputes

20) Coping With Addictions

21) Reduce Child-visitation Conflicts

22) Reduce Sexual Tensions, and

23) Teamwork and (Managing) Major Family Changes.

24) Summing Up and Refocusing.

Let's begin by exploring a surface problem that can stress or enrich all your family relationships: significant *anger*!

13) Make Anger *Work* for Your Family

Convert Co-parent Hostility into Team-building

Is excessive or chronic adult anger and hostility hindering caregiving cooperation between your homes? If so, this chapter suggests common *real* problems underlying those, and 14 options for putting this anger-energy to good use. As we start, reflect on why you're reading this, and what you need (*"I'd feel much better if we could ___"*). Is your Self leading your inner family now?

To illustrate this common post-divorce and stepfamily *surface* stressor, meet . . .

George and Sharon

These are false names for a divorcing couple I met with regularly for almost eight months. They were wearily snarled in a long legal battle over "irresolvable" disputes and mutual hostility around their son ("Marty") and feisty daughter ("Nancy"), both under 10 years old, living with their dad and his ailing Mother. Their mom lived about 45" away with her parents.

The kids' divorce lawyer referred this couple to me, knowing I was a veteran family-communication coach. He hoped that I could help these tormented parents stop the escalating war that was tearing their kids apart and stressing them all. While the details of their story are unique, the themes of "endless" conflict and stress; antagonistic relatives; and expensive, divisive court suits are common to millions of America's divorced and re/married families. Do you know any?

Sharon and George had married nine years earlier, full of love, hope, and wonderful visions. He wanted to become a lawyer, and his bride shared his dreams of building a good life together from his certain future success. She worked overtime to finance his law schooling and their expenses. Their intimacies shifted after their son was born several years later, and again when baby Nancy followed 18 months later. Sharon was working full time to support the young family, while learning the ropes as a dedicated new mom.

George eventually graduated with four degrees, and went to work as a corporate attorney. After several years, he sued his employer for blocking promotions he felt he deserved. Sharon continued to work at her home-management and outside jobs, patiently co-financing their mounting legal bills. For various reasons during those years, they accumulated over $40,000 of credit-card debt. Their sex and social lives dwindled in the face of shared exhaustion, frustrations, disillusionments, and increasing fights and silences. George lost his suit but not his job, humiliated, frustrated, and bitter.

George's version was that Sharon became increasingly blameful, resentful, and explosively angry with him and their young kids. He said she began "threatening" divorce, which terrified him. He initiated joint and personal counseling, which "didn't work," and added new expenses. Sharon railed at him (he said) for his lack of business success, poor sexual skill, "self-centeredness," and ingratitude for her patient sacrifices for their marriage and family.

He charged that she had no empathy for him or anyone else, and was a "control freak" who insatiably demanded of him and the kids that "everything must go *her* way." She vehemently denied each of these, acidly charging that a therapist had implied George was "mentally ill."

Things came to a head when George called the police and got a legal order of protection claiming Sharon had physically attacked him. Jailed briefly, she bitterly denied his claims as totally false, and repeated a long list of his many provocations and distortions over the years. Like a trial attorney, he accused her of many specific instances of verbal and physical child abuse, which she vehemently disputed. Her large family rallied to her, accusing George of being a selfish monster.

Eventually Sharon sued for divorce, all dreams shattered over seven awful years. George won primary custody after a bitter legal fight and a psychological evaluation which his wife hotly contested as unprofessional and highly biased. Both were near their 40th birthdays, their lives half over. I met them several years later, in the midst of ongoing court, co-parenting, and financial warfare. Neither expected this round of forced counseling to work, but came under threat of court sanctions.

Before exploring what was going on with this divorcing family, pause and take a . . .

 # Status Check. Focus on the last six months, and the adults and kids comprising your nuclear (step)family (ref. p. 84). See where you stand with these:

I feel a mix of calm, centered, energized, light, focused, resilient, up, grounded, relaxed, alert, aware, serene, purposeful, compassionate, and clear, so my Self is probably present now. (T F ?)

I'm clear on the difference between acceptable and excessive anger now (T F ?)

Two or more of the co-parents in our multi-home family exchange unacceptable anger or hostility now (T F ?) Here, *hostility* or *antagonism* expands anger to include a local or ongoing intent to harm, punish, or cause discomfort. If accused of the latter, hostile co-parents like Sharon and George often hotly or intellectually deny it.

If excessive anger *is* significantly blocking our co-parental teamwork, I know _ the root causes, and _ what my (or our) options are to resolve them now (T F ?)

I feel no periodic or chronic *excessive* anger, resentment, or hostility toward any of our co-parents now (T F ?)

The _ kids in my life and _ people who know us would agree with this (T F ?)

If another co-parent is excessively or chronically angry at *me*, I'm content enough now with my recent way of reacting to that. (T F ?)

If my partner (if any) feels and/or receives excessive anger from an ex or stepparent, I respect the way s/he reacts to that now (T F ?)

Pause, breathe, and notice any thoughts or feelings that come up from this self-assessment. Have you considered points like these recently? If you feel excessive anger or antagonism isn't a significant teamwork barrier, skip to the next chapter.

Surface Causes of Co-parent Hostility

See if any of these common secondary "anger problems" are roiling your multi-home family:

1) *Blaming* **the other co-parent,** and demanding that s/he change: endlessly analyzing, disparaging, and protesting the deficits, traits, and failings of the other caregiver, vs. accepting personal responsibility for half of the past and present conflicts. Blaming and avoiding seems universal among the many hundreds of unrecovering, shame-based (wounded) co-parents I've met.

An inevitable result is the blamed adult feeling repeatedly misunderstood, attacked, hurt, resentful, and angry—and righteous, guilty, and/or ashamed. Normal responses are to defend by _ withdrawing, _ explaining (justifying), and/or _ c/overtly counter-blaming. Each of these send insulting "I'm 1-up" R-messages, which *amplify* the combatants' toxic . . . (disrespect + distrust) > frustration > hostility . . . spiral.

Another result: dependent kids feel impossibly torn taking sides with one parent or the other, or detaching from both parents and trying independence before they're ready for it. Over time, that promotes their own inner wounding, and many related problems including divisive loyalty conflicts and triangles (Chapter 16).

Lack of objective *awareness* of these dynamics usually causes a spiral of aggressive hostility or avoidance and detachment, amidst other life stressors.

Another secondary problem is . . .

2) Constantly reliving the past, instead of healing and problem-solving in the present, and planning for the future. One or both antagonists (i.e. their false selves) focus endlessly on past injustices, failings, and disappointments, *despite unsatisfying outcomes.*

Like many troubled peers, Sharon and George did this in most of our sessions, despite my repeatedly calling respectful attention to it as wasting their time, energy, and money, and hurting their kids. Their Guardian subselves' intense needs to be heard, accepted, and justified ("I'm *right*, and you're *wrong!*"), and have their opponent repent and grovel, relentlessly prevailed. Logic, "common sense," and even the kids' pain couldn't overcome their false-selves' distorted, short-term focus and obsessions.

Another common surface problem is co-parents' and supporters . . .

3) Seeing the post-separation family as opposing (me/us) vs. (you/them) homes, rather than a *two*-home nuclear biological family united by history, genes, and common love of, and responsibility for, living kids. This one-way or mutual antagonism relentlessly polarizes relatives and others into distrustful, warring camps, promoting situational or ongoing lose-lose combat. This inexorably promotes hurt, distrust, frustration, and *anger*

Yet another common surface cause of hostility is a history of . . .

4) Exchanging confusing double messages, and/or accusing the other mate of *doubletalk, insincerity, lying,* and *never listening.* Example: George and Sharon each (had subselves who) said sincerely *"Our kids' welfare comes first."* Their *actions* (other subselves) said *"Proving to you and the world that*

I'm right and a better parent, and you're wrong, is more important to me than our kids' current agony." Both vehemently denied this and grew to distrust the other as insincere and deceptive (Chapter 9): unawareness and false-self *reality distortion* in action.

5) Giving lawyers, judges, laws, and/or counselors the responsibility for untangling this morass of surface stressors, and endlessly arguing over, blaming, explaining, and justifying that, rather than courageously facing how each co-parent is contributing to the excessive anger. When the legal system and/or the kids' teachers and counselors inevitably fail to heal the *real* causes of anger and hostility (because they *can't*), one or both mates starts to cynically blame "the system," as well as the "deranged, malicious" ex spouse or stepparent. Result: new distractions from the *real* anger problems below, and a series of new legally-related traumas that take adults and kids *years* to heal (Chapter 18). Another common surface symptom is . . .

6) Endlessly arguing about child-related conflicts over schooling, health, visitations, financial support, holidays and vacations, a parenting agreement, activities, religion, and so on. Both _ the conflicting perceptions and values underneath these, and _ the way co-parents express and react to them, cause significant frustration, hurt, and anger.

7) Involving new romantic partners and their kids, if any, can add to ex-mates' distrust, jealousy, disrespect, and resulting hostility. A common theme is all co-parents getting lost in the complex thickets of simultaneous, alien stepfamily adjustment tasks [G], and defocusing from healing the *real* sources of co-parent hostilities (the barriers on p. 109).

Sharon and George (i.e. their false selves) couldn't own or free themselves from their toxic mix of the first six of these surface stresses. Neither had a new partner, partly because their well-meaning false selves were paralyzing their legal divorce process. The odds are that eventually one or both of them will find a new partner, probably with kids and stressors of their own. That will yield a rich new source of confusion, frustration, resentment, conflict, and *angers* to their lives.

These seven are genuine *secondary* stressors resulting from . . .

The *Real* Causes of Co-parents' Hostility

Working with hundreds of troubled ex mates like this mom and dad since 1981, I conclude that a mix of up to six factors causes excessive or chronic anger and hostility in and between them. This brew often affects and is fueled by biased, unaware relatives and new partners. Once understood and admitted, each factor can be significantly reduced. Five core problems are . . .

False-self control and related inner wounds in one or more co-parents. This promotes . . .

Blocked grief: an inability to mourn and *really* accept marital and parental losses, and help kids mourn their own. Plus . . .

Undeveloped communication skills (symptom: endless *avoidances* and/or *fights,* vs. effective problem solving). One result is wounded co-parents staying fruitlessly focused on their surface conflicts, not the real needs underneath them.

These three factors combine to promote . . .

Mutual _ disrespect and _ distrusts, which powerfully inhibit effective problem solving and team-building.

The root cause of all five of these is co-parent and social **unawareness** of their **unawareness** of these five root problems. Until antagonistic co-parents _ understand and accept these five factors, _ adopt a long-range view, and _ agree to refocus on resolving them, they'll experience increasing impatience, intolerance, frustration, weariness, and aggression. These evolve into rage or resignation and hopelessness ("depression"), which trigger many secondary personal and family problems. Vulnerable young kids like Marty and Nancy are the unintended victims, just as their troubled parents were years before.

How can wounded co-parents like George and Sharon, and your kids' caregivers, redirect their anger-energy to better purposes? You have a buffet of choices like these . . .

Healing Options

Like most others I've met like them, Sharon and George ache to find a way to stop their "endless" battles—yet they "can't." Despite my listening empathically to their plaints, and suggesting the ideas above as clearly and respectfully as I could over eight months, this couple drifted out of consultation, locked in new cycles of the toxic battle that was wounding their kids.

Around each other, both these parents were controlled by protective, combative false selves—who hotly denied that. Like "people," ruling subselves guard their status and power. These tormented parents will have to "hit bottom" before they begin to see what's *really* fueling their sacred war.

Some wounded couples I've worked with hit bottom, and began to break free of their toxic hostility cycle. In every case, they chose to do versions of many or all of the steps below. With your kids' faces and lives in mind, reflect on what it would take for you and their other co-parent/s to do most or all of these:

1) Adjust your attitude from "*anger or rage is a negative emotion, and over-angry people are* bad" to "*anger is a normal, helpful reaction to unfilled human needs for affirmation, respect, security, and hope. Expressing anger harmfully means _ a false self is in control, and _ the angry person doesn't know how to communicate effectively yet.*"

Option 2) Try imaging your co-parents' (or anyone's) anger as a powerful jet of water from a big canvas fire hose. Imagine the uncontrolled jet breaking windows, destroying furniture in a room, and knocking over kids, pets, and adults . . .). Feel the *power* of the water jet. Now vividly imagine _ deciding to take charge of the hose, _ using your strength and will to do that, and _ redirecting the jet to put out a roaring fire. Imagine using the jet to clear away debris after a violent storm. Imagine turning the jet off, and putting the hose away safely until it's needed again. Reflect on _ what powers the jet, and _ that the jet itself is neither good nor bad. Muse on your *choice* to allow the hose and water jet to do harm or good . . .

3) Acknowledge that against your wills and (true Selves') "better judgment," **you co-parents are stuck** in a destructive, self-amplifying disrespect > distrust > hostility cycle just like the Israelis and Palestinians. This admission is about healing, teambuilding, and raising your family's nurturance levels, not *blaming* anyone!

Option 4) Admit without excuse that your escalating blame-counterblame hostility cycle hinders and injures your kids and adults, over time. Acknowledge that this harm (inner wounds + ineffective communication + unresolved conflicts + blocked grief and family bonding = low family nurturance) will relent-lessly increase until *each* of you adults takes responsibility to stop your part of the cycle (vs. "You first"). Read and apply [..02/dig-down.htm]. Expect your anxious false selves to sabo-tage this.

5) Evaluate yourself and each "anger partner" for signifi-cant inner wounds, via honest effort at Project 1. See Chapters 5 and 6, and *Who's* Really *Running Your Life?* or [..01/project01.htm]. If your Self is disabled, expect your ruling subselves to resist this. When you feel a mix of *calm, centered, energized, light, focused, resilient, up, grounded, relaxed, alert, aware, alive, serene, purposeful, compassionate, and clear*, your Self is probably in charge. Do you feel that mix *now*?

Work compassionately to identify which subselves in each hostile co-parent are fueling your [disrespect + distrust > blame > defend > counterblame] cycle. Patiently use some form of "parts work" to help each subself trust their Self to take charge of problem-solving with each anger-partner. See Part 2 in *Who's* Really *Running Your Life?*, or [..01/ifs1-intro.htm].

As long as . . .

_ reactive inner children and narrow-visioned, reactive *Avenger, Rebel, Amazon,* or *Warrior* subselves govern your co-parental relations, and . . .

_ protective *Magician* subselves cause you to deny that, then . . .

_ you'll helplessly continue destructive, escalating *hostile* thoughts, images, and actions like George and Sharon did. Your true Selves and *Adult* subselves know how to use your anger "jets" to *help*!

Option 6) Each angry co-parent intentionally **shift** your attitude from "*You're* the problem" to "*We're* the problem." Also shift from defining "the other co-parent's *anger* (or other traits) is the problem" to "anger is a *symptom* that the adults involved don't know how to identify and fill some key true needs (p. 44)." Option: view the web of team-building barriers on p. 109 as "*our* problem." Divorced parents accept that "*Redirecting our mutual hostility (and resolving other Part-2 problems) is our shared responsibility as co-parents linked for life by our child(ren)'s existence.*" Expect strong resistance from your narrow-visioned, distrustful false selves, and notice the results if you allow them to direct your life.

7) Help each other _ adopt and **keep a long-range, wide angle focus**. Choose to help each other shift from habitually _ rehashing past wounds and _ current arguments about surface issues (above) to *learning how to problem-solve current conflicts, vs. fight—specially with child-related values conflicts.* What's the span of your family-focus now?

8) Accept that your minor kids and their descendents depend on *all* you caregivers to model and teach effective communication. Then use the suggestions in Chapter 7 and Resources [H – K] to help each other master these steps. Option: use [*Satisfactions*] as a guidebook for this long-term family-building project. You'll read this same Project-2 recommendation throughout this book.

Option 9) Take responsibility for admitting and dismantling your part in each team-building barrier hindering your multi-home family. *Deliberate decide on the long range pros and cons of hanging on to past hurts and resentments, vs. forgiving* and moving on. Once your Selves are leading, help each other apply Chapter 11.

10) Being stuck in the *anger* phase of grieving can steadily fuel co-parent rage and hostility, and block forgiveness, acceptance, and caregiving cooperation. The losses (broken emotional/spiritual bonds) you need to finish grieving may go as far back as your first five or six years on Earth, not just your former marriage. Help each other study and apply the ideas in Chapter 12 and Project 5 to _ assess for blocked grief, and _ free it up. Restoring your Selves to lead your inner team of subselves, and learning effective communication skills will sharply raise your success with this, over time.

11) As you work on all these anger-redirection steps (and other projects), gather supports (Project 11), and help each other to keep your balances every day (Project 12).

Option 12) Watch for opportunities to affirm your progress _ internally and _ with each other. Have some fun learning to use assertion skill [..02/assert.htm] to give "dodge-proof" win-win compliments and praise to your subselves and family members!

13) Because these steps are complex, alien, and challenging, consider investing in qualified professional help along the way. See [..11/counsel.htm] for ideas and options.

Pause and notice objectively what you're thinking and feeling. Who's in charge of your *inner* family (personality) right now? Once again, we've covered a *lot* here. Before continuing, gift yourself with this . . .

 # Status Check: T = *true*, F = *false*, and? = "*I'm not sure.*"

I feel a mix of calm, centered, energized, light, focused, resilient, up, grounded, relaxed, alert, aware, serene, purposeful, compassionate, and clear, so my Self is probably present now. (T F ?)

I believe we have a significant problem with co-parental anger in our family now. (T F ?)

I _ understand the difference between surface problems and underlying true problems; and I _ accept that our co-parental anger and hostility is a surface problem. I _ see these as chances to identify and fill our co-parents' true needs together. (T F ?)

I understand the difference between first-order (superficial) and second-order (core attitude) changes [..pop/changes1&2.htm], and _ how this relates to our redirecting co-parental anger now. (T F ?)

I fully accept that _ both living parents of each of our dependent kids, and _ any new partners of theirs (stepparents), are full, legitimate members of our multi-home family now. (T F ?) If you don't, see [..03/project03.htm] before trying any options here.

I _ clearly understand the basic ideas and options in this chapter, and I'm motivated to _ discuss them with our other co-parents, and _ apply them to our situation _ now. (T F ?)

I _ understand that "co-parental anger" is a symptom of a mix of the core barriers in Part 2, and that _ helping each other work patiently together to reduce them all over time is our co-parents' real goal. (T F ?)

I'm confidant _ my partner (if any) and _ our key family supporters would answer "true" to each of these items now; *or* if not, _ I know what to do about that. (T F ?)

What did you just learn?

Recap

Anger and hostility are instinctual animal responses to perceived threat and injury. These powerful emotions signal unmet needs, and are *normal*, not good nor bad. Anger and hostility can be used to improve or harm your wholistic healths and family relationships.

The causes and effects of the three-part divorce process, and subsequent re/marriage and stepfamily mergers, cause mosaics of strong emotions for all involved adults and kids. Common among them is situational or chronic anger, rage, and hostility between two or more ex mates and/or stepparents. If it's not confronted, excessive anger will block your family's success at healing, (re)bonding, and (re)building the co-parental teamwork your minor kids need.

From 23 years' study, I propose that excessive anger between divorced and stepfamily co-parents is a surface (secondary) problem. It signals that the adults involved are _ unaware of up to five interactive *real* problems: _ false-self dominance and inner wounds (Chapters 5 and 6); _ ineffective communication skills (Chapter 7); mutually-reinforcing _ disrespects (Chapter 8) and _ distrusts (Chapter 9); which combine to promote _ blocked grief (Chapter 12). These can be amplified if co-parents _ have no consensual (step)family mission statement (Project 6), and/or _ effective strategies to master loyalty conflicts and related relationship "triangles." (Chapter 16).

Seen all at once, this seems pretty complex, doesn't it? So is living in a low-nurturance, multi-home family, and probable re/divorce. Each one of the real team-building barriers above can be reduced in small, patient steps. Do you believe that?

This chapter summarizes 14 options that your co-parents can tailor and apply together to reduce the five problems underneath your "anger problems." If false selves covertly hold any of your Selves hostage, they'll sabotage your efforts, as they did for Sharon and George. Your Future selves will reflect on the outcomes of your current decisions about these options years from now. Perhaps you experienced chronically hostile parents, and may discuss the outcome with *them* in light of what you've learned here.

Your basic choice here is whether or not to make a second-order (core attitude) change, and see co-parent hostility as useful *emotional energy.* If you do, the next decision is whether you want to harness that energy and redirect it to improve your family relationships and co-parental teamwork, over time. Your third choice is whether you want to do this alone, or with other family adults and supporters.

Notice with interest how you feel now, and what your ruling subselves are "saying" . . .

Shift gears. Think about your three or more co-parents, and name the most frequent emotions that some or all of you feel. Is one of them *resentment*? My discussions with hundreds of typical divorced mates and stepfamily co-parents have often been studded by this normal human response. Resentments are specially likely around emotional topics related to kids, money, and legal responsibilities.

The next chapter explores this common secondary stressor, and suggests the typical *real* problems and effective options for your reducing them together.

14) Tame Excessive Resentments

> *I was angry with my friend:*
> *I told my wrath, my wrath did end*
> *I was angry with my foe*
> *I told it not, my wrath did grow.*
> -William Blake

A pre-teen "forgets" her stepmother's request to pick up her toys or clothes from the living room floor *again*. Stepmom snaps at the girl, who tells her father, brother, and biomom that the woman "is mean," "yelled at me," and "doesn't like me." Her dad chides his wife *"Aren't you over-reacting a bit?"* The girl's biomom resents that _ "this other woman" is (reportedly) mistreating her daughter, and _ that her ex "dumped her" to marry the "mean" stepmom.

Stepmom resents _ the girl for ignoring her requests (needs) and enlisting her father "against her," and _ her husband for siding with his daughter. If biomom criticizes stepmom and her husband seems indifferent, the stepmother can resent _ the biomom for not empathizing with her side of the situation, _ her husband for not caring about her feelings and values, and _ her stepdaughter for creating this uproar instead of helping to keep their home neat.

The girl can resent _ her stepmom for "being too mean," and _ her father for (divorcing and) marrying this "mean, nitpicky" woman. The dad can resent his wife and daughter "not handling their own problems," and "always putting me in the middle."

By themselves, the resentments that everyone feels in this scenario may be tolerable. They can feel intolerable when combined with similar frustrations, hurts, and resentments over other issues like meals, chores, money, privacy, visitation, holidays, and discipline.

How often does this kind of chain reaction happen in and between your co-parenting homes? When it does, how well can your co-parents separate the surface and *real* "resentment" problems, and stay focused on resolving them?

See if this chapter is relevant to your family situation by trying this . . .

 # Status Check:

I feel a mix of calm, centered, energized, light, focused, resilient, up, grounded, relaxed, alert, aware, serene, purposeful, compassionate, and clear, so my Self is probably present now. (T F ?)

I'm clear enough on the difference between *resentment, envy, frustration, distrust, disrespect, anger, and dislike* now. (T F ?)

I feel that resentment is a normal, *useful* human response that can help people identify unmet needs, and promote more satisfying relationships among adults and kids. (T F ?)

I feel one or more of our co-parents feels excessive resentment toward each other now. (T F ?) Note: resentment toward (step)kids is covered in the next book in this series.

I often feel significantly resentful toward one or more of our co-parents now. (T F ?) If so, my resentment/s are about a __ on a scale of 1 (trivial, occasional) to 10 (constant, major emotional distraction).

I _ know how to "dig down" below resentment to discover the *real* unmet needs that cause it; *or _* I'm truly interested in learning how to do that. (T F ?)

I'm _ comfortable enough talking to each of our other co-parents now about significant resentments that hinder our family teamwork; *or* _ I'm motivated to become more comfortable about this in the near future. (T F ?)

Each of our other co-parents would answer "T(rue)" to each of these items now. (T F ?)

Reflect: if you just learned something useful or interesting, what is it?

Perspective

Notice your opinion on these basic premises . . .

Needs (discomforts) are normal, healthy, and universal. They cause all our behaviors, including communicating (or not).

All human emotions are valuable signs that some current needs are unfilled.

Relationship conflicts among your subselves and family members manifest as clashing *surface* needs and underlying *true* needs (p. 44).

The human needs for _ self and _ social *respect* are constant and universal.

Ultimately, every adult (like *you*) is responsible for identifying and filling their own true needs—like feeling respected. And . . .

Resentment is the instinctual human emotion that results from feeling disrespected. Feeling ignored, discounted, rejected, excluded, neglected, overruled, used, blamed, deceived, interrupted, invaded, and dismissed all feel disrespectful. Reality-check: think of the last person you resented, and see if you felt any of these common "triggers."

How do you feel about these six ideas?

My clinical experience is that typical divorced and stepfamily co-parents are largely unaware of _ their current feelings and _ the true needs that cause them. Most can identify general feelings like "upset," "bothered," or "mad," and can't clearly identify _ the several emotions comprising them, or _ the true needs that cause these emotions.

I suggest that *resentment* differs from *dislike, contempt (disrespect), frustration, envy,* and *distrust.* Do you agree? Often, these emotional responses bloom together. Distinguishing between each of them can help identify and fill the true needs underneath. The learnable skill of *awareness* can help you make these distinctions *if* your Self leads your inner family of subselves.

Contempt says "I don't *respect* something about you." *Frustration* occurs when someone or something blocks you from filling a current need, and you're unable to remove or bypass the block. *Envy* suggests another person has something you wish you had, and may indicate a distorted sense of entitlement: "I deserve ___." *Distrust* results from the need to feel *safe.*

This implies that significant situational or chronic resentment says "*I need to feel respected by (someone)*." Notice the important distinction between "*You need to respect me more*," and "*I need to feel respected.*" A common (false self) reflex is to blame the disrespectful one as being *wrong* or *bad*. Your Self knows "*I am responsible for _ my self-respect, and for _ asserting my feelings (like resentment) and _ my needs.*" Notice your (subselves') reaction to that . . .

I've seen many (wounded) co-parents sabotage their relationships by believing that "I *deserve* (someone's) respect." Like trust, love, and friendship, respect can only be spontaneous, and must be *earned*. In other words, *you* are responsible for _ earning others' respect, and _ telling others what you need in order to respect them. **Reality check**: think of someone you *don't* resent: do you usually feel respected enough by them? Have you requested or demanded this respect, or have you earned it?

Resentments range between acceptable (no action needed) to intolerable (action required). Each of your co-parents draws their own dividing line. I propose that resentments merit co-parental action when it . . .

- **inhibits** family bonding and making effective co-parenting decisions;
- **promotes** combative us-vs.-them divisions in or between your homes and relatives, and . . .

- **contributes to** loyalty conflicts and PVR triangles some-one feels are significant (Chapter 16).

The bottom line: if *resentment* is among the barriers that hinder your family adults from cooperative caregiving, the *real* issues are someone _ feeling too disrespected, and _ not know-ing what to do about that, and/or _ not taking responsibility for changing that. If you agree and aren't acting to change this, you're *enabling* (avoiding confrontation) is part of the prob-lem.

If you don't agree with this set of ideas, what *do* you be-lieve? Which of your subselves is answering?

Resolve the *Real* Problems

The ideas above suggest some options for *really* resolving your "significant co-parental (and other) resentments":

Help each other keep your Selves in charge of your inner families.

Use awareness and dig-down skills [..02/dig-down.htm] to _ identify your current feelings, and _ use them as pointers to _ sort and rank your current true needs.

Take full responsibility for filling *your* need for respect, *and* _ honor each other family member's need to feel respected enough in local situations, and over time.

Use key ideas in Part 1, _ the communication options in Chapter 7, _ the respect-building options in Chapter 8, and _ the boundary options in the next chapter *respectfully* to help each other get your true needs filled well enough.

These will require you adults to _ *want* to rank co-parental problem-solving high among your dynamic priorities. *That* will require _ your Selves to be guiding your other subselves, us-ing long-term, wide-angle family perspectives for local nego-tiations.

In the example that opened this chapter, patient digging down below surface resentments might disclose a mosaic of key *real* needs like this:

Stepmom needed to _ keep her *self* respect by _ asserting her need to feel respected by her stepdaughter, her husband, and his ex wife. The stepdaughter's littering and "forgetting" were surface (secondary) problems.

Stepdaughter's *real* needs were to test (again) "_ *How much power and status do I have in this house, _ who's* really *in charge here, and _ am I safe here, or will this family break up like my other one did?*" She also needed to feel _ her father and stepmother understood and respected these needs and her dignity. She couldn't articulate any of these, and _ needed empathy and comfort from her biomom for the guilt, confusion, and anxieties she felt. She had many other simultaneous needs, too—see Resource [F].

Dad's *real* needs included _ feeling respected by himself and other family members as a husband, father, and man; _ reducing his divorce-related guilts (Chapter 10); _ lowering his feeling caught in the middle of (another) relationship triangle and loyalty conflict (Chapter 16); and _ empathy from his current and ex wives on these needs.

Biomom had many true needs, including _ assurance that her daughter was being well cared for, and _ wasn't switching her love and allegiance to her stepmother; and that _ her ex husband and _ his new wife respected her needs and feelings as a full, dignified member of their stepfamily.

An Example

Can you imagine taking a recent co-parent "resentment incident" and assessing for everyone's true needs like this? If you did, how could you use Part-1 and effective-communication resources to help fill those needs *respectfully*? Here's a brief example of you and "your ex." Your Self is solidly in charge, and a false self controls your ex:

Your ex (sarcastic false self): *"Well, how are you enjoying the mega-thousand dollar multimedia center you bought with my money?"*

Your Self (calmly recalling your perception that s/he's

wounded, not *rude, insensitive, stupid, or bad* as your Inner Critic declares): *"You sound really resentful."* (metatalk observation, not a criticism).

Ex: *"Me resentful? Just because you and your jerk lawyer walked off with 90% of our assets after you dumped me, you think I shouldn't feel resentful?"*

Your Self: *"You're* enraged *because you feel the whole process and the outcome was so unfair, and you feel justified in resenting me and the process."* (this is empathic listening, *not agreeing!*)

Ex (false-self confused by your calm *respectful* response): *"Well, uh . . . you finally got* that *right."*

Your Self: *"Pat, I can't change your perception, or rewrite our history. I'm truly sad you're burdened by so much anger and resentment."*

Ex (distrusting your sincerity): *"Yeah, sure. And pigs can fly, too . . ."*

Your Self: *"It's hard for you to trust that I mean that."* (More genuinely compassionate empathic listening.)

Ex (again startled by your reaction): *"Of course it is, after all the crap you've dumped on me."*

Your Self (repressing _ your *Inner Critic's* reflex to counter-blame, and _ your *Warrior* subself's instinct to fight): *"Pat, I need to know what you need from me so you'll start to bring down your resentment over past things we can't change. Our kids really need us to get past this together. I know you want what I want for them . . ."* (clear, net assertion, based on your common co-parenting objectives).

Ex (startled and disoriented): *"Huh? You want to know what I need?" That's a first!"*

Your Self: *"I guess you haven't heard that question from me very often, have you?"* (genuinely respectful affirmation, not defending, explaining, groveling, attacking, giving examples, . . .)

Ex: *"That's for sure . . ."*

Your Self: *"Well, I mean it now. What can I do to help lower your resentment of me and our past, so we can give the kids the* *best we've got in the present?"* (reasserting what you need, with a genuine =/= attitude. You calmly *expect* an attacking response now).

Ex: (angrily) *"Well you might start by admitting that you gave me the shaft! I know this is too much to hope for in my lifetime, but you need to apologize to me."* (Suspicion confirmed: your ex seems ruled by an angry Guardian subself, and isn't aware of this).

Your Self (calmly, with steady eye contact): *"You're saying you'd let go of some hurt and resentment at me if you heard me acknowledge how hurt you've been by my actions."* (Note: this an empathic-listening "hearing check," not a question. This tests to see if you're hearing your ex mate clearly, vs. *agreeing* with them! Hearing checks sets the stage for possible problem-solving.)

How does this compare to how you usually think, feel, and respond to a resentful co-parent? If some protective subselves say *"This is unreal. I could never talk like that . . .",* I challenge them: why not? In teaching effective communication, I've seen *many* average adults learn to think and speak like this. With commitment, patience, and willingness to learn from trial runs, you *can* communicate like this, and then teach your kids how to do so! Project 2 *[Satisfactions]* offers concepts and effective tools, and shows you the way . . .

Recap

Divorce and stepfamily formation commonly cause significant *resentments* in adults and kids. This chapter focuses on intentionally reducing excessive resentments to improve caregiving cooperation in your multi-home family. Doing this starts with six basic premises, including the proposal that *resentment* is a normal emotional response to feeling *disrespected*. You read a perspective on resentment, and three criteria for deciding if a "resentment (disrespect) problem" merits adult action. The chapter built on these to propose six options for reducing "significant resentment" problems in and between your kids' several homes.

Based on the concepts in Part 1, key options are _ putting your Self in charge, _ digging down below concurrent surface "problems" to identify your co-parents' *real* needs, and _ using the seven Project-2 skills together to fill those needs—starting with self and mutual *respect.*

Before moving on, pause, breathe well, and recall why you read this chapter. Can you describe what you needed? Did you fill your need/s? Note your options of _ journaling now about reactions to what you just read, and _ taking a body/mind break.

We've now reviewed key options for spotting and reducing the real problems under excessive *anger* and *resentment* among your co-parents. Working together on these worthy projects can help you to reduce a related surface barrier common to many divorced families and stepfamilies: household and personal *boundary* clashes and violations. Do your co-parents have any significant "boundary problems" with each other now? What would each of your other co-parents say? Do your kids know how to resolve *boundary* problems effectively yet? Did your parents?

15) Assert and Enforce Your Boundaries

Define and Negotiate Your Roles and Rules

Years ago, I married a lovely woman and her two young custodial daughters. We naïvely bought a house about five blocks from her former husband and his new wife and step-daughters. We all attended the same church, and we all had cordial-enough relations. Soon after our honeymoon, I came home from work to learn that earlier, my wife's ex husband had walked unannounced into our house to see his girls. When their mom confronted him, he seemed startled: "But Lisa (their daughter) told me on the phone to just come in and see the house." He grudgingly agreed to call or at least ring the bell before doing that again. We had to define our *boundary* with him. Part of this limit-setting involved telling five year old Lisa she could not invite her Dad to "just come on in."

I'll bet that you can describe instances where you and any new partner had to confront an intrusive or unaware ex mate or stepparent on some unacceptable behavior. Multi-home boundary-setting ranges from minor to highly conflictual. If, how, and when you all do it will affect your success at building a high-nurturance family together, over time.

This chapter offers options for effective limit-setting and enforcing with an uncooperative, aggressive, or hostile co-parent or relatives. It complements the prior two chapters on using co-parental anger constructively, and asserting needs for *respect*. We'll review some basic concepts, and illustrate typical surface "boundary" problems with "difficult" co-parents. Then we'll explore and illustrate likely *true* problems, and propose some action options. Boundary problems between co-parents and stepkids are explored in the next book in this series and at [..Rx/spsp/disrespect.htm]. Let's start by reviewing some . . .

Key Concepts

See how these compare to your definitions:

Relationship *boundaries* are the personal dividing lines (limits) each co-parent and child draws between acceptable and unacceptable behavior in _ themselves and _ other people. In high-nurturance relationships and families, key boundaries are clear, stable, mutually respected, and enforced. *Enforcing* a boundary means taking some action that affects a person whose behavior exceeds the limit. Co-parents' behaviors, relationships, roles, and comfort levels are regulated by personal, marital, parental, and household boundaries, or lack of them. A boundary (values) *conflict* occurs when one co-parent or relative disagrees with another's boundary (Chapter 16). A boundary *violation* happens when a co-parent or relative willfully or accidentally disregards an adult's or child's boundary.

Your boundaries range from implied and vague to specific and explicit. Effective boundaries include *consequences*, which may be clear or not, spontaneous or predefined, overt or covert, and be enforced timidly, respectfully, or aggressively.

Aggression occurs when a person puts their needs and worth ahead of another's openly or covertly. Alternatives are *assertion* (my needs and yours are equally valid and important now), and *submission* (your needs and worth are more important than mine now.) Willfully ignoring another person's boundaries is aggression, and sends the toxic R(espect)-message "I'm 1-up here."

Hostility is an aggressive attitude or behavior that seeks to inflict discomfort on another person directly or indirectly. Most co-parental legal disputes result from, and/or cause, significant hostility in one or family members (Chapter 18). Situational or chronic co-parental hostility, e.g. "harassment" and "Parent Alienation Syndrome," is *always* a sign of false-self dominance and ineffective communication.

Intimidation is a form of inner-family or interpersonal aggression based on threat and fear of (boundary violation and) significant discomfort or harm. Some wounded co-parents need to fill their needs by intimidating ("controlling," or "manipulating") adults or kids, because they don't know or trust other alternatives. The most effective response is respectful *assertion* vs. fighting or fleeing.

Assertion is the learnable mental/verbal skill of _ identifying and stating your current true needs _ in a way that another person can clearly hear and understand (vs. agree with) them. Effective assertion [..02/assert.htm] requires _ your Self to lead, _ a genuine "=/=" (mutual respect) attitude (Chapters 2 and 8), _ *awareness* of surface vs. true needs (p. 44), and _ fluency with [..02/awareness.htm] and empathic-listening skills [..02/listen.htm].

Communication is any perceived behavior that causes a significant emotional, mental, or physical change in another person. All behavior, including communication, is powered by human *needs*—emotional, physical, and/or spiritual discomforts. Effective communication occurs when _ all people get their main true (vs. surface) needs met well enough, _ in a way all people feel good enough about. Effective boundary setting and enforcement requires you to communicate effectively. See Chapter 7 and [H].

Boundary violations, conflicts, and consequence-enforcements, usually cause *surface* (secondary) problems. These are symptoms of unrecognized true needs. The learnable Project-2 skills of *awareness, clear thinking,* and *digging down* help to unearth your co-parents' and kids' true needs to help resolve surface "boundary problems."

Problem-*solving* is the mutually-respectful (=/=) process of _ identifying participants' current true needs, and _ brainstorming viable options that fill them well enough. Popular co-parent alternatives are *fighting, arguing, explaining, manipulating (controlling), pleading, rehashing, defocusing, avoiding, repressing,* and *withdrawing.* Defining mutually acceptable boundaries and consequences always involves inner-family and interpersonal negotiating and problem-solving. *Compromising* is a kind of good-enough problem solving where all people get enough (vs. all) of their current needs met.

A confrontation occurs when someone (like you) intentionally asserts their needs, perceptions, or values (like a boundary or consequence) to another person who dislikes, misunderstands, fears, or disagrees with them. Confrontations are inevitable in any relationship, and can range between _ direct (face to face) or indirect, _ respectful or not, and _ effective (need-filling) or not. Confrontations can occur internally (among your subselves), and between co-parents and/or kids. People controlled by false selves often fear or enjoy confrontations, and/or see them as "bad," vs. normal, inevitable, ways of building harmony.

Denial is _ subselves' unconsciously repressing an emotion, awareness, perception, or memory (*"I am not from a low-nurturance childhood!"*), or _ consciously thinking or declaring that some personal trait or behavior is not true (*"I did not lie to you about my herpes."*)

We'll use these basic concepts to form some action-options for setting effective family boundaries and enforcing them. First, let's review some . . .

Typical Surface *Boundary* Problems

See if you and any partner want to reduce current stressors like these:

You feel an ex mate or their new partner is too *aggressive, controlling, manipulative, invading, punishing, uncooperative, harassing,* or *intimidating.* In other words, you feel another co-parent violates your personal, marital, or household boundaries too often; and/or . . .

You ask an ex mate or stepparent to cooperate in reducing any of the team-building barriers in Part 2 of this book, and s/ he "resists" (refuses, postpones, argues, whines, or deflects). S/He may _ deny resisting and/or _ blame you (*"You're too unreasonable and selfish!"*) The larger version of this is refusing to cooperate with you on doing the 11 co-parent projects in [A]. And . . .

You feel you've tried your best to invite or persuade the other co-parent to change their attitudes and behaviors, and "nothing works."

These problems can manifest in many *surface* ways, like these . . .

_ repeatedly asking your child or a relative for personal information about you, despite their discomfort;

_ showing your pre-teen child x-rated videos, despite your strong objection;

_ sarcastically criticizing you as a parent or a person to your child or others;

_ spreading rumors about you and/or your new partner that cause dissention and conflict;

_ "lying" frequently, and denying or justifying that (Chapter 9);

_ frequently sending the child-support check late, and justifying that, playing "victim," or ignoring your protests;

_ insisting on telling you personal information about themselves that you don't want to hear;

_ rejecting or disparaging your new partner, and denying that s/he is a legitimate stepfamily co-parent;

_ repeatedly changing child-visitation arrangements at the last minute;

_ repeatedly making intrusive or threatening phone calls, or refusing to answer the phone or let a child do so;

_ agreeing to do (or not do) things, and not follow through; and . . .

_ often ignoring the terms of the legal parenting agreement, and refusing to discuss that.

Three *Real* Problems

I propose that any combination of these "boundary issues" are symptoms of up to three underlying *real* problems: one or more "difficult" co-parents . . .

is ruled by excessively fearful or shamed subselves, and doesn't know that yet (Chapters 5 and 6); and . . .

isn't using the Project-2 problem-solving skills _ among their *inner* family members (subselves), and/or _ with you other co-parents (Chapter 7). Common symptoms are you adults _ blaming each other, _ fighting vs. problem-solving, _ often defocusing, and _ overfocusing on the past or the future. A third possibility is that these two factors are promoting . . .

you and/or your "difficult" co-parent being unable to grieve key losses from your childhood, divorce or mate-death, and/or re/marriage and co-habiting.

The way you react to behaviors like these depends on your history, your perceptions, and who leads your inner family. Let's re/look at this last factor now.

I suspect the idea of "personalities" (like yours) being an inner family of *parts* or *subselves* is new to you. Recall: your true Self (capital "S") means your innately skilled inner-family leader. A "false self" is two or more other subselves who distrust and disable your true Self, and make well-meaning, impulsive, unwise decisions. Here's a comparison of how a false self and a true Self might handle a boundary violation with an ex mate or stepparent:

Your False self and True Self in Action

To better understand the examples below, first _ re-scan Chapters 5 and 6, and study the Web articles at [..01/ innerfam1.htm], [..01/ifs-faq1.htm], [..pop/f+t_selves.htm], [..01/gwc-meaning.htm], [..02/listen.htm], and [..02/ assert.htm]. Deferring or ignoring this suggests your Self is disabled now.

Relationship partners like you form assumptions and expectations about how the other will think and react in certain situations. *You* means the dominant members of each person's inner team of subselves. Thus *your subselves* will probably have evolved reflexive (semi-conscious) **responses to a co-parent's** violating your boundaries in ways like these . . .

_ "blowing up" (yelling, name calling, threatening, demeaning);

_ sulking, obsessing, and badmouthing (blaming/attacking);

_ numbing out, ignoring your feelings, and "making the best of it" (submission);

_ self-distracting from (avoiding) your hurt, resentment, and anger by using chemicals (including food), overworking, working out, or "getting depressed;"

_ asking a child (or someone) to tell their other parent/s to stop violating your boundary;

_ punishing (hurting) the "difficult" co-parent in some way, and denying, justifying, or flaunting that;

_ praying humbly for patience and tolerance;

_ whining and complaining to others, and avoiding confrontations with the boundary-breaker/s;

_ sending mixed messages like *"I need you to stop that (but I won't do anything if you don't)"*;

_ guiltily relishing wonderful fantasies about awful things happening to this person "some day;" and . . .

_ generalizing critically: reminding the "trouble-maker" angrily or scornfully of all the rotten things they've done over the years.

Responses like these *always* send insulting, incendiary "I'm 1-up!" R-messages, which degrade your co-parenting relationship/s. That lowers your family nurturance level, which scares and wounds your inner and minor kids.

Your true Self will typically react to a boundary conflict or violation by doing things like . . .

_ carefully weighing the overall situation against your current and long-term needs and goals,

_ collecting opinions from other subselves and trusted people,

_ making and reviewing your personal Bill of Rights (p. 514), and . . .

_ deciding *specifically* . . .

* what you need from the other co-parent/s now (define your boundaries);
* when and how to assert your needs;
* how to handle probable reactions without giving in, defocusing, over-explaining, or attacking; and . . .
* what *specific* action s/he'll take if the other co-parent ignores your needs and preferences (dignity).

Then your Self would follow through, by . . .

_ asking your other subselves to counsel and observe, but not interfere; and _ firmly asserting your boundaries and consequence when the other person can *hear* them. S/He means this respectfully as clear, factual *information*, not a threat, manipulation, or retribution.

The ex mate's or stepparent's ruling subselves may need to perceive your assertion and consequences as a threat, attack, or attempt to control them. Your Self compassionately accepts that s/he can't control this, and coaches your other subselves to not over-react.

From these sketches, who usually determines how you react to setting and enforcing your boundaries—your Self, or other subselves?

Example

Here's how typical *inner* and outer dialogs would go for each type if, say, your ex spouse insists on changing visitation arrangements at the last minute, despite your repeated requests not to.

The scene opens with your ex calling 10" before s/he's due to pick up your daughter to say she can't visit because "something's come up." Expecting your daughter Anne to be with her other parent, you're dressed and ready to go to dinner with a special friend. This has happened several times in the past months, with your ex offering insincere apologies, and/or giving no explanation at all. You're on the phone now, Annie is listening, and you're controlled by your . . .

Your False self Governs

All of your subselves "speak" (cause thoughts, images, and emotions) at once . . .

Inner Judge: *"What an insensitive, selfish JERK Pat is!"* (Italics are your thoughts)

Catastrophizer: *"We'll have to put up with this for the rest of our life. We'll never be able to have good social times again!"*

Peace Maker: *"Now c'mon, everyone, calm down. Let's not get into a . . ."*

Rager/Warrior: *"Oh shut up, for God's sake. You are such a pitiful doormat!"*

Righteous One: *"Remember, 'act not in anger . . . ' ";*

Perfectionist: *"People have to do what they commit to!"*

People Pleaser: *"Agh! Sal (friend) will be so disappointed and inconvenienced! We'll send a card, after calling now and explaining that . . ."*

Scared Child: *"Please: is something really bad going to happen? Did I do something wrong?"*

 # True Self: *"Wait a minute! What we need to do now is . . ."*

Judge and **Rager** together (distrustful): *"Be quiet! We'll handle this."* They use your lungs and larynx to say *"I am so sick of you being so unorganized and irresponsible, Pat. You always disappoint the kids, and you make it impossible for me to have a social life. I can't believe how selfish you are! I've already made plans to . . ."* (Implied disrespectful R-message: "I'm 1-up")

Pat's subselves (false self): *"Well, here we go again (sarcastically): demanding your way without ever considering what I need. You didn't even bother to ask why I can't pick Annie up,* *did you? How do you know my leg isn't broken? You really don't give a damn about me, you're just focused on your wonderful social life."* (R-message: "No, *I'M* 1-up!" The old fruitless power struggle is starting to replay.)

Anne looks at you, alert and anxious . . .

Inner Good Parent: *"I have to tell poor Annie what's going on without bad-mouthing Pat . . ."*

Inner Critic *(sarcastically): "Way to go! How come you let Annie get whipsawed by this jerk? She keeps getting hurt, and you never stand up to Pat. Some 'parent'. You are* pathetic."

Shamed Child: *"I know, I know. I'm <u>so</u> stupid and* worthless . . ."

Comforter: (generating a vivid image of a heaping bowl of chocolate ice cream) *"Wouldn't this taste* really *good right now? C'mon, let's . . ."*

Judge: *"So what's your excuse this time, Pat?"* (condescending voice tone implies "I'm 1-up") . . .

It took less than 10 seconds for all this to happen. Neither true Self is in charge, and neither co-parent is _ *listening,* _ aware of their inner and interpersonal processes, or _ intentionally problem-solving. This example omits Pat's inner chaos, which is just as confused and raucous as "yours" above. *There are probably over 20 combined active subselves here, including Annie's inner Worried Girl, Critic, Hurt Girl, Angry Girl, Numb-er, and Good Girl!*

What might this inner and interpersonal exchange have sounded like if your true Self was solidly in charge? You're on the phone, and Pat's just said *"Something's come up."*

<u>Your True Self Leads</u>

 # Your Self: "So you're not coming? Pat, this is really short notice!"

Pat's subselves (false self): "Yeah, I know. I'm sorry, but a key client called just as work was ending, and my boss wants a report on her desk at 9 AM tomorrow. She's a real hardnose, and I have to get on this tonight . . ."

Inner Judge: *"What a jerk! Pat probably wants to drink beer rent a sleazy video."*

Historian: *"This is the fourth time in three months that Pat's cancelled at the last minute."*

Practical Adult: *"We better call Sal right away, and let Annie know what's happening . . ."*

Perfectionist: *"This is wrong! People have to honor their commitments!*

 # Your Self (forcefully): *"Pat, when you tell me of changes at the last minute like this, I feel disrespected, hurt, frustrated, and really irritated!" I need you to give me more warning. I also need you to get more assertive with your boss. I feel like she's running my and Annie's life, because you choose not to draw the line with her."* This is a *need* assertion, not a boundary, because there's no consequence defined if Pat doesn't comply.

Pat's false self (defensively, voice rising): *"I suppose you never had things change suddenly without being able to control anything, eh? Remember all the times you. . . ?"*

 # Your Self (calmly): *"You need me to acknowledge that you couldn't forecast this client's call and the demand from your boss."* (empathic listening, not *agreeing*.)

Pat's false self (feeling *heard* and affirmed): *"Yeah! (pause) I don't like last minute changes either, but I really don't have a choice here."*

 # Your Self: *"I see it differently, Pat. At the least, you could confront your boss factually with your having an important commitment with your daughter, and then brainstorming a compromise. You also could have called me right away, and given me more warning of your choice to change our plans, so I could change mine."*

Inner Critic and other subselves: *"Way to GO!"*

Doubter: *"Easy does it! You know how unreasonable Pat can get if s/he feels guilty . . . Are you overdoing the confrontation thing here?"*

 # Your Self: *"No. This has to stop."*

Pat's false self: *"Well, I'll try. Look, I really have to start on this report, so would you tell Annie that I'm sorry that . . ."*

Inner Judge: *'Well, I'll try': what an indecisive weasel!"*

 # Your Self: *"Two things before you go. I need to sit down with you and work toward changing visitations. I'm not sure you're aware how often you abort, and how that affects Annie and me. I know you don't have time to talk right now. Please check your schedule and call me about whether you can work on this with me next Tuesday or Thursday night, OK?"*

Pat's false self: *"You want to change visitation* again? *You know we've been over and over this. I don't think we need to change anything."*

 # Your Self: *"I know we've struggled. This is* <u>my</u> *need, Pat . . ."*

Inner Judge: *"Tell Pat how unreliable and irresponsible s/he's been!"*

 # Your Self: *"Not right now. That'll only cause defensiveness, and get in the way."* Reasserting to Pat: *"Will you let me know if you can talk next Tuesday or Thursday: say 8:00 or so?"*

Pat's *true* Self: *"Yeah, OK. . . . You said there were two things?"*

 # Your Self: *"Yes. I'd like you to explain to Annie what's happened here. While you do that, I have to call Sal on the other line and say that our dinner's off."*

Pat's false self (feeling guilty and defensive): *"OK, put her on . . ."*

 # Your Self (holding out the phone): *"Annie, Hon? Our plans have to change. Come and talk, OK?"*

Notice the themes in this vignette:

Your subselves trusted your Self to handle this unexpected situation. They were relatively quiet, and didn't interrupt, babble all at once ("mind churning"), or take control, as they needed to in the first example above.

Your true Self . . .

_ was aware, respectful, direct, and assertive (R-message: "=/=") vs. aggressive ("I'm 1-up") or submissive ("I'm 1-down").

_ knew and used several of the seven communication skills, both internally and with Pat and Annie: awareness, empathic listening, and assertion.

_ intentionally stayed focused on the present and near future, and on problem-solving, not allowing other inner-family members to blame, complain, name-call, or rehash the past. S/ He was assertive with Pat *and* your protective (narrow-viewed) *Inner Judge*, which avoided escalating into an argument or a power struggle;

And with the counsel of your *Practical Adult* subself, your Self . . .

_ stayed balanced, and attended the immediate needs of you, Pat, Annie, and Sal; and your Self . . .

_ laid the groundwork for declaring your boundary about aborted visitations with Annie by calmly proposing (vs. dictating) several specific times. Between now and the meeting, your inner family will need to debate what options you and Pat have, clarify what you need, and what consequences you'll need to assert if Pat's governing subselves chooses not to change.

Can you imagine having this kind of Self-managed conversation with your "difficult" co-parent (or kids)? Notice your inner voices now. Which of your subselves are speaking? You *can* learn to do this, with patience, awareness, and practice.

Action Options

Use Resources [D and E] to give you initial feedback on the degree to which you and other co-parents are wounded. Then own your responsibility to act respectfully on your findings—e.g. work at self-healing and reducing your half of other Part-2 teamwork barriers, over time.

Periodically review Chapters 1 through 6 to keep your perspective clear as you declare and enforce your boundaries. Remind each other that doing this "boundary work" is one of several steps in your Project-10 goal of evolving an effective co-parenting team to nurture each other and your kids. Project 10 is one of your 11 concurrent family-building projects [A].

Guideline: your current level of adult teamwork directly reflects the harmony or dissention among your respective *inner* teams of subselves. Coach your subselves and family members to work together patiently: your rewards *will* accumulate and compound over many months!

Learn more of the many adjustment tasks your minor kids each face following separation and re/marriage [F]. Encourage all other co-parents and family supporters to do the same. Then use your awareness to guide and motivate you all to provide the adult support your youngsters need. Also create or upgrade your co-parental "job descriptions," ideally based on a consensual stepfamily mission statement (Project 6). See [C] and *Stepfamily Courtship* or [..10/job1.htm].

If you're ambivalent or weary working on relationship and personal projects like these, nourish your motivation by vividly picturing how you want your grown children to remember these years of their lives. Imagine asking them when they're in their 30s or 40s for their honest feedback on how well all you co-parents did your co-parenting jobs "back then."

As you upgrade your communication effectiveness with your family members (Chapter 7), give special emphasis to digging down to your true needs [..02/dig-down.htm], effective assertion [..02/assert.htm], each co-parent's personal rights (p. 514), and empathic listening [..02/listen.htm]. Based on genuine mutual (=/=) respect and true-Self leadership, these will help you make and enforce effective family boundaries! Help each other _ stay aware of communication blocks (p. 518), and _ tailor the tips on p. 528 to stay on course. Also . . .

Keep your perspective: help each other separate and prioritize your core barriers (p. 109), and work on them one or two at a time. Coach each other to remember and *use* the differences between _ surface and true needs, and _ first-order (superficial, temporary) and second-order (lasting core attitude) changes.

Stay focused on the present and near-term future, rather than the past or the far future, and help each other maintain two-person "awareness bubbles" As you negotiate.

As =/= *teammates* with common goals [C and D], grow effective strategies to avoid and resolve _ values and loyalty conflicts and _ relationship triangles. (Chapter 16). And you can choose to . . .

Seek effective inner and outer supports for yourself (Project 11) and to stay balanced (Project 12), as you improve your boundaries and reduce your other high-nurturance barriers. Stay alert for chances to affirm your and other co-parents' efforts in daily increments, including your learning from "mistakes." Genuine praise and appreciation helps break the blame > counterblame cycle that blocks your team-building. Affirmations can sound like *"Thanks for hearing me out, just now / . . . being on time again / . . . coming to the school conference . . ."*

Review and apply the principles of effective child discipline in *Build a High-nurturance Stepfamily* or [http://sfhelp.org/10/discipline1.htm]. They're about setting clear, respectful boundaries and consequences with *anyone*, including distrustful or overwhelmed subselves, kids, and relatives!

Help each other _ apply the wisdom of the Serenity and Gestalt Prayers (p. 24), and _ avoid black/white (two-option) thinking, as you evolve effective boundaries. As you do, enjoy expecting them to become automatic, even in major conflicts!

Did you realize how many choices you have toward evolving effective co-parental boundaries? These are suggestive, not exhaustive. Pause for a minute to get a sense of where you stand with these ideas now:

I feel a mix of calm, centered, energized, light, focused, resilient, up, grounded, relaxed, alert, aware, serene, purposeful, compassionate, and clear, so my Self is probably present now. (T F ?)

I feel _ no interest in, _ ambivalent about, _ very motivated to put the ideas in this chapter to work for our family beginning this week.

Recap

Relationship *boundaries* are limits adults and kids set un/ consciously with our subselves (*"I will eat no pizza this week."*) and with others, to maintain our self respect, security, and comfort level. Boundaries separate behaviors we will and won't tolerate without a significant consequence. (*"If you choose to drink more than two beers, I won't drive with you."*)

Adjusting to divorce and complex stepfamily mergers requires your co-parents to set new boundaries and consequences with yourselves, your kids, and each other. If an ex mate or stepparent violates your boundaries too often, you may focus on *surface* problems like those on p. 290. At least two *true* problems underlie any of them: significant false-self dominance (loss of true Self), and _ unawareness and/or ineffective use of the seven problem-solving skills in Project 2—particularly effective assertion and *listening*.

Over time, your shared dedication to Project 1 (Chapters 5 and 6) can greatly improve the first of these. Proactively developing your communication skills (Chapter 7 and [H]), improves the second. Then, setting and enforcing clear boundaries with your "difficult" co-parent/s works better if you intentionally reduce other core barriers (p. 109), for your and your kids' *long-term* benefit. You *can* do these, if _ your Self is in usually charge and _ s/he guides your other subselves to shift from seeing the "intrusive" or "insensitive" co-parent as *bad* to respecting him or her compassionately as *dignified, worthy,* and *wounded*. This second-order attitude shift does *not* mean you have to accept or endure the other co-parent's toxic behaviors!

Premise: *you* are responsible for your own comfort level. Putting this responsibility on (blaming, pleading with, or manipulating) another co-parent is ultimately self-defeating, and injures your kids. Suggestion: refresh yourself on Chapters 2 and 3, and (re)read [..02/dig-down.htm] monthly, for a year. (Notice your inner voices!)

Take a comfort break now if you need one. Then join me in exploring ways to master two of the most common divorced family and stepfamily *surface* problems . . .

16) Loyalty Conflicts and Triangles

Clarify and *Live by* Your Priorities

Larry's parents were strict about "table manners" when he was a boy. So insisted that his two sons say "please" and "thank you" at the dinner table, "take small bites," "chew with your mouth closed," and "finish what's on your plate."

After divorcing and several years of non-custodial fatherhood, Larry started dating an alluring single Mom. He was "uncomfortable" with Laura's indifference that her pre-teen daughter Mandy "ate like a wild animal," but didn't comment. "It wasn't my place to correct Mandy," he said later.

They remarried, and Larry moved into Laura's busy home. One night soon afterward, the new stepfather said "*Mandy, I think it'd be better if you chewed with your mouth closed.*" Startled, his wife and stepdaughter both stared at him. The girl turned to her mother. "*Do I have to, Mom?*" Laura was suddenly in the middle of what may be the most common *surface* stepfamily stressor: a **priority or loyalty conflict**. Any answer to her daughter's question, including "*I don't know,*" risked displeasing someone important to this woman.

This vignette illustrates a potential cause of re/divorce. in a series of conflicts, who's needs rank higher with a bioparent—their mate's or their child's? Routine and special conflicts *force* re/married bioparents to choose, over and over again. If Larry perceives Laura siding with her daughter too often (despite his protests), he feels disrespected and "second best."

Until Laura settles her own ambivalence (*inner*-family conflict), she'll grow resentful and/or anxious that Larry "makes me choose." Until young Mandy quells her abandonment fear, she'll automatically test and retest to see who her Mom prefers, how much power she (Mandy) has in the new family (*"Who's in charge here?"*), and whether she's lost status (priority) with her Mother.

If Laura and Larry don't admit and compromise their underlying *values* conflicts over "good parenting," a related stressor will surely appear in many forms: a **PVR relationship triangle**. Larry is the "**Persecutor**," criticizing Laura's parenting values and Mandy's behaviors. Mandy feels like a "**Victim**," being judged and forced to change; and Laura will unconsciously assume a "**Rescuer**" role, defending her daughter (and her mothering values and behaviors).

If Larry grouses about this to a friend or co-worker who sympathizes (rescues), *he* can feel like the Victim (*"I feel ignored"*), and Laura and Mandy are cast as his Persecutors. If Laura's father or Mandy's biodad side with Laura or Mandy, *they're* assigned Persecutor roles, Larry becomes the Victim, and may seek or welcome a volunteer Rescuer. Each person can be in a different role in several triangles at once.

From 23 years of consulting with over 1,000 typical divorced-family and stepfamily members, my hunch is your adults and kids are experiencing a dynamic series of stressful _ values and _ loyalty conflicts, and _ relationship triangles. If you co-parents don't evolve an effective strategy to deal with these three toxic *surface* problems, your re/marriage/s are at real risk and your nurturance level will drop sharply.

This chapter _ offers perspective on these three stressors and _ illustrates them; _ summarizes common *real* problems underlying them, and _ suggests action-options and resources for resolving the latter. The chapter is equivalent to the one on Project 9b in *Build a High-nurturance Stepfamily* [xlibris.com]. To get more from this chapter, I suggest that you all read and discuss four Web articles first, as partners: [http://sfhelp.org/09/project09.htm], [..09/lc-intro.htm], [..09/triangles.htm], and [..10/kid-needs.htm]. If you can't access these, key points are summarized below.

To further prepare, raise your awareness of each of your co-parents' recent priorities. Bookmark this page, and thought-fully fill out [..08/priority.htm] and Resource [L]. As you do, notice how you feel, and where your thoughts go. Do you know why you're reading this chapter?

Perspective

Needs are emotional, physical, and/or spiritual discomforts. Needs can clash between _ two or more subselves (an *inner-family* conflict) or _ persons (interpersonal conflict). Most stepfamily relationship "problems" are concurrent _ internal and _ interpersonal conflicts. So to *really* resolve minor to major "stepfamily conflicts" you need to identify and fill each person's true (vs. surface) needs (p. 44) as partners. Do you co-parents and kids *do* that now?

Besides conflicting needs, co-parents like Larry and Laura—and your adults and kids—experience inevitable clashes over . . .

Values, Preferences, and Beliefs

A *value* **is an opinion on** _ how important something is (its priority), or _ whether something is good or bad, right or wrong, or acceptable or not. Family loyalty conflicts (below) are a type of values conflict. A *preference* is which of several things brings you more comfort or pleasure. A *belief* is something you cur-rently feel is *true* or *real*. Building a new stepfamily requires your three or more co-parents to admit and resolve *hundreds* (thousands?) of minor to huge values, preference, and belief conflicts as you merge your biofamily cultures, traditions, and assets [..09/merge.htm].

The emotional intensity of complex, dynamic mixes of these

disputes in and between your homes ranges from annoyance to rage. Your minor kids depend on you adults to help them resolve their current values conflicts, and teach them how to do that for themselves.

Because these inevitable conflicts are more emotional than logical, they require your co-parents to _ admit (vs. deny or ignore) them, and _ *want to* compromise (agree to disagree), to _ promote personal and household harmony and stepfamily bonding.

The intensity and complexity of your values, preference, and belief conflicts depends partly on the size of your multi-generational stepfamily, which may include a hundred or more people (p. 437). In my experience as a stepfamily consultant since 1981, under 5% of typical courting or troubled co-parenting couples like Laura and Larry have evolved an effective strategy to resolve family-merger conflicts over these three stressors. Have you yet?

When your subselves or family members clash over needs, values, preferences, and beliefs, they often experience a related invisible stressor. Family therapist Murray Bowen and followers dub them . . .

PVR Relationship Triangles

Persecutor—Victim—Rescuer triangles involve three roles, like those in a drama. The person in the *Persecutor* role says or does something that causes the *Victim* significant discomfort. Typical Victim-role players don't know how to identify and assert their boundaries, needs, and opinions, so they explain, defend, collapse, cry, whine, plead, submit, defy, freeze, counterattack, or flee. Then a *Rescuer* feels compassion or alarm for Victim, distrusts that they can care for themselves, and comes to their aid loudly or covertly. The Rescuer may feel responsible for the Victim, and/or identify with their 1-down ("underdog") role.

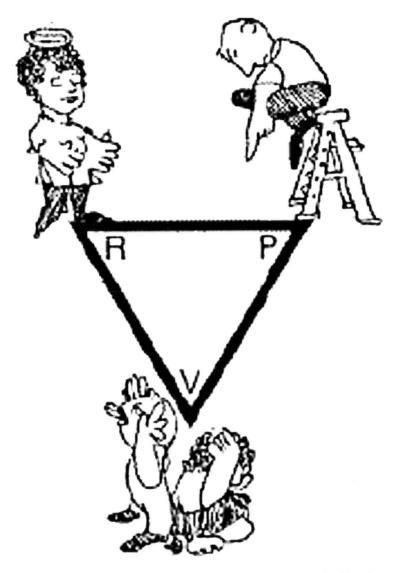

PVR triangles are caused by _ unawareness, _ ineffective communication, and _ each person's (or subself's) primal needs for *respect, comfort,* and *safety (security)*. Your triangles are stressful because none of the three PVR roles fill these core needs well enough. Adults or kids in the Persecutor and Rescuer roles are 1-up ("*I'm right, and/or my needs, opinions, and/or values are better or more important than yours.*") People assuming the Victim role feel 1-down (rejected, vulnerable, powerless, disrespected, and discounted).

From this view, PVR triangles might be better labeled *respect* conflicts. Most divorces partially result from, and cause, triangles. Parental re/marriage often generates a web of new triangles, specially if co-parents _ aren't aware of them, and _ have no cooperative strategy to resolve them and related values conflicts. This seems to be our current U.S. norm. Have you ever seen a class or program on "Avoiding and Resolving Relationship Triangles"?

My experience as a therapist since 1981 is that typical co-parents (like you), and many health, education, clergy, and family-law professionals, are unaware of _ these triangles and what causes them, _ their effects, and _ how to avoid or resolve them. That means your minor kids remain ignorant of these four things. That promotes _ false-self dominance, _ stress and lower family nurturance, and _ passing on the unawarenesses and wounds to future generations.

Reality check: did your childhood caregivers teach you about relationship triangles and how to "de-triangle"? Did your mate's early caregivers? Do your kids know about triangles now? "No" is *normal*—and you have some work to do!

Most (all?) family relationship triangles come from, and generate . . .

Loyalty (Priority) Conflicts

Here are some key points from Project 9b in *Stepfamily Courtship* and [..09/lc-intro.htm]:

A loyalty conflict involves a person or subself "in the middle," feeling s/he must choose between two or more other important people or subselves. Any choice, including choosing not to choose, will displease one or more of the others, and risk disapproval, hurt, and possible rejection or retribution. In this chapter's opening vignette, Laura was "in the middle."

Loyalty conflicts are inevitable in all families and groups. When they happen, *no one is wrong or bad*! Stepfamily loyalty conflicts are more common and complex than those in intact biofamilies, because they involve *your* or *my* ex mate or child, not *our* child. Often, courtship politeness, tolerances, and "good behavior" mask deep loyalty conflicts that emerge only after re/wedding and cohabiting.

All members of your multi-generational divorced family or stepfamily can feel impossibly caught "in the middle." Kids and many adults have no language to describe how these stressors feel, or what the person needs.

Typical stepfamilies are riddled with loyalty (priority) conflicts *for years* over things like names, titles, assets, roles, rules, expectations, pets, holidays and celebrations, customs traditions, memories, genes, food and meals, parenting, and dwellings. The surface details differ, but the underlying dynamics are universal.

Bioparents *must* often choose between pleasing or supporting themselves (acting on their integrity), their child(ren), or another co-parent. The hardest choices are between biokids and a new mate. Choosing not to choose frustrates *everyone*, and usually causes guilts, hurts, resentments, and anxieties. Childless adults and non-steppeople can only guess at how agonizing this feels to typical biomoms and dads.

Loyalty conflicts are specially likely and intense if a dad or mom hasn't resolved their divorce-related guilts (Chapter 10) and shame (Project 1). I recall one agonized biofather's creative attempt to resolve this impossible choice. He demanded of his new wife *"Can't you see that you're* <u>all</u> *'first' with me?"* The inference was that *she* was at fault for feeling rejected and hurt by his siding with his kids. He was ruled by guilty and fearful subselves who couldn't face having to displease one someone he loved. Neither mate knew this consciously.

Unaware and shame-based (wounded) stepparents often feel significantly guilty that they "make" their bioparent-mate choose. They may also feel guilty and confused at the "unreasonable" jealousy" they feel over their mate's attention to their minor or grown kids, ex mate/s, and/or relatives. This is specially so if their (defensive) mate labels the stepparent *unreasonable, selfish, oversensitive,* or *childish.*

New stepkids of any age are instinctively motivated to *test* their family status, power, and security by forcing each bioparent to demonstrate (vs. say) *"Who comes first with you now?"* They'll keep testing until they feel sure of the answer. This need for security can be prolonged or amplified if the child hasn't had time or encouragement to grieve their *many* concurrent family changes (losses). This also happens if _ their other bioparent or a powerful relative discourages their accepting the new steppeople (a family *membership* or *inclusion* conflict).

Similarly, non-custodial bioparents need to learn (test) whether a new stepparent will _ *want to* nurture their custodial or visiting kids well enough, and _ respect the bioparent's dignity and parenting role, needs, style, and values. If your (step)kids' other bioparent lacks true-Self leadership and effective communication skills (Chapters 5-7), her or his actions will probably trigger loyalty conflicts and relationship triangles in and between your homes. Bio and step relatives may detach or take sides, adding new conflicts and triangles, and hindering co-parenting teamwork and bonding. **Reality check**: do you think any of your divorced-family or stepfamily adults know what you're learning here? What does that mean for you all?

Because stepfamily roles are usually alien to everyone, a key cause of loyalty conflicts is co-parents' (and supporters') lack of _ awareness and _ empathy. For example, a childless stepparent may understand, but has never *felt*, the agony of choosing between a stepfamily mate and a child. Unless their mate has kids too, the bioparent often can't *feel* what the stepparent is experiencing. Often neither can empathize with what minor kids, ex mates, and grandparents are feeling, and vice versa. If you mates aren't aware of your feelings, or lack the vocabulary to describe them, achieving even intellectual understanding of loyalty-conflict stress can be hard. This is specially likely for survivors of low-nurturance childhoods who aren't recovering.

Note that well-meaning clergy, counselors, and other human-service providers can unintentionally become part of, and/or promote, loyalty conflicts and triangles. They can be seen as, or choose to be, Rescuers, which implies some of your family members are Persecutors and Victims. Fetuses, infants, dead ancestors, media "authorities," and past or present mentors can also be active members of triangles and loyalty conflicts. (*"I feel torn between what Ann Landers, my Mother, and my mate say."*)

The roots of your loyalty conflicts are _ unawareness of feelings and these concepts (above), _ psychological wounds, and _ core emotional-spiritual *needs*. As with conflicts over values, preferences, and beliefs, **attempts to resolve loyalty conflicts and triangles with *logic* or persuasion won't work**. This implacable reality usually breeds mounting confusion, distrust, self-doubt, and anxiety (or numbness), specially if your co-parents are ruled by false selves.

When viable compromises don't appear, your conflicted bioparents can avoid guilt by accepting the paradox that putting their re/marriage first over their kids' current needs really puts their kids first by protecting them long-term from another family-breakup trauma. This is specially true if there are young "ours" kids involved.

Finally . . .

Untended loyalty-conflict discomforts accumulate. Until you mates _ admit these normal stressors without blame, and _ forge an effective co-operative strategy to resolve them, the hurt, distrust, resentment, disrespect, anger, anxiety, and guilt they cause will mount in your adults and kids as months go by. As they grow, withdrawals and avoidances are likely to increase, and gradually one or more of your co-parents may lose hope there's a viable solution. This is specially true if any of you deny or ignore _ that you're a *step*family [..03/identity.htm], and/or _ your mounting personal and re/marital stress. Such denials are clear symptoms of co-parent unawareness and false-self dominance.

The bottom line: your inner-family harmonies and stepfamily relationships (including re/marriages) *will* inexorably be stressed by conflicts over _ values, _ beliefs, _ preferences, and _ loyalties; and by _ related, interlocking PVR relationship triangles. These stresses will accumulate until you co-parents intentionally develop cooperative =/= strategies to resolve them together.

Your resident and visiting kids depend on you grown ups to find a workable solution to these normal stressors, and help them manage theirs. Adult children and relatives probably need with loyalty conflicts and triangles too.

Back away from these ideas for a moment. Breathe well, stretch, and notice your thoughts and feelings. Did you know what you just read before you began this chapter? Do these ideas make sense to you? Do _ each of your other co-parents and _ key supporter/s, including professionals, know them?

Typical Symptoms

How can you tell if significant PVR triangles and loyalty conflicts are present? Common symptoms include . . .

One or more of your co-parents feels too ignored, unheard, blamed, and/or discounted (disrespected) by someone in your multi-generational stepfamily, including a child, mate, ex mate, or key relative.

One or more of your co-parents withdraws, and/or becomes increasingly "indifferent" to child and family welfare.

A spouse feels that their mate is over-indulgent and/or over-allied with a biochild, an ex mate, or a relative. ("*You pay more attention to your sister than you do to me.*")

You co-parents accumulate "endless" arguments over the welfare or behavior of *your* or *my* kids, ex mates, and/or relatives. [*"You just won't face the (my) truth, Chris."*] The fights may accelerate addictions, and cause court suits.

One or more of you feel increasing anxiety, frustration,

and discomfort over _ normal family events like meals, child visitations and school events, home chores; and/or _ holidays, vacations, and family celebrations. You may feel similar emotions over your attempts to discuss and resolve these discomforts together.

One or both mates feels _ a "wall" or gulf is growing between them, and _ efforts to reduce it aren't working. A related symptom is feeling significantly drawn to another empathic adult emotionally or sexually. Another is sleeping in different beds, or losing sexual desire and shared pleasure. Another is indifference.

More common symptoms of unresolved triangles and loyalty or values conflicts:

A resident or visiting minor child is increasingly "acting out" at home and/or school, and your best efforts aren't reversing that trend. "Best efforts" may include working with a school or independent counselor.

A resentful, weary stepparent decides silently or vocally stop nurturing one or more stepkids, and/or a stepchild starts hinting, asking, or demanding to live with their non-custodial parent.

One or both mates experience significant physical/emotional discomforts, like migraines, stomach upsets, rage explosions, sleep disorders, or "depression" [..Rx/mates/depression.htm].

And/or . . .

One or more co-parents avoid spending time together and/or discussing "family things." S/He may admit, justify, minimize, or deny this, or argue about it and blame another co-parent for it.

Each of these are real *secondary* stressors that hinder co-parental teamwork and family nurturance. I propose that dynamics like these are *symptoms of . . .*

Four *Real* Problems

Underneath any triangle or clash over loyalties, preferences, values, or beliefs are . . .

Ignorance of _ these concepts, _ stepfamily norms and realities, and _ effective communication skills; and . . .

Unseen false-self dominance, causing excessive shame, guilt, anxiety, and distrust; plus . . .

A mix of the other core barriers on p. 109, specially co-parental disrespect and distrust; and perhaps . . .

Blocked grief in one or more co-parents or kids.

The solutions to these epidemic American problems are simple to describe, and challenging to implement in your busy lives. Build a shared commitment to:

_ **Courageously do Project 7,** if you haven't already. Honestly done, this will disclose whether one or more of you chose the wrong people to re/wed, for the wrong reasons, at the wrong time. If you did, the rest of these options probably aren't relevant.

If you partners made three *right* re/wedding choices, then co-commit to . . .

_ **Do co-parent Project 1** together (p. 430), to empower you mates to meet and harmonize your inner families under the wise guidance of your true Selves and Higher Power/s. Your odds of mastering and avoiding toxic loyalty conflicts and triangles go *way* up if your true Selves are solidly at the helm.

_ **Do Project 2** over time, to increase the effectiveness of your problem-solving *any inner*-family or stepfamily need-conflicts.

_ **Do Projects 3 and 4** to help you forge realistic stepfamily relationship and role expectations. **Learn** about (1) stepfamily norms and realities, including _ values and _ loyalty conflicts, and _ PVR relationship triangles; and (2) their current impacts on you all.

_ **Do Project 5** together, to help you identify and free up and blocked grief.

_ **Help each other assess** whether divorce-related guilts

are biasing any bioparent toward their kid/s over your re/marriage. If so, evolve an intentional strategy to reduce your guilts, over time. This requires your Selves to be in charge, and fluency in all seven Project-2 skills. See Chapters 7, 10, and 11 for perspective and options.

The odds that these steps will provide real relief rises steeply if you mates also **co-commit to Project 6**: evolve a meaningful stepfamily mission statement [C], and *use* it to evolve workable co-parenting job descriptions, based on assessing what each of your minor kids really needs [F].

If you began these Projects during courtship and kept at them, this will make sense to you. If you're new to the Projects, see Resource [A] for an overview. Then go to [http://sfhelp.org/12-overvw.htm] and follow the links for perspective, concepts, resources, and suggestions. The guidebook for the first seven projects is *Stepfamily Courtship* [xlibris.com, 2001]. See *Build a High-nurturance Stepfamily* [Xlibris.com] for the five post-re/wedding projects.

Later projects require progress on earlier ones, so I encourage you to tackle them in order. If your true Selves aren't usually leading your inner families, none of the other projects are likely to be very effective.

Examples

Have you ever argued with someone over religious or spiritual beliefs? If so, I suspect you know how impossible it is to persuade someone to change core beliefs with "facts," logic, or manipulation. *Good parenting* is a kind of religion, in the sense that it's a set of beliefs and behaviors based on accumulated experience, others' opinions, and faith in long-term outcomes.

One co-parent says "*Child discipline works best if you use* punishment *(cause discomfort).*" The other parent says "*I disagree: that causes guilt, hurt, resentment, and defiance; and it teaches the child that using power and causing pain is the way to solve problems. I think natural consequences are much bet-*

ter, in the long run." Partners ruled by false selves will be un-aware of being caught up in "being right" and "not caving in." They will argue, sulk, withdraw, blame, or punish each other for not agreeing.

Mates guided by their true Selves will find a mutually-re-spectful ($=/=$) way to compromise this values conflict without anxiety, guilt, or resentment: "*OK, I'll go along with occasional punishments, if you go along with some natural consequences . . .*" If this example resonates with you, see [..10/discipline1.htm].

A loyalty-conflict + PVR triangle example:

Stepmother Nina scowls and says to her husband David, "*Your son is unbelievably insensitive and self-centered. I say 'Hi, Nate,' and he just walks right by me without a look or a sound. I'm getting real tired of being treated like a piece of furniture unless he wants something.*" The unspoken add-on is "*Do you care enough about my feelings (me) and our mar-riage to confront Nate on this?*"

If this couple is progressing on the several co-parenting projects above, they might continue like this:

David: "*That really hooks me. I feel criticized as a bad Dad, protective of Nate, and like defending me and him. Nate's the Victim, you're the Villain (Persecutor), and I'm the White Knight (Rescuer).*" Helpful first steps in "de-triangling" are to _ admit the triangle, and _ name who's in what role, *without blame.*

Nina: "*You're right, Hon. I don't want a triangle either. I think what I really need here, first, is to feel you can hear that Nate's behavior hurts and frustrates me. Then I need you to want to do some win-win problem solving with me. I want to honor Nate's needs too.*" Nina uses the communication skills of _ awareness, _ clear thinking, _ digging down to her true needs, and then _ assertion [H] to _ avoid forming a triangle, and _ to ask David *respectfully* to problem-solve this loyalty conflict.

If he's of like mind, they'll focus together and brainstorm a win-win-win compromise, vs. fight, deny, or adopt triangle roles.

Success is more likely if they both know _ stepfamily realities, norms, adjustment tasks [G], and _ stepkid's typical needs [F]; and _ share "=/=" (mutual respect) attitudes.

Do you feel you and your beloved could learn to think and talk like this example? Could all your nurturers? You can *if* you commit to doing the projects together, starting with helping each other to empower your true Selves.

Five Options

Keys to avoiding or resolving _ values and _ loyalty conflicts, and _ triangles are:

Help each other to _ replace false-self dominance with the wisdom of your true Selves, and _ keep a long-range, big-picture attitude.

Learn together _ what each of these three re/marital stressors is, and _ how to spot them in your relationship and co-parenting homes. Reading and discussing this chapter is a great start! Reality check: try describing each of the stressors now to another adult or an older teen ("Wanna hear something that'll help you get more of your needs met?").

Develop a vocabulary to describe and discuss these conflicts and triangles together. Typically this will include terms like *values conflict, need, loyalty conflict, communication-need conflict, surface problem, effective communication, (relationship) triangle,* and *Victim, Persecutor, and Rescuer* roles. Use your *awareness* skill to distinguish between an adult or child and a *role* they're choosing. Thinking or saying "*I am a victim, and you are a persecutor*" promotes 1-up and 1-down guilt, shame, and defensiveness, not win-win (=/=) problem-solving. It sounds and feels different if you say without blame "*I'm choosing to play the Victim role, and I'm putting you in the role of Persecutor here.*"

Learn and use the seven communication skills in Project 2 [H] to resolve your inner and mutual conflicts and triangles *as teammates.* You two can do this if _ your Selves are in charge, _ you each genuinely feel "=/=" ("*Your needs and dignity are*

just as important to me as mine are."), and _ you learn to distinguish between surface problems (need clashes) and the *real*
problems underneath them.

Get and stay clear on your priorities, as partners. If your
Selves are in charge, you'll agree that usually putting your personal wholistic health (inner-family harmony) first, your re/
marriage second, and all else third, actually puts your kids first
long term by protecting you all from eventual psychological or
legal re/divorce trauma.

Once you're underway with these four, **then give priority
to teaching the kids and other adults** in your stepfamily homes
(and elsewhere) about them, and invite them to join you! Forg-
ing effective strategies to combat values and loyalty conflicts
and related PVR triangles is a *stepfamily-wide* project!

Does this all make sense to you? If so, is there anything
blocking you and your co-parents from committing to these
five steps, if you haven't yet? If you're not sure, review p. 109.

Recap

Perhaps the most common and vexing *surface* problems
between divorced-family and stepfamily co-parents are conflicts over parenting and financial _ *values* and _ *loyalties* (relationship priorities). These usually combine to produce stressful _ Persecutor-Victim-Rescuer (PVR) *relationship triangles.*
Without _ awareness of these three stressors and _ a consensual plan to resolve each of them, your co-parents' needs to
feel *understood, accepted,* and *respected* by each other are likely
to feel increasingly unfilled. That promotes many secondary
relationship problems.

This chapter _ describes these three relationship stressors,
_ illustrates common personal and stepfamily symptoms they
cause, _ proposes the *real* problems (unfilled needs) beneath
them, and _ suggests what your caregivers can do to fill your
real needs: commit together to doing co-parent Projects 1
through 6, and reduce the core barriers in Part 2 together, over
time. The chapter closes with five over-arching suggestions.

Reminder: reducing these three stressors is Project 9b in the guidebook *Build a High-Nurturance Stepfamily.*

Status check: Take stock of where you are now:

Now I feel some mix of *calm, centered, energized, light, focused, resilient, up, grounded, relaxed, alert, aware, serene, purposeful,* and *clear.* That means my true Self is probably answering these questions. (T F ?)

I can clearly describe _ a *values* conflict, and _ how we caregivers can best resolve ours now. (T F ?)

I can clearly describe a _ *loyalty* conflict, _ why they're toxic to our multi-home family's harmony and growth, and _ how we should resolve our loyalty conflicts now. (T F ?)

I can clearly describe a "PVR relationship triangle," _ how to spot them, and _ what our co-parents should do to avoid or dissolve them now. (T F ?)

I can describe _ the difference between a *surface* relationship problem (symptom) and the *real* problem underneath the it; and _ I can name the three *real* needs underneath typical loyalty conflicts and PVR triangles. (T F ?)

I can describe (at least) each of the first six co-parent projects proposed in this re/divorce-prevention series, and _ I know where to find more detail, options, and resources on them now. (T F ?)

I believe each of our co-parents _ will answer "True" to each of these items now, and _ is willing to discuss and cooperatively apply these ideas in our relationships and linked homes; *or* _ I know how to promote this effectively among our family adults. (T F ?)

Take some time to notice your thoughts and feelings now . . . What are you aware of?

Another common *surface* problem in many U.S. divorced families and stepfamilies is a co-parent appearing "indifferent", "uncaring," or "uninvolved" in their kids' lives. Often that's not an accurate indication of what's *really* going on. If you have one or more psychological or biological parents that aren't "active" caregivers, the next chapter offers perspective and suggestions.

17) If a Co-parent is "Uninvolved"

Is it Disinterest or Inner Wounds?

Children of divorced parents suffer when their noncustodial parent seems "uninterested" in them. The implied message to them is "You're not important to me." This was a shaming reality young Sarah McLean was growing up with, as her biofather Ted showed little consistent interest in how she was doing. [http://sfhelp.org/example.htm].

This chapter explores your options toward reducing three *surface* teamwork barriers: your ex mate seems indifferent to _ you and/or _ a minor biochild, or _ your *partner's* ex seems to ignore your stepchild/ren. Each of these fosters loyalty conflicts and relationship triangles, and lowers the nurturance level in your kids' several homes. See Chapter 15 for setting and enforcing boundaries with an *over*-involved non-custodial biomom or dad. For conflicts over child support, see Chapter 19.

Premise: the *real* causes of post-divorce relationship cut-offs are usually co-parents' combined _ inner wounds, _ unawarenesses, and _ ineffective communications. These are often amplified by ex mates' disrespect, distrust, and unhealed guilts. Chapters 8-10 suggest specific things you can do to reduce each of these.

If you want to reduce stress related to an ex mate's "indifference," you have a surprising range of options.

Prepare

Promote positive change by doing things like these:

Even if you're not "spiritual," use the theme of the Serenity Prayer often, to help you discern and accept what you can control, and what you can't. (p. 24)

Adopt a 10 to 20-year outlook, and make co-parent team-building a steady high priority.

Develop your awareness of high-nurturance family traits [D], and use that and Resources [F and G] to evolve a (step)family mission statement [C].

Use the ideas and resources in Parts 1 and 2 to gradually improve any of the three surface barriers above.

Periodically remind yourself and any partner of the difference between first-order (surface behavior) and second-order (core attitude) changes. To encourage your "indifferent" ex mate to grow their co-parenting involvement, you'll need to *want to* make one or more second-order changes . . .

Assess whether you or your ex are in protective denial of significant inner wounds. Start with Resource [E], and use the resources in the Project-1 guidebook *Who's* Really *Running Your Life?* or at [..pop/assess.htm] to assess *yourself.* Then use Chapters 5 and 6 and these tools to assess your ex mate for significant wounds. Note the possibility that some behaviors of your ex may activate your false self ("*I turn into a different person when I talk to Jamie.*") The reverse may be true of your ex.

If your ex bears significant wounds from a low-nurturance childhood, explore the possibility that these injuries manifest as an inability to care about (bond with) other people [..01/bonding.htm]. Know that people afflicted with this horror typically _ aren't conscious of it, _ deny it, and _ don't know what to about it. A crippled ability to bond usually means they have all six inner wounds (p. 448)—i.e. they're significantly controlled by a false self, and don't know it. Also note that adults and kids who can't bond well have little to grieve when relationships weaken or end. This helps explain why they may seem "cold," "hard-hearted," "selfish," and "indifferent." No, they're tragically *wounded* and *empty*.

Another preparation option you have is to . . .

Change your attitude about your ex from blame, criticism, rejection, or pity (I'm 1-up) to *compassion* for their wounds, unawareness, and limitations. This doesn't mean condoning or ignoring behaviors that have hurt or frustrated you or the kids. Your odds of making this second-order attitude change rise as your own self-love and self-confidence improve, and your and your child(ren)s' divorce and stepfamily grief progresses. As you shift toward a genuine attitude of compassion and =/= respect, your communication will shift, and so will the outcomes. See Chapters 5—7.

Review the Personal Bill of Rights (p. 514), and see if you believe that it applies to your ex and yourself equally. If your Self guides you, you'll see the ex mate as having as much human dignity and worth as you do, *despite her or his behaviors*. You'll also be able to see your situation as "*our* (family) problem," rather than something other co-parent mate must fix. *Your* unawarenesses, and perceived 1-up attitudes and past and/or recent behaviors are probably causing up to half of this teamwork barrier!

In conflicts and impasses, evolve and review a list of the core needs that each adult and child in your family tries to fill every day, including your ex mate. See the example on p. 44.

And you and any partner can choose to . . .

Empathically evaluate whether your ex is blocked in grieving key divorce or other losses, and _ doesn't know that or _ what to do about it. See Chapter 12 for starters. If s/he seems blocked, consider telling her or him non-judgmentally why you think so. Accept that thawing frozen grief is the other parent's responsibility, and is beyond your control. Freeing your own blocked grief and helping minor and grown kids free theirs, *are*! Blocked grief and underlying wounds and unawareness appears to be a common contributor to re/divorce.

If your ex was or is addicted to a substance (including food), an activity, a relationship (co-dependence), or an emotional state, review your options in Chapter 20. Any addiction strongly suggests major inner wounds, and a desperate (unconscious) attempt to self medicate from intolerable inner pain. Addiction signals low family nurturance and *family* pain, *not* a personal moral failing, "weak will," or "character defect." Assess *yourself* and each minor child for the six inner wounds that low family nurturance promotes (p. 448), and do what you can to guard and heal your kids.

Premise: You can proactively choose to change some things about yourself, *without losing your integrity or dignity*, that *may* increase real co-parenting teamwork between you and your and/or your mate's ex. Limitation: if your or your partner's ex is significantly wounded and denies that, her or his governing subselves may stay "uninvolved" no matter what you or the kids do.

Lets add special options for two teamwork barriers, starting with . . .

Your Ex Mate Ignores or Rejects *You*

The symptoms are unmistakable: _ unanswered phone messages and emails; _ silences and curt responses in person, with _ little or no eye contact; _ communicating via writing or third parties (including kids) . . . Behaviors like these send the provocative 1-up R-message "*Your thoughts, feelings, and needs don't matter to me.*" That's being *ignored*. A more hurtful message is: "*I think you're a bad (wo)man / parent / person, and I want nothing to do with you.*" That's *rejection*.

Both are painful *surface* problems which block the nurturing teamwork your minor kids depend on. Neither is likely to improve until *you want to* change some attitudes and unawarenesses. Then your behavior will change, and your ex's *may*. This also applies to you and your partner's ex mate/s.

If you two mutually chose to conceive kids, being ignored or rejected later by your co-parenting partner can painfully cheapen the love and dreams you shared in co-creating a new life. It can also feel like your partner duped you, and/or you deceived yourself. Both promote guilt, shame, and self-doubt.

Special Options

If your child's other parent ignores or rejects you and you want to change that, evaluate six more choices:

Choose to believe that trying to improve relations with your ex mate is a gift to yourself and your kids. It is *not* submitting to, pleasing, or saving your ex, or sacrificing your values. Test the idea that communications are circular. if you change *your* attitudes and behavior, you'll eventually get a change in your ex mate's behavior. You don't have to be a passive victim or martyr, unless your false self persuades you to be.

Honestly own your half of what (you think) caused your divorce. Option: tell your ex, when s/he can really hear you. If you feel guilty about some past behaviors that affected your ex, consider making a genuine apology to her or him *to free yourself.* See Chapters 11 and 12.

Ask your ex directly what s/he's needed recently from you and isn't getting. In particular, ask if s/he feels you _ respect, _ trust, and _ *hear* (vs. agree with) her or him. If s/he's willing to tell you, really *listen* [..02/listen.htm], even if it sounds like criticism. Deepen your awareness and empathy by using the communication skill of "digging down" [..02/dig-down.htm]. Strive for an attitude of genuine compassion and mutual re-spect *for both of you*, rather than blame. Encourage your *in-ner*-family members to not get defensive, resentful, or into self-blame. And . . .

Ask someone who knows you and your ex and you can trust for an honest, objective opinion, what they see about your relationship that may promote your ex mate's ignoring or re-jecting you and/or your child(ren) recently. Do this when your Self is in charge, and *listen* for ideas and *aha's*, rather than defending, explaining, guilt-tripping, focusing on past hurts, or blaming! Finally . . .

Review the legal battles you and your ex have endured together, starting with your divorce. Note that people hire lawyers when they feel _ powerless to get their needs met, _ unheard and disrespected, and _ hopeless and/or exhausted. Unless your legal experiences were genuinely co-operative, you're each probably harboring some residual hurts, resentments, disrespects, and distrusts from them. Unhealed, these can amplify co-parental avoidances and cutoffs. See Chapters 9, 10, 11, and 16.

If you or your ex had an affair that contributed to your divorce, suspect that unresolved reactions to that are contributing to your ex's rejecting you. Consider the attitude that marital affairs usually occur because of one or more of these:

_ **one** or both mates survived low childhood nurturance (deprivation), and the affair is a symptom of unseen false-self dominance and inner wounding. The person initiating the affair was or is unable (vs. unwilling) to bond, give and receive love, or commit; and/or . . .

_ **mates** can't communicate and problem solve effectively, so core relationship needs go unfilled, and one (usually wounded) mate eventually seeks to fill them with another partner; and/or . . .

_ **one** or both mates had unrealistic needs or expectations of their partner, and didn't know it, or couldn't admit it.

Note the themes of these six special options. Because your situation is unique, you may have other useful choices. If you're resistant to any of these options, they're probably the most valuable! Let's look at two of them briefly . . .

Admit Your Half of Prior Divorce/s

First, clarify the scope of what you associate with the term "our divorce": mull [..pop/divorce.htm]. It takes courage and vision for wounded ex mates to do this without blaming, justifying, whining, minimizing, numbing out, playing "if only," and avoiding personal responsibility. If your ex feels you blame him or her for ending your commitment, genuinely owning your part in it *without seeking a payoff* can encourage better co-parenting relations.

If you choose to work at this difficult, rewarding option, I suggest you start with Project 1 to see if your false self has run your half of the relationship *without your knowing it.*

Another option: review the reasons that mates commit to each other [..07/rt-reasons.htm], and see if your false self chose your former partner. For more perspective, read Dr. Harville Hendrix's book "Keeping the Love You Find," and Hal and Sidra Stone's paperback "Embracing Each Other." You may also find some *aha's* in Dr. Deborah Tannen's informative book "You Just Don't Understand." She illuminates male and female differences in priorities and perceptions.

If you're false self is in charge, be alert for (protective) subselves sabotaging this option. If one or more of your zealous inner crew distrusts or fears _ your true Self and _ any good outcome from owning your half of your relationship with your ex, they'll work hard to distract you, distort your conclusions, scare or shame you, or unbalance you toward analyzing, justifying and explaining too much. From life-long habit, most of your Guardian subselves care far more about *your* safety than about your kids' or your ex mate's.

Useful exploration themes are: _ *"What specific needs did I hope to fill by marrying my ex? _ How balanced was I in focusing on my partner's needs, vs. mine? _ Did I unconsciously choose my ex to help resolve old hurts and resentments with my parent/s? _ What was the R-message s/he usually got from me?"* (p. 510).

_ *"How did I approach conflict resolution with my ex— skeptically? haughtily? timidly? _ How empathic was I, usually, to her or his feelings and needs? _ To my own? _ Did I assert my needs honestly and promptly, or bury them and build resentments? _ In conflicts, did my ex feel heard and respected by me, though we disagreed?"* Finally . . .

Stay clear that your goal here is to be genuinely accountable and reduce *unrealistic* ex-mate blame. If your judgmental attitude about your ex moderates (a second-order change), so will your— and eventually their—behavior. Note that the way you *present* your conclusions to your ex will affect how s/he receives you. You can be defensive (1-down), intellectual (no feelings), vague, humorous, ashamed and guilty, or genuine and mutually respectful. You can be open or closed to feedback during or after your sharing. Respectful empathic-listening skill is a great help here! [..02/listen.htm]. Another is learning to give effective feedback on emotional topics [..02/evc-feedback.htm]

Stay focused on why you're doing this (improve nurturance teamwork), rather than how *bad* you were! If your ex distrusts and/or disrespects you, work to improve those first (Chapters 8 and 9).

Clear self examination is hard because of our subselves' protective self-deceptions. Option: hire a professional counselor to help you safely reduce your divorce-related denials, guilts, and misperceptions, and reveal your truth.

In my experience, unseen frozen mourning is often one of several reasons people avoid or reject each other. This is usually a result of _ inner wounds, _ unawareness of the requisites for healthy three-level grieving, and _ lack of inner and outer permissions to grieve. So if you want to shift your relations with your ex)or another person) . . .

2) Assess for Blocked Grief

Your separation and divorce process, and what led to it, have caused you adults and kids major losses—broken emotional/spiritual bonds. Divorce is usually a sign that one or both mates is significantly ruled by a false self. *That* means one or both of you probably doesn't feel safe to move through all three levels of healthy grief.

So your ex's "ignoring or rejecting" you may *really* be dominant subselves avoiding intolerable feelings of hurt, anger, sadness guilt, shame, and remorse that come up when communicating with you. If so, your ex's ruling subselves are avoid-

ing this unbearable blend of emotions, not *you* or your child/
ren!

Part or much of this may be due to the (wounded) ex being
stuck in the *rage* phase of mourning. This often has to do with
repressed childhood anger, and undeveloped inner permission
to express hurt and anger without guilt, shame, or anxiety. If
so, your opportunity is to learn how to keep your true Self in
charge, and your boundaries clear and firm (Chapter 15), when
your ex's false self needs to rage (Chapter 13).

The good news: if s/he's blocked in grieving, that's not your
problem. The bad news: as long as s/he's stuck, you and your
kids must adapt to the blockage's effects, while working to avoid
blaming your ex for unconscious self-protection. We wounded
people don't *choose* to disable our true Selves or get stuck in
our grief. Each of these can be healed, once admitted.

See Chapter 12 and Project 5 (p. 432) for many helpful
resources and options.

We've been exploring your options if your former lover
seems to ignore or reject *you*. A more emotionally-complex
nurturance barrier occurs if . . .

Your Ex Mate "Ignores" Your Child/ren

Are you a single or re/married custodial bioparent whose
child/ren rarely see or hear from their other parent? This section hilights options you have toward _ changing this, or _
accepting and making the best of it.

What's the *Real* Problem?

Start by getting clear on _ what you want to change, _
what's in the way, and _ what you can affect. If your goal is to
have your ex mate *want* more contact with your kids, then your
challenge is to change *your* attitudes and behavior in a way
that _ raises your ex's motivation, and/or _ reduces her or his
discomfort.

Try standing in your ex's shoes. I suspect one or several things may be causing his or her co-parental "disinterest":

your ex mate is so wounded s/he can't genuinely bond—*attach* emotionally and spiritually. If so, pretending to *want* contact with your kids (a double message), will probably evoke confusion, distrust, and frustration. Another possibility is that . . .

s/he feels too much *pain* when she interacts with your kids—e.g. agonizing guilt, sadness, frustration, incompetence, and regret. Often the problem underneath this is blocked grief, which is a symptom of false-self wounds. If you have a new partner, a variation of this is that contact with your kids forces facing that another adult is sharing and shaping your kids' growing-up years. And/or . . .

Your ex is weary of combat, and feels hopeless that you and s/he can ever agree on child-related conflicts. If so, the solution is for you two to *want to* improve your communication skills via Project 2, for all your sakes (Chapter 7). And/or . . .

Your ex is in a loyalty conflict with a new partner who discourages him or her from seeing or talking to your kids or *you*. In my experience, the real problems in this case are _ unseen false-self dominance in both or all you co-parents, _ ineffective communication skills; and _ unawareness of the topics in this book. Another root problem may be . . .

your child/ren's behavior causes too much pain. If they dislike, distrust, fear, disrespect, or don't care about your ex, then spending time with them is hardly fun and satisfying. A variation of this is your ex may not know how to interact comfortably with your child/ren because of inadequate or toxic parenting in their own childhood.

A special barrier exists when a judge rules that your ex's visitations with your kids must be supervised by another adult in a public place, to protect your child/ren. Merited or not, this is demeaning and restrictive, and blocks enjoyable, spontaneous visitations for everyone. Professional counseling for all of you is probably required to sort out your mix of causes and impacts, and promote gradual healings.

A final possibility is your ex's "disinterest" is due to a mix of uncomfortable relationship distractions with you, your kids, and/or other significant people like grandparents. Option: work patiently at reducing your half of the core problems in Part 2, for your own sake. Be open to discovering (vs. expecting) that your efforts over time may make it safer and easier for your ex to *want* more contact with your kids.

Pause and reflect. We've just reviewed some possible *real* causes of your ex mate's "indifference" to contact with your kids. Were you aware of these before you began reading? Do you see any new options?

<u>Action Options</u>

Your choices boil down to: _ identify what you *really* need here, _ accept what you cannot change, and _ work patiently to change the things you can. I propose that you can't change _ the past, _ your mate's wounds, _ local and natural laws, _ your family members' true needs (p. 44), and _ the weather. You *can* affect everything else, including . . .

- how you view your ex mate's "indifference"—i.e. how you define "the problem;"
- your knowledge, attitudes, and behaviors; and . . .
- your kids', relatives' and supporters' knowledge and options.

Fully exploring your options for each of the real problems above would take its own book. Much of that book exists in the volumes in this series and the related Web articles at [http://sfhelp.org/..]. The rest of this chapter hilights some key options and resources.

See which of these seem useful in your situation:

Adjust your expectations. If you've felt stumped or powerless to increase your ex mate's co-parenting involvement, adopt the open "mind of a student," and try *"Maybe I can find a way."* Avoid black/white thinking, and widen your goal from changing your ex mate's behavior to building an effective co-parenting team over time (Project 10).

Review the proposed *real* problems above, and identify those you feel are true in your situation. Focus on improving them one or a few at a time.

Decide how important this problem is to you, in the context of your other short and long-term goals.

Read and apply _ Chapters 1-4, and _ the baseline options above. If you're reluctant or ambivalent, assume that a false self dominates you. Empowering your true Self becomes your highest-payback goal. And you may . . .

Review your motivation and status with your core team-building barriers (p. 109). Confront the probability that *"I am probably contributing to my ex mate's attitudes and behaviors."* Give yourself a "status check" on your attitude and progress with the baseline team-building barriers.

If you have a new partner, invite her or him to take the steps above, and join you in your long-range teambuilding effort. If s/he resists or is ambivalent, cynical, or pessimistic, you have another team-building barrier see chapters 5 and 6, and *The Re/marriage Book* [xlibris.com].

Empathically assess how you've generally reacted to this situation, and new alternatives . . .

_ I silently or vocally criticize and blame my ex, and keep telling him or her what s/he must do. This is probably self-defeating, because it inexorably sends inflammatory R-messages: *"You're wrong and bad, and I'm 1-up."*

_ I pity my child/ren, and overindulge them to offset their hurt. This may stress you all indirectly by fostering loyalty conflicts and relationship triangles. See Chapter 16.

_ I disparage my ex to friends and family (and/or the kids), and justify or deny this. This makes your problem *worse*! Option: learn *why* you do this—e.g. to avoid guilt and shame, and stop it. See Chapters 2 and 10-12.

_ I reassure our kids that their other parent's disinterest is not *their* fault. This is helpful if you don't also blame their parent (or yourself), specially if the kids are developing a shame-based inner family.

_ I make excuses for my ex's actions to our kids. This may be an unintended form of *enabling,* and may cause your kids guilt and self-doubts. Alternatives are to affirm your kids' feelings and needs, be honest about your own, and try and educate your kids factually on the *real* problems in your multi-home family (e.g. Part 2) with compassion, vs. blame.

_ I ignore, defer, or minimize this problem, because it's so painful and confusing. This is understandable, and may change as you review all your options here.

_ I over-analyze my ex's choices and actions, and avoid assertions or confrontations. This suggests that fearful subselves control you, and minimizes the odds that your kids will get all that they need from you caregivers.

_ I dwell on the terrible wounds this (parental disinterest) is causing our kids. This may be a symptom your *Catastrophizer* dominating your inner family and helping to disable your Self. It may also indicate that *you* experienced similar childhood pain. Do Project 1!

_ I obsess about how *I* felt when my parent ignored or abandoned *me.* If this is part of a personal healing (recovery) program, stick to it! If it's not, it's a vivid heads-up that you need such healing. Your protective false self may be avoiding the discomfort of that by over-focusing on your kids and/or ex mate.

Is there a best way for you to react to this complex situation? I propose that your true Self knows the answer. See what s/he thinks about options like these . . .

Acknowledge (vs. deny or minimize) that you feel your ex is ignoring or rejecting your child/ren.

If you feel your ex is significantly wounded (Chapter 5 and 6), consider the possibility that s/he may not be able to form genuine bonds (caring) for some or all other people. Most such people have learned to deny and disguise their wound well, because it's so horrifying and shameful. Reality: if your ex has this wound, reducing it is not subject to will, logic, persuasion, court decree, or demand. Genuine (vs. dutiful or strategic) compassion and empathy *may* help you all adapt to what's possible.

Invite your kid/s to talk, often, about how they *feel*, and what they *really* need (vs. *surface* needs) from their other parent. And . . .

Teach and encourage your child/ren to assert their feelings and needs clearly and directly to their other parent, vs. you acting as their spokesperson. If they're scared to, model and teach them _ their human rights (p. 514), _ empathic listening [..02/listen.htm], and _ respectful assertion [..02/assert.htm] skills.

_ **Be on high alert** for loyalty conflicts and relationship triangles with other family members, and adapt the options in Chapter 16 to fit your needs and situation. Keep your personal and family priorities clear as you do this.

_ **See if** there's a "surrogate parent" (mentor) available who needs to give the nurturance that your child/ren's other parent can't provide now. If there's a local chapter of Big Brothers / Big Sisters of America [www.bbbsa.org/], they can be a wonderful resource!

_ **Work patiently** at Projects 1, 2, 5, and 10 for your and your kids' sakes, inform your ex, and invite (vs. demand) him or her to consider joining you for the kids' sake.

_ **If you're a stepparent** and the "disinterested" parent is your partner's ex; adapt these options to fill your needs, and use them as a framework for supporting your mate and stepkids. The same applies if you're a caring relative or professional supporter.

_ **Periodically affirm** your efforts and progress at all your Part-2 team-building barriers, including this one. A final powerful option is to periodically redefine what you cannot change, and release those things to your Higher Power or "fate."

You have many choices!

Recap

A troubling dynamic in divorced American families is one co-parent seeming to ignore or reject their ex mate and/or a non-custodial child. The media tends to highlight "deadbeat dads," and focus on dollars and legal actions vs. *feelings* and underlying causes. There's also a silent subculture of divorced Moms, who either can't bond because of early-childhood trauma, and/or are deprived of custody for various reasons.

This chapter proposes that such parental "indifference" or "uninvolvement" is a *surface* symptom of the underlying real problems in Part 2. The chapter offers summary suggestions on understanding and adapting to the *true* causes of an ex mate's "ignoring" or "rejecting" their conception partner and/or their kids.

A core premise here is that the ex mate's attitudes and behaviors are usually only half of the (surface) problem. The other half belongs to you and perhaps other family adults. The good side of this is that you have many options to improve your caregiving teamwork over time (within limits), and raise your family's nurturance level.

A common *surface* stressor in millions of divorced biofamilies and stepfamilies takes place in and around family-law attorney's offices and courtrooms. The next chapter offers perspective on these toxic dramas and their impacts, and suggests _ what legal suits between co-parents *really* mean, and _ how to reduce or avoid them.

18) Avoid or End Legal Battles

Find Better Ways to Fill Your *Real* Needs

A large minority of the hundreds of divorcing and re-married couples I've consulted with were struggling with, or trying to recover from, legal fights between two parents. The bitterest fights occurred when one parent charged the other with addiction, child abuse or neglect, preventing appropriate visitation, and/or "brain-washing" a child to reject them. Some conflicts were amplified by biased, aggressive stepparents and/ or relatives.

In 21 years' consulting, I have never met one bioparent or stepparent who thought these legal battles helped to nourish their personal serenity or their long-term family relationships and security. Their comments usually were some version of *"My ex mate just won't cooperate or negotiate (so I have to use legal force)."*

Legal intervention and force is justified to protect (1) a dependent child from co-parental abuse or neglect, and/or (2) a co-parent from harassment or violence from an ex mate. All other disputes between divorcing parents are *far* better resolved, long-term, by self-motivated _ personal healing and _ education.

This chapter proposes typical _ surface and *true* causes of court fights between ex mates, _ long-term problems resulting from them, and _ better alternatives to legal combat.

Typical Surface Problems

For perspective on what follows, re-read the premises in Chapters 2 and 3. One is that most role and relationship "problems" are surface symptoms of unmet true needs. So effective problem-resolution requires conflicted people to _ "dig down" to their true needs (p. 44), _ agree on who's responsible for filling them, and _ use problem-solving skills to do so cooperatively.

Because typical American parents seem to be significantly wounded and unaware of these options, many (you?) hire lawyers to force solutions to *surface* impasses like these . . .

Divorce causes and property settlements;

Ex-mate aggression and harassment (boundary violations);

Child visitation, custody, financial support, health, education, or religious practices. Extreme cases can includes a parent kidnapping a child, or threatening that.

Alleged child abuse and/or neglect, sometimes because of alleged _ parental addiction, _ "mental illness, and/or _ "immoral (sexual) behavior" with a new partner.

Allegations that a parent is maliciously biasing a child against the other parent. ("Parental Alienation Syndrome").

The terms of, or compliance with, a legal parenting agreement.

A custodial parent moving out of state.

A grandparent claiming their rights to see or talk with a grandchild are being violated.

Combinations of these cause concurrent . . .

Secondary Surface Problems

. . . like these:

The parent initiating the legal suit becomes the *Persecutor* in a **relationship triangle**, and kids and/or the other co-parent assume Victim roles. The attorneys, judges and related professionals become Rescuers and/or Persecutors. Compound relationship triangles and **related loyalty conflicts** (Chapter 16) *add* family stress, and inhibit problem solving.

Legal fights are financially expensive. This often adds new resentments, anxieties, and conflicts between parents, attorneys, and others over "money." These conflicts are *always* surface symptoms. See Chapter 19.

By personality and role, **lawyers are aggressive and combative**. They're motivated and paid to *win*, which guarantees that both co-parents are going to feel attacked, and one or both—and any allies—will feel like *losers*. *Embattled parents can conclude* that one or more lawyers, including a court-appointed Guardian ad Litem (child's attorney) and/or a "biased" or "ignorant" judge are significant parts of "the problem." This can lead to new problems over firing and hiring attorneys, and/or arguing with *the local legal system to change jurisdictions or assigned judges. These are effective ways of avoiding the real problems below.*

Another common secondary surface problem is . . .

Parents, attorneys, or judges may call for **expert psychological evaluations** of kids' mental health, and/or parental stability, sobriety, and caregiving competence. These expensive and often embarrassing formal evaluations by clinical strangers *always* raise parents' (and often kids') anxiety, insecurity, resentments, and weariness (or determination). They often increase hostility between affected relatives, including stepkin. Defensive parents and attorneys can charge that the evaluating clinicians are biased, incompetent, and/or unethical, which adds to the mayhem. Fees for these forced professional evaluations add to surface financial conflicts, which increase the core problems in Part 2.

Typical family-law attorneys, judges, mediators, and child psychologists have little or no practical training in stepfamily norms and realities. Though legally or clinically competent and well-intentioned, these unaware (and often wounded) professionals often create legal rulings based on *biofamily* norms *and short-term* family outcomes. Because these rarely address the real issues below, such **well-intentioned, distorted rulings** often *increase* the scope and duration of divorced-family and stepfamily stress.

Another common secondary stressor in stepfamily situations can be . . .

Stepparents are affected in many ways by ex-mate legal fights. From allegiance, self-protection, and/or moral concerns, they **often amplify or create related loyalty conflicts and relationship triangles**. These can increase "the other (bio)parent" feeling ganged up on, misunderstood, blamed, and attacked. This *increases* their motivation to use legal power to righteously defend themselves and "win," which prolongs the divided family's toxic attack > defend > counterattack spiral. Also . . .

Prolonged, bitter, and/or sequential court conflicts between ex mates often cause **cynicism about our legal system**, which may foster pessimistic, cynical adults and kids. Kids learn that adults use legal force to get their needs met, rather than admit and resolve the real problems below.

An overarching secondary surface problem can be **emotional and mental overwhelm** from the turbulent, complex mix of primary and secondary stressors like those above. When false-selves rule, this overwhelm can promote desperate, impulsive decisions or indecisiveness; defocusing or numbness; frustration and rage, and/or depression. These promote *more* stressors, like generalized anxiety or anger, lower job or school performance, psychosomatic health problems, relationship breakdowns, and addictions.

Do you see your situation here? If so, I propose that _ *none* of these are your true problems, and _ as long as you co-parents focus on these surface stressors, they will *increase* your long-term personal, re/marital, and family discomfort. I assume you wonder *"Then what are our* real *problems, and how can we resolve them?"*

Before reading my opinion, I encourage you to read about digging down to true problems in the Project-2 guidebook *Satisfactions* (xlibris.com), or the several Web articles at [http://sfhelp.org/02/dig-down.htm]. Then see if you agree with these . . .

Four *Real* Causes of Legal Combat

I hope this will look familiar by now. If no parent or child is in clear, significant danger now, protect your kids from the *long-term* toxic results of legal conflicts by shifting your efforts to . . .

1) Assess for, and heal, **significant psychological wounds** in each of your co-parents (and any legally-combative relatives). Starting points: Chapters 5 and 6, and the Project-1 guidebook *Who's* Really *Running Your Life?*

2) Banish **unawareness of, or confusion over, each of the topics in Chapters 1-3**, and how they apply to your unique situation. Each of you co-parents can commit to eliminating a keystone unawareness by learning to communicate effectively— Chapter 7. Your kids depend on you adults to show them how to do this! Use these as foundations to . . .

3) Work intentionally and patiently at helping each other _ admit and _ reduce your web of **core co-parent teamwork barriers** (p. 109). Do this for your descendents' sakes, if not your own.

Another factor that usually amplifies the affects of these three stressors is . . .

4) Uninformed advice. Typical relatives, friends, human-service providers (including lawyers and judges), and media producers aren't aware of these three core problems or the mosaic of concepts in Chapters 1-3. Their well-meant opinions and suggestions can mislead and distract you co-parents from resolving the three interactive problems above. This promotes the core problems in Part 2, and increases weariness and hopelessness. As you co-parents _ free your Selves to lead your inner families and _ gain education and awareness (e.g. Parts 1 and 2), you'll automatically discern and reject uninformed advice, and guard your kids from them.

Status Check: If you have had, or are now having, legal disputes with an ex mate, your descendents need you to assess whether these four core stressors are hindering your internal and co-parental teamwork:

I feel a mix of calm, centered, energized, light, focused, resilient, up, grounded, relaxed, alert, aware, serene, purposeful, compassionate, and clear, so my Self is probably in charge now. (T F ?)

I _ understand the concept of surface and underlying true problems, and _ I agree that our legal battles are surface *symptoms* of the four true problems above. (T F ?)

I have honestly evaluated _ myself for the six inner wounds (Project 1), and _ am proactively working to heal any significant false-self dominance now. (T F ?)

I have _ read Chapters 5 and 6, and _ am using relevant options in them to adapt to any significant wounding in my ex mate/s now. I am _ actively working toward replacing scorn and resentment for them with compassion, while _ asserting my co-parental needs and boundaries. (T F ?)

I _ have studied Resources [H-L] or the guidebook *Satisfactions*, and _ am intentionally growing my fluency with the seven Project-2 communication skills now. (T F ?)

I am actively studying and applying relevant items in Chapters 1-3 to improve my knowledge and awareness for my and my kids' sakes now. (T F ?)

My partner (if any) would answer each of these items "T(rue)" now. (T F ?)

I _ have respectfully encouraged my ex mate/s to read this book, and join me and any new partners in healing and building our long-range parenting teamwork for our descendents' sakes. If not yet, _ I intend to do this in the next two weeks. (T F ?)

I'm committed to doing everything I can to avoid increasing our family stress and lowering our nurturance level by invoking the legal system to resolve our co-parenting disputes. (T F ?)

If you answered "F" or "?" to any of these, you have some work to do!

Four Options

Based on the above, you can choose to promote long-term co-parental teamwork by _ intentionally healing from past legal fights, _ working to end current fights, and _ avoiding new ones. You have many alternatives . . .

Your odds for attaining these goals rise if your Self is in charge, you keep a steady, long-range view, and you're applying the ideas in Chapters 1-3 toward building the best co-parenting team your circumstances allow. If these aren't true for you yet, I suggest working on them first.

Heal From Past Legal Fights

If your legal divorce process was significantly antagonistic, or you've had rancorous legal fights since then, you parents probably have some residual resentments (blame), guilts, and regrets to release, and losses to mourn. If so, these add to your mix of the co-parenting blocks on p. 109.

Begin by affirming the specific long-term benefits to you and your kids of healing your half of these residual stressors. Common payoffs are increased self-respect and serenity, improved co-parenting teamwork, and reducing or avoiding expensive legal combat. These strengthen re/marriage, and raise your family's nurturance level.

Another key is whether you see this as *my* healing project, or *ours*. Can you see you two ex mates as dignified, wounded, unaware parenting (vs. marital) partners who each love your kids and want to nurture them? Do you *want* to value your ex spouse's needs, feelings, and dignity as equal to your own, despite major disputes? If you don't yet, shift your efforts to applying Chapters 5-12.

What specific stressors do you want to release? What blocks you from doing so? Your answers probably depend on which of you initiated past legal combats. If you can approach this as *our* healing project your targets probably include some or all of these:

A **reciprocal-blame** mindset: "*The legal trauma was your fault! "No, it was* yours!*"* I suspect you *both* caused the litigation because of unseen false-self dominance and unawarenesses. Rancid blame may extend to relatives or friends who sided "against me." Usually reality distortion and toxic shame and guilt block admitting your half of this. If so, see Project 1, and Chapters 5, 6, and 10 for perspective and options.

Disrespect: your legal combat probably added to prior reasons that you scorn or pity each other, as persons, mates, and/or parents. Within the larger goal of regaining respect and compassion for each other, see if there are specific legally-related actions each of you took that your *Inner Critics* delight in reviewing. Focus on them one at a time, and see if Chapters 8 and 11 offer effective ways to let go of scorning or pitying yourself and/or your ex.

Resentment and anger. Do you periodically replay your favorite court-related outrage/s and nourish old resentments? If so, how does that help build the teamwork your kids need from you both? If you "can't help it," a false self surely rules your inner team. See Chapter 13 and Project 1.

Distrust: my compassionate hunch is that both you parents increased various distrusts of yourselves and each other because of past legal combat. If so, it may help to identify specifically what you distrust/ed, and then clarify specifically what you need now toward (re)building teamwork. See Chapter 9.

Reality distortions: it's common for wounded co-parents whose hostility or guilt goes public (as in a courtroom) to misassume, misinterpret, and subjectively misjudge the attitudes, motives and behaviors of their opponent/s—specially if there's little real *listening* going on. If you parents can reduce the barriers above enough, you'll be able to review what you thought was happening, and correct major distortions. The target here is not to blame, vindicate, or justify, it's to remove sources of ongoing resentment, disrespect, and anger and improve communication effectiveness for all your sakes.

Another common barrier to healing from prior legal battles
is . . .

Blocked grief: litigation between parents *always* causes or
amplifies important losses (broken bonds) for all involved family
members. Option: meditate on what you each lost because of
each legal dispute (resource: [..05/abstract-loss-inv2.htm]), and
use Chapter 12 and Project 5 *[Stepfamily Courtship]* to assess
how you each are progressing with your three grief-levels. Do
the same for each of your children, and perhaps key relatives.
Blocked grief signals false-self dominance, and often promotes
"endless" resentment, anger, and avoidances, and harmful compulsions like addiction.

The results (decrees, orders) of past legal fights may contribute to these healing targets also—e.g. unwanted and "unfair" visitation, custody, and financial constraints. If so, who's
responsible for reducing such stressors, and what prevents you
from doing your half, for your kids' sakes?

Besides healing prior legal injuries, you partners share the
option to . . .

Learn From the Past

You can _ try to "forget" your court fights, _ endlessly
obsess about them, or _ *learn from them.* To do the latter, your
Self must be free to lead "your inner orchestra" (personality).
Learn *what*? Alone or with objective support, reflect honestly
on core questions like these . . .

Q1: "Specifically how did my ex and I each cause lawyers
to get involved?" Dig down below generalities like *"We just
couldn't agree"* (ask *"Why not?"*) to specifics like *"Because s/
he and I don't trust or respect each other, and neither of us can
listen to the other without getting angry (losing our true Self)."*
Recall: this is about learning, not blame!

Q2: *"Was my Self initiating or responding to the legal action? How do I know?"* To answer this, you'll need to have
progressed well on Project 1. You'll also be able to answer *"Was*

my ex mate being controlled by a false self, in initiating or responding to our legal conflict?" See Chapters 5 and 6.

Q3: *"How did the process of the court conflict effect each of our minor and grown kids, specifically?"* (Option: list benefits and stressors.) See Resource [F] for perspective.

Q4: *"What did each of our minor and grown kids learn about interpersonal conflict-resolution from their perception of our legal fights? Is this what I want them to learn?"*

Q5: *"All things considered, was the time, effort, and money we both put into our legal fights a net plus in my and our kids' lives? Would I do it again?"*

Q6: *"How would my ex answer these?"*

Meditation, journaling, and/or exploring questions like these with an objective counselor can help grow your awareness of what your legal conflicts and their outcomes mean to you all *long term*. That clarity can help motivate you to avoid similar long-term stresses, wounds, and expenses that new legal combat will cause you all.

Pause and reflect on your reaction to what you just read. If your self-talk is some form of *"Yes, but . . .",* or *"I can't (or won't) . . .",* I doubt that your true Self is making your decisions . . .

End Current Legal Battles

Pause, breathe well, and reflect: do you feel some mix of calm, centered, energized, light, focused, resilient, up, grounded, relaxed, alert, aware, serene, purposeful, compassionate, and clear now? If so, read on—your Self is probably leading your inner crew. If you don't feel this, or "anything," I respectfully suggest you shift to reading *"Who's Really Running Your Life?"* What follows will only have practical benefit if your Self is making your decisions!

If your or your child's wholistic health is in clear, current danger (a subjective judgment), and a former spouse won't respect your boundaries or can't responsibly protect your child, then qualified legal intervention may be the best short-term choice. Otherwise, I suspect . . .

. . . the surface reasons for your court battle are not the *real* reasons (above), and . . .

. . . one or both of you parents is ruled by a false self, and . . .

. . . you're both too distracted and upset to weigh the toxic *long-term* personal and family costs of legal combat against the imagined short-term gains.

Legal aggressions and decrees imposed by uninformed strangers *always* increase co-parental distrust, disrespect, guilt, hostility, frustration, and family disharmony. Parental legal suits corrode empathy and compassion, hinder future cooperation, and often *increase* the toxic blame > counterblame cycle you're trying to avoid or end.

The emotional and financial impacts of current legal fights will detract significantly for many years from the co-parenting teamwork your minor kids urgently need. Legal fights will probably add major stress to any new primary relationships. The odds are that the cumulative effect of your warfare will *lower* the nurturance level of your family. A crude analogy is trying to fix a flat car tire by puncturing another tire.

When you're approaching your death, will you look back and say *"Our legal fight was the right thing to do."*? Will your grown kids and their kids agree with that?

Even if you agree with these ideas, I assume you see no better short-term options, or you feel you're powerless to dissuade your ex from her or his legal campaign. See if any of the options below offer viable ways to stop your courtroom warfare, and/or to . . .

Avoid New Legal Fights

Premise: by patiently _ doing co-parent Projects 1 and 2, and _ reducing your mix of other teamwork barriers (p. 109) over time, you parents can give your kids the caregiving teamwork they need without resorting to legal force. Do you agree

with that yet? I trust the short and long-term benefits of doing
this are obvious.

In my experience, troubled parents (and others) ignore both
projects because _ their false selves rule them and _ don't know
(or care) _ what the projects are, _ what priceless benefits they
bring, and _ how to do them. Typical co-parents' guilty and
shamed subselves usually don't want to take full responsibility
for their past and present choices and outcomes. Until your
Self begins to guide them toward recovery, your other subselves
have no reason to trust that a far better life is *safely* available to
them (you).

To augment your efforts at wound-healing (Project 1 and
Chapters 5 and 6), and improving communication effectiveness (Chapter 7), consider **options** like these:

Accept that *you* are responsible for your decision to initiate or conduct yourself in a legal fight. Lawyers, your ex, or
anyone else may have strong opinions, but *you* are ultimately
responsible for your attitudes and actions. If your mind replies
"*Yes, but . . .*", that's probably a Guardian subself trying to
protect you without seeing the big picture.

Confirm the reality that hostility and aggression ("I'm 1-
up") causes reciprocal hostility and aggression ("*No, I'M 1-
up!*"). True Selves choosing steady, mutually-respectful (=/=)
assertion [..02/assert.htm] have a far greater chance of promoting genuine negotiation and win-win compromise. False
selves stubbornly focus on short term relief ("winning"), and
blame the "enemy" when hostility harvests counter-hostility.

Pay special attention to the concept of digging down below surface problems to discover _ the real needs "beneath"
them (p. 44), and _ who's responsible for filling them. See
"Dig Down" in [*Satisfactions*] or [..02/dig-down.htm].

Appreciate that when you and your ex (or anyone) try to
negotiate conflicts, there may be well over a *dozen* combined
subselves clamoring and arguing for their (different) viewpoints
[..01/innerfam2.htm]. That's why it's essential that your true
Selves take charge and coordinate your co-parenting communication and negotiations!

More options for avoiding future legal combat:

Read Hal and Sidra Stone's useful book "Embracing Each Other" to learn how your and your ex mate's subselves interact. Then read Deborah Tannen's insightful "You Just Don't Understand" to broaden your awareness of how typical females and males react differently to life. For deeper awareness, read Dr. Anne Moir and David Jessel's interesting, controversial book "Brain Sex," which explains in lay terms why each of us has a "male brain" or a "female brain," and what that *means* in our relationships.

Get clear and honest: are you focused on short term goals like *"Get the court to force my ex to increase child support,"* or *long-term* goals like *"Improve co-parenting teamwork with my ex, for our child/ren's sakes?"* Short-term legal victories usually cost you long-term teamwork and heartache: *all* of you adults and kids lose. Consult with your Future (old age) self for perspective..

Use *awareness* skill [..02/awareness.htm] and communication *mapping* [..02/evc-maps.htm] to learn where you and your ex typically focus: _ the past, the present, or the future; and on _ your needs and feelings, theirs, both of yours, or something else [..02/a-bubble.htm]. Focusing together on identifying and filling your respective current *true* needs as =/= co-parenting partners will work the best for you all. Some focus on the past can be helpful *if* you learn from it, and use it to form needed forgivenesses (Chapter 11) and to grieve (Chapter 12) .

Use the Serenity Prayer (p. 102) when you get stuck. as you work patiently at these steps. As you do, give yourself permission to rest and stay balanced along the way (Project 12)!

Clarify your main life priorities. Then assess honestly: are your legal-battle choices and actions consistent with your key *long-term* life goals? Do your recent actions match your stated goals? This is about *discovery* and healing, not *blame*! Use [..08/priority.htm].

Still more anti-litigation options . . .

Work toward understanding and cooperatively resolving (or avoiding) _ loyalty conflicts and _ relationship triangles _ within your inner family [..01/innerfam1.htm], and _ between you and other family members. Legal battles follow and create both of these potent surface stressors. Encourage your other co-parents, involved kin, and key professionals to join you in this. See Chapter 16 and Project 9b in *Build a High-nurturance Stepfamily*.

Review Resource [D], and assess how past and current parental legal battles are affecting your family's nurturance level. If you're in a stepfamily, use [G] to assess how such battles are affecting your biofamily-merger progress (Project 9). Do this to discover and plan, not blame!

Consider your web of core team-building barriers on p. 109, and face that legal combat *increases* them.

Honestly assess how legal aggression between you parents affects each of your kids. It's likely to force them to feel less secure and impossibly torn in siding with one or the other of you parents, and hinder their progress with their daunting developmental and adjustment needs [F]. Unless someone's safety is clearly at stake, legal aggression teaches your kids that *force* is the way adults solve major disputes. When you're old, will you be proud of doing that—and acknowledge there's a better alternative (Projects 1 and 2) ?

If options like these aren't enough to avoid legal combat, try to find an attorney who has genuine empathy for the major distrust, disrespect, resentments, and avoidances that courtroom battles always promote. One trait of such a person is s/he steadily values what's best *long term* for your whole family (win-win), rather than beating your ex mate's attorney now at all costs (lose-lose).

Were you aware that you parents had options like these 13? What prevents you from discussing these with your ex, in the spirit of long-term satisfactions?

In the context of co-parent teambuilding, We just reviewed practical ways to _ heal and _ learn from past legal disputes between ex mates, _ end current battles, and _ avoid future litigation.

Recap

Like the other chapters in Part 3, this one focuses on a *surface* barrier to co-parenting teamwork. It hilights common primary and secondary reasons for parental legal battles. The chapter then proposes four *real* reasons why exasperated, frustrated co-parents choose legal force to fill their surface needs:

dominant false selves, and related inner wounds;

unawarenesses of _ inner wounds and recovery, _ *true* needs (p. 44), _ effective communication skills [H], and possibly _ healthy three-level grieving;

the combined effects of core co-parental relationship barriers (p. 109); and . . .

misguided advice from (wounded, uninformed, biased) relatives, friends, and human-service professionals.

Based on these, the chapter offers four sets of options to reduce these core stressors. Key among them are you each _ empowering your true Selves to lead your inner family (Project 1), and growing fluency in effective thinking and communication skills (Project 2). The overarching goal is to promote long-term caregiving teamwork in your multi-home family, and raise your nurturance level together.

A clear symptom of false-self control is a divorced parent choosing legal aggression and short-term *winning* over long-term co-parental teamwork and high family nurturance. Exceptions: the long-term costs of legal intervention and force are probably justified if it's clear that _ a parent's and/or _ minor child's safety and welfare is at risk because of the other parent's wounds and behaviors. If that's true for you, apply all the relevant ideas in Parts 1 and 2 to your legal decisions to minimize the major *long-term* psychological costs to you all.

Option: put your Self in charge, and mediate and journal about _ your reactions to this chapter, and what it means to you (all), and _ what actions you want to take as a result.

Among the thousands typical divorced and stepfamily dramas I've heard since 1981, one of the top four *surface* conflicts is about *money* and *assets.* The other three are strife over _ marriage, _ ex mates, and stepparent-child relations. The next chapter overviews typical surface "money" conflicts, the real issues beneath them, and suggestions for identifying and resolving the latter.

Before continuing, do you need a break?

19) Resolve "Money" Disputes

Discover and Fill Co-parents' *Real* Needs

Do your co-parents have significant disputes over earning, spending, and/or saving money now? If so, I suspect they really *aren't* about "money." (Notice your reaction.) This chapter _ reviews common financial conflicts between divorced and stepfamily co-parents, and _ proposes seven possible *real* problems, and practical options for resolving them.

Unaware, wounded, co-parents I've met focus repeatedly on surface "money" problems, which usually prolongs them and fosters new ones. Anyone, like *you*, can learn to discern and help each other fill the unmet needs below "money" battles. To see this in action, bookmark this page and read [http://sfhelp.org/02/dig-down.htm]. That will help you understand what follows.

Typical *Surface* Problems

There are lots of post-divorce "money problems": _ dividing assets in a legal property settlement, _ fights over paying kids' expenses like clothing, education, health, and insurance; and _ living adequately on less money after divorce. Ex mates who sue each other can fight over _ who causes the legal bills, and who should pay them. Any of these can flare if an ex mate loses a job or they or a child incur major new expenses.

Ex mates and stepparents can feel conflicted by these internally and interpersonally, a little to a lot, temporarily or chronically. Property-settlement fights usually fade away, though hurt, resentment, and anger can remain. Battles over child support, aggravated by other mutual conflicts, can continue for years well into the kids' early adult years or beyond.

On top of these, re/married mates can fight over _ prenuptial agreements; _ separate vs. joint checking and saving accounts; _ child allowances, expenses, and money management; _ bill-paying and checkbook-managing; _ asset titles and insurance; _ who should earn what; _ major investments, including college fees; _ estate plans, and _ "standing up to" a financially-uncooperative or hostile ex mate.

Whatever the details, most financial disputes in divorced families and stepfamilies have common themes. See if you see yourselves here . . .

Theme 1) Co-parents can argue over multiple *topics* like those above, **and the way they communicate** with the other (or doesn't) about financial conflicts ("*If I bring up anything to do with money, Janice hangs up.*"). Often, communication problems are aggravated by sets of values and loyalty conflicts, and relationship triangles (Chapter 16). Typical co-parents aren't aware of these, and have no effective strategies to manage them. (Right?)

When each new stepparent enters the post-divorce picture (with or without kids and ex mates), new "money" conflicts can bloom over topics and communications.

Theme 2) One or more kids involved react to the (perceived) adult strife. They can numb and withdraw; get scared and overwhelmed ("act out" at home or school); try to distract their adults from fighting; and/or take sides. Each child's reaction is shaped by their age, security, wounds, perceptions, and status with their daunting mix of developmental and family-adjustment needs (p. 464).

Kids' reactions may amplify adult blame and scorn: "*Alex, if you weren't so irresponsible about the money you owe, Jenny wouldn't have these stomach aches!*" This blaming gets amplified if a child's reactions costs someone money (e.g. for counseling or exams and medicines). It also escalates if co-parents don't know how to manage loyalty conflicts and persecutor-victim-rescuer (PVR) relationship triangles—which is common (Chapter 16).

Co-parents' frustrations and polarities over these can rise if . . .

Theme 3) Relatives and friends take sides, try to mediate or intervene, or distance (*"I don't appreciate your sister calling me a 'deadbeat dad'"*). This shifts the support that each co-parent feels, and can contribute to feeling "ganged up on," misunderstood, attacked, and/or rejected. Another shift occurs if one co-parent hires a lawyer who increases antagonisms by imposing their or the law's ideas about "what's (financially) fair and reasonable."

Theme 4) Overwhelm: typical wounded, distracted co-parents can feel locally or chronically paralyzed by simultaneous _ family-adjustment tasks [G], _ helping kids with *their* concurrent needs [F], _ (hopefully) their versions of the 11 ongoing Projects in [A], while _ attending many other responsibilities and tasks. If co-parents have _ no guiding life-goals and mission statement, and _ don't know what's in this book, or how to focus and prioritize their lives, inner-family and inter-home chaos becomes the norm. "Money problems" are just a part of this welter of stressors.

Theme 5) Temporary or no resolution. Regardless of the details, typical "money" fights don't get resolved—at all, or for long. A common response is to become resigned to them (and repress the frustration that merits).

Premise: these topics and dynamics are real stressors, and *none* of them is the real problem! As long as your co-parents focus on surface issues like these, "money" conflicts will recur and probably increase. Does this seem realistic in your situation?

Identify and Resolve the *True* Problems

As with every surface stressor in Part 3, I propose that the underlying *real* sources of your "money" stresses are your personal and co-parental mixes of the core problems on p. 109. The three main shared contributors are _ unawareness (vs. stupidity), _ unseen false-self dominance in one or more co-parents, and _ undeveloped communication skills among you all. Once you caregivers are aware of these, and accept personal responsibility for improving each one, *you can do* so, over time!

Options

Reflect on your choices now. You're reading this chapter to fill some needs. Are you clear on what you *really* need about "money" with your other co-parent/s? See which of these appeal to you, or suggest "the next right thing to do":

Confirm that your Self is solidly in charge. When s/he is, you'll feel a mix of calm, centered, energized, light, focused, resilient, up, grounded, relaxed, alert, aware, serene, purposeful, compassionate, and clear. Invite other wounded co-parents to do assess for false-self dominance, and take responsibility for personal recovery (ref Chapter 5 and 6). If you or they ignore this, the options that follow will be of little lasting use.

If you're re/married, honestly review the worksheets in Project 7. If two or more of you re/wedded the wrong people for the wrong reasons, at the wrong time, resolving "money problems" may distract you from more fundamental unmet needs. For perspective, read [..Rx/mates/redivorce1.htm].

Use your awareness, clear-thinking, and dig-down skills from *Satisfactions* or [..02/dig-down.htm] to validate the true problems under your particular "money" problems.

Meditate and/or journal about what you read here. Free associate, listen to the different "voices" inside your mind, and capture them objectively like a reporter would. Be open to new awarenesses, without judgment.

Alert your other co-parents and any professionals you're working with to this book and chapter, or the related Web articles at [http://sfhelp.org/Rx/ex/money.htm], [..Rx/mates/money.htm], and [..Rx/kin/money.htm].

_ **Do** that, _ discuss these proposed core problems with them, and then _ *cooperatively* assess you and your other co-parents for possible "fits."

_ **If you** haven't yet, Try one or more of the 12 co-parent projects [A] by yourself, or _ ask your ex mate to join you as a co-parenting partner in doing one or more of the projects, for your kids' sakes. I urge you to start with Projects 1 and 2 . . .

_ **Add your learnings from this chapter** to others from these books and Web articles, and choose to act on relevant options in Part 2 with the resources in Part 4.

_ **Choose** and apply relevant options from Chapter 16, to identify and reduce money-related values and loyalty conflicts, and relationship triangles *as teammates.*

_ **Postpone** any of these choices until you're less distracted (by what?), and re-evaluate your options "sometime."

_ **Do** what you've always done, in hopes for a better outcome.

_ **Imagine** in detail a future life for your kids in which you and your other co-parents raised the level of co-parenting harmony among you all.

_ **Imagine** asking your kids as grown adults what they wish you and their other parent had done for them at this time in your lives.

_ (other options) . . .

If your Self guides you now, and you and I have done our jobs well, you should feel clear that _ your stressful "money" conflicts are *symptoms*, and _ you *can* identify and resolve the true problems "under" them, and _ grow real co-parenting teamwork, by patiently tailoring and using options in Part 2.

Notice your self-talk (thoughts, images, and emotions) now. Which subselves are 'speaking"? What do they need?

Recap

Typical U.S. co-parents in divorced families and stepfamilies argue over money-related issues, or avoid discussing them. Because money and financial assets represent status, control, freedom, power, and security, such arguing can be fierce and polarized. So are it's effects on co-parents' egos, and any kids and relatives involved.

This chapter sketches a brief context for viewing financial conflicts between co-parents, and outlines common *surface* clashes that they commonly fight about. The chapter proposes the *real* problems under most "money" disputes are the combined Part-2 stressors on p. 109. The chapter closes with an overview of typical options you can choose from now.

Resource: "Money Advice for Your Successful Remarriage—Handling Delicate Financial Issues With Love and Understanding"; by Patricia Schiff Estess; Betterway Publications paperback, 2nd ed.; 1996. Patricia is the remarried founding editor of Sylvia Porter's Personal Finance Magazine, and a Stepfamily Association of America Board member. Her practical advice can augment what you're reading here.

A high percentage of the divorced and stepfamily co-parents I've met say that their lives are or were impacted by key people struggling with some kind of toxic addiction. If that's true in your multi-home family, the next chapter offers perspective on this important *surface* problem, and suggestions for what you can do about it.

20) Coping With "Addictions"

Set Compassionate Boundaries

I'm the son of two "functional" alcoholics, and the recovering survivor of a *very* low-nurturance childhood. Learning this in 1986 has led me on a life-changing discovery about _ the causes and _ personal and relationship impacts of addiction, and _ the levels of recovery "addicts" (wounded adults) and their kids and mates can choose.

My clinical experience since 1981 suggests that addictions and the myriad personal and relationship problems they cause are common in typical U.S. divorced-family and stepfamily trees. How about in yours? Answering that question factually requires your knowing the symptoms of a true addiction.

This chapter introduces the complex topic of addictions (compulsive, toxic self-medications), and overviews key options if any of your co-parents were or are afflicted with one. As you can guess from this chapter being in Part 3, I propose that any addiction (including co-dependence) is a secondary (*surface*) problem. Let's begin by clarifying . . .

What Is An *Addiction*?

I define "an addiction" as any repeated action which significantly harms the addict psychologically, physically, or spiritually, *which (s)he cannot control.*" "Significantly" is a subjective judgment. How does this compare with your definition? If you equate addiction with drinking ethyl alcohol, know that *alcoholism* is the best known of . . .

Four Types of Addiction

Mood-changing substances, including alcohol, some foods (sugar and fat), nicotine, prescription and street drugs, and some industrial chemicals. These are often the easiest addictions to identify because these substances are tangible.

Compulsive activities like excessive busy-ness, sexual fantasizing or actions, gambling or spending, personal-computer use, "working out," and worship. A related condition is hyper-dedication to some "causes," like "spiritual warfare," feminism, preventing abortions, gun ownership, safe sex, gay rights, and (some) political activism.

Mind/body "states" like excitement (*"Jack's a thrill seeker."*), power ("winning"), pain, "success," rage, sexual arousal and release, and disorientation; and . . .

Human and spiritual relationships, like co-dependence and "devil worship."

All four of these are caused by the overpowering need to self-medicate (reduce or distract from) intolerable inner pain. The pain is a relentless brew of excessive shame, guilt, fear, rage, confusion, emptiness, hopelessness, and sadness. I believe this brew *always* comes from a protective false self born in a low-nurturance childhood.

In some substance addictions like alcohol and nicotine, body cells grow dependent on the drug, adding physiological craving to compulsive self-medication from psychological discomfort. Science confirms that *some* alcoholics' bodies metabolize ethyl alcohol differently than non-alcoholics, which genetically predisposes (vs. dooms) them to addiction.

An *obsession* is an intense mental-emotional preoccupation with some thing, person, or idea that may significantly unbalance the person's life. **A** *compulsion* adds the element of irresistible action. The compulsive one *does* something repeatedly, like hand washing, praying, masturbating, stalking, or nail biting. The key word is *irresistible*—not under willful mental control.

Obsessions and compulsions range from trivial to lethal in their effects on the person and people around them. True *addictions* are moderately toxic to lethal compulsions. They hurt addicts and their families emotionally, physically, and spiritually, and (the underlying wounds) often promote toxic (or no) relationships, disability, illness, and premature death.

Addiction is at one end of a spectrum that ranges through *excessive* to *disinterest* (*"I've never wanted to chew tobacco."*). Judging the behavior of someone you care about on this continuum is subjective. That causes confusion and conflict in deciding whether behavior is truly addictive, or just "overdoing it at times."

Because our unaware and wounded ancestors misunderstood, scorned, and pitied *addiction*, it's important to note how the word is used and interpreted. *"Pat's an addict"* sounds much different than *"Pat is struggling with the toxic compulsion to medicate daily inner pain."* If you were Pat, which would you prefer?

I recommend calling addiction _ a *condition*, and _ a symptom of psychological wounding and false-self control. Labeling addiction as a *sickness* or *disease* promotes anxiety, repugnance, shame, and denial (*"I am NOT diseased!"*). These *increase* inner pain, and discourage awareness of inner wounds and their healing. Yes, some chemical addiction does have physiological roots.

Seven Key Traits

Though details vary widely, several things are true about typical addictions. They . . .

are "irrational" and unconscious, so *you can't reason with an addict.* Expect double messages, distortions, and deceptions, and earnest *denial* or justification of these.

are progressive: the "medication" relentlessly *increases* the original shame, guilt, and anxiety, over time, so addicts need to medicate more and more. From behavioral patterns, informed observers can assess an addiction's status as early, mid-phase, or advanced. Accurate assessment can help provide appropriate help to the wounded person and his or her family. And true addictions . . .

are fiercely minimized or denied by the afflicted person's false self: "*Sure I work a lot, but that doesn't make me a workaholic.*" The underlying dynamic is unconscious reality distortion, which convinces the addict they're OK, when objective others disagree. Typical addicts (i.e. their ruling shame-based false selves) need to deny their compulsion, and blame others for their behavior ("*Edith, I work 65 hours every week because you just won't shut up when I come home!*")

These distortions, plus and fear of *discovery* and major losses, usually cause addicts to act furtively, and to lie to themselves and others about their behavior and what it means. This secrecy and deception breed shame, guilt, conflict, and anxiety, which *increases* their pain.

And true addictions . . .

result in premature death or "hitting the wall," and finding a healthier way to manage the inner pain. "Hitting the wall," or "hitting bottom," is usually some kind of climactic trauma like (re)divorce, job loss, injuring or killing a loved one, or public legal action. The accumulated stress and this trauma finally shatters the wounded person's protective denials, and s/he confronts stark reality: change, or die early. And addictions . . .

cause significant emotional pain, anxiety, and psychological damage to the wounded one, people they live and work with, and sometimes to strangers. *This is specially true for an addict's vulnerable, dependent children.* Addiction is a powerful *unconscious* vehicle for transmitting low-nurturance parenting and psychological wounding down the generations, until death, sexual dysfunction, or true recovery stops it.

And true (vs. pseudo) addictions . . .

can be controlled (vs. cured) *when the wounded person is* *ready* (self-motivated), by a major change in awareness, core beliefs, and priorities; including _ seeking and accepting help from a Higher Power and informed others (like professional healers and other recovering addicts).

Since 1935, the new lifestyle that evolves from this change has come to be known broadly as "working my recovery program" through the global impact of Alcoholics Anonymous. Reaching stable *recovery* ("sobriety") is a process that often includes one or more painful relapses back into distorted thinking, compulsive self-medication, guilt, anxiety, and shame.

Finally, it appears to me that . . .

"recovery" has three levels: pseudo, preliminary, and full. In pseudo recovery, a compulsive medicator may hit the wall and stop gambling, and their false self will take up (say) compulsive sex to mute their inner pain. Alcoholics may achieve *sobriety*, but deny or joke about an addiction to nicotine, sugar, fat, and/or porn. These are first-order (surface) changes *which leave the underlying pain and emptiness unhealed.* Replacing one addiction with another is sometimes called "cross addiction."

Preliminary recovery includes major awareness of the inner pain, and a genuine second-order (core attitude) change in priorities, beliefs, and thinking. Protective denials and distortions are gradually replaced by clear, honest awareness, and spontaneously taking full responsibility for personal health, and addictive behavior's harmful impacts.

I propose that most people working relapse-free 12-step addiction-recovery programs are in *preliminary* recovery. This is a genuinely healthier lifestyle, *and stops well short of full healing.* Evidence: based on direct experience, testimonials, and/or tradition, most recovering addicts and supporters feel if they quit attending 12-step meetings they'll relapse. They're "*sober*" (clear headed) and still ruled by a protective false self.

After 16 years' personal and professional experience, I believe ***full* or *true* recovery** _ reveals the tireless false self that paradoxically causes and tries to self-medicate the person's inner agony; and _ restores the person's true Self to harmonize their *inner*-family and permanently reduce their agonies and wounds. This promotes _ realizing and pursuing the recoverer's true life purpose, _ protecting others from inner wounding, and _ living a fuller life span.

The bad news is there's little current lay or clinical awareness of the prevalence of the six psychological wounds from inadequate parenting (p. 448). Therefore, only *inner*-family therapists and a few others espouse this three-level recovery concept, so far. The good news is that awareness is accelerating in our time. I believe we're on the brink of a major social epiphany that can set millions of sufferers free, and protect unborn generations.

The courageous founders and promoters of all 12 step recovery programs were and are, to my knowledge, unaware of true-Self empowerment as the core *full*-recovery target. Fortunately, this is starting to change!

About Co-addiction . . .

Since the advent of family therapy in the 1950's, society has begun to see that typical addicts' partners ("co-addicts") grow predictable, psychologically-toxic traits of their own. Three stand out:

Co-addicts typically grow their own reality distortions about _ the addict's behavior and _ it's harmful impacts ("*Carl is a little overzealous about sex, but he's certainly not addicted to it.*").

Many co-addicts become compulsively focused on the welfare and behavior of their partner. This is a symptom of the widespread psycho-spiritual condition recently called **co-dependence**. This condition (vs. sickness or disease) is a form of relationship addiction, in that it is an uncontrollable behavior that harms the wholistic health of the people involved. In a family, this means the (spiritual + physical + emotional + mental) health of dependent kids is being affected by *two* wounded caregivers, not one. And . . .

Until their own compulsion is owned and controlled, co-addicts usually **enable** their addicted partners: unintentionally promote the compulsion's progress. They do this by fearing to confront their partner on their harmful behaviors, and setting healthy limits (*"Janice, trust me. If you go on one more credit-card binge, I'm going to file for divorce and seek custody of the kids."*)

The unmistakable implication of all of the above is that "**addiction**" is a *family* **affliction**. I believe its roots *always* lie in unintended early-childhood neglect (low nurturance), some-times combined with genetic predisposition. Co-parent addic-tions and denials re-create low childhood nurturance, which inexorably passes the inner pain and adaptive psychological wounding on to the next generation.

All of the above nets out to this: each of the four addic-tions is a symptom of the real problems: _ unawareness, and _ the unseen dominance of a protective "false self" and related inner pain. Most lay and clinical people focus on the addictive *behavior* and it's impacts, not this hidden root cause. This can result in pseudo or preliminary recovery, and accidentally *in-creasing* inner pain.

What does all this mean to you?

If a Co-parent is *or Was* Addicted

You have many options . . .

Accept that any of the four addictions is _ an inherited *family* (vs. personal) condition, and _ a *symptom* of the real problem: psychological wounds, *not* "character defects." This condition merits compassion, education, and confrontation, not shame. Encourage all your co-parents to get clear that your real targets are _ admitting and patiently healing the excessive shame, guilts, and fears that power false-self control ("compul-sion"), and _ building a high-nurturance team together for you and your descendents (Chapter 4 and [D]).

Accept that if any of your co-parents were addicted but seem to be "in recovery" now, s/he's probably not in *full* recov-ery from false-self dominance and the five related inner wounds.

Also note that if your parents or grandparents were active or recovering addicts but you co-parents weren't or aren't, false-self rule is usually inherited anyway. If so, you'll have many of the symptoms in [E] and related Project-1 checklists [http://sfhelp.org/pop/assess.htm].

Option: invest time creating a family genogram (multi-generational map) like the one on p. 437. Use [..03/geno1.htm] to help. Then invite your other co-parents to join you in assessing all the people in your diagram for traits of addiction (false-self dominance).

Honestly assess yourself, and each ex mate, stepparent, and child, for symptoms of inner wounds (Project 1) and blocked grief (Project 5). Based on your findings, take appropriate action as teammates. Avoidance and procrastination suggest significant false-self control. *The ideas in this chapter and book will be of little use if your Self is not trusted to lead your inner family.* Is s/he now?

Assess if you have re/wedded the wrong people (too wounded and unaware), for the wrong reasons, at the wrong time. This is likely if any of your co-parents is or was addicted, and isn't clearly in preliminary (probably 12-step) recovery now. See the articles and worksheets at [http://sfhelp.org/07/links07.htm]. to help you do this: If you (your false self) made any wrong choices, you probably need to focus on Project 1 *now*.

And if a co-parent is or was "addicted" . . .
Learn more about . . .

- family nurturance [D],
- psychological wounding and inner families *Who's Really Running Your Life?* or [http://sfhelp.org/01/gwc-meaning.htm] and [..01/innerfam1.htm], and . . .
- addiction, co-dependence [..01/co-dep.htm], and full recovery [..01/recovery1.htm].

Invite your other co-parents and kin to do the same, and teach your kids relevant information, over time.

If people you love (does that include *you?*) are ruled by a false self, _ seek spiritual guidance and *informed* lay and professional support for you and your kids, and _ use those to patiently evolve and work a *full*-recovery plan.

Strengthen your co-parents' communication skills (Chapter 7), and teach your kids and supporters. Part of this option is to _ evolve a personal Bill of Rights, (p. 514), and _ use it to help assert *compassionate* boundaries and consequences with your wounded co-parent/s (Chapter 15). Do this partly to avoid enabling (not confronting) them, and coach your kids to do the same, without guilt or anxiety.

Develop your spiritual awareness, and respectfully encourage other family members to do the same. Full recovery is, by definition, a spiritual-psychological-mental growth process.

The rest of this chapter explores each of these, and offers perspective, options, and resources.

1) Learn More

One of five family hazards you co-parents and kids face (p. 429) is *unawareness.* Much anguish and stress from addiction comes from ignorance. The old myth (ignorance) that addiction is a personal problem is being replaced by the perception that it's an inherited *family* affliction, based on unseen inner wounds in *both* mates and often their parents.

Adopting this attitude (e.g. *"Maria's addiction to shopping affects* all *of us."*) and teaching it to your kids and supporters will help all your other relationship efforts pay off across future years. Choosing blame, pity, or disinterest toward your wounded co-parent will distort your communication, and breed mutual disrespect, distrust, and distortion (e.g. denial and lying). These are likely to block the grieving and forgiveness essential to your and your kids' wholistic health.

Learn about _ family nurturance and inner wounds [D], _ the causes and progression of *family* addiction, _ how it affects each adult and resident or visiting child, and _ about family recovery. Ignorance promotes guilt, shame, misunderstandings, frustration, and unrealistic expectations. Those promote painful, harmful relationships.

Your local library, bookstores, and the Internet offer wealth of current information about survivors of "toxic" parents and "dysfunctional" (low nurturance) childhoods, addiction, and recovery. Search any Web bookseller's site (e.g. [amazon.com], or [bn.com]), for titles under "Adult Children," "addiction" and "addiction recovery." Also search on the specific type of addiction you're focusing on—e.g. "workaholism" or "compulsive overeating.")

Hazelden [www.hazelden.org] and the Johnson Institute in Minneapolis are reputable providers of accurate information about all kinds of addiction and recovery.

As you acquire knowledge about family addiction and what it means, another healthy decision you can make is to . . .

2) Assess Yourself and Your Kids

A significant past and/or present relationship with an addicted partner strongly suggests . . .

You may now be denying compulsive self-medication, including over-eating, spending, or working; and/or co-dependence (relationship addiction to a wounded person). If so, your *real* problem is a mix of the six psycho-spiritual wounds on p. 448; and . . .

You have wounded sibs, relatives, and ancestors in your and any ex mate's family trees who's *inner* families are covertly controlled by myopic, well-meaning false selves; and . . .

Your minor and/or grown kids have mixes of these wounds from unintended low childhood nurturance [D and F]. This manifests as recurring school, relationship, legal, financial, and health problems; and it suggests . . .

One or more of your co-parents and kids may be blocked in grieving prior family changes (losses). This lowers wholistic health, and hinders growing healthy new emotional/spiritual bonds. See Chapter 12 and Project 5.

Do you think any of these apply to you and other family

members? Unless you're already in effective personal (full) recovery, you're at high risk of your ruling subselves' distorting your reality to avoid more pain and anxiety. If you're held in protective custody by a false self, you'll probably answer "*No*," or "*I don't really care*," or "*I don't want to think about it*", or blank out the question.

Defensive answers like these put you and each dependent child at risk of living with unfilled core needs, and unsatisfying or toxic relationships. To avoid this, you can assess yourself now for false-self dominance, and then for blocked grief. Project 1 *Who's* Really *Running Your Life?* and Project 5 *Stepfamily Courtship* offer you clear options and resources for assessing yourself, other co-parents, and your kids. What is more important to you than doing these vital projects now? Who is answering?

As you _ redefine "addiction," _ learn about recovering from the wounds that underlie this family affliction, and _ start to heal *your* wounds, you'll profit if you . . .

3) Find Lay and Professional Supports

If your family was or is afflicted with addictions and underlying psychological wounds, you can use up to four types of support:

- discovery and recovery from inner wounds;
- adapting to addiction and co-addiction;
- three-level grieving; and . . .
- divorce recovery, and/or stepfamily co-parenting.

Think of the last time you experienced "support," including giving it to another person. It means "compassionate, respectful help reducing significant discomforts." Personal support has many forms: acceptance, reassurance, encouragement, empathic listening, hugs, brainstorming, useful information, respectful advice, and caring confrontation. These can come from within you, and from your mate, relatives, and friends, your Higher Power and church community, and from concerned professionals.

The initial challenge for most of us, specially men, is to publicly acknowledge that we *need* support. Many of us who grew up too fast learned self-sufficiency very early. Others learned to play the helpless "victim." We also learned to help or ignore others, and discount or deny our own needs and feelings. In divorced families and stepfamilies, this significantly hinders reducing the four stressors above (and others).

If you're a wounded survivor of too little early nurturance (a Grown Wounded Child, or GWC), you may not want to admit aspects of your past or present life to yourself or others. Your childhood family rule may have been *"We keep family affairs to ourselves."* If so, it's hard to reveal publicly that your family is afflicted by one or more toxic compulsions, and the underlying wounds. This is specially likely if you were (wrongly) taught that addiction is *shameful.*

Most communities have free and fee support groups, classes, and counseling for addiction recovery. Many have lay and professionally-led groups and programs to facilitate grieving in kids and adults (e.g. "Rainbows."). Your community may also have support for "Adult Children" (recovering from childhood abuse or neglect—low nurturance). The Internet has an expanding array of support resources, including discussion groups, articles, booklists, and selected Web site links. For a thorough review of key support options, read and discuss the series of Web articles in Project 11. See the guidebook *Build a High-nurturance Stepfamily* or the Web resources at [..11/links11.htm].

If "addiction" (unawareness and psychological wounds) afflicts your multi-home family, another powerful option you co-parents can choose is to . . .

4) Strengthen Your Communication Skills

All four types of addiction cause and are fueled by the core co-parental barriers in Part 2. If your multi-home family is afflicted with past or present addiction/s, your co-parents and relatives probably can't problem-solve effectively yet. Divorce is a stark symptom of this. Identifying and healing your mix of co-parenting barriers hinges on effective inner and behavioral communication among you adults. The wound-symptom of addiction provides *another* reason your kids depend on all you adults to commit to Project 2 together. See and apply Chapter 7!

As you progress on these four Project-10 options, you'll become more able to . . .

5) Set Effective Boundaries

People burdened with false-self domination and related toxic compulsions are often difficult to live and work with. Their choices and actions often breed distrust, disrespect, anxiety, resentment, hostility, guilt, and confusion.

If that describes any of your co-parents (including *you)*, you can use your Self and Project 2 skills to assert and enforce respectful boundaries with _ impulsive subselves, and _ aggressive or disabled co-parents and kids. Many of us wounded survivors of low childhood nurturance have never learned to do this without aggression, timidity, anxiety and guilt, or double messages. That often means we can't teach dependent kids how to respectfully set and defend their boundaries. Are your children learning how to do this?

Active "addiction" is a high-return opportunity to practice firm boundary-setting (Chapter 15). Well done, this is a win-win choice. It _ helps you fill your and your kids' needs, and _ helps the "addict" by confronting them and avoiding toxic enabling. A powerful *family* (group) boundary-enforcement with an active addict is called an "intervention." See [..Rx/mates/ addiction2.htm] for an overview and resources on this.

6) Develop Your Spiritual Awareness

The 12 addiction-management steps espoused by the various "Anonymous" recovery programs are built on faith in a benevolent, active personal Higher Power. These steps have clearly worked better than other schemes to help many addicts control toxic compulsions (preliminary recovery). Core themes in these steps are _ admitting your life is out of conscious control, _ asking for and _ accepting spiritual help, and _ respecting other people's views of God and spirituality. The Serenity Prayer (p. 24) adds clarity and direction to these healing attitudes.

Lacking any spiritual guidance or inspiration from my alcoholic (wounded) parents, I drifted into atheism. My recovery since 1986 has brought me bedrock faith in the validity and value of these 12-step themes and a benign, attentive, *real* Higher Power. My experience and the stories of hundreds of recovering clients, many of whom were recovering compulsives, founds this sixth option.

I propose that your consciously valuing and developing your spiritual (vs. religious) *awareness*, is a priceless help in your working patiently at _ options like the five above, and _ building co-parental teamwork within your situational limits. The paradox is, you won't experience the personal and family value of doing this until you try it. If a Guardian *Cynic* or *Pessimist* subself persuades you to ignore this (intense anxiety: fear of aloneness and loss of self-sufficiency), ask adults in active recovery to describe how spirituality affects their progress. See if you can find anyone in effective personal recovery who doesn't have an active *nurturing* (vs. fear and shame-based) spiritual faith.

Note the important difference between *religion* (usually centered on the rules, hierarchy, and worship practices of an organization like a church), and *spirituality*—a personal faith in, and intentional interaction with, Guardian Angels or Guides, Higher Selves, and a responsive Supreme Being. I suspect you know people who are pious and religious, but not spiritual . . .

Reading these words will probably not cause you to "develop your spiritual awareness." If you weren't coached to begin doing that as a child, you may need to experience "hitting bottom," and using agony to finally admit "my life is unmanageable (beyond my conscious control)."

Some inner-family advocates believe that your Self, or Higher Self, is your soul. Others believe your inner family always includes a quiet subself who is the local "representative" of God, or "the God or Spirit within." True progress at empowering your Self to lead and harmonize your other subselves (Project 1) promotes natural spiritual awareness and growth.

These are six of your options if your *family* is burdened with the wounds and unawarenesses underlying any of the four addictions. Popular alternatives are to defer action and "get busy on other things;" endlessly analyze, worry or catastrophize ("yes but . . ."); pray and "hope for the best;" overfocus on someone else; collapse; stoically endure; and/or "get depressed and apathetic." Another option is to gain (temporary) comfort from *your* favorite compulsion/s. Choices like these probably mean you're dominated by a protective, distrustful false self.

To help sort through these choices, meditate and interview your older Self—i.e. the person you'll be just before you die. Ask that wise person what s/he feels you should do in this difficult family situation. S/He knows how it all turns out for you and your child/ren. Your current and future decisions determine the quality of her or his life. Implication: even childless people have at least one dependent!

Get quiet again, and listen for the counsel of the Wise One within you. S/He speaks briefly, with a "still, small voice." Recall the important difference between first-order (surface) and second-order (core attitude) changes, as your governing subselves decide what to do.

As you decide how to adapt to past or present co-parent or ancestral addiction, use Project 12: coach yourself and each other to balance your many goals and priorities, and design each day to avoid overload and overwhelm. Veteran 12-steppers remind each other "H.A.L.T." Four things that trigger addiction (false self dominance) are being too **h**ungry, **a**ngry, **l**onely, and **t**ired. *Awareness* and an empowered Self are your best protections!

Recap

Premise: Past or present co-parental "addiction" is a surface symptom of underlying psychological wounds and major unawarenesses. These harmful compulsions amplify, and contribute to, the core co-parent-teamwork barriers in Part 2. The physical + emotional + spiritual + mental condition called *addiction* is very common in divorced-family and stepfamily trees. Does it appear in *yours?*

Compulsive self-medication with substances, mood states, activities, and relationships aim to provide temporary relief from relentless shame, anxiety, guilt, loneliness, emptiness, and despair. Paradoxically, addiction relentlessly causes *more* of these, until some trauma ("hitting bottom") sparks surrender, breaking old denials, and beginning preliminary or full recovery— second-order change. Pseudo recovery is a surface-behavior (first-order) change often triggering a cross addiction.

This chapter outlines _ seven traits of a true addiction (compulsion), _ three levels of recovery (pseudo, preliminary, and full), and outlines _ six options if you feel a co-parent is or *was* addicted. These include . . .

Choosing to see addiction as a *family* affliction, and learning more about it;

Learning, using, and teaching effective communication skills; and then . . .

Using them, plus personal recovery from false-self dominance, to set effective boundaries with your "addicted" (wounded) co-parent/s and disrespectful or insensitive (wounded) others.

Researching and using the local and Internet support available for grieving, "single" parenting, relating to an "addict," and stepfamily co-parenting. And . . .

Intentionally growing your spiritual awareness.

An overarching option in doing these and your many other daily activities is to value and manage your daily **balance** of work, play, and rest, and help your kids and co-parenting partners to do the same. Project 12 *[Build a High-nurturance Stepfamily]* offers resources to help do this.

"Addiction" is an inherited, widespread multi-generational *family* affliction. It promotes the six inner wounds in adults and vulnerable children, blocks "good grief" and effective communication, and weakens or prevents healthy bonding. Each new day is a chance to face these in your family, adopt a long-range mindset, and take compassionate action. The first target must be to empower your true Self, and harmonize your inner family (commit to *full* recovery).

A common highly-visible *surface* stressor in typical divorced families and stepfamilies is uproar and conflict over child visitations. The next chapter offers perspective and options toward reducing these in your homes.

21) Reduce Child-visitation Conflicts

Help Each Other Fill Your True Needs

A common source of anger and frustration in multi-home nuclear families is disputes over minor kids visiting their non-custodial parent. Regular and special (e.g. holiday) visitations are rich sources of relationship triangles and rancorous values and loyalty conflicts (Chapter 16). This chapter proposes that typical arguments over visitation frequency, timing, transportation, duration, expenses, and other details are never really about those things at all. It suggests the *real* problems underneath all of these, and hilights options for your co-parents resolving them "well enough."

Let's start at the beginning . . .

What Is "Child Visitation"?

What follows is based on the premise that minor kids of parental divorce need "enough quality time" with each primary caregiver for emotional health and growth. Each child and caregiver has a unique definition of "enough," and is the only person really qualified to judge. Though "enough" changes with age and circumstance, "quality time" does not. More on that in a moment.

Let's define regular and special "child visitation" as a complex sequence of personal and interpersonal events in a minor child's two homes. The events effect every person living in each dwelling, based on *many* factors like these:

1) the _ true (vs. surface) pre-visitation needs of each person involved, and _ how these needs are ranked by the decision makers; plus . . .

2) the _ values, _ attitudes, and _ mental/verbal skills that each involved person has which shape the overall visitation experience, plus . . .

3) the mosaic of responsibilities, schedules, and obligations of each child and adult in both homes; plus . . .

4) the _ internal and _ interpersonal discussions that occur among all involved about "the coming visit," plus . . .

5) the verbal or written _ agreements and _ expectations that result, and _ the communication process required to inform everyone of them; plus . . .

6) the roles of each adult and child (who's responsible for what), plus . . .

7) the several sets of household rules (shoulds, oughts, musts, and have to's) that shape how each role is acted out (*"You have to see that Jackie wears her dental retainer every night"*), plus . . .

8) the visitation-preparation process (e.g. packing, cleaning, food buying) in each home, plus . . .

9) the "goodbye" process at the child/ren's custodial home, plus . . .

10) transporting the child/ren to the receiving home, plus . . .

11) the "welcoming" process or ritual at the "other home," plus . . .

12) the stabilization process in both homes; plus . . .

13) the planned and impromptu activities that occur between the "hellos" and preparing to leave, including conflicts and any inter-home communications; plus . . .

14) the preparations in both homes for the child to leave/arrive; plus . . .

15) the "goodbye" process at the visited home, plus . . .

16) transport back to the original home, plus . . .

17) the "hello" process upon arrival, including "debriefing" (*"How was it? How are you?"*); plus . . .

18) the restabilizing of both homes, and the co-parents' and kids evaluating privately and together whether it was "a good visitation" or not; and finally . . .

19) any inter-home and other communication needed to "finish" the visitation (*"Frank, Marcy left her gym shoes and wallet at your house. Can you . . ."*). This can also include a web of conversations and reactions with peers and relatives about visitation events and reactions.

Have you ever seen a generic "child visitation" cycle dissected like this? Each part is a potential source of stress or satisfaction. Would you change this outline in some way? If you're not involved in such a post-divorce ritual yourself, can you empathize with the kids and adults that go versions of this several times a month, for years? Note that typical intact biofamilies don't face these 19 factors and their impacts on everyone.

Newly-separated biofamilies have to invent and stabilize their version of this complex sequence over months, amidst many other personal and family dynamics. Their cycle must restabilize each time someone _ moves in or out of each house, and _ has a "significant' lifestyle change, like starting school or graduating, re/marriage, cohabiting, custody change, illness or disability, childbirth, job loss, etc.

Even if all concerned achieve "OK stability" in both homes, their basic visitation cycle can have special variations like "six-week summer vacation," and "year-end school-break visitations." Thus regular visitations in your family may be "OK," but "special visitations" aren't, or vice versa, according to someone. Cycles involving family birthdays, anniversaries, and other special events usually generate unique true needs in members of both homes.

Based on this . . .

What's an *Effective* Child Visitation?

Why do some visitation cycles feel better than others? I propose that an *effective* child visitation is one which . . .
_ all involved kids and adults . . .
_ thoughtfully agree afterward . . .
_ everyone's key true (vs. surface) needs got filled . . .
_ in each part of the cycle . . .
_ "well enough," including . . .
_ each person feeling *respected* enough by . . .
_ themselves and _ all others involved.
How does this compare to your definition of an effective child visitation? If you co-parents haven't discussed and agreed on a common definition, doing so now is one way to start building visitation harmony.

Let's clarify some of these factors.

" . . . **all involved kids and adults** . . ." means the three or more people living regularly in the sending and receiving homes, not just the visiting child. It may also include relatives or baby sitters who don't live in either home.

" . . . **thoughtfully** . . ." means each child and adult meditates on what they genuinely think and feel about the last visitation cycle before forming an opinion;

" . . . **everyone's key true** . . . **needs** . . ." This is the heart of successful visitations. It proposes that each adult and child involved has true needs, like acceptance, respect, stimulation ("fun"), security, freedom, and affection, underlying surface ones like "I need to have a nice time."

People who learned to be shamed and emotionally numb as kids have a hard time _ knowing their *true* needs, _ validating and asserting them, _ empathizing with others' needs, _ cooperatively resolving need conflicts, and _ discerning whether their own needs got met well enough or not. When such people are asked "How was your visitation?" they truly don't know how it was.

" . . . **in each part of the cycle** . . ." implies that each of the three or more adults and kids have a set of true needs that may change at each of the 19 stages of the visitation process. One view of this is that your standard cycle has six or more phases where people's needs may not be met. Another view is there are almost 20 places to improve your visitation need-filling process (glass half full).

For instance, a child may feel good about going to and being in their "second home," but feel rudely ejected or tearfully enmeshed when it's time to leave one or both homes. "I hate visitation" may really mean "I hate the feelings I have when I say goodbye."

"... **in a way that** ..." means that the *way* each person got their true needs met is just as important as the needs themselves. For example, getting a goodbye hug feels better if it's desired, spontaneous, and genuine, vs. getting hugged dutifully and half-heartedly.

"... **leaves each person feeling respected enough** ..." Each adult and child is the only person on the planet qualified to judge "enough." Feeling included, valued, considered, and appreciated (respected) *enough* are primal needs of each person at each step in the visitation process. Are each of your kids and adults aware of these needs?

"... **by _ themselves and _ all others involved**." So if there are six people involved in a visitation, each needs to feel respected enough by five others and themselves for their visitation to feel effective. Premise: If any child or adult is shamebased (doesn't really respect themselves), the others' respect probably won't feel like enough.

How do you feel about these ideas? How would each of your other co-parents and kids feel? If factors like these define child visitation "success" (effectiveness), then what hinders co-parents (like you?) from achieving it? Let's explore common ...

Surface Visitation Problems

In over 17,000 hours of clinical consulting, I've heard hundreds of divorced and stepfamily co-parents describe child-visitation complaints like those below. Check any that apply to your unique family:

"**My ex mate won't** cooperate / listen to reason / give in or compromise / empathize with our child's needs / apologize / respect my needs / keep me informed / set healthy boundaries and limits / provide reasonable consequences / provide consistent, appropriate caregiving / follow the legal parenting agreement / obey the Order of Protection / stop badmouthing me / stop harassing me / get appropriate medical or emotional help / problem-solve / protect our child from _____ / stop using chemicals / drive safely / follow through / be on time / stop using the kids as spies / appreciate my sacrifices and compromises . . ."

The implied surface problem is *"Our visitation problems are my ex mate's fault, and I'm helpless or forced to confront him or her.*

Or visitations are "a problem" because . . .

"**My child doesn't like** going to their other parent's home / spending time with their other parent, stepparent, stepsibs, and/ or steprelatives / all the complicated planning, packing, and traveling / the rules and expectations in that house / adapting to a very different set of house rules than ours / leaving their pet / not having their own room over there / not having enough privacy / being left with a sitter over there / never doing fun stuff / feeling bored, ignored, and/or used / disliking the food / being quizzed . . ."

The implied *surface* problem is: *"The people in the other house do things that make visitations painful, scary, unpleasant, or boring too often for my child(ren). It's their fault, and I'm helpless or forced to confront them."*

Or visitations are unpleasant because . . .

"**My (stepparent) mate says** I'm . . . being walked on by my ex / not protecting my child from my ex / giving too much time and energy to visitation issues / worrying more about my kid/s than hers or his / making too big a deal out of visitations / being too sensitive, aggressive, passive, or cooperative / still attracted to my ex / attached to my child at the hip / letting guilt run my life / overprotective / ignoring my mate or my child when s/he visits / 'unnaturally close' to my child / inconsiderate of someone . . ."

The implied surface problem is: visitations are stressful because my (stepparent) partner criticizes me for my values and/or behavior, rather than filling my needs for empathy and support.

And typical co-parents say visitations are a pain because . . .

Stepsiblings fight / whine / complain / are too noisy / don't like each other / won't obey house rules / are too picky about food / gang up on each other / ignore each other / compete / stay up too late / trash the house / seem over-sexual / are rude and disrespectful . . ."

The implied surface problem is: *one or more kids' behaviors cause our visitation problems.* Another surface stressor may be with . . .

Relatives: my mother / father / mother in law / father in law / ex mother in law / ex father in law / other relative criticizes me / my child(ren) / my present partner / my ex mate / all of us for some visitation choices and behaviors without understanding / listening / being asked for their opinion / empathizing / knowing the details / caring what I need or feel . . .

Implied surface problem: *"It's my relatives' fault that visitations are stressful, and I'm helpless to reduce that."*

A final group of surface visitation problems sounds like . . .

The lawyer(s) / judge / legal system / mediator made this ridiculous schedule / is completely unreasonable / is totally biased / made us use this expensive psychological expert who said . . . / forced us to see this counselor, who said .. / cost us thousands of dollars we don't have, to get (no solutions) / threatened me with . . . / won't stand up to my ex about . . ."

Implied surface problem: *"Our visitation stresses are caused by the legal system, not us or me!"*

Did you see elements of your situation here? The average visitation conflict is a mosaic of these stressors, with adults and kids in each home having different perceptions, priorities, and

different sets of criticisms and complaints. My opinion is—
none **of these are the real problems!**

What do you notice about these reasons individually and
all together? What I notice is the complaining co-parents are
critical of, and frustrated with one or more *other* people, and
rarely acknowledge _ their part in "visitation problems" and _
the underlying *real* problems. I have rarely met co-parents who
were aware of everyone's *true* visitation needs, and could problem-solve family-members' unmet visitation needs effectively.

If you're having major trouble sorting and resolving your
version of these stressors, let's use the ideas in Parts 1 and 2 to
explore . . .

Real Visitation Problems and Solutions

You may be uncomfortable with what you're about to read,
because _ *you* are probably part of the "visitation" problems,
and _ some of the *real* problems may feel scary or overwhelming at first. Though you're situation is unique in detail and history, I suspect that your "child visitation problems" are caused
by a mix of these:

1) You all are focusing on the wrong things. I'd bet that
you co-parents are caught up in a cyclic series of blame > defend > counterattack visitation sequences focusing on *surface*
irritants, partly powered by unhappy or "acting-out" kids. Your
real "visitation" problems are probably a mix of these:

2) False-self dominance: one or more of your co-parents
(including *you*) survived a low-nurturance childhood, and suffers from significant psychological wounds. This guarantees
reality distortions, ineffective communications, and ongoing
distrust, disrespect, and frustrations in all your stepfamily relationships, not just visitations!

Long-term solution: starting with you, use the ideas and
tools in Project 1 to assess each of your co-parents for signs of
false-self dominance and related wounds. Then assess each of
your kids. If you find signs, _ learn how these wounds degrade
communications and relationships, _ replace 1-up criticism with

"=/=" compassion, _ take responsibility for healing your own wounds, and _ avoid enabling wounded co-parent partners, including your mate. See Chapters 5 and 6, and the guidebook [Who's Really Running Your Life?].

Another probable underlying *true* source of visitation conflicts is . . .

3) Unawareness: one or more of your co-parents don't yet know some or all of these . . .

_ **how to judge** if a child or adult's true Self is in charge of their inner family (starting with yours!), and _ what to do if a false self is in control—e.g. when a visitation dispute arises. Solution: adopt a long-range view, read, discuss, and apply the chapters in Part 2, and help each other work at them and Project 1 together, over time.

_ **your stepfamily identity** and _ what it means, so some or all of you have unrealistic (visitation) expectations of yourself and other stepfamily members. Solution: do Projects 3, 4, 6, and 7 together, over time, invite your other co-parents to join you after Project 1 is well under way. Then teach your kids, relatives, and family supporters what you're learning.

_ **the seven mental/verbal skills** required for effective planning and problem-solving _ in general, and _ in helping you all meet your true visitation needs. Long-term solution: tailor Chapter 7 to your situation, and commit to helping each other do Project 2. Start by reading [H], then follow up with *Satisfactions*. Specifically:

_ learn the difference between surface needs and underlying true needs (p. 44). Then help each other use awareness and dig-down skills [..02/dig-down.htm] to discern everyone's *true* visitation needs.

_ review [J], and map your typical adult communication sequences about visitation. Help each other use the seven skills and the tips in resource [K] to gradually improve how you all communicate about visitation needs and plans.

_ read and discuss these examples: [..02/lose-lose.htm] and [..02/win-win.htm].

And you co-parents are also probably unaware of . . .

_ **how blocked grief** may be impacting your visitation sequences, and _ what to do about that. Long-term solution: starting with you and your partner, do Project 5 together. Then invite your other co-parents to do their version, and help your kids to become "good grievers." See Chapter 12 and Project 5.

And you adults probably can't name . . .

_ **your (step)kids' four sets** of developmental and change-adjustment needs, and _ how they affect each of your kids' general and visitation true needs. Solution: read and discuss Resource [F] with all your co-parents and older kids. Help each other assess each child for their status with these many needs. For perspective, also share [..10/kids-want.htm] and [..10/kid-memo.htm].

And one or more of you co-parents may not be able to . . .

_ **spot and resolve** _ values and _ loyalty conflicts, and _ (persecutor—victim—rescuer) relationship triangles. I suspect your visitation vexations are partly due to each of them. Solution: read, tailor, and apply Chapter 16, and invite other adults and kids affected by visitations to do learn how to reduce these three related *surface* problems.

Finally, you all may be unfamiliar with . . .

_ **the concept of** first-order (superficial) behavioral changes and second-order (core attitude and priority) changes. If so, you're used to trying to solve your *surface* visitation problems (above) by making first-order changes. As you're wearily aware, they don't work for long, or at all. Solution: read and discuss [..pop/changes1&2.htm], and then review the way you all have been trying to solve your visitation "problems" (need and values conflicts). Accept that most of us make second-order changes only after we "hit the wall," and are so weary, hurting, disgusted, and hopeless that we "break through" old (fear-based) barriers to make fundamental attitude and value changes.

Besides _ one or more of your co-parents and kids being ruled by a false self, and _ several of you being unaware of the seven vital topics above, another probable source of ongoing child-visitation distress is . . .

4) Your three or more co-parents aren't a well-functioning team yet, with common goals and clear roles ("job descriptions") yet. Solution: commit to reading, discussing, and applying this book together, for all your sakes!

Pause and regroup. You've just read a *lot* of ideas, and may feel overwhelmed or discouraged. All together, the above ideas may seem a lot bigger than "getting my ex to pick Sally up on time."

The point here is (again): what seems to be the (visitation) problem probably *isn't* the problem. If one or more of you has recurring heartburn over some aspect of child visitations, I urge you to . . .

Take a long-term view (e.g. 10 or more years), instead of focusing on the last few visitations and the next one;

Help each other accept that for more *long-term* visitation harmony and satisfaction, you co-parenting partners will have to *want to* make some scary second-order (core attitude) changes; including . . .

Adopt a "we" (team) vs. antagonistic "us vs. you" attitude for your kids' sakes and your own; then . . .

Accept that "visitation problems" are probably a composite of several to many smaller surface and true problems (above). Then help each other patiently identify each one, separate and prioritize them, and resolve them one or a few at a time. If you don't, the collective complexity may well progressively overwhelm and traumatize you and your kids, over years of stress and unhappiness. And . . .

If you co-parents are snarled in a legal battle over *surface* child visitation, custody, and/or money disputes, face that the inexorable acrimony and resentment from this will amplify your mix of wounds and team-building barriers for many years. Hiring a legal gunslinger may win the visitation battle at the enormous cost of lowering your family's nurturance level (Chapter 18). That puts your kids at high risk of major current and future health problems [..01/research.htm]. The patient long-term solutions above and in Part 2 are a *far* better investment!

Is this what you expected (or hoped for) when you began

to read this chapter? Pause, breathe, and notice what your subselves are saying now . . .

Recap

Most of America's millions of post-divorce families wrestle with conflicts over child-visitation routines between two homes. These conflicts can be bitter, frustrating, and complex, because of intense parent-child bonds, major values conflicts, unhealed guilts and unmourned losses, and post-divorce feelings. They're part of the larger system of divorced-family and stepfamily relationship "problems" on p. 109.

This chapter proposes . . .

- a 19-part definition of a generic child visitation cycle,
- a multi-part proposal of what it takes to make a *successful* visitation,
- a review of common *surface* "visitation problems," and . . .
- options for resolving four key *true* visitation stressors: _ focusing only on short-term surface problems, _ significant false-self dominance and other psychological wounds in adults and kids, _ unawareness of the ideas and resources in Parts 1 and 2 (specially how to think and communicate effectively), and _ not being able to resolve your set of team-building barriers, so far.

Give yourself time to digest all these ideas. Journal about and/or discuss them, and consider alerting _ your other adults and older kids involved in your child visitations. and _ any professional consultants you've hired. Refer others to the Web version of this chapter at [..Rx/spl/visit.htm.]

See your visitation conflicts as _ opportunities (a glass half-full attitude), and _ normal parts of the larger multi-family merger you're co-managing (Project 9). Keep focused on your shared long-term targets, hold hands, and keep your knees bent and your senses of humor. Stay aware of your many strengths

[..07/strnx-intro.htm], and help each other keep your daily balances as you work on all your projects together (Project 12).
You (all) can do it!

Some divorced-family and stepfamily co-parents face another emotionally-charged *surface* problem: excessive sexual
attraction between ex mates. The next chapter offers perspective on this, and some key options.

22) Reduce Sexual Tensions

Learn What's *Really* Going on, and Act

Depending on many factors, sexual desire, fantasies, anxieties, and behavior may cause significant co-parenting-teamwork barriers in and between your kids' homes. This chapter _ offers background perspective, _ illustrates typical surface problems, _ suggests five underlying primary problems, and _ outlines key options for resolving each of them. If you feel you have a sexual problem with your *mate*, see *The Re/marriage Book* (xlibris.com) or [..Rx/mates/sex.htm].

Status Check. To set the stage, respond to these:

I feel a mix of calm, centered, energized, light, focused, resilient, up, grounded, relaxed, alert, aware, serene, purposeful, compassionate, and clear, so my Self is probably present now. (T F ?)

We have no significant sexually-related problems in or between our kids' co-parenting homes now. (T F ?)

The sensuality of our adults and older kids raises the nurturance level of our multi-home family. (T F ?)

All our family members _ are knowledgeable enough about sexual matters now, and _ can talk freely with each other about sexual aspects of their relationships. (T F ?)

I know why I'm reading this chapter. (T F ?)

Perspective

Sensual pleasures and sexual needs and fantasies are primal responses in healthy teens and adults. They're not subject to will power, Holy Book commandments, or divorce decrees. They're not intrinsically good or bad, any more than digestion or breathing are. The survival of our species depends on us acting on periodic sexual impulses.

How your family members _ behave sexually, and _ react to other members' perceived sexual attitudes and behaviors, *is* (usually) subject to conscious control. Merging one or more stepparents and their kids and relatives with a multi-generational divorced family raises the odds that some people will feel significantly conflicted over sexual values or behaviors.

Our Victorian heritage of idealized romantic *love* and sexual "propriety" has gradually lost ground because of _ female "emancipation," _ religious liberalism, and _ pervasive, relentless media focus on sexual images and thrills. Our society has become more sexually "liberal," with pockets of fierce protest from various groups. One recent effect has been the horrifying discovery of how widespread sexual abuse of children has been in our country, and of the massive psychological wounding it causes and passes down the generations.

The ancient prohibition against sexual intercourse among genetically-related people also shapes your family's sexual attitudes and boundaries. This incest taboo does not extend to most stepfamilies, since stepkin share no genes, and usually haven't grown up with each other.

American freedom of expression allows the print, film, advertising, and electronic media to profit from our insatiable, primal demand for sexual titillation. This relentlessly exaggerates and distorts normal sexual thoughts and behaviors, and may amplify or conflict with the sexual attitudes and values that adults gave each of your co-parents as kids. Reflect: where did each of your parents fit between _ sexually liberal and permissive, to _ numb or confused and ambivalent (double messages) to _ massive shame, guilt, and anxiety)? What sexual attitudes are *you* modeling for your minor kids and others?

So what does all this mean to you co-parents? Divorced families and stepfamilies like yours can have a mosaic of . . .

Typical Surface Problems

Though details vary infinitely, sexually-oriented co-parent barriers fall into categories like these:

Alleged or admitted past and/or present sexual abuse—forcing unwanted or harmful sexual experiences on a naïve or helpless (vulnerable) child or adult.

Unwanted sexual behavior between ex mates, like language, threats, advances, innuendos, and harassments.

Excessive guilt, shame, anxiety, and confusion over sexual desire for, or fantasies about, ex mates, biokids or stepkids, and/or other people. This includes "unfinished business" about prior or current extra-marital affairs. More on that below.

Suspected, perceived, or actual sexual behavior between children.

Major values conflicts between co-parents and relatives over _ adult sexual preferences and behaviors, and _ guiding minor kids to healthy sexual values and practices. These can include conflicts over religious values.

Marital and household conflict over _ pornography, and/or _ alleged or actual hiring of prostitutes.

Jealousy, suspicion (distrust), and/or disapproval among co-parents about imagined or real sexual thoughts or behaviors.

Discord over _ adult or child bisexuality or homosexuality, _ masturbation, or _ adults exposing children to sexual behavior too soon.

Using a child as a sexual spy, confidant, or messenger (triangling).

Alleged or clear "promiscuous behavior" in one or more adults and kids.

Sex-related drug usage.

Adults shaming kids for normal sexual curiosity and experimenting.

Unwanted pregnancies, which cause a mosaic of complex home and family problems. And . . .

Sexually-transmitted disease (STDs), sexual hygiene, and "safe sex" values and practices.

These stressors are real, and complement the normal range of sexual _ need and _ values conflicts between mates. The stress usually doesn't come from sexual impulses themselves, but from the emotions and behaviors they cause. Two of them deserve special perspective:

Perspective: Sexual Abuse

Clinical literature and my therapeutic experience suggest that sexual abuse is among the most psychologically damaging traumas a child or young adult can experience. Many lay people are unaware of what sexual abuse is and isn't, and what to do about it's effects on a person and family.

True abuse, vs. _aggression_, must meet the three conditions on p. 26. _Sexual_ abuse involves a "power person" gratifying their emotional, and _perhaps_ physical, sexual needs in a way that wounds the helpless victim. There are many more sexual traumas than forced body-penetration or sensual skin contact. For example . . .

Allowing or forcing a child to witness live or media sexual acts, including masturbation, torture, and rape;

Allowing or forcing a child to expose their genitals, or to witness others' genitals, without any skin-on-skin contact;

Seducing or forcing a child into sexually-suggestive or provocative interactions with adults, kids, objects, and/or animals;

Exposing children to human or animal sexual images without age-appropriate explanations, before they understand their bodies, and human sexuality and procreation.

Intentionally misguiding children on sexual information, morality, or consequences, including associating sexual thoughts or actions with malevolent spirits, gods, or other emotionally-loaded spiritual or fantasy images; and . . .

Using sexually explicit or provocative language, and/or sexualizing situations, ideas, or objects.

In general, any sexual behavior that significantly shames, frightens, misinforms, disorients, or physically injures, a compliant or unwilling child, and/or causes them significant guilts, can qualify as true sexual abuse. Often, abusive adults amplify the trauma of any of these by threatening major pain if the child tells anyone about them. Not instructing a child accurately on human sexuality, and/or not supervising their sexual experimentation, is caregiving *neglect*, and may qualify as indirect sexual abuse.

Whatever the details, childhood sexual trauma _ usually occurs amidst other low-nurturance stressors, and _ *always* promotes major false-self development and related wounding. Victims' common (false-self) protective strategies are "forgetting," denying, minimizing, projecting, and/or intellectualizing _ abusive events and _ the intense related agonies and impacts. One moral of this: be very cautious about accepting any co-parent's belief that sexual abuse in their early years "is totally healed."

Secondly, if any of your co-parents or their parents are accused of sexually abusing someone, pay serious attention to the allegations *and their impact/s*. True or not, the *accusation* of sexual abuse will galvanize false selves. Look for significant psychological wounds (p. 448, and Resource E) _ in the accused person *and* _ their alleged victim/s *and* _ related family members. Be specially alert for _ significant distrust, disrespect, guilt, shame, and repressed or obsessive anger and blaming, _ addictions (Chapter 20), and _ "depressions" (Chapter 12). All of these suggest a dominant false self.

A well-regarded resource for sexual-abuse survivors and supporters is "The Courage to Heal," by Ellen Bass and Laura Davis. There are many other books and helpful Web sites, and probably local clinicians with special sex-abuse recovery training and experience. When any co-parent has significant concern about possible or sure sexual abuse, seek qualified professional help without delay.

Another common barrier in divorced families and stepfamilies is significant emotional residue from . . .

Extra-marital (Sexual) Affairs

A significant minority of the hundreds of co-parents I've consulted with mentioned extra-marital affairs as a major stressor in their childhood, past marriage, and/or re/marriage. Shelves of learned and anecdotal books and tapes are devoted to exploring this age-old human trait, from tabloid, psychological, moral, religious, and sociological perspectives.

Do any of your co-parents admit or deny a suspected past or current affair? If so, in the context of this series and chapter, several major points are probably worth considering and discussing:

Premise: all animal behavior is cause by *needs* (discomforts) and instincts (primal neural programs). So a romantic or sexual affair suggests that both participants had needs that weren't filled enough elsewhere. This implies that a spouse choosing an affair lacks something in their primary relationship. This leads to the tough question "Which mate is responsible for filling their respective *true* relationship needs [*The Re/marriage Book* or ..08/remarriage2.htm]?"

Shame-based false selves will insist that their mate is responsible for choosing an affair, and that they are blameless. If the accused mate is also wounded, s/he will probably invite an endless [avoid or explain > defend > counterblame . . .] behavioral sequence. This short-sighted strategy is *guaranteed* to leave everyone's true needs unfilled, and amplify family surface conflicts. Typical true Selves will _ minimize self or mate shaming and guilt, and _ calmly look for who's true needs weren't getting filled, why, and what can be learned from these.

Starting with *you*, if any of your co-parents had (or have) secret, alleged, or admitted romantic or sexual affairs, I suggest that . . .

Both partners and the third person probably _ came from low-nurturance childhoods, and _ were or are often dominated by a false self. If so, I propose spending your energy on proving, analyzing, or moralizing about the affair is *far* less productive than assessing for major inner wounds, owning them, and healing them. Working to release major guilts, shame, disrespect, and distrust (of self or another) are useful targets, within the context of Project 1—true-Self enabling, and inner-family harmonizing. And . . .

All participants in the affair probably couldn't communicate and problem-solve effectively, which merits compassion and empathy, not scorn; and . . .

Kids, relatives, and key friends may have "unfinished business" about the allegations and/or realities. These deserve _ identifying, _rank-ordering, and _ respectful confrontation and resolution among you all, in the interest of co-parental team-building.

If there are sexual or romantic affairs among you and your respective siblings and parents, A fundamental question each of your co-parents must answer is: "*Is someone who participates in an affair a* bad *(weak, irresponsible, promiscuous, lecherous, sly, dishonest, immoral, shameful, despicable, pathetic . . .) person—or is s/he* wounded *and* unaware?" If any if your active subselves feel the former, that will inexorably promote "1-up" R(espect) messages (p. 510) in your behavior. Those *always* degrade communication effectiveness, relationship quality, and caregiving teamwork. The more your co-parents ruling subselves hold the latter attitude, the more pronounced this degradation and related problems will be. Do you agree?

Moralizing, preaching, and c/overtly blaming co-parents about affairs or other "misdeeds," and *ignoring them*, will cause or magnify your secondary family problems and inhibit your teamwork. Everyone loses, specially your minor kids and their descendents.

I assume you're reading this chapter because one or more of the "sexual situations" above concerns you directly or indirectly. If you have specific questions and needs about your family's versions of these stressors, what are they?

I again suggest that sexually-oriented family problems like these are symptoms of underlying *primary* problems. If so, trying to solve the secondary (surface) problems by making first-order (behavioral) changes probably won't fill your immediate or long-range needs. What *can* work permanently is identifying, owning, discussing, and resolving your half of . . .

The *True* Problems

From prior chapters, I hope you can now predict the five probable primary causes of typical sex-related problems like those above:

Psychological wounds: one or more of your co-parents is dominated by a protective false self, and most or all of you aren't aware of that and it's implications. When surface sexual problems exist, they often relate to unhealed sexual traumas in childhood and/or early adulthood. Such traumas usually resulted from primary caregivers' wounds and unawarenesses and low-nurturance early childhoods. These wounds in your co-parents promote all the core problems in Part 2, amplified by . . .

2) Unawareness: one or more of your co-parents doesn't yet know how to . . .

spot and react appropriately to _ sexual abuse and/or _ sexual "addiction" (Chapter 20);

spot and reduce excessive _ guilt, _ shame, and/or _ anxieties about human sensuality or sexuality;

define, model, and teach healthy sexual information, responsibilities, and limits to resident and visiting kids;

find qualified clinical, medical, and legal help with marital or family sexual problems, including recovery from past sexual traumas;

spot and resolve sex-related _ values and loyalty conflicts and _ relationship triangles (Chapter 16); and . . .

communicate effectively (Chapter 7).

Personal and family "sexual problems" occur among a

welter of other simultaneous stressors. So a third core problem in your family can be . . .

3) Blocked grief. The two primary problems above can contribute to one or more of your co-parents being unable to fully accept some major broken bonds (Chapter 12). That _ will inhibit stabilizing family relationships and roles after death, divorce, and re/marriage, and _ can promote addictions, including to sexual excitement and orgasm. These three stressors can combine and contribute to . . .

4) Overwhelm: your unique mix of psychological wounds, unawarenesses, needs, and core barriers (p. 109) can paralyze, demoralize, scare, and "depress" (overwhelm) some adults and/ or kids. I've heard some unaware co-parents describe this as "laziness" or "apathy." Feeling chronically overwhelmed adds another real *secondary* problem to your family mix, which hinders resolving your set of the core barriers. I propose that lasting or recurring overwhelm is usually a symptom of significant false-self dominance + unawarenesses + low-nurturance environments.

A last core problem may be . . .

5) Neuro-chemical problems. My 23-year (non-medical) training and experience as a psychotherapist suggests a strong correlation between psycho-spiritual wounding in childhood, chronic false-self dominance, and many "chemical imbalances" and psychosomatic illnesses in adults and neglected kids.

If this premise is true for your family, then any significant "sexual problems" that inhibit your co-parenting teamwork are really symptoms of _ psychological wounding, plus _ unawareness (ignorance), plus _ ineffective adult thinking and communicating, plus _ possible neuro-chemical factors. Once you understand and assess for these four, you can choose to intentionally reduce at least the first three over time. Medication may help regulate (vs. "cure") the fourth. Distrustful, unaware, myopic false selves will often persistently try to divert or dissuade you from taking action on these until your discomforts become intolerable.

Options

You've already taken the first option by acknowledging that one or more of your co-parents has "a sexual problem." Related options include _ learn more now, and develop more options; _ defer any action to "later;" or _ accept things the way they are now. If your subselves elect the first of these, some choices you have are to . . .

Disregard the idea that there are core problems, and work to resolve what I propose are *surface* problems. If you do, I predict that you'll eventually admit that your core needs haven't been satisfied "well enough," or have reappeared in another form. Pursuing surface solutions teaches you long-term _ what won't work, and _ what your *real* targets are. You and I make second-order (core belief and priority) changes when our despair is great enough, and we've tried all the "easy" safe solutions . . .

Another option you may choose is to . . .

Research the five primary problems above to see if they fit your situation and warrant action.

To learn whether any of you co-parents are significantly controlled by a false self, start by assessing *yourself* via [E], and the Project-1 resources in *Who's* Really *Running Your Life?* or [..pop/assess.htm]. If you feel *your* Self is disabled, evolve and work patiently at a high-priority personal recovery plan. If you feel another co-parent is significantly wounded, select options like those in Chapters 5 and 6.

Option: use "parts work" (inner-family harmonizing) to identify which subselves "activate" over major surface "sexual stressor/s." What does each such subself think, feel, and *need*? Do any distrust or blend with (take over) your true Self when sexual conflicts or needs arise?

If you feel that *unawareness* of any of the factors above is a significant primary problem, the next step is developing your motivation to seek and learn. We live in an Information Era, where knowledge has never been so available to so many people, and is expanding so fast. Consider this paradox: you can't appreciate the personal and family importance of accurate information on the factors above until you learn about them. What you don't know *can* hurt you and your loved ones!

To assess your knowledge of the seven communication skills, take this quiz: [..02/evc-quiz]. Then review Resources [H—K] in Part 3, and decide if you want to learn more. If so, study the guidebook [*Satisfactions*] or the resources at [..02/links02.htm].

Premise: interpersonal disputes often have up to three parts: *inner-family* conflicts in _ you and _ your partner, and _ disputes *between* your teams of subselves. So the first place to try out your upgraded communication skills is among your inner-family's subselves [..01/ifs8-innr_cnflct.htm]. This will probably seem alien to you. Once you define who composes your inner family [..01/ifs3-prep.htm], try it and see what happens over time! An interesting, useful resource is "Embracing Each Other," by Hal Stone and Sidra Winkleman.

Because sexual topics are usually emotionally-loaded and volatile, talking clearly and effectively about your "sexual teamwork barriers" can be hard. To help identify and correct sex-talk "problems," try recording and mapping the communication sequences among your subselves [..02/evc-maps.htm]. Include avoidances, vaguenesses, and silences, and pay special attention to E-levels, R-messages, and awareness "bubbles." Does your sequence qualify as *effective* (inner) communication (p. 509)? If not, what *within your control* would make it more effective? Then try mapping the "sex-talk" sequences between your co-parents or important others. Do they qualify as effective communication? If not, what *within your control* would make your discussions more effective?

Another research option is to . . .

Identify your attitudes about your and/or someone else's sexual impulses, fantasies, and behaviors. Part of the core problem may be that one or more of your co-parents have been taught to feel excessive guilt, shame, or anxiety about these normal human responses. If so, these attitudes will c/overtly reduce self and/or mutual respect (Chapter 8). These inevitably degrade effective co-parental communications and relations.

Excessive shame, guilt, and anxiety are signs of _ misinformation or unawareness, plus _ false-self dominance, plus (perhaps) _ a low-nurturance environment [D]. Once aware of these, your co-parents can reduce each of them over time, *if* their Selves are in charge. Suggestions:

Because they're healed differently, refresh your discernment between *shame* (I'm a bad, worthless person) and *guilt* (I break important shoulds, oughts and musts).

Meditate and decide honestly if you feel that shame and guilt are each _ healthy and normal, _ *negative* and *bad*, or _ helpful or toxic depending on situational factors. I propose each is a normal, useful human emotion signaling some needs are unfilled. *Excessive* shame and guilt is common in survivors of low-nurturance childhoods, and can cause major harm to bodily health and family relationships.

Reflect on your reaction to statements like these. T = true, F = false, "?" = "I'm not sure" or "it depends":

I feel a mix of calm, centered, energized, light, focused, resilient, up, grounded, relaxed, alert, aware, serene, purposeful, compassionate, and clear, so my Self is probably present now. (T F ?)

Sexual thoughts or fantasies about people other than your primary partner are *always* wrong and bad. (T F ?)

Sexual thoughts or actions other than for procreation are *always* wrong and bad. (T F ?)

Sexual thoughts, fantasies, and impulses are normal and OK, as long as I don't *act* on them with someone other than my primary adult partner. (T F ?)

Divorced parents who have strong sexual feelings for their ex mate and/or children are *sick* and/or *bad*. (T F ?)

Healthy, mature ("good") men and women should be able to control their sexual thoughts, fantasies, and feelings (vs. actions). (T F ?)

Adults who need to masturbate, hire prostitutes, and/or use pornography are *bad* and *wrong*. (T F ?)

I feel no significant shame or guilt now about past sexual incidents or choices; *or* if I do, I'm actively working to heal them now. (T F ?)

Each of my parents _ accepted, appreciated, and enjoyed their sensuality and sexuality, and _ felt no significant shame or guilt about either of these or their gender. (T F ?)

I'm comfortable talking about sexual issues with _ family adults (including any ex mate), _ older kids, _ close friends, and _ any counselors and clergy who support us. (T F ?)

I responded to these questions honestly, calmly, and without major doubt, anxiety, or uncertainty. (T F Mixed)

What did you just learn? If you want to reduce excessive guilt, see Chapters 10 and 11. If *you* feel significant shame or embarrassment about sexual (or other) issues, _ do Project 1 *Who's* Really *Running Your Life?*, and _ read and apply relevant ideas in "Healing the Shame that Bind You," by John Bradshaw.

In addition to assessing for false-self dominance [E] and building awarenesses (Chapter 1), you co-parents can choose to agree on the _ symptoms and _ effects of personal "overwhelm." Then use those to assess for it, and reduce it in your related homes. In my experience, key symptoms are _ significant indecisiveness, passivity, or aggression; _ rigidity (black/white thinking); _ isolation and avoidances; _ relying on medications for daily functioning, including fats and sugar (carbohydrates); _ "irritability," _ "mood swings," _ "depression," and _ difficulty focusing.

All these are symptoms of false-self dominance and the other five related psychological wounds. They contribute to the web of core co-parental barriers on p. 109, which promote "overwhelm." Note the cycle: _ false-self dominance and _ unawarenesses cause a web of core problems (Part 2), which promote Part-3 surface problems (including "sexual"), which interact to _ amplify false-self dominance and wounding others, including your kids. If unseen and unbroken, this cycle silently spreads down the generations . . .

Self-motivated true personal **recovery** (Project 1) **and** proactively **learning** about the topics in Chapters 1-3 (and healthy sexual attitudes and practices) **can break this toxic cycle** by reducing your mix of core barriers, over time. Your odds of progress rise when _ your co-parents' Selves are leading, you all are growing _ =/= (mutual respect) attitudes and _ effective communication skills, and you _ separate and rank your concurrent barriers and family-adjustment tasks, and patiently work together on a few at a time. Are you tiring of reading this?

To discern whether blocked grief in any of your co-parents or kids is contributing to your "sexual problems," read Chapter 12 and Project 5 in *Stepfamily Courtship* or [http://sfhelp.org/05/links05.htm]. Whether you find blocked grief or not, a helpful option is to consciously evolve a family "Good Grief" policy (p. 255) and help each other apply it in and between your homes.

Two final overarching options:

Grow your shared awareness: invite each of your co-parents to read this chapter or book, or the Web articles at [..Rx/mates/sex.htm], [..Rx/ex/lust.htm], [..Rx/spsc/lust.htm], and [..Rx/sibs/lust.htm]. Then discuss whether any of the stressors and ideas in those articles apply to your family, and warrant co-operative action. Help each other _ avoid blame, loyalty conflicts, and relationship triangles (Chapter 16); and _ focus on long-range teamwork that builds your multi-home family's nurturance level.

Remind yourself to reread this chapter on some specific future date (when?), to assess and celebrate your progress on any of your action-options above.

Recap

Primal sexual desires, fantasies, and pleasures—and related guilts, shame, and anxieties—can promote a wide range of *secondary* (surface) personal and relationship stressors in divorced families and stepfamilies like yours. Where so, these often follow sexual neglect and traumas in childhood and/or young adulthood. These secondary stressors combine with others in Part 3 to hinder _ personal recovery from false-self dominance, _ grieving prior losses, and _ bonding and building co-parental teamwork. Until identified and patiently reduced, these all lower the nurturance level of your multi-home family. *That* promotes unconsciously passing on the toxic bequest of false-self dominance and related inner wounds.

This overview chapter summarizes common sex-related family stressors, and proposes that they're all symptoms of up to four inter-related underlying problems:

* false-self dominance in one or more co-parents;
* a mix of unawarenesses, specially of communication skills;
* mental/emotional overwhelm in one or more family members; and possibly . . .
* organic and/or psychosomatic medical conditions.

The chapter suggests representative options you co-parents have to _ identify and _ reduce each of these four, starting with assessing for false-self dominance. Once again, **the options net out to**: help each other _ avoid focusing on your *surface* "sexual problems" and _ identify and reduce your family's unique mix of the underlying primary problems in part 2. This vital work starts with Project 1 (empower your Self and harmonize your inner family), and Project 2 (learn effective thinking and communication skills together, and teach your kids).

Stretch and breathe. Do you need a break? We're in the home stretch of reviewing common *surface* barriers to the co-parental teamwork your kids need. The next one is common to all families: arguing over major family changes. When your ready, let's explore . . .

23) Teamwork and Family Change

A Payoff for Reducing Your Barriers

Your nuclear family is composed of adults and children living in two or more homes. As your family evolves, your co-parents and kids are likely to experience membership, role, ritual, and other significant changes that affect everyone. Your first major family changes after divorce or mate death may include new jobs, homes, and communities; a parent's courtship and re/wedding, and/or people cohabiting. Serious courtship starts an amazingly complex process of merging (changing) three or more biofamilies, over many years. To review 14 sets of things that families like yours must merge, scan the chapter on Project 9a in *Build a High-nurturance Stepfamily*, or [..09/merge.htm].

When (not if) major changes to family structure or process occur, your co-parents' level of teamwork will determine how stressful these changes will be, and how they affect your family's nurturance level. Conversely, how your family members react to major changes may build or hinder co-parenting teamwork.

This chapter invites you to become more aware of the inevitable process of family change, and how your co-parents' teamwork barriers may affect it. We'll look at _ the changes you may encounter, _ factors that affect how stressful they may be, and _ key choices that can minimize your stress from future changes.

Lets start by reviewing . . .

About Family Change . . .

Your family's "structure" is built from people, roles, rules, goals, assets, and boundaries. A "structural change" involves one or more of these things shifting a little or a lot. When they change, everyone affected must adjust their expectations, priorities, and routines. Structural changes affect your family's *dynamics*—how you all interact in normal and special situations. *That* affects your family's current and long-term nurturance level: how well each adult and child gets their true needs met, over time.

All families change expectedly or suddenly because of child conceptions, deaths, graduations, kids leaving home, promotions and retirements, relocations, natural disasters, disablements, bankruptcies, and so on. Typical divorced families and stepfamilies also encounter special structural changes like these . . .

a child's bioparent courts, re/weds, or re/divorces a stepparent; or . . .

a new stepparent initiates major child-related changes in and between the child/ren's two homes; and/or . . .

an ex mate and stepparent conceive or want to adopt one or more children; and/or . . .

important relatives politely or rudely exclude new stepfamily members from biofamily traditions or rituals; and/or . . .

physical custody of one or more minor kids transfers to the other co-parent/s' home by agreement, demand, or court order.

And intact-biofamily members don't have to adapt to . . .

stepsibs or stepparents and stepkids feeling or acting sexual together; and/or . . .

an exasperated stepparent refusing to nurture a disrespectful, defiant resident or visiting stepchild; and/or . . .

an ex mate or new couple moving significantly closer to or away from the child's other home; and/or . . .

an ex mate or other couple having major occupational and financial shifts, including bankruptcy or sudden wealth; and/ or . . .

a co-parent initiating a legal suit about child visitation, support, or custody; or . . .

the special complexity of change-related loyalty and values conflicts, and relationship triangles (Chapter 16); and/or . . .

an ex mate trying to block contact and/or bias a child against their other bioparent and/or a stepparent ("Parent Alienation Syndrome).—PAS").

Have you all experienced any of these—yet?

Perspective

Changes like these happen in the midst of your multi-year biofamily merger, and your physical and social environments constantly shifting. Even if foreseen or chosen, changes like these can combine to upset the rhythms and balance of your whole multi-home family for weeks or months. If changes cause major losses (broken bonds) for one or more members, the upset includes healthy or blocked grief (Chapter 12). Disruptions are greater and last longer if several changes happen at once, aren't expected, and/or some of you haven't stabilized from prior changes.

Disruptions are also bigger if any family adults deny _ your identity as a stepfamily, _ the related norms [..03/facts.htm] and _ five re/marital hazards (p. 428), and _ your kids' and adults' many adjustment tasks (pp. 464 and 493). Family disruption and it's impacts (a secondary problem) can also be magnified by kids' and relatives' reactions to co-parent changes like these, like anger, "rebellion," relationship cut-offs, taking sides (triangles), or depression. Special stress from changes is likely in bi-racial, same-gender, and ethnically or religiously mixed stepfamilies.

The high probability of complex stressful family changes like these is one reason it's vital during co-parent courtship to _ acknowledge *"We're forming (or joining) a *step*family"*

(Project 3), and then _ work together to convert up to 60 unrealistic (bio-family-based) myths [..04/myths.htm] into realistic stepfamily expectations [..04/60expect1.htm]. One such expectation is *"We must expect that major changes may happen to us all with or without warning."*

Details of family changes vary infinitely. **The core challenge** your co-parents face is: when such changes happen, do you have a "you vs. us" attitude, and get tangled in defocusing, blaming, resenting, and disrespecting each other; or do you empathically help each other adapt and stabilize *our family* changes? The answer depends on whose needs each of your adults feel are most important locally and overall. *That* hinges on how well all of you are progressing on your version of the 12 family-building projects on p. 430—specially Project 10: building a caregiving team by reducing your mix of the barriers on p. 109. Does this seem realistic to you? To bring this point home, try this . . .

#Status Check:

I feel a mix of calm, centered, energized, light, focused, resilient, up, grounded, relaxed, alert, aware, serene, purposeful, compassionate, and clear, so my Self is probably present now. (T F ?)

I include each of our children's living parents and stepparents as full members of our multi-home family now. (T F ?) If you don't yet, work on Project 3 *in Stepfamily Courtship* or [..03/project03.htm].

All our co-parents can describe the five hazards we and our dependent kids face now (T F ?)

All our co-parents _ can name, and _ are fully committed to, the 12 projects we need to work on together to build a high-nurturance multi-home family. (T F ?) If not, _ what's in the way, _ who's responsible for fixing that, and _ what may happen if it's not fixed?

I believe all of our co-parents are making reasonable progress on our version of these projects, *or* we're actively working on reducing any barriers to our progress. (T F ?)

If *all* your co-parents can't clearly answer "T(rue)" to these items, focus your efforts on reducing applicable barriers in Part 2. If you all *can* answer "True," then tailor the guidelines below to help each other manage major family changes effectively. To prepare for that, let's explore. . .

10 Stress Factors

"Stress" means some mix of anxiety (worry) + confusion + doubt + resentment + sadness + excitement + frustration that is judged to significantly effect someone's wholistic health and/ or role performance. Significant stress can occur in and between your homes when . . .

. . . significant structural change is proposed or declared, but hasn't started (*"Max and I are thinking about moving to Alaska"*); and . . .

. . . the change is in process (effects are first experienced); and . . .

. . . after the structural changes "end," and your individual and combined homes restabilize their roles, rules, rituals, and relationships. The degree and duration of stress in these three periods depend on your mix of 10 or more factors. Options: _ using a scale of 1 to 10, rate your family on these factors now, and/or _ be alert for (false-self) overwhelm as you read.

How your several homes are structured—i.e. who's in charge, and how effectively they're managing normal and special tasks. Discover your family's structure with this tool: [..09/ map-str1.htm].

How stable (calm, balanced, confident, resilient, aware) your family system is before the changes happen. In typical post-divorce families, this depends on _ how well kids and adults are doing with their respective adjustment tasks (pp. 467 and 496), and _ how *balanced* your co-parents are (Project 12). Those factors depend on _ how each of your co-parents are doing at empowering their true Selves, (Project 1) and _ how informed they are (Chapter 1).

_ **Who** initiates the change/s (one or two of your co-parents, or all of you); and _ why (what surface and true needs are being filled); and . . .

Whether the changes are _ chosen or _ forced by uncontrollable events like major illness or disability, accidents, natural disasters, job upheavals, and riots; and . . .

_ **Who's affected** by the changes and _ *how* they're affected (a little to a lot). Personal and family stress is proportional to change/s filling family members' key needs vs. creating major *new* needs (discomforts).

Other stressors include . . .

Members' *attitudes* **about change**: where each affected adult and child falls on the line between "family change is safe, enriching, exciting, and rewarding (glass half full)," and "family change is always scary, hurtful, confusing, and stressful (half empty)." Often _ the degree of animosity and conflict during co-parents' divorce/s, and _ key childhood experiences with change shape your adults' and kids' attitudes about major family-structure changes. Where do each of your co-parents fall on this "attitude scale"?

Whether the change/s are _ well planned and _ discussed with everyone affected, or imposed suddenly or aggressively by one or two co-parents (*"I've had it. Sandy is coming to live with you next Tuesday."*), Stress also depends on . . .

How well your family members can support each other in grieving the losses (broken emotional bonds) that major structural changes cause (Chapter 12 and Project 5); and . . .

How effective your co-parents are at _ planning and _ communicating and resolving the conflicts (unmet needs) that structural changes cause (Chapter 7); and finally . . .

Environmental factors affect your stress—local safety, the availability and effectiveness of relevant community supports, and perhaps geographic factors like climate, locale, pollution, allergens, and pests.

Reflect on the last major family change you experienced (birth, death, wedding, divorce, retirement, graduation, geographic move, adoption, disablement, etc.). Did each of these factors contribute to the harmony or chaos during and after the change? Were there other factors that played a key role? In your opinion, how well did your family plan for, manage, and adjust to the change/s? How long did it take for your family to restabilize? Would other members agree with you?

Add your own factors to these 10 to form a change-planning checklist.

Change-Management

Here, "family-change management" means you co-parents (ideally) agreeing on how to _ plan major changes effectively, and _ resolve significant problems (fill members' main true needs) before, during, and after the change takes effect. Shared progress on Projects 1 through 6 and 9 will help you do this together.

As you know, an effective plan requires _ someone to accept leadership responsibility, who _ collects and ranks the needs of everyone affected, and then _ defines what the end goals are and _ what's needed to achieve them. Your leader/s then _ gather resources, _ initiate the change, _ monitor progress, and _ resolve conflicts effectively until family stability returns. Reality: each of your two or more co-parenting homes has one or two leaders, who may or may not value co-operative (team) planning, or be able to *do* it.

Core Problems

If your three or more co-parents are having trouble managing major family structural changes, you probably have some of the real (vs. surface) problems below. Use this summary to help _ identify manageable targets, _ prioritize them against your family's *long term* goals (Project 6) and other responsibilities, and _ help each other work patiently to reduce each of these over time . . .

Too little teamwork. One or more of your co-parents is wounded and indifferent (or overwhelmed) and antagonistic. A symptom of that is not really caring how their major lifestyle changes will affect other related adults or kids outside their home. if *the way* a co-parent proposes or causes a major change in your multi-home family is perceived by other members as "*my (or our) needs are more important to me (or us) than yours*"; then teamwork barriers like disrespect, distrust, and hostility (anger) will probably grow.

They'll also grow if the co-parents who must adapt to the changes respond with "1-up" behaviors like blame, criticism, sarcasm, resistance, and/or retribution—specially if they (you) use kids as spies, pawns, or agents ("*You tell your Dad you won't visit him if he moves to Nevada.*)"

Incidentally, I'm assuming that you co-parents are solidly in charge of your respective homes, vs. a strong-willed (needy) child or relative, or *no one*. [..09/map-str1.htm].

Bottom line: you caregivers can't begin to manage major family changes effectively until you've made major progress on each relevant teamwork barrier on p. 109. You'll have trouble doing that if two or more of you made . . .

Wrong re/marriage decisions. If you re/wedded without doing some version of the first seven projects in [A] during courtship, either of you partners may have committed to the wrong (wounded, unaware) people, for the wrong reasons (e.g. to rescue or end loneliness or overwhelm), at the wrong time (e.g. before healing inner wounds, learning Chapter-1 topics, and grieving well). (Re)read a true vignette illustrating this in "One Stepfamily's Story" *Stepfamily Courtship* or [..example.htm].

If this is true for you, seeking co-parental harmony and/or stability from major co-parental changes now may be unrealistic or fruitless. You can still learn much from your experiences, heal personal wounds, and live more authentically as you admit your losses, grieve, and decide on your best options. To see if this factor may apply to you, see Project 7 in *Stepfamily Courtship* or [..07/links07.htm]. If it does apply, mull the options in [..Rx/mates/redivorce1.htm].

If your co-parents each made three *right* re/marital deci-

sions, your next possible change-management problem may
be . . .

Family identity and membership conflicts. If an ex mate
and/or new stepparent . . .

. . . doesn't accept your potential or actual group identity
as a *stepfamily*; and/or . . .

. . . doesn't care what that identity *means* [A]; and/or . . .

. . . rejects other co-parents or excludes themselves from
stepfamily membership; then . . .

. . . they won't be motivated to evaluate how and when to
manage major family changes for all your sakes. If this is true
in your case, it's highly likely the real problem is denied psychological wounds in the co-parent/s, and key unawarenesses.
Recall that adults ruled by false selves tend to pick each other
repeatedly, until well along in true (vs. pseudo) recovery. Chapters 1 through 6 point the way . . .

A fourth core change-management problem you may have
is . . .

Nuclear-(step)family instability. A *mobile* is a network of
objects hanging by threads or strings from rods of different
lengths When any object is moved, the whole network oscil-
lates until gravity gradually restores balance (no motion) to it.
Your multi-home family is like a mobile, with the bars and
strings being bonds and relationships among your infants, kids.
and adults.

Picture your mobile with the "objects" being 50 to 100+
small dolls or photos of the adults and kids living in your present
family's many multi-generational homes (p. 437). This mobile
began when one or more smaller mobiles (prior first-marriage
families) were restructured by divorce or mate-death. It took
some *years* for each disturbed mobile to rebalance. Before or
after rebalancing, a new co-parent's mobile (biofamily) was
added when you mates courted and re/wedded. Rebalancing
the larger system takes more years than before, because there
are many more elements, strings, and bars.

A stepfamily-merger of three or more multi-generational
biofamilies is stunningly complex. It spans up to 14 sets of

physical and invisible factors [..09/merge.htm], among scores of people whose individual lives are changing at the same time—in changing social and biospheric environments!

Each of the changes on p. 403 represents a major disruption to your "big mobile." If your family network hadn't stabilized from prior significant changes (divorce, relocations, grieving losses, role changes), adding a new change too soon may make restabilizing "too long" for some people to tolerate.

Restated: if any of your co-parents initiate major family changes like those above before *all* your affected adults, kids, and relatives have had a chance to . . .

accept your new family identity and agree on who belongs (Projects 3 and 4), and . . .

learn new realities and life-skills (Chapters 1-4), and . . .

assess and begin healing from psychological wounds (Chapters 5 and 6), and . . .

grow effective communications (Chapter 7), and . . .

grieve prior losses, and help kids mourn their own, (Chapter 12 and Project 5), and . . .

reduce prior adult disrespects, distrusts, and guilts, (Chapters 8, 9, and 10) and . . .

clarify, negotiate, and stabilize new family roles, rules, relationships, and expectations—i.e. progress well together on [..09/sf-task1.htm], and . . .

understand the new change/s (like an ex-mate re/wedding a single parent) and what they'll *mean* to individuals and your whole extended-family system . . .

. . . then *everyone* in your big mobile will be stressed to varying extents, slowing or blocking your family's rebalancing and merging. Premature and/or excessively violent "disturbances" (changes) may cause parts of your mobile (family system) to collapse (major depressions and "breakdowns," illnesses, separations, desertions, cutoffs, and divorces). For perspective on the factors that determine the right (stable-enough) *time* to implement any of the co-parent changes above, read and discuss [http://sfhelp.org/07/rt-time.htm].

Another (common) core problem may be . . .

No viable change-management policy and/or plan. A related problem is having a reasonably-discussed policy and plan, but no cooperative implementation or follow through—probably a symptom of false-self control.

Some key elements of your "family change-management policy" include . . .

Who comprises your family—i.e. who's needs shall be considered in planning important family changes? And . . .

Whether your members view major changes as risky and scary (glass half empty), or inevitable, manageable, and sources of valuable learning and growth (glass half full). If the former, do you think it's feasible to change basic attitudes like these? Review Chapter 3. And . . .

Which family member/s are responsible for _ planning and _ managing important family changes in identity, membership, roles, rules, rituals, assets and debts, securities, locations, and boundaries; and . . .

Whether members should or can distinguish between *changes* (no major broken emotional bonds) and *losses*, which justify helping each other grieve (Chapter 12); and . . .

Whether members should help each other distinguish between surface planning goals (needs), and underlying *true* needs.

And . . .

_ **What** are the primary true current needs of your adults and kids (pp. 44, 467, 496, and 508), _ what is an appropriate time-frame (immediate vs. long-term needs), and _ how shall both of these determine what constitutes an *effective* change-management plan.

Each of these four change-management problems is a set of smaller core problems that amplify each other. If you acknowledge this, you'll see the value of helping each other to break big problems into parts, prioritize them together, and stay focuses on a few at a time, unless higher priorities call.

I invite you to pause, close your eyes or look away, breathe, and stretch. Notice your thoughts and emotions now, and see if any subselves need anything from your Self. Attend their needs, and then recall why you began reading this chapter. With that in mind, see if you can summarize the main ideas you've read here so far. As you do, notice if your energy rises on any particular topics.

Based on the ideas above, let's look at your options if _ you initiate family change, or _ other co-parents do.

Options

As usual, these suggestions are illustrative, not exhaustive. Use them to inspire ideas that fit your unique situation . . .

If *You* Initiate Major Changes

_ **Ensure** your Selves are (increasingly) leading your inner families (Project 1);

_ **Help** each other maintain a *long term* (e.g. 10-20 year) outlook.

_ **If you** haven't, check to see if you each made three right re/wedding choices. Use Project 7 ideas and tools in *Stepfamily Courtship* or [http://sfhelp.org/07/links07.htm]. If you didn't choose *right*, you have higher-priority problems than planning (step)family change, unless it's re/divorce [..Rx/mates/redivorce1.htm].

_ **Check** your attitudes, key knowledge, and problem-solving beliefs. Reread Chapters 1, 2, and 3, and discuss them with your partner/s. Option: read them out loud to each other.

_ **Confirm** that you value the needs and dignity of each other family co-parent equally with your own, despite major values differences. If you don't, check for false-self dominance (Project 1).

_ **If you're** re/married, confirm that _ the five re/marital hazards apply to *you*, so _ the 12 co-parent projects do too (p. 429). Then _ Invest time in gauging where you stand on each project.

_ **Re/read** your family mission statement out loud (p. 438), and discuss whether the changes you're considering are in keeping with your vision. If not, what needs revising, and by whom? If you have no mission statement, is anything in the way of you co-parents drafting one now?

_ **Reaffirm** your long-term priorities [..08/priority.htm] to help negotiate conflicts your change may cause. I recommend choosing your wholistic healths, recoveries, and integrities first, your re/marriage second, and all else (usually) third. This helps protect all of you from the high odds of re/divorce trauma.

_ **Use** your dig-down [..02/dig-down.htm] and other Project-2 communication skills with your partner and other family members to illuminate what *true* needs (p. 44) this proposed change aims to fill, and who's responsible for filling them. If false selves dominate they're often expert at distorting the real problems, and focusing on first-order (superficial) changes as "the answer" to major family problems. See Chapter 7.

_ **Refresh** your awareness of stepfamily realities by reviewing and discussing these: [..03/compare.htm], [..04/myths.htm], and [..04/60expect1.htm].

_ **Review** _ the 14 sets of things that your proposed change may impact in [..09/merge.htm], and _ the common adjustment tasks for stepfamily co-parents on p. 493. Discuss honestly with all co-parents and others affected if you feel your homes are stable enough to weather a new major change.

_ **Recall** that blocked grief can promote psychological or legal (re)divorce, and review your family Good-Grief policy (p. 255). If you have none, draft one together. Then *use* it to inventory how each of your co-parents and kids are doing on grieving their losses. Restated: check your several homes' progress on Project 5. See *Stepfamily Courtship* or [..05/links05.htm].

_ **Review** the set of adjustment needs that each of your minor kids is working on (p. 464). Discuss *honestly* how your proposed change/s impact each child. What new needs may arise for her or him, and how will you adults help fill them? Recall that kids have an instinctive need to *test* their status, limits, and security after every major family change—specially if prior changes traumatized them, and/or they're not sure who's

in charge. Usually, major structural family changes like conceiving a child, relocating, adopting (a stepchild), changing
custody, and similar shifts will cause each child and adult to re-
do prior adjustment tasks. That takes *time* and energy!

_ **Review** the right-time worksheet from Project 7 together
(*Stepfamily Courtship* or [..07/rt-time.htm]), to double-check
for factors you haven't thought of. Recall that active false-selves
try to protect your Inner Kids by convincing distortions and
denials.

_ **Before** or if you co-parents (or any family members)
develop significant disagreements over your proposed changes,
review Chapter 16 and check for *surface* loyalty conflicts and
PVR relationship triangles.

_ **If the** change/s you propose are financial, see Chapter
19. If they have to do with child visitations, see Chapter 21.

_ **Use** all the above and the other ideas in this book to evolve
a consensual change-management plan. Discuss it thoroughly
with all affected people, and assess any special supports you'll
need to implement the plan well—e.g. legal, insurance, psychological, spiritual, or financial counseling, education, and
validations (Project 11).

_ **Add any other steps** to your plan that fit your creativity
and unique situation. If all lights seem green enough, help each
other keep your personal, re/marital and household balances
as you implement and stabilize your changes (Project 12.) *Keep
your kids and key supporters informed every step of the way,
starting in the concept stage.* The alternative is a high price
hurt, in resentment, distrust, disrespect, and antagonism. All of
these _ indicate false selves at work, _ hurt the family bonding
(I assume) you want, and _ take a *long* time to heal!

_ **Note the effect** of this whole process on the degree of
teamwork you co-parents feel. Also note that your working to
reduce any major co-parenting teamwork barriers in Part 2 is a
significant family-structure change

Finally . . .

_ **When** things have settled down enough, review your
change-planning and implementing process together. Enjoy

genuinely affirming what you did well, and identify what you'd do differently *without blame*. Note your option to use this whole complex experience as a way of modeling and teaching dependent kids how to manage changes in *their* lives!

Think of the most likely major family-structure change you (and any partner) may initiate in the near future. Option: identify the next major change a minor or grown child or their other co-parent/s may initiate. Thoughtfully scan the suggestions above, and notice what your self-talk (thoughts, images, emotions) is like. What does that mean?

Another scenario occurs if en ex mate and/or their new partner initiates major change in your dynamic, complex family system. How can you and any mate best adapt to that?

Other Co-parents Initiate Major Changes

_ **With** your Self in charge of your inner crew, note your attitudes toward each co-parent. If you feel anything other than "=/=" (mutual respect), downsize your expectations on _ teambuilding and _ successful change-management. See chapters 1-12 for viable strategy-building options.

_ **If you're upset** by a family change the other adults initiated, you mates help each other identify what's causing the upset: _ is it the change/s and their effects, _ the *way* the changes were proposed or declared (e.g. arrogantly, covertly, without warning, and/or without regard for your feelings, interests or concerns); or _ both? Help each other keep alert for the *real* (Part-2) problems that fuel your upset.

_ **If you feel** the other co-parent/s violated one or more of your _ values and/or _ boundaries in choosing, announcing, or implementing the change/s, consider your option to confront them *respectfully* to let them know the effects of their behavior. First re-study Chapters 13–16 to see if they apply. Your healthiest goals are to _ nourish your integrity and self worth, and _ avoid enabling the other co/parent/s. Trying to "beat" them, get "even" and/or "revenge," and/or "have the last word" are each *clear* signs of a false-self controlling your inner crew. See Project 1!

If you do assert, _ make sure your Self is leading, _ use awareness, clear thinking, and dig-down skills to clarify what your *real* needs are in confronting, and _ use all seven Project-2 skills (p. 512) to plan and deliver your assertion and handle expected responses. Start by reviewing Resources [H-K], and then *Satisfactions* (xlibris.com) or [..02/a-bubble.htm], [..02/dig-down.htm], [..02/assert.htm], and [..02/listen.htm].

_ **If your** and your partner's Selves feel it's the right time, invite your other co-parents to read this series of books and Web pages—or at least this one [..10/change.htm]. Invite them to do so for your kids' sakes, not because "*we know better than you.*" A major factor here is whether the other adult/s accept your shared stepfamily identity, and are willing to learn what that means for all your sakes. If other co-parents have identity and/or membership conflicts, invite them to study Projects 1 through 4 (at least) in *Stepfamily Courtship* to protect their re/marriage, *not* to please you!

If another co-parent disbelieves, distrusts, and/or disrespects you and refuses this invitation, consult the chapters in Part 2 to own and reduce your half of your co-parental barriers. Keep a long-range outlook, and recall it takes most stepfamilies four or more years *after re/wedding* to stabilize. Small steps add up, here! Patience, patience, patience . . .

_ **If after** thorough discussion you feel the other co-parents' proposed or declared change/s _ put your kids at risk [F] and/or _ significantly degrade your prospects for long-range co-parental teamwork, *exhaust all other alternatives* before choosing to use legal force to "win"! Except in clear cases of child abuse and neglect or criminal activity, using the legal system to force your way on other co-parents indicates _ false-self dominance, _ undeveloped communication skills, and _ denial of the toxic long-term effects (Chapter 18).

Recap

Over time, all families choose or adapt to minor to major, planned and unexpected changes (e.g. births, deaths, relocations, illness, retirements, adoptions) to their membership, roles, rules, assets, goals, and rituals. Typical multi-home nuclear families face these normal changes *and* a web of special local changes (p. 403) while they progress at their complex multi-year biofamily-merger (change) process.

This chapter proposes that depending on their degree of teamwork, your co-parents can take effective proactive steps to manage the stresses that family-structural changes will generate in and among your homes. Your teamwork and change-management strategies affect each other. The chapter outlines 10 factors that your caregivers can use together to help design an effective change-management plan, and offers suggestions if _ you and your mate or _ other co-parents initiate major family-structure changes. All these suggestions aim to _ reduce local stress, and improve long-term co-parenting teamwork and nurturing success.

Bottom line: help each other to _ expect major, complex family-structure changes along the way, and _ patiently build your co-parenting teamwork (Part 2—Project 10) so you can _ evolve effective change-management *attitudes* (change is good) and consensual *plans* to promote your security, mutual trust, and bondings, over time.

Pause for a time. Reflect on what you learned here,, what you're feeling, and anything you want to do now. Is your Self in charge of your inner family?

Our last chapter recaps the purpose and key premises in this book, and refocuses you on the larger perspective of your 11 ongoing, long-term family-building projects.

24) Summing Up and Refocusing

Can you recall why you bought this book? I hope you got clearer on—and filled some—true needs, as you absorbed these chapters. Did you develop some new needs?

After 23 years' clinical study, I believe the tragic U.S. divorce and re/divorce epidemics indicate the prevalence and combined power of five (re)marital hazards:

Psychologically-wounded co-parents, and . . .

unawareness of key knowledge (Chapter 1), and . . .

blocked grief in co-parents and kids, and . . .

courtship neediness and reality distortions, and . . .

little *informed* community and media **help** for naive or troubled co-parents and kids.

This book is the sixth in a series dedicated to helping co-parents and their supporters build high-nurturance family relationships. **This is the guidebook for co-parent Project 10—** one of 12 projects which can help you all overcome these five toxic hazards.

A basic premise in this series is that any family, including yours, falls somewhere on a line between very low-nurturance to very high. Nurturance means "filling adults' and kids' true current needs (p. 440)." Growing up in a low-nurturance family seems to promote kids' automatically developing a survival-oriented unseen "false self," and up to five related psychological wounds. Until intentionally enabling their competent true

Self, false-self dominated people tend to _ choose similarly wounded partners, _ reproduce low-nurturance environments for themselves and their kids, and _ (re)divorce psychologically or legally.

Typically, protective false selves focus on immediate comforts. They don't look beneath the surface symptoms of local personal and relationship problems to identify and resolve the *true* needs beneath them. That results in making ineffective first-order (superficial) changes (e.g. a fad diet), which leaves your core needs unfilled. A common sign of this is that the (surface) problems recur in one form or another. The books in this series are about identifying and resolving your *true* problems via empowering your Self to lead your other subselves, and making second-order (core attitude) changes to attain life goals. One such goal is building co-parental harmony and co-operation.

Another premise here is that half of the focus of a high-nurturance family is on filling the true needs of family adults. The other half is filling dependent kids' needs. On top of ~25 normal developmental needs, typical stepkids are challenged with filling *many* concurrent adjustment needs that biofamily children don't face (p. 464). So divorced-family and stepfamily kids depend on their several co-parents (bioparents and stepparents) to _ understand these special needs and _ work *co-operatively* to provide informed guidance and support for them—i.e. a high-nurturance environment.

The first half of Project 10—and this book—focuses on building this vital co-parental teamwork, by admitting and overcoming a group of interactive barriers (Part 2 here). The second half of Project 10 *[Build a High-nurturance Stepfamily]* focuses on using your teamwork to develop effective child discipline in your kids' related homes.

The first three chapters in Part 1 _ oriented you to this book, and invited you to upgrade _ your knowledge base, and _ clarify your key beliefs and attitudes about resolving relationship problems. Chapter 4 provided perspectives on your co-parent team-building challenge, and summarized some key options. Reading these chapters and the five prior books in this series (p. 555), will help your co-parents get the most value from the rest of this book.

Part 2 offered specific options for identifying and reducing **seven core team-building barriers**. Two of these barriers affect all five others: _ unseen psychological wounds in one or more co-parents (Chapters 5 and 6), and _ unawareness of effective communication concepts and skills (Chapter 7 and p. 507). If present, these two factors will significantly lower your _ inner-family's and _ physical family's nurturance levels, regardless of the cooperation among your co-parents. Projects 1 and 2 provide you with concepts and tools for reducing them.

Part 3 hilights 11 common *surface* (secondary) teamwork-barriers. Each of these can lure unaware co-parents into escalating conflicts that make their underlying Part-2 barriers *worse*. Each surface barrier (e.g. loyalty conflicts and legal battles) *is* a real secondary problem, and a symptom of several of the true barriers in Part 2. Project 10 is about you co-parents learning the true barriers and options for resolving them, and then discerning surface problems from the true needs "beneath" them.

The paradox you caregivers face is learning to overcome these core and surface barriers while they hinder you from doing so. Your integrities, commitment and knowledge; parental and spousal love; and *informed* supports can power you all to overcome this "barrier of barriers" and help nurture your kids and each other effectively!

Part 4 provides 15 resources to help you implement the suggestions in Parts 2 and 3. All these chapters include references to related articles, worksheets, and resources in the companion Web site at [http://sfhelp.org/].

Like the other volumes in this series, this is meant to be used as a modular reference book as your stepfamily roles and relationships evolve. The long-term benefit you get from the series and this book depends directly on several things: *all* three or more of your co-parents . . .

willingness to _ take full responsibility for the quality and outcome of your own lives; _ make second-order (core attitude) changes, and _ assess honestly for six psychological wounds. This aims to protect your vulnerable kids and their descendents from inheriting the wounds. And all of you adults need to . . .

accept _ your identity as a normal multi-home *step*family, and _ your high vulnerability to the five re/divorce hazards which justifies _ co-committing to some version of the 12 projects in the next chapter.

Without these basic factors, expecting to build high-nurturance, long-term family relationships after divorce and/or re/marriage is like expecting a coat of paint to cure termites in your house foundation. Notice your thoughts and feelings now . . .

One way of sensing whether each of you caregivers *really* has these factors now is re-taking the quiz in Chapter 1. For "extra credit," take the similar quizzes at [..02/evc-quiz.htm] and [..05/grief-quiz.htm]. Another way is noting whether you can clearly describe the five hazards and 12 projects to someone who doesn't know about them. A third way you can tell is whether each of you co-parents can clearly describe _ the six psychological wounds you may have inherited, and the _ traits that suggest your true Self is leading your inner family.

Pause and see if you describe each of these now . . .

Just reading this book will probably do little toward building the effective co-parenting team your kids need you to want. Starting with you, your co-parents will need to commit to evolving a proactive plan to assess for and reduce the seven core barriers in Part 2. You've already taken the first key steps by reading these books and Web pages. Keys to an effective plan include . . .

wanting to respectfully help each other keep your true Selves in charge. If you don't (yet), focus on Project 1 and Chapters 5 and 6.

giving steady, high life priority to *wanting* to _ keep a long-term outlook in the face of immediate problems, and to _ build a high-nurturance family (p. 440) for you and your descendents. Do your recent *actions* (vs. words) demonstrate those priorities?

wanting to help each other work steadily at the 11 concurrent projects you need to build high family nurturance;

being able to name _ most of the development and adjustment needs your kids have [F], and _ *wanting* to assess and monitor each custodial and non-custodial child for their status with their unique mix of these needs.

being able to name _ the goals and steps of co-parent Project 10, and _ the traits of an effective team (p. 85); and _ *wanting* to honestly assess whether you co-parents have these traits _ now and _ over time. And . . .

wanting to assess all of your co-parents for each of the seven core barriers on p. 109 *now*, and . . .

wanting to _ maintain an "=/=" (mutual respect attitude, and _ discuss your results with each other, and you co-parents . . .

wanting to invest time and effort planning how you all will use ideas and resources like those in Part 2 to reduce your team-building barriers a few at a time, based on _ personal recovery plans, and _ helping each other grow effective thinking and problem-solving skills together, and . . .

acknowledging **that** you each need supports as you do these and your other concurrent co-parent projects, and _ using Project 11 to get them, while you caregivers . . .

proactively work to _ keep your daily balances as persons, marital partners, and caregiving teammates, and _ often _ affirm your progress, and _ *enjoy* each other, your kids, and your complex family-building challenge—i.e. *want* to help each other work steadily at Project 12.

If this feels like a tall order—it *is*. So is re/divorce! Notice your self-talk now—your dynamic mix of thoughts, emotions, and *awarenesses*.

Back away from all these barriers, projects, tasks, ideas, steps, and options now. Clear your mind. Bookmark this page, and review the 28 traits of a high-nurturance family on p. 440. Then reread the sample family mission statement on p. 438, perhaps out loud. Then return here, and read the following exercise. Put the book down, breathe well, relax, close your eyes, and do something like this . . .

Imagine yourself in old age, a week before you or your partner will die. Imagine being alone together in a safe, comfortable place. Reflect quietly on the lives you've led, and all that you've dreamed, experienced, and accomplished together across your years. If you wish, sense the comforting presence of your Higher Selves and/or God. Imagine confronting that your re/marital journey together is almost done, and it's time to savor your years of effort, heartache, joy, and adventure. Look into each other's eyes wordlessly, and notice the rich emotions that well up in you each. Say or do anything that you need to. Breathe well, and be at peace with your thoughts and memories.

Now imagine each of your grown children joining you, one at a time. Include any who have died or live far away. If they have children, imagine them joining you, one at a time. If you wish, imagine each of your own parents joining you, and any other adults who mentored you and your mate as a child and adult. Then imagine each of your kids' other co-parents joining the circle around you, one at a time.

Notice your emotions, as your family assembles. Greet them each and all, and ask for some moments of silence. Look into each of their faces, and be *aware* of your thoughts and reactions . . .

The nurturing decisions and efforts you co-parents made years ago have indelibly shaped the values, dreams, and lives of each of these younger people. They'll pass on parts of your legacy to an expanding fan of descendents and others far into the future.

Reflect on whether your co-parents and relatives were able to provide many of the high-nurturance traits for your young people. Imagine you and your beloved mate speaking from your hearts, and telling your kids and grandkids what you tried to do for them across your years. Vividly imagine your thoughts and emotions as you do this. Notice their reactions, without judgment. Invite each of your other co-parents to comment on their caregiving intentions, feelings, and memories, one at a time. Sense the growing mood among you all, as you begin to finish this part of your family experience.

Now notice what you feel in this inner scene. Is it _ deep love and satisfaction, shared pride, and contentment; or _ numbness; or _ regret, sadness, anger, and guilt? What is your mate feeling? Each other person? Imagine the looks in their eyes, and whether you all can hold direct eye contact or not . . .

Imagine asking any questions you have, listening, and responding. Take all the time you need. When you're all ready, say goodbye to each of these special people, one at a time, and see them leave. Picture you mates being alone again, and looking into each other's eyes. Breathe well, and see what wants to happen . . .

When you're ready, flex your muscles, take a full, comfortable breath, open your eyes, and come fully back into your body and the present moment. What are you aware of now? Consider journaling now or soon about this experience. Recognize that by your stream of personal and family-management decisions in the present, you co-parents are determining how your future experience will turn out.

You mates share the responsibility for how you'll each feel in whatever version of this scene occurs in your future.

We've come to the end of our path together in this book. Recall that this is the guidebook for Project 10—one of 11 ongoing family-building projects. If you've read all 24 of these chapters thoughtfully, I congratulate you! This is hardly light reading! As a parting suggestion, I encourage you to reread the true stepfamily vignette at [http://sfhelp.org/example.htm] now. When I was working with (some of) them, these six average co-parents (p. 84) weren't able to overcome their set of barriers and forge an effective team for their five young people. These wounded men and women didn't know what you know now, and had fewer choices. I believe the biggest single reason they couldn't team up was that at least five of these worthy people were often dominated by a false self. Two of them were learning what that meant, and choosing to work at true recovery.

You mates and ex mates control how *your* vignette will read. Keep a clear image of any live experience you've had being part of—or leading—an effective team, as your days unfold. Imagine your kids saying proudly in middle age – "*Our family is a really great* team!"

Go for it!

Part 4) Resources

Use these to help each other reduce the teamwork barriers in Parts 2 and 3, as you all work patiently at all your co-parenting projects a day at a time:

A) Re/marital Hazards and Protections
B) A Stepfamily "Genogram" (Map)
C) Sample Family Mission Statement

D) High-nurturance Family Traits
E) Worksheet: False-self Behavioral Traits
F) Summary: What Your Kids Need Now

G) Common Stepfamily-merger Tasks
H) Summary: Communication Basics
I) Sample: Personal Bill of Rights

J) Worksheet: Common Communication Blocks
K) Summary: Tips for Effective Communication
L) Worksheet: How We Handle Loyalty Conflicts

M) Summary: What's Unique About *Stepparenting*?
N) Selected Readings
Index

A) Re/marital Hazards and Protections

5 Unseen Stressors, and 12 Defenses

This resource chapter summarizes . . .

five factors that combine to cause well over half of typical American stepfamily couples to divorce, psychologically or legally; and . . .

12 projects co-parents like you can do together over time to prevent re/divorce. The projects are sequential. The first seven are best done *before* deciding whether to re/wed, because they promote choosing the right *people* to commit to, for the right *reasons,* at the right *time.* They're still very helpful after re/ wedding. The "/" in "re/wed" notes it may be a stepparent's first union.

To inform others of these hazards and projects, print or email the Web pages at [http://sfhelp.org/5reasons.htm] and [..12-overvw.htm]. References to other resources in this book are shown in brackets: [X].

Five Re/marital Hazards

Typical unaware stepfamily co-parents risk psychological or legal re/divorce from a mix of these factors:

Up to six significant psychological wounds (p. 448) in one or more co-parents and kids, who survived (or are living in) low-nurturance ("dysfunctional") childhoods. The core wound is the dominance of a reactive, unwise "false self." The other injuries are excessive shame, guilt, fears, and reality and trust distortions. These can combine to cause an inability to bond emotionally and spiritually, tolerate intimacy, and exchange love. And . . .

Unawareness in co-parents and supporters of _ these wounds and what to do about them, _ stepfamily norms and realities, and _ grieving, _ communication, and _ relationship fundamentals (ref. Chapter 1). Plus . . .

Blocked grief in one or more co-parents and kids. All stepfamilies follow two or three sets of profound losses for all people involved, adding to many childhood losses. Plus . . .

Excessive courtship neediness and reality distortions (repressing, idealizing, exaggerating, minimizing, rationalizing, projecting, and denying); and . . .

Little or no *informed* stepfamily help available to co-parents and kids in their local communities or the media.

Until admitted and reduced, the first four hazards combine to cause typical co-parents to _ make three wrong re/wedding decisions, and _ unintentionally co-create low-nurturance families, and wound their vulnerable kids. To avoid this, aware caregivers can choose to work together at . . .

12 Co-parent Projects

My 23 years' clinical research indicates that co-parents' committing to 12 inter-related, multi-step tasks steeply raises their odds of neutralizing these five hazards, and building a high-nurturance family (p. 440). To access referenced Web pages below, add the pointers [..**/***.htm] to the base address [http://sfhelp.org/..]—e.g. [http.//sfhelp.org/**/***.htm]. Omit the brackets.

Seven Projects (Ideally) *Before* Re/wedding

These multi-step tasks are outlined in the guidebook "*Stepfamily Courtship—Make 3 Right Re/marriage* Choices" [xlibris.com, 2001]. In these summaries, each "_" is a sub-task.

PROJECT 1) Each co-parent (bioparent and prospective stepparent) _ learn the ~30 traits of high-nurturance family health [D]. Then _ **assess yourself for symptoms of six psychological wounds** from a low-nurturance childhood [E] and [..pop/asses.htm]. If you find enough, _ evolve a *self*-motivated, high-priority, personal healing (recovery) plan. _ Commit to your plan, and begin.

Then thoroughly evaluate the odds that _ your prospective partner and _ any ex mate/s are significantly wounded. If they are, and if at least your partner is not *clearly* in solid emotional recovery, settle for friendship. *Unrecovering survivors of low childhood nurturance unconsciously pick each other, and often break up, over and over again. "Who's* Really *Running Your Life?"* [xlibris.com, 2000] is the guidebook for this keystone project. See Chapter 5.

PROJECT 2) _ **Expect** that building your multi-home stepfamily will generate *many* **inner-family and interpersonal conflicts, for years**. Couples _ honestly assess how well they accept and resolve *values'* and *resource* conflicts with each other (Chapter 16) and key others. _ Help each other **develop seven communication skills together**: awareness, clear thinking, digging down to the primary problems, *metatalk* (talking about *how* you communicate), empathic listening, effective assertion, and win-win problem solving. Help each other _ learn to apply these skills to conflicts within your *inner* families, and _ model and teach the skills to your kids and other co-parents. *Typical psychologically-wounded people don't resolve inner or interpersonal conflicts effectively.*

Courtship romance often disguises deep *values* disputes

on parenting, money, family priorities, and home management. These *will* surface after your re/wedding! The guidebook for this vital project is *"Satisfactions—7 Relationship Skills You Need to Know"* [xlibris.com, 2002]. Alternative: [..02/links02.htm]. Success with this essential project depends on significant progress on empowering your true Self via Project 1 above. While you work on these first two tasks, also do . . .

PROJECT 3) _ Accept your (prospective) identity as a normal multi-home *step*family together, vs. *"We're just a (bio)family."* Then _ all three or more of your co-parents and all minor and grown kids work to agree on who *belongs* in your nuclear and extended stepfamily (p. 436). In particular, _ accept that each minor and grown child's other living bioparent, and any new stepparent/s and stepsibs, will remain full members of your multi-home stepfamily until you die or re/divorce.

_ Admit and work to resolve strong stepfamily-*identity* and *membership* conflicts. Avoiding this promotes _ members using inappropriate *bio*family norms and expectations when confused and conflicted, and _ excluded members feeling hurt, angry, and resentful. See *Stepfamily Courtship* (xlibris.com, 2001), or [http://sfhelp.org/03/links03.htm].

PROJECT 4) Form realistic stepfamily expectations. _ Learn how your multi-home stepfamily differs in over *70* ways from typical one-home intact biofamilies [..03/compare.htm]. Then _ study and discuss 60+ common stepfamily *myths* and realities [..04/myths.htm], and _ **draft *realistic* expectations for each of your key stepfamily roles and relationships**. _ Reality-check your expectations with veteran co-parents. _ Learn together what comprises a high-nurturance nuclear-*step*family structure [..01/health.htm] and [..09/map-str1.htm]. Then _ compare your two or more related co-parenting homes (p. 84) against that model. Key stepfamily reality: *Without your steady, high-priority work on your version of these 12 projects, you and your kids will probably re/divorce.* See *Stepfamily Courtship* or [..04/links04.htm].

PROJECT 5) Assess for blocked grief. All three or more co-parents _ learn the three levels of healthy grieving, and the *specific* symptoms of blocked grief. Then _ inventory yourselves, each other co-parent, and each minor and grown child for their major prior divorce and/or death losses.

If anyone is seriously blocked, _ *all* your co-parents agree on a plan to correct that. _ Act together on your plan. _ Consider specifically what each child and adult will *lose* by your re/marriage and cohabiting. If you do re/marry, _ **evolve a clear Good-Grief policy, and** _ *use* it to guide and support you all through your inevitable stream of life losses. See *Stepfamily Courtship* or [..05/links05.htm].

PROJECT 6) Define long-term goals and who's responsible for what. _ Consult your other co-parents and key relatives, and rough-draft a stepfamily *mission* or *vision statement* together [C]. _ Learn typical stepkids' post-divorce and new-stepfamily emotional-adjustment needs [F]. Then _ all co-parents decide specifically what each adult is responsible for with each minor child.

_ Rough draft each of your co-parents' "job descriptions" (nurturing responsibilities), and _ share them with key relatives and other supporters. _ Review and refine these over time, and _ begin to identify potential loyalty conflicts and relationship triangles (Chapter 16). See *Stepfamily Courtship* or [..06/links06.htm]. If you re/marry, continue this work with Project 10.

PROJECT 7) *Now* (not before): _ you and your partner **explore six vital pre-re/marriage questions honestly**:
"*Is my true Self making my decisions?*"
"*Why should I re/marry at all?*"
"*Why* now*?*"
"*Why* this *person and their kids, ex mate, and psychological baggage?*"
"*If I have to, can I often put this special adult's needs ahead*

of my own kid/s' needs without major resentment or guilt?"
(Re/wedded bioparents are forced to choose, *often*).
   "Can this adult really do that for me?" (if they have biokids)
   "What are my other options now?"
   See *Stepfamily Courtship* or [..07/links07.htm].

Five Post-re/wedding Projects

   If you partners choose to re/commit, continue Projects 1-6 as required, and add five more. They're outlined in the guide-book *Build a High-nurturance Stepfamily* (xlibris.com, 2001) and the Web pages noted:

   PROJECT 8) Partners protect your living and future kids from re/divorce by _ **intentionally nurturing your re/marriage often enough**. Make (vs. *find*) enough time for undistracted intimacy, play, sharing, planning, and problem solving. _ Keep your relationship consistently *second* only to individual per-sonal integrity, spirituality, and growth, including inner-wound healing (Project 1). See *The Re/marriage Book – Master Com-mon Stressors Together* (xlibris.com) or [..08/links08.htm]. And . . .

   PROJECT 9) _ **Merge and stabilize your three or more co-parents-biofamilies'** assets, beliefs, habits, values, rituals, priorities, and lifestyles ("cultures"). Over time, _ invent and stabilize up to 15 new multi-home stepfamily *roles*, and _ re-vise most of your old 15 biofamily roles. _ Evolve new intra- and inter-home *rules* for all 30 of these roles. Evolve an effec-tive way to resolve the _ values conflicts and _ relationship "triangles" that *will* result from your merger (Chapter 16). _ Accept that each bioparent *must* clearly decide which usually comes first with them in conflicts, when no workable compro-mises appear: _ their personal integrity, _ their re/marriage, or _ all else, including their child/ren. See *Build a High-nurturance Stepfamily* or [..09/links09.htm].

PROJECT 10) _ **Evolve an effective co-parenting team, and** _ **nurture your kids.** _ Help each other admit and grieve key personal losses as you do this. Co-operatively _ refine and *use* your stepfamily job descriptions (goals and responsibilities) for *each* active co-parent. _ Regularly affirm your multi-home stepfamily's specific strengths and benefits. This builds on Project 6. Use this book or [http://sfhelp.org/10/links10.htm].

PROJECT 11) Over time, intentionally build a support network of *successful* veteran (e.g. re/married five or more years) stepfamily co-parents, and stepfamily-informed relatives, friends, and professionals: e.g. clergy, counselors, school staff, and an attorney. Join or start a nurturing co-parents' support group. See *Build a High-nurturance Stepfamily* or [..11/links11.htm]. And while you work at all of these together, help each other do . . .

PROJECT 12) Every day, **mates** _ consciously **balance and** co-manage all ongoing projects above, plus *many* other responsibilities, well enough. As you do, _ keep your goals clear and ordered, _ build a solid, hi-priority re/marriage, _ enjoy your kids, _ keep growing emotionally and spiritually as persons (based on *inner*-family recovery, if needed); and _ *laugh, play, relax, and* **enjoy the whole adventure** *together enough* while you do all this! See the guidebook above or [..12/links12.htm]

Here's how these projects fit together:

balance yourselves,
your relationships, and your homes,
as you do all these projects
and other life activities - and
enjoy the whole adventure!

heal divorce wounds, & build a co-parent team	build a support network and use it together!

if you re/wed, steadlily nurture your re/marriages,
as you merge 3 or more biofamilies over 4+ years
and resolve **many** conflicts and relationship "triangles"

develop 7 communication skills	learn stepfamily realities & tasks	learn grief basics; & assess all members for blocked grief	learn kids' needs & assess their status; then draft co-parent "job descriptions"

accept your stepfamily identity and your 5 hazards;
agree on who belongs to your stepfamily

assess co-parents for psychological wounds
and start needed recoveries

12 co-parent projects for building a high-nurturance
stepfamily, overmany years. Read from the bottom up.

B) A Stepfamily "Genogram" (Map)

This is a *partial* diagram of a real stepfamily. See [http://sfhelp.org/03/geno1.htm] for background and suggestions on how to map your multi-home family, and ways to *use* your map to strengthen your relationships. Also see [..09/map-str1.htm] for another way to map your family.

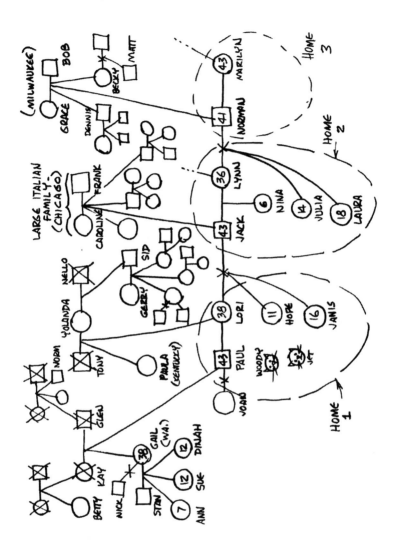

C) Sample Family Mission Statement

One trait of an effective team (Chapter 4) is the members share clear long-term goals. Building an effective co-parenting team (Project 10) is of limited value without you all agreeing on what you're trying to achieve over time for you and your descendents. Project 6 focuses on evolving an effective *mission* or *vision* statement to guide the development of your complex new multi-home family. This foundation promotes designing effective roles ("job descriptions") as caregivers and mates. See [http://sfhelp.org/10/job1.htm].

Do you know co-parents in any kind of family who drafted and *used* a mission statement to guide them through family changes and crises? Did your caregivers do this? Did your partner's? Can you describe _ who belongs to your present family, _ who leads it, and _ what they're trying to accomplish over time?

If you have trouble imagining what a family mission statement might look like, mull this example from the "Personal Leadership Application Resource" for Stephen Covey's excellent book "The Seven Habits of Highly Effective People":

"The mission of our family is . . .
to create a nurturing place of order, truth, love,
happiness, and relaxation; and . . .
to provide opportunities for each person
to become responsibly independent, and
effectively interdependent, . . .

in order to achieve worthwhile purposes.
Our Family Mission
To *love* each other . . .
To *help* each other . . .
To *believe in* each other . . .
To wisely use our time, talents, and resources
to bless others . . .
To worship together . . .
Forever."

This brief charter clearly states what the leaders of this family want to do together. In crises and major decisions, do you think rereading and reaffirming this would help partners decide what to do? What would it feel like to take part in a family whose leaders really followed these ideas? Would a charter like this work as well for a stepfamily as a biofamily?

Perhaps the co-authors of this declaration started with a shared dream to fashion a "good life" for themselves and their children. It looks like they felt responsible for making this dream happen, rather than assuming that it would "somehow." Finally, the authors evidently spent a lot of time thinking and talking about specifically what comprises the "good life" they wanted to co-create over time. Do you agree?

With this example in mind, scan the stepfamily map in the last chapter, or (better), your own map. Do you think a mission statement would be useful in raising all members' satisfactions, and promoting strong bonds? For perspective and options for creating your own family mission statement, see *Stepfamily Courtship* or [..06/mission1.htm].

Note your option to evolve and use a similar mission state-ment for your *inner* family of personality subselves. See *Who's Really Running Your Life?* or [..01/innerfam1.htm].

Awarenesses . . .

D) *High-nurturance* Family Traits

Unawareness is one of five widespread re/divorce hazards (p. 428). In my experience, many co-parents aren't aware of . . .

– what childhood *nurturance* really means,
– how to realistically assess the nurturance level of a family or relationship, and . . .
– how to maintain a high nurturance level for all adults and kids in a multi-home divorced family or stepfamily.

Psychological or legal divorce implies that the mates couldn't answer the last two of these well enough. If you co-parents aren't informed on all three topics, and/or if your opinions seriously conflict, you risk major stress among your *inner* families, adults, and kids. From 23 years' study of many researchers' and clinicians' opinions, this chapter offers perspective on the first two topics. The 12 projects in on p. 430 offer a framework for understanding the third one.

Use this checklist to help fashion an effective mission statement (p. 438 and Project 6) for _ harmonizing your *inner* family of subselves (Project 1), and _ doing all 10 or 11 of your other family-building projects.

Let's start by defining a *family* as "an adult and one or more other people of any age who _ prize and maintain significant emotional and spiritual bonds, and _ consistently *want* to (vs. have to) help each other fill their current needs." Family members may or may not share common genes and ancestries.

Why Do Families Exist?

I've opened scores of relationship seminars and co-parenting classes with this seemingly brainless question. People sputter a little or look into space, then say something like "Well, *obviously* to have and/or raise kids, and uh, to be happy, healthy, and productive." I ask "Do you have to have children involved to be a family?" People have mixed opinions about this. After some discussion I ask: "What can a family (potentially) do better than any other human group?" I'm sobered by how vague typical co-parents are on this vital question. Many have never thought about it. Have *you*?

A *need* is an emotional, physical, or spiritual discomfort that may cause action. Each of us has conscious and unconscious, and physical needs. Psychologist Abraham Maslow proposed that we instinctively prioritize, or rank, our current needs in a five-level hierarchy [..02/needlevels.htm]. This guarantees dynamic conflicts and harmonies _ within and _ between us all. "Conflict" and "problems" are based on unfilled or clashing needs. Do you agree?

Though humans vary infinitely, we all seem to feel a mix of these concurrent . . .

Core Spiritual/Emotional Needs

- To give and receive love.
- Self _ awareness, _ acceptance, and _ respect.
- Spiritual _ awareness, _ faith, and _ communion.
- Clear personal and group *identities* and *boundaries.*
- A coherent life purpose, and resources to pursue it.
- Social _ acceptance, _ respect, and _ companionship.
- The chance to develop effective life skills.
- Comforts (support) during _ crises and _ losses.
- Knowledge of the world, and freedom to learn.

- To be able to "make sense of" our experiences.
- Clear feedback ("mirroring") from other people.
- Opportunity to _ conceive and _ nurture new life.
- Balanced work, play, and rest.
- _ Recognition, _ validation, and _ appreciation.
- Encouragements to _ grow and _ persevere.
- Enough _ emotional and _ physical *securities.*
- Enough nurturing sensory stimulation, like hugs.
- Enough *hope* for satisfaction and comforts; and . . .
- Enough nurturing (vs. shaming) laughter.

Mull this set of needs and edit it to fit your beliefs and experience. Where else but in a family can you (ideally) get most or all of these met? You can (potentially) fill some of these needs in good friendships, your workplace, and religious and social communities.

Do you agree that *"families exist to nurture (fill a set of core spiritual-emotional needs) each member over time, in a way that other human groups can't"?* In this book, we're concerned with families that include minor and grown children. Now let's refine this to propose . . .

Families of procreation, re/marriage, foster care, and adoption exist to (1) produce wholistically-healthy, socially valuable, self-sufficient new adults, while (2) filling the core needs of all their members (above) well enough, as they and the Earth evolve.

Would you revise this? Would your parents, ancestors, and mentors agree with this definition? Each of your other co-parents? This two-part definition enables us to answer . . .

What is a *High-nurturance* family?

Depending on their leaders' _ wholistic health and _ knowledge, some families are more effective at filling their members' true needs than others locally and over time. So every family can be judged somewhere between very low nurturance to very high nurturance. Let's say . . .

A high-nurturance (functional or healthy) family is one which _ all members and _ knowledgeable outsiders agree has met the above two conditions well enough. A dysfunctional, toxic, unhealthy, or low-nurturance family is one that doesn't meet one or both of these conditions well enough, according to someone.

What does it take to produce a "wholistically-healthy, socially-valuable, self-sufficient adult"? A **basic premise** here is that to achieve this amazing feat, a child's nuclear family must have one or more adult co-parenting leaders who consistently provide enough key factors over time. Ideally, all the adults in a young child's multi-generational (extended) biofamily provide these factors. What factors?

Traits of High-nurturance Families

Using our definition above, can you think of a past or present family you judge to be "high-nurturance"? What factors or traits merit that judgment? See how many specific traits you can identify, and then compare your ideas to the 28 traits below. Use them to form your own thoughtful set of traits. This compilation comes from my six decades of life experience, including 15 years' personal recovery from a low-nurturance childhood; 19 years' formal education; over 17,000 clinical hours with over 1,000 co-parents and (some) kids, and hundreds of hours of post-graduate professional study. (Whew).

See if you think the combined traits below would probably help fill *all* family-members' sets of true needs (above), not just those of minor kids. This chapter illustrates how many factors affect your long-term family-building success. If you use this as a checklist, check the main items if you can confidently check all sub-items. Add the bracketed pointers below [..**/ ****.htm] to [http://sfhelp.org/..] to see a Web-page resource. Omit the brackets.

Directions

Reduce any bodily or environmental distractions, and decide if your Self is leading your other subselves. See the *status check* below.

Decide who to rate: your birthfamily, past marriage family, single-parent family, present household or family, school or class, work group, church community, or several of these. If you're rating a group, substitute "group" for "family" or "household", and "leaders" for "parents" below.

Pick a time frame: now or a specific earlier period (e.g. childhood); then . . .

Decide specifically who comprises this family or group: just the people who live/d or work/ed together, or psychologically-important absent members too, including living and dead grandparents and/or other relatives or special friends. Decide who led this group during this time.

Thoughtfully note this family's or group's nurturance traits. Check each item below that fits "well enough," in your judgment. If you're unsure about an item, use "?"

Take your time: this is not a trivial exercise! Option: star or hilight which items give you the strongest reactions, and when you're done, explore why . . .

Make notes, underline, star, or hilight key items as you go. Note that two people can use this worksheet (__ __), or you can rate two homes or families.

Use this inventory to discover what is or was real, not to blame. Family leaders and other members (i.e. their ruling subselves) try to make the best choices available at the time! Option: discuss this inventory with your other co-parents and supporters, to help build and motivate your team.

Option: if any items don't merit a clear yes or no answer, use a scale of one to five to rate the degree of "trueness."

Status Check

I feel a mix of calm, centered, energized, light, focused, resilient, up, grounded, relaxed, alert, aware, serene, purposeful, compassionate, and clear, so my Self is probably present now. (T F ?)

I believe that my birthfamily's emotional-spiritual nurturance level was _ very low _ fairly low ._ average _ fairly high _ very high.

I believe this had _ very growthful _ no significant _ very harmful effects on my wholistic health and development as a young child.

Common High-nurturance Traits

___ ___ **1) The** family leaders consistently _ value, _ seek, and _ promote _ personal and _ family-relationship wholistic (mental + spiritual + physical + emotional) healths. The leader/s _ have few traits of false-self dominance [E] *or* _ they are well into true (vs. pseudo) personal recovery [..01/recovery1.htm].

___ ___ **2) All** adult and young members _ are clear on who leads the family, and _ genuinely respect and follow their guidance often enough. Each leader is consistently effective at promoting _ teamwork, _ harmony, _ respect, and _ loyalty among all family members.

___ ___ **3) The** leaders _ hold clear, long-term family goals, and maintain clear _ priorities and _ effective plans to meet them. The leaders are consistently able to _ adapt and re-stabilize these in the face of significant family, social, and environmental changes and crises.

___ ___ **4) All** family members share strong *nurturing* spiritual (vs. religious) faiths. _ Individual spiritual preferences are respected and nurtured, rather than having to adopt someone's definition of "*the* one Way." _ Spiritual beliefs and practices are not based on fear, guilt, or shame.

___ ___ **5) All** child conceptions are well researched, discussed, and planned. There are no disputed adoptions _ unexpected conceptions, _ abortions, or _ major ambivalences.

___ ___ **6) All** family members usually feel _ included, _ valued, _ respected, and _ loved *unconditionally.* At times, that can manifest as _ caring confrontations, and _ helping by not helping (not enabling).

___ ___ **7) All** members prize their _ personal dignity, _ self and mutual respect, and _ individuality. There are no significant c/overt _ male-female or _ age biases.

___ ___ **8) All** family members generally _ trust each other, and _ exchange the truth _ promptly. There are _ no major family secrets or _ "no talk" rules implied or declared.

___ ___ **9) All** members consistently feel _ emotionally, _ spiritually, and _ physically safe *enough.*

___ ___ **10) The** family leaders consistently _ model and _ encourage _ feeling and _ expressing *all* emotions. Members _ usually distinguish between *feeling* emotions, and *acting* constructively or harmfully on them. _ No emotions are judged as *bad* or *negative.*

___ ___ **11) The** family leaders are _ clear on the principles of healthy three-level grieving, _ usually model them spontaneously, and _ encourage other family members to _ learn and _ practice them. The family has _ a clear pro-grief policy (p. 255 and [..05/griefpol.htm]).

___ ___ **12)** _ **Interpersonal** communications and _ conflict resolution are usually _ prompt, _ mutually respectful, and _ effective: i.e. members usually _ assert and _ get enough of their needs met, _ in a way that feels good enough to them all. _ Disagreements are seen as normal, not *bad* or *wrong.* See p. 507 and Chapter 7.

___ ___ **13) All** family members _ assert and _ respect _ each other's and _ their family's boundaries (limits) and _ related privacies. They _ equally respect the boundaries of _ guests and _ other homes and families. See Chapter 15.

___ ___ **14) All** members grow real (vs. pseudo) emotional-spiritual bonds with (attachments to) _ each other and _ selected others. [..01/bonding.htm]

___ ___ **15) The** main family *roles* (responsibilities) are _ clear enough to all, _ appropriate in age and ability, _ negotiated respectfully, and _ firmly flexible—i.e. adaptable to change.

___ ___ **16) Within** age-appropriate norms, all family members usually accept personal accountability (responsibility) for their life choices and actions.

___ ___ **17) Household** and family *rules* are _ usually clear enough to all. The *consequences* of breaking the rules are _ enforced by the family leader/s, _ clear, _ respectful, and _ consistent *enough*. Leader/s are _ open to renegotiating the rules and consequences as members and life conditions evolve.

___ ___ **18) All** family members highly _ value and _ promote physical health by balancing _ diets, and _ work, play, exercise, and rest.

___ ___ **19) All** family members _ get enough *nurturing* (vs. toxic) physical touching, and _ practice wholistically-healthy sexual _ values, _ limits, and _ behaviors.

___ ___ **20) All** members evolve clear _ personal and _ dyad (mate-mate, parent-child, sib-sib) identities, and share _ a clear multi-home, multi-generational family identity.

___ ___ **21) Family** members frequently _ take safe risks, within their limitations. Mistakes are _ accepted and _ *valued* as useful chances to learn, vs. sources of shame and ridicule. Members are _ generally comfortable and sincere in apologizing, and _ usually receive others' apologies and genuinely forgive.

___ ___ **22)** All members feel *non-elitist* _ personal and _ family _ pride and _ loyalty.

___ ___ **23) Members** are generally open to new _ people, _ ideas, and _ experiences.

___ ___ **24) Family** members take _ local and _ global _ social welfare and _ ecology seriously but not obsessively.

___ ___ **25) Spontaneous** _ play and _ non-shaming laughter are common _ in and _ outside the family's home.

___ ___ **26) Family** members often _ seek and _ enjoy time together, while _ respecting individual solitudes and privacies. Members usually _ *want* to congregate, vs. feeling obliged to.

___ ___ **27) Family** members share consistent attitudes of _ realistic optimism and _ hope, without _ denying or minimizing anxieties or confusions.

___ ___ **28) Each** family leader _ can describe most of these traits spontaneously, and _ came from a childhood family which consistently had most of these traits.

This is not meant as a complete or "absolute" compilation of high-nurturance family traits. I suggest it is "right *enough*." Shelves of books, reams of learned articles, and endless conferences debate these factors, and there are many viewpoints.

The basic premises here are: _ some families are "healthier" (higher nurturance) and "more successful and productive" (more functional) than others; _ there are specific factors that combine to shape any family's nurturance level, over time; and _ through awareness and determined effort, informed, motivated leaders can increase their family's nurturance level over time. How do you feel about these ideas?

Effects of Low Nurturance: Inner Wounds

After 23 years' clinical study and 16 years' personal recovery, I (and many other researchers) believe typical young kids who get too few of these nurturance factors adapt by "fragmenting" our personalities. We do this instinctively to *survive*, vs. thrive. Depending on many variables, this causes two to six moderate to major psychological wounds. The universal wound is . . .

Forming a protective "false self" – a group of semi-independent subselves or personality parts that have a distorted view of the world, and make impulsive, short-sighted local decisions. This happens because _ our true Self (capital "S") is undeveloped and ineffective, and _ our caregivers' true Selves are disabled. See the next chapter.

Significant false-self dominance causes mixes of five more wounds . . .

Excessive shame (I'm worthless, inept, and unlovable) **and guilts** (I do bad things). Adults and kids who are dominated by

subselves who feel primally worthless and protect against awareness of that are called "shame-based" in this series of books
and Web pages. For more perspective, see Chapters 8 and 10,
[..01/shame.htm], and [..01/recovery1.htm].

Excessive fears of _ abandonment, _ the unknown, _ emotional overwhelm (and hence fear of conflict and intimacy), _
"failure" (shame and guilt), _ success ("I'm a fraud and don't
deserve it."), and _ admitting these wounds, and what they mean.
A compound stressor is fear of too much fear and being unable
to reduce it. Children and adults who are frequently controlled
by fearful and fear-activated (Guardian) subselves are called
"fear-based" here. See [..01/fears.htm].

Reality distortions, including exaggerating, minimizing,
projecting ("You *have the problem, not me!*"), numbing, "forgetting," idealizing, exaggerating, catastrophizing, intellectualizing, rationalizing ("*My behavior is OK because . . .*"), and
denying. The most insidious distortion is denying these. See
[..01/distortions.htm].

Dis/trust problems: _ trusting too easily, and getting repeatedly used and betrayed; or _ not trusting people and groups
who really are safe, caring, and reliable. Toxic distrust can include _ excessive self-doubt, and/or _ skepticism and cynicism about relying on a benign Higher Power. See Chapter 9.

These five wounds promote a sixth in some people:

Difficulty *feeling* and **bonding** —forming genuine emotional-spiritual attachments to ("caring about") selected or all
other living things. One manifestation of this is the inability to
feel, express, and receive _ empathy, _ intimacy, and _ *love*.
Another is being unable to grieve. See [..01/bonding.htm], and
Chapters 17 and 20.

Three implications of these wounds: until in real (vs.
pseudo) recovery, adults who have them (1) pick each other as
partners repeatedly, and have significant relationship problems;
and co-parents (2) unintentionally recreate low-nurturance environments, and (3) pass these wounds on to their young kids.
Recent research at UCLA (2002) strongly suggests that the lat-

ter has serious health consequences for such kids, and short-
ens their lives. See [http://sfhelp.org/01/research.htm].

I propose that adult and societal *unawareness* of _ these
six wounds, _ where they come from, and _ what they *mean*, is
one of five reasons that most Americans can't form high-
nurturance family relationships (e.g. co-parent teams). Once _
aware and _ motivated, any co-parent (i.e. *you*) can asses for
these wounds, and evolve an effective recovery program. For
more perspective and resources, **see Project 1** in [A], *Who's
Really Running Your Life?*, or [..pop/assess.htm]. If you feel
any of your other co-parents are significantly wounded, see
Chapters 5 and 6.

Options:

_ invest some time in journaling your reactions to this chapter.

_ If you're working with a therapist, review this with them.

_ If you want to share this chapter with someone, refer
them to [http://sfhelp.org/01/health.htm].

_ to assess the nuturance level of an organization you be-
long to or work in, see [..01/hi-n-org.htm].

Awarenesses:

E) Worksheet: False-self Traits

49 Behavioral Symptoms of Inner Wounds

This is one of 12 self-evaluation checklists you can use to assess for psychologically wounds (p. 448) from being raised in a low-nurturance ("dysfunctional") childhood. The other checklists are in the Project-1 guidebook *"Who's Really Running Your Life?"* and on the Web at [http://sfhelp.org/pop/assess.htm]

Premises

Young kids raised in low-nurturance homes [D] don't get important needs met. To survive (vs. thrive), we automatically adapt by developing a group of Vulnerable and Guardian *subselves* or *personality parts*: a protective "false self" that regulates our perceptions and behaviors without our or our caregivers' awareness. Until healed, false-self control cripples the development and functioning of the person's true Self.

Every newborn has an undeveloped true Self (capital "S"). That subself has the innate ability to learn and make increasingly wise, wide-angle, long-range healthy decisions in calm and chaotic times. Because this talented subself knows little of the world at first, young kids depend on the their caregivers' dominant subselves to guide and protect them.

If caregivers' are Grown Wounded Children (GDCs) with disabled true Selves, they can't provide the consistent high nurturance their kids need. So young kids automatically develop "false selves" to compensate. These well-meaning, short-sighted subselves regularly make unwise or unhealthy choices. Later, these including marrying the wrong people, for the wrong reasons, at the wrong time. One common result is psychological or legal (re)divorce.

False-self dominance seems to be our unseen societal norm. It ranges from minor to significant to extreme ("Multiple Personality Disorder," now called "Dissociative Identity Disorder"). I believe many *character, mood,* and *personality* "disorders" are symptoms of significant false-self dominance.

Mates unaware of significantly false-self dominance risk *unconsciously* _ co-creating low-nurturance homes and _ promoting psychological wounds in their kids as their unaware ancestors did.

Adults and kids significantly ruled by false selves display characteristic behaviors that Self-led people usually don't. Since learning of these traits in 1986, I've consistently found clear mixes of the behaviors below in over 80% of my hundreds of divorced and stepfamily therapy clients and students. Many report coming from low-nurturance early years. Others (i.e. their false selves) anxiously or aggressively deny that because of excessive fear, shame, and guilt (reality distortion).

Once people become aware of false-self dominance and wounds, they can intentionally *recover*: i.e. empower their disabled Self to harmonize and safely direct their *inner* family of personality subselves, over time. Co-parent Project 1 in this series of books and Web pages is one way to do that. Generally, those who work at recovery report that their health, relationships, clarity and focus, productivity, spiritual awareness, zest, and serenity increase over time.

Results from this worksheet alone may *not* be a reliable indicator of whether you're significantly wounded and your Self is disabled. That's because the protective subselves controlling your inner family may need to distort your understanding of these items, and/or your response to them. If so, that distortion will feel *normal* and legitimate to you.

You can get a more accurate reading by merging the results from all 12 checklists in *"Who's* Really *Running Your Life?"* and at [..pop/assess.htm]. Doing this worksheet honestly can give you a useful overview of how average adults and kids from low-nurturance childhoods conduct themselves, before electing true (vs. pseudo) recovery from their personality wounds (vs. "character defects.") I emphasize: such burdened, unaware people are *injured,* not *sick, psycho, weird,* or *crazy!*

I've compiled the behaviors and traits below from over a dozen veteran mental-health authors who have written on co-dependence, Adult Children of Alcoholics, toxic childhoods, addictions, and recovery from childhood trauma and neglect. My clinical and personal experience consistently validate these traits and their origins.

Suggestions

To get the most from this resource . . .

Choose a non-distracted time and place to do this worksheet, and satisfy any physical needs you have. Reserve at least 30".

Adopt the questioning, unbiased "mind of a student." Choose a win-win attitude: anything you learn here is useful!

Pick an adult or child you want to assess for false-self dominance. Pick a time frame: e.g. "the last six months," or an earlier period. Then take your time, and thoughtfully check each item that feels solidly "true." The "__ __" symbols allow you to assess two people. I suggest assessing one person at a time, starting with *you.*

Take notes as you do this worksheet. Your thoughts, feelings, and awarenesses as you respond are as valuable as your checkmarks and blanks.

If there are others who might benefit from this checklist, copy it first from the Web site at [..01/w1-gwctraits.htm].

The aim here is discovery and potential recovery, not *blame.*

These traits are not good or bad, they're symptoms of adaptive false-self dominance, just as vomiting is a symptom of your body trying to purge toxins. **Check** each sub-trait "_" before deciding whether to check the main trait. Option: use 1 to 5, instead of a check or blank. **Asterisk** or hilight any items you feel are specially important. Write margin notes or symbols to add to your learning. **When you feel** some mix of *calm, centered, energized, light, focused, resilient, "up," grounded, relaxed, alert, aware, alive, serene, purposeful*, and *clear*, your Self is probably leading your inner team of subselves. If you don't clearly feel a version of these now, other (short-sighted, protective) subselves are about to fill out this worksheet. To protect your several Inner Children [..01/innerfam2.htm], they'll probably skew your results, so also use the other 11 checklists to better see "the truth."

These false-self behavioral traits are in no special order.

me / you

___ ___ **1) S/He** _ usually thinks in black/white *bi-polar* terms: i.e. s/he sees things as either right or wrong, good or bad, relevant or not, logical or stupid, not somewhere between, or a mix. In internal or social conflicts, s/he tends to see only two options, and has trouble brainstorming. S/He's _ moderately to very uneasy with ambivalence, vagueness, or uncertainty, and _ may deny or joke about that.

___ ___ **2) S/He** is _ often a compulsive perfectionist ("I can't help it"). Achieving perfection _ feels unremarkable and merits no praise, but achieving less rates guilt and shame. S/He _ has trouble enjoying her or his own achievements, and _ is often uncomfortable receiving merited praise.

___ ___ **3) S/He** is _ often rigid and inflexible. S/He _ thinks obsessively and/or _ acts compulsively, even if personally unpleasant, unnecessary, or unhealthy; *or* _ s/he is often overly passive, cautious, and compliant, fearing to take personal, social, and occupational initiatives and risks.

___ ___ **4) S/He** is usually _ serious, intellectual, and analytic, wanting to *understand* life and situations, and know in great detail why things are as they are. S/He _ may be interested in psychology and counseling, and/or _ read about, analyze, and discuss human behavior "endlessly."

___ ___ **5) S/He** is often _ confused, disorganized, overwhelmed, dependent, and "helpless;" *or* s/he _ is fiercely independent, domineering, over-organized, and overcompetent. S/He _ depends excessively on *or* _ stubbornly avoids medical, psychological, social, financial, and/or spiritual help.

___ ___ **6) S/He** is _ uncomfortable being silly, spontaneous, or child-like ("doesn't know how to play"); *or* s/he _ is often silly, simplistic, playful, jolly, and superficial.

___ ___ **7) S/He** is _ *very* responsible (over-willing to take charge, organize, and fix things, even if personally taxing); *or* s/he _ is frequently irresponsible and undependable. S/He probably _ denies, _ minimizes, and/or _ rationalizes (justifies and defends) either behavior.

___ ___ **8) S/He** often has trouble _ feeling and/or _ expressing strong emotions, and/or _ tolerating them in others—specially anger, hurt, fear, and sadness. S/He _ often feels "nothing" *or* s/he _ has unpredictable or inappropriate surges of rage, sadness, weeping, "depression," or anxiety. S/He may _ never apologize, *or* _ apologizes "all the time" and unnecessarily.

___ ___ **9) S/He** compulsively needs to *control* personal emotions, key relationships, and interpersonal situations. S/He is either _ overly aggressive, rigid, and domineering *or* _ subtly, persistently manipulative (e.g. using guilt trips or a "helpless victim" stance) to "always" get her or his way. Where true, s/he probably _ denies, _ minimizes or jokes about this, _ rationalizes it ("I can't help it," or "I have to, because . . ."), or _ blames someone else.

___ ___ **10) S/He** has _ significant memory gaps about early childhood years and events, and one or both parents. S/He _ knows little about one or both parents' childhood experiences and feelings, and _ views that as unimportant or unremarkable. If s/he asks about these, senior family members may deflect or "not want to talk."

___ ___ **11) S/He's** socially _ very shy and awkward, *or* _ very charming; and _ has few or no real (intimate) friends. S/He has a history of relationship _ avoidances and/or _ "failures," including divorce/s. S/He demonstrates _ high discomfort with interpersonal commitment and/or intimacy, and consistently _ denies, _ minimizes, or _ rationalizes this.

___ ___ **12) S/He** _ may be sexually dysfunctional (e.g. impotent, addicted, "frigid," or non-orgasmic) and/or _ compulsively avoid sexual contact; *or* _ s/he is overly seductive, voyeuristic, and/or promiscuous ("oversexed"). S/He may be secretly confused about and/or ashamed of her or his _ gender, _ body (parts), sexual _ feelings, _ behaviors, _ preferences, and/or _ fantasies.

___ ___ **13) S/He** _ "never gets sick" *or* _ suffers chronic illnesses like migraines or other headaches, back, neck, or other muscle pain; insomnia or apnea; obesity; asthma; gastric, intestinal, or colon problems; anxiety attacks; phobias; allergies; or other emotional or physical maladies which may not respond to appropriate medications or therapies. S/He _ may rely on medications to provide daily rest, digestion, comfort, mental focus, and mood-stability.

___ ___ **14) S/He** is _ highly uncomfortable about revealing personal thoughts, feelings, and experiences (excessively distrustful); *or* s/he _ often discloses personal things inappropriately (naïvely over-trusting).

___ ___ **15) S/He** is _ uncomfortable giving, getting, and/or observing affectionate touching and embracing (*stiff* or *cold*); and/**or** _ s/he touches others dutifully, awkwardly, or inappropriately. S/He may _ joke about, _ explain, _ apologize, or _ deny this.

___ ___ **16) S/He** _ often avoids personal conflicts with or between others by changing or controlling the conversation, getting intensely angry, "collapsing," or withdrawing physically and/or emotionally ("numbing"); *or* _ s/he seems to often *enjoy* triggering or experiencing conflicts (i.e. *excitement*) with or between others.

___ ___ **17) S/He** is _ very opinionated and reactive about,

and/or _ was or is compulsive about or addicted to one or more
of these:
 _ Ethyl alcohol in some form (liquor)
 _ Prescription drugs or _ illegal ("hard") drugs
 _ Sugar, fats, and carbohydrates (junk foods)
 _ Food, dieting, eating, and/or nutrition
 _ Caffeine and/or nicotine, and attempts to quit either
 _ Risk, excitement, and drama
 _ A special hobby, including computer use
 _ Pain, illness, and/or death
 _ Another person (codependence)
 _ Cleaning, neatness, lists, and/or organization
 _ Health, fitness, and/or exercising
 _ Work, "busy-ness," and/or "being *productive*"
 _ "Justice" and/or "fairness"
 _ Protecting one or more children, or social "underdogs"
 _ A social "cause" like abortion and gun control
 _ Material possessions (shopping and comparing)
 _ Psychological "recovery" (e.g. Project 1 here)
 _ Sexual arousal and orgasm
 _ God, worship, church, salvation, hell, and/or Satan
 _ Lying, secrecy, truth, and/or honesty
 _ Personal image, and/or others' opinions
 _ Money, wealth, saving, spending, and/or gambling
 __ __ 18) S/He has _ children, _ relatives, and/or _ past or
present partners who _ excessively obsess about, or _ are or
were addicted to, one or more of the above.
 __ __ 19) S/He has recurring _ "depressions," _ apathy,
and/or _ exhaustion "for no reason." S/He may have _ "Seasonal Affective Disorder" or periodic sleep disorders like _ insomnia, _ apnea, _ narcolepsy, and/or _ unusual nightmares.
 __ __ 20) S/He often feels vaguely *empty, "something's
missing (in me),"* or *"I'm different than other people somehow . . . ,"* without knowing why.
 __ __ 21) S/He is _ significantly uncomfortable being alone;
or s/he _ prefers solitude to an unusual degree, and seems socially isolated.

me / you

_____ **22) S/He** _ has consistently low self esteem; _ is often harshly self-critical; _ discounts her or his own successes and/or merited praise; _ is constantly apologetic or defensive; _consistently avoids making or keeping solid eye contact with some or most men / women / authorities / people. S/He _ commonly uses "you" or "we" rather than "I" (*"You get angry when some idiot . . ."*)

_____ **23) S/He** _ often experiences mind-racing or churning: i.e. ceaseless "inner voices" (thought streams) which _ are frequently anxious, fearful, critical, self-doubting, argumentative, and/or chaotic. S/He may _ have chronic trouble concentrating, and _ have been assessed as having "Attention Deficit Disorder" (ADD) and/or a reading or learning "disability."

_____ **24) S/He** is _ often anxiously alert to the present and future opinions, feelings, and actions of other people (hypervigilance). S/He tends to _ assume others' (usually critical) beliefs or intentions, and _ often reacts to things that haven't happened as though they had. (*"I* know *you'll have an affair"*)

_____ **25) S/He** often _ smiles and/or chuckles inappropriately when nervous, hurt, confused, scared, angry, or worried (i.e. often). S/He _ is usually unaware of this habit or _ can't explain it; and _ may minimize, intellectualize, defend, or joke about it to hide related anxiety.

_____ **26) S/He** _ often feels vaguely or clearly victimized by others or "fate," _ regularly avoids taking responsibility for her or his own choices, and _ denies or _ endlessly rationalizes doing so; *or* s/he _ assumes *too much* responsibility, and _ obsessively feels guilty and *bad* for things beyond her or his control.

_____ **27) S/He** is _ highly sensitive to real or imagined criticism from others, _ frequently self-doubtful, and _ unnecessarily rationalizes, explains, and/or justifies his or her own opinions, values, and actions. S/He is _ quick to blame others *or* _ often empathizes with "the other guy's" situation, and defers to them.

_____ **28) S/He** commonly _ fears, distrusts, is tense around,

_ criticizes, and/or argues with people in authority roles. S/He either _ feels very anxious without clear instructions *or* _ compulsively resists instructions and acts independently, even if self-harmful.

me / you

____ **29) S/He** often _ fears saying "no" and setting appropriate limits (boundaries) with others. S/He _ feels guilty about asserting her or his own _ needs, _ tolerances, and _ ideas; and may do so _ expecting others to discount, ridicule, or ignore them.

____ **30) S/He** semi-consciously _ confuses love with pity, control, or need; and/or _ associates love with pain. S/He _ usually focuses on others' needs first, and tends to _ rescue or "fix" them; *or* _ s/he is overconcerned with her or his own needs ("self centered" or "Narcissistic"). S/He _ avoids intimacy or _ cyclically seeks, then runs from it—i.e. s/he has a history of "approach-avoid" relationships.

____ **31) S/He** _ hangs on desperately to toxic relationships which cause significant shame, anxiety, guilt, confusion, and pain. S/He _ may repeatedly cycle between intense jealousy and guilt. Her or his _ major personal relationship-choices are often largely based on fears of criticism, "being wrong," rejection, and abandonment [..01/co-dep.htm].

____ **32) S/He** _ feels bored, restless, or uneasy without current personal or environmental crisis, drama, or excitement. At times _ s/he seems to seek or *make* crises, and _ denies, minimizes, jokes about, or justifies this.

____ **33) S/He** _ is often passive, timid, self-doubting, and reactive to other people and situations; *or* s/he _ is often self-harmfully impulsive, spontaneous, and aggressive. S/He _ may claim *"I can't help it."*

____ **34) S/He** often _ feels alone, disconnected, or lonely, even in a social group. S/He _ seldom feels s/he really *belongs* anywhere, and may or may not disclose that to others.

____ **35) S/He** _ often seeks pleasure and gratification (comfort) *now* vs. later, even if self-harmful. S/He _ may defend or minimize this, _ rationalize by saying "*I can't help it*," or _ deflect from it by joking.

me / you

__ __ **36) S/He** prefers to work independently (e.g. as a consultant, craftsperson, or entrepreneur) and/or in a solitary setting. S/He either _ changes jobs often *or* _ stays at the same job for years. S/He _ may work in a human-service occupation or avocation (nurse, doctor, teacher, counselor, mediator, lawyer, beautician, case worker, clergyperson, realtor, accountant, coach, nanny, day care worker, professional consultant, customer-service rep . . .)

__ __ **37) S/He** _ rarely *or* _ frantically initiates social activities. S/He habitually _ avoids *or* _ compulsively seeks being the center of social and/or occupational attention.

__ __ **38) S/He** is often _ self-centered, grandiose, and hyperconscious of health and/or appearance; *or* s/he is _ subtly or clearly self-abusive, self-deprecating, self-sabotaging, and self-neglectful (e.g. seeing a doctor, dentist, gynecologist, oculist, or therapist only in crises).

__ __ **39) S/He** _ habitually withholds, shades, or distorts the truth (lies) to avoid expected criticism, rejection, loss, or "hurting others." S/He _ denies doing this, and _ secretly feels righteous and justified and/or guilty and ashamed.

__ __ **40) S/He** is _ secretly or openly critical or ashamed of her or his "looks," appearance, or body. S/He may be _ extremely modest *or* _ very immodest. S/He consistently grooms and dresses either _ shabbily and drably *or* _ gaudily, over-formally, or perfectly.

__ __ **41) S/He** is _ notably pessimistic, skeptical, gloomy, cynical, and "negative;" *or* s/he is _ idealistic, unrealistically optimistic, relentlessly cheerful (including crises and traumas) and rigidly focuses on "the bright side" of things.

__ __ **42) S/He** frequently _ gives confusing double (mixed) messages by word and behavior; and _ denies, whines, justifies, jokes, or intellectualizes about this.

__ __ **43) S/He** notably _ avoids making major decisions, _ procrastinates, and/or _ doesn't "follow through" on promises and intentions; and _ rationalizes, whines, complains, defends, blames others, and/or intellectualizes about this.

me / you

__ __ **44) S/He** _ exhibits unusual "mood swings" (like elation > depression), _ may react unpredictably, and _ may have been diagnosed as *bi-polar, manic,* or *manic depressive.*

__ __ **45) S/He** _ disparages or is indifferent to church, one or all religions, God, and worship; *or* s/he _ is excessively pious, zealous, righteous, rigid, and aggressively biased about "the Only God, religion, or Holy Book." If the latter, s/he believes immovably in a punitive, judgmental Deity, and Hell, demons and the Devil, the "Rapture," "spiritual warfare," and "mortal sin."

__ __ **46) S/He** often chooses people with many of these traits as mates, friends, and associates.

__ __ **47) S/He** _ denies having many or most of these traits *to excess,* _explains them defensively, and/or _ minimizes their personal significance; and _ s/he probably denies this denial, _ jokes about it, or _ is defensive or reactive about it.

__ __ **48) S/He** _ unconsciously promotes persecutor-victim-rescuer (PVR) relationship triangles, and resists _ acknowledging this and _ "de-triangling" (Chapter 16).

__ __ **49) Unless** already in true wholistic recovery from psychological wounds, s/he will _ discount, avoid, intellectualize, disparage, or distort Project 1 in this series (assess for inner wounds), and _ deny, justify, or trivialize that.

+ + +

Because none of us grew up in perfect childhoods, *everyone* has mixes of these traits in varying degrees! Note how many of these 49 behaviors you checked about yourself: ___. **The more of these items you checked, the higher the odds** you're often controlled by personality subselves who don't know or trust your skilled inner leader, your Self.

Cross-check your results by reviewing the 28 traits of high-nurturance families on p. 440 or in [..01/health.htm], and the six common psychological wounds on p. 448. My clinical experience is that the fewer high-nurturance factors you grew up with in your first four to six years, the higher the odds that you developed a protective false self then, which has felt *normal* ever since.

Note that a protective false-self strategy is "amnesia" of early traumas. Note also that major psycho-spiritual neglect can be a series of small daily traumas over a long period that may not merit individual memories. The latter helps explain why many seriously wounded people fervently claim their early years were "fine," and their family was "loving," and "very healthy." That's augmented by the tendency for many wounded members of low-nurturance families to share protective denials and distortions ("*Grampa would NEVER molest a child!*")

Your Guardian subselves [..01/innerfam2.htm] are used to deceiving you "for your own good" via covert denials, distortions, and repressions. To guard against that and gain a clearer estimate, fill out the other 10 Project-1 self-assessment checklists. If you feel you *are* often controlled by a false self, read "*Who's* Really *Running Your Life?*" (xlibris.com) for recovery suggestions and resources. If you feel your *partner* has significant false-self traits, see Chapters 5 and 6 or [http://sfhelp.org/Rx/mates/split.htm], and mull why your false self is devoted to her or him.

Option: focus on your main childhood caregivers one at a time, and judge how many of these 49 wound-traits they have or had. Psychological wounding migrates unseen down the generations until it's spotted and healed. Do you have kids?

 # Status check: which of these do you feel are clearly true now? "T" = *true*; "F"=*false*, and "?"="*I'm not sure.*"

I feel a mix of *calm, centered, energized, light, focused, resilient, up, grounded, relaxed, focused, alert, aware, serene, purposeful*, and *clear*, so my true Self is probably answering these questions. (T F ?)

My childhood family had over 20 of the high-nurturance traits in Resource [D]. (T F ?)

I'm _ clearly wounded, psychologically, and _ I'm committed to learning more about personal recovery from false-self dominance now. (T F ?)

I _ have few of these traits, and _ feel I don't need to focus on personal healing. (T F ?)

I'm _ not clear whether I have "significant" inner wounds, so _ I'll do the other Project-1 self-assessment checklists to get clearer. (T F ?)

I believe _ my partner is often ruled by a false self; I'm comfortable _ saying that openly, and _ asking him or her to _ verify that, and _ choose personal healing. (T F ?)

My partner _ has few of these traits, and _ often displays symptoms of true-Self leadership (above). (T F ?)

I'm _ not sure if a false self dominates _ my partner or _ another co-parent now, and _ I need to do more of the 11 checklists to widen my perspective. (T F ?)

For what to *do* about significant false-self dominance, see the Project-1 guidebook "*Who's* Really *Running Your Life?*" or [http://sfhelp.org/01/recovery1.htm].

Awarenesses . . .

F) What Your Kids Need

~60 Growth, Healing, and Adjustment Tasks

Psychologist Judith Wallerstein has studied effects of divorce on a group of average California adults and children over many years. She concludes that dependent kids that are at special risk of developmental slowdown from parental divorce (and what led to it) are . . .

"**latchkey**" kids (no competent, supervising adults consistently home after school);

kids supporting an overwhelmed (i.e. false-self dominated) custodial parent and/or troubled younger siblings;

kids caught in "endless" parental post-separation battles and court disputes over child custody, visitation, and/or financial support; and . . .

kids *of parental re/divorce.*

If Wallerstein is right, this last group is specially sobering, since well over half of U.S. stepfamilies divorce psychologically or legally. [..pop/epidemic.htm]

In their book "Second Chances," Dr. Wallerstein and Sandra Blakeslee propose that depending on many factors, *it may take an average minor child 10 to 15 years to fully master their overlapping biofamily-breakup adjustment tasks.* In making that estimate, they don't acknowledge false-self wounding, what causes it, how it affects grieving, or the sets of needs you're about to read.

After extensive research, a team of UCLA scientists recently reported (2002) strong evidence that children who grow up in "risky families" often suffer major health problems including cancer, heart disease, hypertension, diabetes, obesity, depression and anxiety disorders. The research also found such kids die prematurely.

The UCLA scientists found large numbers of studies that reveal a pattern of serious long-term health consequences for children who grow up in homes marked by conflict, anger and aggression; that are emotionally cold, unsupportive; and where children's needs are neglected [D]. Some diseases do not show up until decades later, while others are evident by adolescence. For more on this, see [http://sfhelp.org/01/research.htm] or the Psychological Bulletin, v. 128, #2, pp. 330-336.

Preparation

One at a time, focus on each minor and grown child who matters to you and/or your partner. Write down each child's main current *needs* as you see them. List as many as you wish. Next . . .

Name the adults you feel are responsible for helping each child fill their mix of current and long-term needs (i.e. for *nurturing* them). Refresh your perspective by re-scanning the traits of high-nurturance families in [D]. Then . . .

Read and discuss these [http://sfhelp.org/..] Web articles with your co-parenting partners: [..06/mission1.htm], [..10/co-p-goals.htm], [..10/co-p-dfrnces.htm], [..10/co-pinv1.htm], and [..02/needlevels.htm]. There are other useful, relevant articles at [..10/links10.htm].

Use this worksheet to help you partners discuss and draft knowledgeable "job descriptions" for each co-parent in your courtship or present stepfamily. See and discuss this sample: [..10/job1.htm]. Also use this for conferences with teachers,

and any counselors or tutors you hire to help nurture your custodial or visiting kids.

Premises: stepfamily re/marriage requires each mate to
accept the role of *co-parent* (stepparent and/or bioparent) for
someone's minor or grown child/ren. Co-parents want their resident, visiting, and grown kids to become healthy, self-support-
ing, productive young adults. To achieve this, young kids in
any family need adult help to fill ~ 25 developmental needs,
over ~20 years. *Typical minor kids of divorce and parental re/
marriage face two to five* additional *sets of family-adjustment
needs* (below). Often many of the needs are simultaneous.

If co-parents, kin, and other supporters can name and describe their kids' _ developmental, _ wound-healing, and _
adjustment needs, they're better able to nurture their youngsters effectively toward healthy adult independence. Do you
agree?

My experience as a stepfamily researcher and therapist since
1979 is that typical divorced-family and stepfamily co-parents,
and many clinicians, can't name most of the adjustment needs
that their minor kids have. Many can't name most or all of kids'
normal developmental needs. That implies that they can't accurately assess and effectively help their boys and girls to master their mixes of *up to five dozen* concurrent needs. That puts
most minor kids at major risk of slowed or blocked development and up to six psychological wounds (p. 448).

That implies that such kids _ will feel bewildered and overwhelmed as they struggle for mastery of all these simultaneous
challenges; so they _ may have major trouble succeeding as
productive adults, and _ they're at significant risk of *unintentionally* creating new low-nurturance families [D] like their
ancestors did, _ passing on the protective false-self dominance
[E] that that they inherited.

**Average minor kids of re/marrying parents face sets of
needs from . . .**

Healing psychological wounds from an *unintended* low-nurturance childhood; plus . . .

Adjusting to birthfamily reorganization from parental separation, divorce, or death; and . . .

Adjusting to extended-biofamily reorganization when one bioparent re/marries, and . . .

Adjusting to *another* wave of losses and role, relationship, and family-ritual changes if their other bioparent re/marries and/or cohabits. Then over half of these kids . . .

Must also adjust to their stepfamily disintegrating seven to ten years after their parent's re/wedding.

These sets of needs usually overlap each other and the kids' ~25 developmental needs (below). They require co-parental awareness, *teamwork*, and dedication for kids' attaining healthy independence. This happens while each of their siblings, two to four co-parents, and up to eight co-grandparents are adjusting to their *own* versions of the same family-reorganization changes, compounded by the five hazards on p. 428. Pause, breathe well, an notice what you feel and think now . . .

This chapter is a summary checklist of kids' normal developmental needs and three sets of adjustment needs. The young people in your life depend on you adults to understand and help with all of these, so they can become healthy, responsible, independent adults. This checklist is suggestive vs. "perfect," so edit it as you see fit. It's based on 64 years' life experience, and 23 years' clinical research and consulting experience with well over 500 average Midwestern, Anglo divorced families and stepfamilies.

What's an *Effective* Co-parent?

Based on this summary, an *effective* co-parent may be defined as *"an adult who _ understands each of these sets of needs, and is _ motivated, _ able, and _ skilled at providing consistently-effective guidance with them, so dependent kids _ fill them well enough (in somebody's view) when they live independently."* A longer-range definition is: *"an effective co-par-*

*ent is someone who nurtures each dependent child to grow up
and _ pick a wholistically-healthy (minimally-wounded) partner, and _ provide a high-nurturance family environment [D]
for their dependent kids so _ the kids aren't faced with the
family-adjustment needs summarized below."*

Whew!

Alert: this summary is dry, complex, and may feel overwhelming. To get the most from this resource chapter, pace
yourself, and stay aware of your thoughts and feelings as you
read. This summary is as much about *you* as a child as about
kids in your life now. If you get boggled, pause and refresh
yourself. Consider taking notes as you read and react. Take as
much time as you need!

1) Kids' Normal Developmental Needs

Edit this summary against your own life experience and
training. It is generic and not specially prioritized. Satisfying
some needs depends on progress with others. *Satisfying* is a
subjective concept. Try rank-ordering these needs and relating
them to kids' age-zones (e.g. pre-school, middle school, high
school). Gain perspective on these needs from Dr. Erik Erikson's
timeless book "Childhood and Society." Family therapy and
the U.S. post-war divorce epidemic were blooming as he wrote
it. Two generations would pass before "personality splitting"
(false-self development) began to be acknowledged and understood. That awareness is in it's social infancy as I write this.

+ + +

Reality Check: as you read, reflect whether *you* had to
fill each of these needs to succeed as an independent adult.
Each of your girls and boys needs to . . .

1) Learn how to think effectively to make sense of the
world and make effective daily decisions. This includes *many*
subtasks, like perceiving, classifying, and articulating abstract
concepts; growing fluency with an expressive vocabulary, syn-

thesizing unrelated ideas, objectively discerning information patterns and inconsistencies, discerning process from content, staying focused, and logical induction and deduction. Most of the co-parents I've met think "fuzzily": [http://sfhelp.org/02/fuzzy1-wks.htm]. And kids need to . . .

2) Learn how to _ be clearly aware of, _ focus among, and to _ balance (prioritize), dynamic emotions, thoughts, hunches, intuitions, and current *needs*; in order to _ react to life challenges and opportunities in healthy, safe, and satisfying ways. And they need to . . .

3) Learn to monitor and shift their "bubble of empathic awareness" from focusing only on *their* current needs, feelings, and thoughts, or only on other people's (*"Always think of the other guy!"*), to automatically being aware of themselves *and* selected other people [..02/a-bubble.htm]. The ultimate phase of this developmental task is to develop an empathic awareness of all living things. And your kids need to . . .

__ **4) Forge a realistic identity** to satisfy core human questions like *"Who am I?"*, and *"How am I like and different from* _ *my parents,* _ *other people, and* _ *others of my gender?"* Part of this developmental task is _ developing and asserting personal *boundaries*: finding a stable, peaceful way to separate with minimal anxiety and guilt from caregivers' _ needs and _ visions of who *they* want the child to be. This includes kids' needing to evolve realistic understanding of their own _ unique talents and _ personal limitations _ without undue egotism, guilt, shame, and anxiety. And your (step)kids and any grandkids need to . . .

5) Forge genuine _ **self-respect**, _ self-care, _ self-trust, and _ self-awareness as foundations for filling their daily and long-term personal and social needs well enough. This implies all their personality subselves' learning to trust and cooperate with their Self, other Regular subselves, and a benign Higher Power.

And your kids also need to . . .

6) Learn how to communicate effectively [H] with peers, authorities, and strangers of any gender and race, in calm and conflictual situations. This includes learning how to _ identify and _ assert their current true (vs. surface) needs (p. 44), while _ respecting and appreciating the current needs of others. Ineffective communication is an epidemic societal and family stressor (Chapter 7). And kids need to . . .

7) Learn to understand, appreciate, and care effectively for their changing body, to promote ongoing wholistic (spiritual + physical + emotional + mental) health and healing. This includes kids' _ understanding, _ valuing, and _ controlling their _ sensuality and sexuality. And kids also need to . . .

8) Learn _ how to form nourishing (vs. toxic) emotional **attachments** to (i.e. *bond* with) selected people, ideas, visions, and principles [..01/bonding.htm]; and _ learn how to grieve well when such attachments break (Chapter 12). And your youngsters need your help to . . .

9) Learn to _ discern and _ make balanced daily decisions between . . .

_ short-term pleasure vs. long-term satisfaction;

_ pleasing others vs. themselves;

_ inner and environmental realities, vs. tempting illusions and distortions (like denials);

_ attitudes of pessimism, idealism, and realistic optimism ("glass half full"); and . . .

_ work, play, and rest.

And each of your boys and girls needs to . . .

10) Learn effective social (relationship) skills like tact, empathy, intimacy, selective trust, assertion, cooperation, and respectful confrontation, to "get along well" with other people, including an eventual mate and dependent kids. Developing kids also need to . . .

11) Learn how to _ *want to* take non-shaming responsibility for the impacts of their actions, vs. denial, projection, repression, blaming others, numbing out, and "confusion;" while they learn to _ respectfully grant other people full responsibility for their own decisions, behaviors, feelings, health, and welfare (avoid toxic *enabling*). And they also need to . . .

12) Learn _ how to learn, evaluate, retain, sort, prioritize, and use (apply) new concrete and abstract information; and learn _ how and _ where to get needed information. Perhaps the hardest part of this task is learning how to _ identify and _ *unlearn* old attitudes, beliefs, habits, and values that no longer fit current life reality and goals.

And you're probably helping your kids to . . .

13) Evolve meaningful answers to core life questions about spirituality and religion (*"Is there a God? What does S/He want? Does S/He really care about me?"*), life and cosmic origins, destiny, fate, good and evil, health and death; and _ learn to revere and develop the spiritual part of their nature in their life decisions. And . . .

14) Learn how to _ accept and *learn* from _ personal **mistakes and failures,** and to _ keep their mental + spiritual + emotional + physical balances. And immature people need to . . .

15) Evolve an authentic (vs. borrowed) framework of **ethics and morals**: deciding what's "right and wrong" and "good and bad" in any situation, and _ apply those judgments effectively toward filling daily and long-range personal and social needs; while they . . .

16) Learn _ how to earn and responsibly manage money and other assets, debts, and _ respect and care for what money buys, including power and freedoms; as they . . .

17) Learn to make responsible, healthy short and long-term decisions about _ sex and _ child conception; and learn about _ (these) kids' development phases and needs, and _ effective parenting (above). And young people need to . . .

18) Learn how to understand, negotiate, and **balance the responsibilities and limits of key social roles** like child; grandchild; sibling; student; friend; sexual partner; parent; local, national, and global citizen; team member; neighbor; employee; taxpayer; consumer; spiritual being; debtor; and eventually independent, responsible (wo)man. And ideally, kids learn to . . .

19) _ Acknowledge _ that they have a unique, worthy life mission or purpose, and _ stay alert for "evidence" (thoughts, feelings, hunches, outside feedback), about what it is; while _ trying out as many "personalities" and roles as possible, as an explorer. That can help them . . .

20) Value and evolve meaningful _ visions and _ life goals, and _ a meaningful plan to attain them. The alternative is living each day as a disconnected random experience, and dying with regrets over a wasted life. (*"If only I had . . ."*). And your kids need to . . .

21) Learn how to _ need, _ ask for, and _ receive _ human and _ spiritual help, *without excessive guilt, shame, and anxiety,* when life becomes chaotic and overwhelming. And . . .

22) Learn _ to discern who and what to trust; and _ how to adapt to people, ideas, and circumstances they *don't* trust enough. Part of this task involves _ learning to live comfortably enough with inevitable ambiguities and insecurities. And to gain effective independence, your kids need to . . .

23) _ Master basic life skills like cooking, sanitation, hygiene, understanding contracts and laws, time management, and (usually) driving a vehicle; while they _ learn about the physical world, and _ how to value nurturing the Earth, vs. plundering it.

24) <u>Over all:</u> shifting from dependence on the ruling subselves of caregivers to confident reliance on their unfettered true Self and Higher Power. The alternative is a fragmented personality dominated by a well-meaning group of myopic subselves: a *false self.* A good start on mastering this keystone task in childhood is unlikely if false selves control one or more of your child's primary caregivers—e.g. *you.* It then becomes an adult recovery task (Project 1) that *may* activate in middle age if circumstances allow.

25) Progress on filling all these needs over time, mirrored and affirmed by key caregivers, helps a developing child to _ **feel, _ spontaneously express, and _ receive real** *love,* including _ healthy *self-*love. A common alternative is unconsciously developing a protective false self, and adapting to reflexive shame, guilt, anxiety (fears), and self-doubts. That dedicated group of subselves quickly learns to pretend and people-please to gain essential caregiver approval and primal nurturance. The latter is likely if the caregiver/s are usually ruled by their own false selves.

Add your own developmental tasks . . .

Notice how you feel now, and where your thoughts go. Did *you* get enough help filling these basic developmental needs before you tried living on your own? Did each of your early caregivers satisfy these needs as kids? In future years, do you think your kids will thoughtfully answer that question "Yes"? This is about *awareness*, not blame!

I propose that *all* kids instinctively struggle to master concurrent growing-up tasks like these, regardless of their family, ancestry, and social environment. **Children who grow up in low-nurturance homes** and families **must** (eventually) find an effective way to *also* . . .

2) Admit and Heal Psychological Wounds

About 90% of typical U.S. stepfamilies now form after the divorce of one or both re/marrying mates. I now believe parental separation and divorce is a strong sign of significantly low psycho-spiritual nurturance in one or both mates' early years. I believe that typical kids like Patty McLean (*Stepfamily Courtship* or [..example.htm]) growing up in significantly low-nurturance environments automatically adapt by developing an unwise, protective false self. In cases of extreme parental neglect and abuse, this manifests as Multiple Personality Disorder—called "Dissociative Identity Disorder (D.I.D.)" by the American Psychiatric Association since 1994.

This neurological adaptation is powered by the primal instinct to *survive* now, vs. grow (fill these developmental needs). It results in the child's decisions, attitudes, and perceptions being significantly governed by a protective false self [E]. Over time, the growing child's experiential view of "normal" forms around this false self's perception of life, and how the environment reacts to its decisions and actions.

Bottom line: I believe most parents who _ separate or divorce, or _ avoid intimacy and true relationship interdependence and commitment, are significantly controlled by protective false self. They haven't been able to satisfy many of the developmental needs above—specially # 24. Until they understand this via Project 1 or equivalent, and work to empower their true Self to manage their *inner* family of subselves (personality), they risk unconsciously causing their kids to develop a false self too, like their ancestors.

Premise: typical kids of parental divorce must satisfy some mix of the inner-healing needs below, *on top of their normal developmental needs*. Their psychological wounds and low-nurturance environment combine to hinder developmental progress. These *recovery* needs can be viewed as steps to _ recognize and _ free their true Self to _ lead and harmonize their team of personality subselves. Recognizing and mastering these healing tasks is a life-long process. It usually starts in middle age, after years of pain and "hitting bottom." In some way. The other family-adjustment needs below are usually encountered before this personal healing begins. That makes inner-family harmonizing harder to acknowledge and master.

My experience is that tragically, our false-self dominated media and educational systems aren't aware of these ideas, so most fragmented people never perceive their or their kid's six psychological wounds (p. 448). Typical unaware caregivers are at high risk of mis-diagnosing or minimizing what their troubled kids *really* need. Fortunately, the 1980s "Adult Child" and "Inner Child" movements, facilitated by the Internet and TV expansions, are combating this.

Numbering continues from above, because all these needs overlap. Numbers in parentheses refer to developmental needs above. The needs you're about to read are not ranked in importance. Together, they form the goal of Project-1 *recovery* [..01/recovery1.htm]. Each survivor of low childhood nurturance has a unique mix of healing needs like these:

26) Break protective denials that they _came from a low-nurturance childhood, _ developed a false self to survive, and _ have been often or chronically controlled by it which _ is significantly stressing them and the people around them (24).

In my experience since 1986, most co-parents and many family professionals aren't aware of this essential group of needs.

27) _ Value and _ take responsibility for their own life and wholistic health; and evolve an effective way to _ enable their Self, _ acknowledge a meaningful Higher Power, and _ grow inner-family harmony. Restated: this keystone need is _ to recognize that need 24 above was never filled, and _ choosing to satisfy it as a self-responsible adult. Related needs are to:

28) Heal toxic shame: intentionally _ reverse low self-esteem and self-respect over time, and _ develop unconditional love for themselves and selected (or all) others (5). A related need is to . . .

29) Change reflexive self-neglect (self-abandonment) **to authentic** (vs. dutiful or fearful) **self-care** and self-nurturance. (7)

30) Replace primal fear and *expectation* of abandonment by key caregivers, **with steady faith in** a loving and reliable Higher Power, key adults, and true-Self reliability. Concurrent needs are to reduce excessive fears of _ the unknown, _ normal interpersonal conflict, _ "failure," and _ overwhelm from intense emotions. (5, 22, 24)

31) Convert vague or distorted senses of Self (personal identity), including male/female identity, to clear, healthy, and appropriate senses of true Self. This includes developing and accepting a realistic body image, and accepting personal talents and limits. (4, 5)

32) Reverse distrusts of _ personal perceptions and judgment ("self doubt"), and of _ the dependability and good intentions of most caregivers and adult authorities (22). A related need is to _ improve accurate discernment of who justifies average and special trust.

33) Learn that _ there are no "negative" emotions, and _ **develop** the anxiety and guilt-free **abilities to fully _ feel and _ express *all* emotions within safe limits**. Also learn _ to be comfortable enough with others doing the same, specially with frustration, anger, sadness, confusion, anxiety (worry) and fear, and despair. Failure to fill these needs will seriously inhibit the wounded person's ability to _ grieve, _ communicate, and _ resolve inner and interpersonal conflicts well. (2)

34) Develop the ability to usually tolerate _ change; _ uncertainty (ambivalence); _ inner-personal and interpersonal conflict; _ imperfection; and _ selective, healthy intimacies. This depends partly on learning to _ discern and _ accept what can be affected, vs. what is beyond the person's control (p. 24, and tasks 24, 25, and others above). Typical false selves usually can't do some or all these well and consistently.

And wounded kids need to learn to . . .

35) *Want to* replace self-harmful (toxic) ways of self-soothing and self-comforting (e.g. addictions, reality distortions, and avoidances) **with self-nurturing habits** and healthy sources of comfort and reassurance (7, 21, 23). And . . .

36) Strengthen their ability to _ form and _ maintain genuine (vs. faked or strategic), emotional attachments to (bond with) high-nurturance people and goals. This is one essential for genuine social intimacy and effective re/marriage and co-parenting. (8 and others, and [..01/bonding.htm])

A final over-arching adjustment need for kids raised with significant nurturance deficits is to . . .

37) Develop faith that their lives have intrinsic worth, promise, and real meaning, vs. old nihilism ("nothing matters"), worthlessness, pessimism, and inner emptiness. (5, 19, 20)

Add your own healing tasks . . .

Minor kids and young adults have little chance to recognize and fill these recovery needs if _ their main caregivers and mentors don't see and understand them, and _ deny their own psychological wounds. Again: I propose that **first divorce is a strong suggestion that** one or both mates _ got too little nurturance as a young child; _ weren't able to satisfy enough of their own developmental needs; and _ were unaware of their set of these inner wounds, or _ didn't know how to heal them.

Most U.S. re/weddings follow the divorce of one or both partners . . .

How are you doing? This is pretty heavy going, isn't it? Do your subselves need a mind-body break? When you're ready, refocus on the key kids in your life again. If and when their biofamily reorganizes (vs. "breaks up"), they must fill unsatisfied needs above while they try to . . .

3) Adjust to Biofamily Reorganization

Many American kids are under 20 when their birthfamily reorganizes from the separation or desertion of a parent. Far fewer minor kids must adjust to a parent dying. The complex emotional, financial, and legal divorce *process* (vs. event) adds new stress to _ years of trying to survive inadequate emotional/spiritual nurturance. Often, a parent leaving or being ejected from home breaks kids' protective denial of "family trouble," and their personal stress (inner-family chaos) soars. Other kids' stress soars because it's *not* safe to break their denials. Both situations strengthen false-self dominance and related wounds, which hinders filling concurrent developmental, healing, and these adjustment needs.

Many factors shape each child's reactions to birthfamily restructuring from parental death or separation. These include age, gender, birth-order, extended-family presence and coherence, ethnicity, finances, education, local social conditions (support), and so on. Generally, the lower the child's emotional nurturance [D] has been before parental separation or death, the more trouble s/he will have in filling the developmental and personality-harmonizing needs above, and the family-adjustment needs below. Does this make sense to you?

Note that *these change-adjustment needs are concurrent with any unfilled developmental and recovery needs.* Depending on many factors, it may take an average minor child five to 15 years to *stabilize*, vs. *satisfy*, their mix of the needs above and below. Kids who have adjusted and begun bonding in a stepfamily must fill these needs *again* if their stepfamily breaks up.

Again, numbering continues from above. Reflect on which of the developmental and healing tasks above would need to be mastered "well enough" in order to fill each one of these new needs. Also mull what "mastered" means . . .

38) Make stable sense out of why one parent left them, and why their biofamily came apart. Progress with this is greatly shaped by whether each bioparent is _ often led by a true Self; and honest with _ themselves, _ their ex mate, and _ with the child. If a protective false self controls the child, parental honestly about their family's break-up may not be received clearly or at all because of excessive shame and guilt, distrusts, and reality distortions.

39) _ Accept that *they* didn't cause their biofamily's re-organization, and _ clarify and accept that someone else is responsible, without anxiety. And each child needs to . . .

40) Grieve *many* concrete and abstract losses (broken emotional bonds), over many years. Parental dwelling moves, and child visitations may cause waves of new losses for adults and children alike. Success here depends on caregivers providing an effective "good grief" policy (p. 255). And . . .

41) Change their views of one or both bioparents from hero/ine to "flawed and still lovable" special adults. This task depends on _ personal and family grieving progress; _ may include *forgiving* one or both parents; and is shaped by _ the post-divorce relationship between ex mates, and _ their abilities to think clearly and communicate effectively (Project 2).

And typical kids of parental separation or death need to . . .

42) Heal _ unwarranted guilts ("I did bad things that made this happen") **and new _ shame** ["I'm unlovable and *bad* (worthless), so Dad (Mom) left me / us."]. And also . . .

43) Draw clear new personal boundaries: _ separate themselves from their parents' and relatives anxiety, needs, and conflicts _ *without undue guilt, anxiety, and shame.* And . . .

44) Re/build trust that adult caregivers and authorities will not reject or abandon them, despite the child's major problems and self-perceived "flaws." And . . .

45) Build new trust that living bioparents and key sibs and relatives are safe, healthy, and happy enough as their family reorganization stabilizes. And . . .

46) Adjust to many new _ roles, _ rules, and _ living conditions, including _ (eventual) parental dating, and _ new household responsibilities like taking more care of their home, themselves, younger sibs, and/or an overwhelmed bioparent.

This need often is compounded by learning _ new and sometimes clashing roles and rules in two bioparental homes, plus _ inter-home visitation rituals. *If a child came from a significantly low-nurturance biofamily, s/he will probably shuttle between* two *low-nurturance homes after parental separation.* There are exceptions. And many minor and grown kids of birthfamily reorganization need to . . .

47) Cope with one or both bioparents using them as a weapon, spy, lure, confidant, or courier in ongoing relations with their other bioparent and/or key relatives. This is specially likely when _ parents battle in court over child support, custody, and/or visitations; and when _ one or both bioparents verbally attack or revile the other parent in front of the child.

Typical kids of parental divorce or death also must . . .

48) Adjust their personal and family identities over time to "*OK* divorced or bereaved (boy / son / brother / relative) or (girl / daughter / sister / relative)." And . . .

49) Find and accept surrogate nurturance, if biofamily parenting is inadequate. This is specially vital if their custodial caregiver/s are overwhelmed and regressed (dominated by a false self). A related need is to _ adjust well enough to any guilt, shame, or anxiety over _ seeking and _ accepting surrogate caregiving.

And over time, minor kids of birthfamily neglect and reorganization need to . . .

50) Re/build authentic feelings of personal security, confidence, optimism, and hope for their future, and as a competent future _ adult, _ spouse, _ wage-earner, and _ (potential) co-parent.

How long do you think the average child of parental divorce or death would take to fill their set of these 12 adjustment needs, while progressing on their 26 developmental needs, burdened by up to six psychological wounds?

Before continuing, breathe, look away, and see where your thoughts want to go with what you just read. Did your ruling subselves blank out? Can you name at least six of the 12 needs you just read about? Take your time absorbing and integrating all these needs and what they mean in your family!

If their custodial biomom or dad cohabits and/or re/marries before _ the child and _ each bioparent has progressed well on filling their mix of needs above, a typical child now experiences their absent-parent family "breaking up" (reorganizing *again*). Kids (and adults) now face an array of . . .

4) Typical *Stepfamily* Adjustment Needs

Once again, the nature, mix, and complexity of stepfamily-adjustment needs for a given child depends on their age, sex, relations with each bioparent, understanding of parental divorce, and many other factors. Key factors are the nurturance-levels in their pre-and post-divorce homes, schools, churches, and neighborhoods [D]. These depend largely on _ the degree to which true Selves lead the child's main and secondary caregivers, and _ the availability of *knowledgeable* stepfamily supports. In my experience since 1979, few communities have any, and the media offers little.

These new needs often overlap those above, so the numbering continues. These stepfamily-adjustment needs arise during parental courtship and co-habitation, and may amplify or repeat some of the needs above. Generally, the more *develop-*

mental needs each child has made major progress filling, the more apt s/he is to fill these new needs:

51) Mourn and accept less (custodial) bioparental attention and accessibility. This may coincide with teens' growing focus on socializing with friends and gaining early independence.

52) Redefine _ personal and _ family identity *again*, and _ decide clearly *"Who comprises my family now?"* This is often in the face of co-parents' and relatives' confusions over their version of this task, including people rejecting, unsure about, and being excluded from stepfamily membership.

53) Negotiate and stabilize several to many forced (unchosen) **stepfamily _ roles and _ relationships**, like custodial or visiting stepchild and step-sibling, step-cousin, step-grandchild, half-sibling, etc. Typical biofamilies have 15 common roles; multi-home stepfamilies have ~30. Co-parents often are as confused and conflicted about these as their kids, and may *add* to kids' confusions.

54) _ Adjust to new _ privacy and __ sexual norms and conditions in their one or two homes. Norms in one home may conflict with those in the other, and with those in the prior absent-parent home. While they're working on all these, your kids must also . . .

55) _ Continue grieving prior losses, and _ start mourning a complex set of *new* abstract and concrete losses from the ending of their prior living situation. Usually this includes adjusting to a new dwelling, and perhaps a new neighborhood, school, and church. See [..05/physical-loss-inv.htm]. Kids also need to . . .

56) Form and act from clear, stable personal boundaries without guilt or anxiety, in case key relatives' or friends' disapprove of their bioparent's _ divorce, _ re/marriage, and/or _ cohabiting.

57) _ Test for, _ learn clearly, and _ accept:

What are the _ rules and _ consequences in my _ two co-parenting homes and _ complex new extended stepfamily?

Who's *really* in charge at each of my co-parenting homes? Who _ makes and _ enforces the rules, if anyone?

What's my _ rank (importance) in each home, and _ how much power do I have now to get others to fill my needs in each?

How do I handle the (inevitable) differences in the _ values (preferences and priorities), _ rules, _ roles, and _ consequences between my several step homes?

And typical minor kids in new stepfamilies need to . . .

58) Build stable trust that "This home and family are *safe* to participate in and rely on, because I believe they won't break up like my *all* my other ones did."

59) Adapt to feeling alone, confused, and weird because most of the child's relatives, teachers, and some friends don't *really* understand what it's like to live in a stepfamily like theirs. Friends' stepfamilies will *always* be structured very differently [..03/compare.htm]. And kids also need to . . .

60) Adjust their _ identity, _ power, _ loyalties, and _ "rank" in their _ home/s and _ stepfamily each time _ their co-parents have a new child (i.e. a half-sib); or _ a biosib or stepsib moves in or out of their home; or _ a key person dies, moves away, re/marries, or re/divorces. These boys and girls must also . . .

61) Re-fill most of these needs (with more experience and knowledge) **if their other bioparent re/marries** *or re/divorces*. Average stepkids may have four co-parents, eight co-grandparents, several half and/or step-siblings, and dozens of co-relatives. See the sample genogram on p. 437.

62) The Stepfamily Association of America guesstimates that over 60% of typical U.S. stepfamilies re/divorce within 10 years of the nuptials. That suggests that **a high percentage of stepkids must re-fill many** of needs 38-50 above, concurrent with any unfinished prior tasks.

Typical stepfamily co-parents have their own version of most of these adjustment needs [G]. Stepfamily literature suggests that it commonly takes co-parents and kids four or more years to stabilize (vs. satisfy) all these stepfamily-adjustment needs well enough. Many factors determine how "fast" a family like yours will take [..09/develop1.htm].

In over two decades of stepfamily research, I've never seen any coherent acknowledgement of these five overlapping sets of typical kids' developmental, healing, and family-adjustment needs. Have you?

Note what you're (subselves are) thinking and feeling. On a scale of 1 to 10, how thorough and realistic do you feel this summary is? What changes would you make? How many of these needs could you have named before you read this?

Think of the minor kids in your life: do you know which of these needs they've satisfied, and which they currently need help with? What kind of help do they need? From whom? What kind of help do *you* partners need to help your kids? Does the importance of building an *informed* co-parenting team make more sense to you now?

Stretch, breathe, and re-center. When you (your ruling subselves) are ready, let's consider your . . .

Options

If *you* and/or your current partner are survivors of low-birthfamily nurturance [D] and/or of biofamily breakup, **use the checklist above to assess yourselves**. How are each of *you* doing with your version of these needs? _ Do the same for your ex mate/s, and any new partners of theirs. _ Discuss this assessment and what it *means* with relevant family members. _ Review your life priorities [..08/priority.htm], and decide if you want to change something.

Give a copy of this summary [..10/kid-needs.htm] to each caregiver who affects each minor child in your life, including ex mates, concerned kin, teachers, tutors, and counselors. Consider tailoring this checklist to suit each individual child.

Agree with your partner to use this summary to _ identify which needs each of your minor kids need help with, and then

_ evolve co-parent job descriptions in Project 6 if you're courting, and Project 10 if you're re/married [..10/job1.htm]. Ideally, you'll have forged a family mission statement to guide
you in this. See p. 438, *Stepfamily Courtship*, and [..10/co-
pinv1.htm].

If you may re/wed _ a bioparent whose kids haven't progressed well on "too many" of these tasks (in your opinion), or
if _ your partner isn't aware of these needs or _ seems to minimize their relevance or importance, then *seriously* question the
wisdom of re/marrying them (all). Your partner has the same
option. See [..07/links07.htm].

Here are some options for . . .

Assessing Your Kids' *Needs* Status

You've just read a summary of over *60* developmental,
healing, and family-adjustment needs that typical minor stepkids
often have. Girls and boys whose parent died face most of the
same needs. Depending on many factors, most of the needs
will overlap. They can easily overwhelm the staunchest co-parent or supporter, let alone a child or young adult.

How can you partners realistically gauge where each child
stands with their mix of these many needs?

Basics

An early goal in co-parent Projects 6 and 10 is to "learn
what your dependent kids need." That's a simple phrase for a
vital, complex effort; partly because it challenges you to realistically evaluate some psychological aspects of your custodial
and visiting kids. An advantage you may have is that typical
stepparents may be more objective about this assessment than
biomoms and dads.

A core Project-10 goal is "build an effective co-parenting
team over time, to help fill your and your kids' (many) needs."
This challenge looks like . . .

- accept your stepfamily identity and your five re/marital hazards, and . . .
- work patiently on up to 11 concurrent protective projects, including . . .
- identifying and _ reducing your mix of co-parenting teamwork barriers (p. 109), while you caregivers . . .
- assess your kids for their status and needs on their three to five sets of overlapping needs, and then . . .
- try to agree on how to help each child, while . . .
- working on your personal adjustment and recovery tasks, and . . .
- balancing *many* other goals and responsibilities.

Thoughtfully apply this framework to your unique situation, and notice how you *feel*...

Reality: there are *many* multi-home stepfamilies in your area who are succeeding at their version of this challenge. With knowledge, patience, and commitment—and your true Selves in charge—your co-parents and supporters can do the same!

As a fledgling engineer, I learned to start a complex design project by defining the desired outcome clearly, and working backwards to see what was needed to achieve it. In "co-parent engineering," that becomes "D*efine _ the questions about each child you want credible answers to, and _ how you co-parents want to feel about _ yourselves and _ your research process when you're done. Then work backwards to see how your several co-parents and concerned kin can do those together.*"

Because typical divorced families and stepfamilies are complex, stressed, and emotionally volatile, I suggest you start with *"How do we want everyone to feel as our child research progresses?"* Compare my proposed answer with yours:

"We want _ our co-parents and kids to each feel respected, aware, harmonious, and hopeful; and to feel _ united and motivated on a common, worthy project."

If you co-parents ignore getting clear on this question together, you risk unrealistic results in drafting your co-parent job descriptions. *How* and *when* you co-parents approach

Projects 6 and 10 are just as important as what they yield and what you do with the results!

First Steps Toward Assessing Your Kids' Status

Some of what follows is available at [..10/kid-dx.htm]. To begin, you co-parents will need clear, *consensual* answers to . . .
"When should we do this child needs assessment?"
"Who will participate, and who will lead?"
"Which kids, specifically, are we going to assess?"
"What preparation do we need?"
"What specific questions are we trying to answer?"
"Who's responsible for acting on our results?"
"How will we resolve disputes among us?" And . . .
"How can we optimize our efforts together, over time?"
Suggestions . . .

When Should We Do This Needs Assessment?

Ideally, well *before* you make any re/marriage decision, as the second half of Project 6. Whatever your situation, every day that passes without you adults (including co-grandparents) learning your kids' status on their daunting sets of these many needs increases their risk of psychological wounding, stepfamily stress, and possible re/divorce trauma.

Who Will Participate and Lead?

Which of your extended-(step)family adults are *really* interested in helping with this important needs-assessment, once they understand it? Are there counselors, tutors, coaches, mentors, or close family friends who want to contribute? If some co-parents or key relatives are blocked from supporting your kids by barriers like those in Part 2, your options include _ using the Serenity Prayer (p. 102) and a long-term view, and _ keeping them respectfully informed of _ what you're trying to do, _ why, and _ how you're progressing. They may get interested along the way.

Someone has to initiate, plan, and facilitate this child-assessment (nurturing) project. Ideally, all of you will share motivation to do this together. In real life, your mix of teamwork barriers may inhibit that. *Leading* implies planning, coordinating, and deciding what to do with your assessment's results.

Which Kids Will We Assess?

I recommend: each minor *and grown* child of each of your related bioparents and stepparents. "Ours" kids (half siblings) have all the developmental needs, and a subset of the stepfamily adjustment needs. Beware of *assuming* that an apparently happy, "well-adjusted" child has filled their several sets of needs, specially healing psychological wounds! False selves expertly camouflage pain and unmet needs from their host person and the people around them.

"What Training and Preparation Do We All Need?"

Your best preparation is progress on _ knowledge building (Chapter 1) and on _ your version of the 12 projects on p. 429. The four most important co-parent prerequisites for assessing your kids are _ empowering your Selves to lead, _ growing fluency in the seven Project 2 communication skills [H], evolving an effective family mission statement [C], and significant progress on building an effective nurturing team (Part 2).

A vital preparation is for all your co-parents and key relatives to evolve an effective family strategy to avoid or spot and reduce _ values and _ loyalty conflicts, and _ relationship triangles. Use Chapter 16 as a framework to help. Another vital preparation is to learn about healthy three-level grieving, and evolve a family-wide "good grief" policy. See Chapter 12.

What Questions Are We Trying to Answer?

Have all your active co-parents and key supporters _ review copies of this checklist. _ Discuss and edit the list to fit your values and situation, and _ agree on a set of specific child-needs that you all believe are important. Try to avoid black/white (either-or, right-wrong) thinking, and _ be alert for normal values differences (p. 161). Your basic questions are: _ which of (your version of) these ~60 needs does each of your custodial, visiting, and independent kids need your help with now, and _ what kind of help? Option: use the worksheet at [..10/co-pinv1.htm] to help.

Who's Responsible for Acting on Our Results?

You'll judge that each child is "OK enough," "*maybe* OK enough," or "not OK enough now" with each of their respective needs. Once you do, who will act on your results, how, and when? The answer largely depends on _ your caregivers' progress reducing the barriers in Part 2, and _ where you all are in the stepfamily development cycle [..09/develop1.htm].

Help each other stay focused, for you'll have *many* daily-life distractions. Then based on your family mission statement (Project 6) and your assessments, help each other evolve meaningful "job (role) descriptions" [http://sfhelp.org/10/job1.htm] to clarify and document your chosen responsibilities and targets.

You've probably never seen bioparents use child-care job descriptions. This is likely because in typical intact biofamilies, there are _ one or two primary caregivers, not three or more; _ probably fewer kids than you all have; and _ the kids only have one set of (developmental) needs to satisty, not three to five concurrent sets! *How* to help your kids with selected needs would fill another book. See the *Solutions* series of articles at [http://sfhelp.org/Rx/dx.htm], and books and Websites in [N] and at [..11/resources.htm] for ideas and resources. Also read about picking a qualified stepfamily clinician at [..11/

counsel.htm], and periodically discuss whether professional help with some or all of these needs is warranted.

Adults and kids in typical divorced families and stepfamilies need more outside help than peers in high-nurturance biofamilies. Seeking and using professional help in a divorced or re/married family is a sign if wisdom and *strength*! See need 21 above. Exception: using combative lawyers to substitute for effective co-parental problem-solving *guarantees* that false selves are running your show. See Chapter 18.

"How Will We Resolve Disputes Among Us?"

Your child need-status research *will* be hindered by values and loyalty conflicts, and triangles, in and between your adults' teams of subselves. If each of your co-parents have _ progressed on Projects 1 and 2, and _ read and discussed the chapters in Part 2, you co-parents *can* evolve effective ways of resolving these hindrances together. Two keys: each of your co-parents _ must want to adopt an ("=/=") attitude of mutual respect, and then _ agree that your minor kids depend on you *all* to overcome your barriers and differences to give them their best chance for independent living. Build on the ideas in Chapters 7, 8, and 16 together, using all the resources in Part 4 and the related Web materials. Recall that *Satisfactions* [xlibris.com] is the guidebook for growing effective thinking and family communications.

"How Can We Optimize Our Efforts Together?"

I believe you co-parents will be far more apt to share old-age satisfaction and contentment if you help each other . . .

Adopt the attitudes that . . .

_ mastering "co-parenting" together is a priceless long-term adventure and opportunity, vs. an ego-contest, power struggle, or an onerous obligation and chore; and . . .

_ each of your kids' needs and spirits, and each of your co-parents' needs and spirits, are of equal importance to you all; and the adopt the attitude that . . .

_ each of you adults are students in a new, challenging stepfamily environment, so helping each other *learn* (Chapters 1-3) is a priceless gift to you and your future generations. Periodically do "attitude checks" by rereading and discussing Chapter 3.

Learn _ how to tell if your Selves are leading your respective inner families, and _ what to do if they aren't (Project 1). Make true-Self empowerment a high *family* priority.

Focus steadily on how you adults want to promote the high-nurturance traits in [D] *long-range*, via acting from your family mission statement and job descriptions (Projects 6 and 10).

Evolve and *use* a shared definition of "effective co-parenting" (p. 467) based on understanding each of your kids' developmental and adjustment needs. Resource: [http://sfhelp.org/10/co-p-goals.htm].

Keep your perspective: Projects 6 and 10 are two of 11 ongoing co-parent tasks [A]. They all contribute toward your building a high-nurturance stepfamily together over many years. Help each other patiently take small steps on these, and affirm *"Progress, not Perfection!"*

Recap

Parenting is the decades-long process of intentionally filling childrens' kaleidoscope of mental, emotional, spiritual, and physical needs, while filling your own. *Nurturing* means "filling current and long-term true (vs. surface or secondary) needs." Long-range co-parenting success after divorce and/or re/marriage is *far* more complex and difficult than rearing kids in intact high-nurturance biofamilies. Project 6 is a series of initial steps for all your kids' co-parents to take together toward such success, and Project 10 continues them after re/wedding.

The first half of this resource chapter proposes four sets of concurrent, interactive needs that each of your minor kids needs informed adult help with. The second half suggests how you co-parents can assess how well each of your minor and grown kids is doing with their unique mix of these many needs. No matter how competent or stable they appear, your kids *really* need your wisdom, heart, awareness, empathy, patience, and humor here!

If you're considering stepfamily re/marriage (or you may), use this chapter as a resource to help you complete Project 6 with your beloved. I strongly encourage your efforts on evolving a stepfamily mission statement (p. 438) to guide you in complex, confusing times. Adult unawareness of what typical stepkids need (among other things) is one of five roots of potential re/divorce.

If you're already re/married, use this chapter as an inspiration and guide for the first half of Project 10: building an effective co-parenting team, and nurturing *all* your kids and adults. The second half is evolving effective child discipline in and between your homes. See *Building a High-nurturance Stepfamily* or [..10/discipline1.htm].

If you're a professional who supports families, _ weave key ideas and resources from this chapter (and book) into your work, and _ encourage your colleagues, funders, trainers, and employers to do the same. For a larger perspective, see [http:// sfhelp.org/prevent/prf1.htm].

Status Check: Relax from all these details. Breathe well, stretch, and see where you stand now. T = true, F = false, and "?" means "I'm not sure."

I feel a mix of calm, centered, energized, light, focused, resilient, up, grounded, relaxed, alert, aware, serene, purposeful, compassionate, and clear, so my Self is probably present now. (T F ?)

I could name over 30 of these 62 needs before I read this chapter. (T F ?)

I believe this is a reasonably accurate summary of the normal developmental and family-adjustment needs that average kids of parental death or divorce and re/marriage face. _ If not, I know how to improve this summary. (T F ?)

For each minor and grown child I care about, _ I'm clearly aware of their status with these needs *or* _ I'm very motivated to assess that in the next several weeks. (T F ?)

I'm clear enough now on _ my and _ my partner's (adult) status with each of these needs. (T F ?)

I see significant value in using the ideas in this chapter now to help meet the needs of _ me, _ my co-parenting partners, and _ each custodial or visiting child that depends on me or us. (T F ?)

I can clearly describe _ co-parent Project 6 (and if you're re/married, _ Project 10) to an interested stranger now; and _ I genuinely want to work at our version of these projects *now*, vs. "soon" or "sometime." (T F ?)

I feel comfortable enough discussing the ideas and suggestions in this chapter now with _ my co-parenting partner/s, _ other family members, and _ any professional supporters. If not, I know _ why and _ what to do about this. (T F ?)

I accept that without informed help from me and my caregiving partners, _ the minor kids that depend on us may not satisfy their set of these needs over time. I further accept that _ my and my partners' passive acceptance of this amounts to child neglect. (T F ?) If you don't agree, what would you call it?

I accept without ambivalence that if I re/marry, I share ongoing responsibility to help each minor child in our multi-home stepfamily fill their set of these needs over many years. (T F ?)

G) Common Stepfamily-merger Tasks

31 Alien Adjustment Projects

Your complex multi-year stepfamily merger begins when any bioparent starts to date seriously. To build your perspective, first read about co-parent Project 9 (merge three or more multi-generational biofamilies) in *Build a High-nurturance Stepfamily* [xlibris.com], or in the Web articles at [..09/links09.htm]. Give special attention to [..09/merge.htm]. To show other people a summary of these tasks, invite them to read [..09/sf-task1.htm]. Ongoing or recurring tasks are asterisked (*).

Each typical stepfamily **SF)** task below is compared to any equivalent tasks in forming a first-marriage biofamily **BF)**. As you'll see, most of these tasks are more complex, or have no equivalent. Options:

_ as you read, star (*) each task you already knew;

_ hilight each task you feel is of special importance; and . . .

_ note which of these tasks your other family adults and supporters are – or aren't – aware of.

As you read, consider how the degree of genuine co-parental teamwork will affect your multi-home family's mastery of these many tasks over time . . .

+ + +

Task 1) Couples negotiate courtship with existing kids, ex mate/s, and ex in-laws in the picture: **SF)** *Required.* Logistics and emotions are often far more complex than typical first-marriage courtship. **BF)** Usually *no equivalent task,* so courtship is simpler, more focused, and less conflictual.

2*) All adults and kids **accept the new identity "We're members of a multi-home *step*family**." Then _ each of you decide "who is included in my stepfamily now?", and _ resolve major conflicts over this. **SF)** *Required* (Project 3). All your three or more co-parents must _ learn and accept your stepfamily identity, and _ agree on who's needs, feelings, and values deserve your ongoing consideration. Your kids and adults must resolve disputes over stepfamily-identity and membership definitions (see Chapter 16). This task recurs if another ex mate re/marries or any re/divorce. **BF)** *No equivalent task.* Biofamily identity and memberships (inclusions) are usually clear to all. Memberships change only with births, weddings, adoptions, and deaths. Low-nurturance biofamilies may have conflicts here.

Task 3*) Co-parents _ learn "What's *normal* in an average multi-home *step*family?" and _ change up to ~ 60 common myths [..04/myths.htm] into realistic expectations. Then _ teach these realities to key others. **SF)** *Required* (Project 4). Avoiding this greatly raises the odds of your members' holding inappropriate (*biofamily*-based) role expectations of each other. This learning continues as your stepfamily evolves [..09/develop1.htm]. **BF)** *No equivalent task.* Relatives, society, and the media have taught biofamily norms to caregivers since early childhood.

4a*) All members identify and grieve prior tangible and invisible losses from _ divorce and/or death, and (later) _ re/marriage and _ co-habiting. **SF)** *Required* (Project 5). Prior grieving styles, values, and rules must be merged. Co-parents ignoring this vital project promote personal stress, stepfamily conflicts, and eventual re/divorce. **BF)** *No equivalent task.* Biofamily members do have other losses to grieve.

4b) Co-parents help minor bio-kids grieve (normal) fantasies of bioparent and birthfamily reunion. **SF)** *Very common.* If unmourned, this dream can block kids from accepting a step-parent and any stepsibs and relatives, inviting loyalty conflicts and triangles (Chapter 16). A bioparent's re/marriage can _ shatter the dream, or _ create determination to sabotage it. **BF)** *No equivalent task*, though kids in troubled low-nurturance biofamilies can dream about more family harmony until they lose hope.

4c) Bioparents, biokids, and often bio-grandparents **resolve guilts and shame** from prior divorce and/or parenting "failures." **SF)** *Required* unless the former mate died. Ignoring this task [..Rx/ex/guilt.htm] can skew co-parenting priorities, and cause divisive loyalty conflicts and relationship triangles (Chapter 16). **BF)** *No equivalent task.*

Task 5*) Family adults _ blend your styles of verbal communication, and _ **develop effective problem-solving skills together. SF)** *Required and more complex* (Project 2). Without progressing on this project *early*, all your co-parents are greatly hampered in accomplishing all other personal and family adjustment tasks in and between your homes. This project recurs if another ex mate re/marries. **BF)** *Required and simpler*: only two co-parents need to do this, not three or more. The U.S. first-divorce statistics suggest most first-marriers don't master this task, because our legislators and educators didn't prepare their parents well enough.

6) Courting adults each decide _ "Are these the right people to re/marry? _ Is this the right time? _ Am I re/marrying for the right reasons? **SF)** *Required, and far more complex* (Project 7). The U.S. re/divorce epidemic implies that _ most couples don't research and evaluate these key questions well enough, and _ our society condones this. **BF)** *Simpler.* Couples have no kids or ex mates to consider in answering these questions, (often) more idealism, and less life experience.

More stepfamily-biofamily adjustment-task differences . . .

7*) Couples _ make pre-nuptial-agreement decisions, and _ resolve any related family conflicts: **SF)** *More common.* Wealthier re/marriers often want to guard against possible re/divorce asset-conflicts and losses, specially after bitter prior divorces. Such legal contracts can breed distrust, hurt, anxieties, and resentments. This task may recur if assets change substantially. **BF)** *Unusual.* Most first-marriers aren't wealthy enough to worry about this, and don't believe divorce could happen to them. Including *psychological* divorce, over half are wrong.

Task 8) Re/marriers plan and hold a commitment ceremony for "the (step)family" and supporters. **SF)** *More complex.* Who should come? Who should "stand up"? There are no social norms to guide engaged couples, their parents, and/or clergy with inevitable values and loyalty conflicts, and relationship triangles. **BF)** *Simpler.* Social norms and traditions are much clearer. There are usually no biokids, ex in-laws, and fewer legal relatives involved. See *Stepfamily Courtship* and [http://sfhelp.org/Rx/spl/wedding1.htm].

9) All family members adjust to any kids', ex mates', and ex in-laws' disapproval of co-parents re/marrying and merging assets and families. **SF)** *Required.* Kids, ex mates, and/or kin can range between critical, hostile, rejecting, and intrusive to genuinely delighted and supportive. **BF)** *No equivalent task.*

10*) Negotiate acceptable dwelling, furnishing, decorating, and space-allocation (e.g. bedroom) decisions. Merge physical and financial assets, ownerships, traditions, rituals, and values. **SF)** *far more complex*: "Your home, mine, or a new one?" More people are affected, with more belongings, so these choices are usually logistically complex and conflictual. Major concurrent values conflicts and relationship triangles are common throughout your family system (p. 161 and Chapter 16). Versions of this task recur each time a couple moves and/or a child changes custodial homes. **BF)** *Simpler.* The first dwelling is usually new to both mates, and there are far fewer belongings, assets, and rituals to blend.

11*) Members resolve name and family role-title confu-

sions: *"What should we call each other?"* **SF)** *Required.* These are often conflictual, stressful, and frustrating in and between linked homes, and with kin and friends. These can recur if kids change dwellings, new kids are born, and/or other co-parents or kin re/marry. **BF)** *No equivalent task.*

12*) Cope with a co-parenting ex mate and/or key relatives **who won't accept** their divorce, the re/marriage, and/or the new stepparent (i.e. hasn't grieved; see #4a above): **SF)** *Frequent.* When present, usually the ex _ felt abandoned and/or mistreated in their marriage, and _ is dominated by a false self (see # 28). Until personal recovery and intentional progress reducing the barriers in Part 2, ex-mate rejection and hostility can seem "endless" and insoluble. **BF)** *No equivalent task.*

13*) Minor stepkids' key task: *test* to learn clearly _ *"Am I safe in this new family, or will it break up too?"*; and _ *"Who's really in charge of this home?"* (See #16a). The co-parent-half of this task is to respect and empathize with kids' need to test, and react appropriately. **SF)** *Required* if stepkids experienced prior birth-family trauma, and parental abandonments and/or divorce. Appropriate testing is often mis-labeled "acting out" or "rebellion," and the kids are shamed and punished. That promotes defiance or apathy, and *increases* kids' false-self control and wounds. This task can recur when _ the child's other bioparent re/marries, _ either bioparent conceives a new child, and/or when _ a child changes custodial homes. **BF)** *No equivalent task*, but it can develop in a low-nurturance biofamily home.

14a*) Non-custodial *bio*parents grieve and accept that _ they're missing much of their kids' growing-up events, and that _ another adult with different values is co-raising their child/ren. **SF)** *Required* unless this other bioparent is dead or "uninvolved" (Chapter 17). Bioparents who resist grieving (clues: ongoing hostility or "indifference") are probably controlled by a false-self (Chapters 5, 6, and 12). This task is ongoing, as each parent-child pair moves through their developmental stages. **BF)** *No equivalent task.*

Task 14b*) Non-custodial **dual-role** (bioparent + stepparent) **caregivers cope with significant guilt, resentment, and**

sadness that they're co-parenting others' child/ren instead of their own. **SF)** *Possible* if adult-child visitations and communications are infrequent, unsatisfying, and/or blocked by others. Childless stepparents and relatives don't face this, and may lack empathy for co-parents who do. This task often recurs as special milestones and events happen. **BF)** *No equivalent task.*

15*) New mates decide *"Shall we have one or more 'ours' kids?"* **SF)** *Probable* and *far* more complex [..Rx/spl/ourschild.htm]. Mates are older than first marriers, and odds are higher that a bioparent says *"No, I have enough kids."* More adults and kids are affected emotionally, financially, and logistically. If *"Yes,"* new conceptions and births (or deaths) cause many multi-generational changes, losses, and loyalty conflicts. This task _ may occur more than once, and _ be triggered by a wife's aging. **BF)** *Simpler decision.* The co-parents are younger, have fewer financial issues and assets, and no stepkids, ex mates, and ex in-laws who are affected.

16a*) All co-parents _ learn and _ help kids fill many complex family-adjustment needs, concurrent with their normal developmental needs [F]. **SF)** *Required.* Most co-parents can't name all these needs (unawareness), which hinders their effectiveness (p. 467) and leaves kids' needs unfilled. This task continues as each child matures. **BF)** *No equivalent task.* Bioparents strive to guide minor kids on many normal developmental tasks.

16b*) Co-parents agree on caregiving goals, plans, priorities, and responsibilities for each minor child: **SF)** *Far more complex*: three or more co-parents and six or more co-grandparents are involved, in two or more nuclear-stepfamily homes. Post-divorce hostilities and distrusts, ineffective communication skills, blocked grief, and adults' unawarenesses of step norms and unique stepchild tasks often interfere. This task continues as the stepfamily develops. **BF)** *Far simpler.* Only two co-parents and fewer relatives are involved, so the odds of conflict are lower. Bioparenting role-norms are clearer. There are fewer kids and tasks involved, and no parenting, visitation, financial, and/or custody agreements to comply with and rene-gotiate.

Pause, breathe, stretch, and recall why you're reading this. This is detailed, *important* reading, so pace yourself! More stepfamily-biofamily adjustment-*task* differences . . .

Task 17*) All your extended-family members **resolve a stream of values and priority (loyalty) conflicts** in and be-tween your many linked homes. **SF)** *Required and much more complex.* Re/wedded bioparents must choose their mate "first" enough vs. biokids, kin, or work; or the stepparent grows re-sentful and eventually may detach or legally re/divorce. This ongoing task can get easier *if* your co-parents understand and admit these conflicts and related PVR triangles, and evolve a cooperative strategy to avoid or resolve them (Chapter 16). **BF)** *Uncommon and simpler,* unless the extended biofamily is significantly low in nurturance [D]. Often, biokids and parenting values are not the key marital conflict.

18*) Mates make enough quality couple-times to nourish their (re)marriage, discuss family goals and plans, problem-solve, and co-manage the family: **SF)** *Often much harder,* due to more homes, more people with busy schedules, more con-flicting needs (responsibilities), and more concurrent adult and child adjustment tasks. This is part of Project 8 (nurture your re/marriage), which is ongoing. **BF)** *Easier,* unless one or both mates are wounded and shun intimacy. There are significantly fewer people, relationships, needs, and tasks to interfere and prioritize.

19*) Resolve _ relationship and _ role problems between new and prior co-parenting mates, stepsibs, and/or step-kin and "ex" in-laws: **SF)** *Required.* Common conflicts: money; parenting values, responsibilities, and priorities; kids' educa-tion; religion; power and authority; time allocation; possessions; sexuality and privacy; health; and holidays. This is part of the reason why courtship Projects 1-7 are vital. **BF)** *No equivalent tasks.* There *are* relationship problems to resolve, among fewer people, with less old baggage, and fewer concurrent tasks and conflicts.

20a*) Financial decisions I: Shall I (a stepparent) include your child/ren in my will? In my health and/or life insurance? Shall I help pay for your kids' education and special needs? **SF)** *Required.* Stepparents' decisions here can cause gratitude, warmth, and bonding; or resentments, guilts, angers, and relationship triangles in and between extended-stepfamily homes. These decisions may recur as family membership, relationships, roles, and assets change. **BF)** *No equivalent tasks.*

20b*) Financial decisions II: all three or more co-parents agree enough on child-support amounts, timing, and allocations. Resolve conflicts co-operatively, without putting the minor kids or relatives in the middle. **SF)** *Required.* This is a complex, conflictual project requiring all co-parents' _ clear priorities, roles, and goals; _ forgivenesses of prior-family wounds; and _ shared effective negotiating skills (task # 5). This task is ongoing until the youngest child attains legal majority or dies. **BF)** *No equivalent task.*

20c*) Financial decisions III: mates evolve a harmonious way of managing operating income and expenses, investments and savings plans; insurances, and deciding on asset titles (e.g. vehicle, securities, and real estate ownership). **SF)** *Required, and far more complex.* Common debates: separate his, hers, and ours asset accounts, and/or one "common-pot" account; and separate or joint savings and investment accounts. This ongoing task requires mutual trust, time to talk, and effective communication skills. **BF)** *Required, and far simpler.* The common tasks are co-managing *our* checking and savings accounts, investments, and shared asset-ownerships.

21) Decision: "Shall I (a stepparent) legally adopt your child/ren?" SF) *Possible.* There are many emotional, financial, and legal complexities to this decision, including getting the other bioparent's legal consent to release parental rights and responsibilities. **BF)** *No equivalent task.*

22*) All co-parents manage regular and special child visitations between two or more co-parenting homes [..Rx/spl/visit.htm]. **SF)** *Ongoing*, unless the other bioparent/s are dead or "detached" (Chapter 17). This task often lasts until kids are late teens, and can be very conflictual in and between homes. **BF)** *No equivalent task.*

23*) Co-parents re/negotiate child-custody and legal parenting agreements as conditions change over time. **SF)** *Frequent*, unless the other bioparent is dead or all stepkids are living independently. Many causes for adjustment are possible. This task is often significantly conflictual without _ clear, stable adult roles, _ prior losses well grieved, and _ effective adult problem-solving skills. This task can recur, depending on many factors. **BF)** *No equivalent task.*

24*) All family members adjust to minor children changing homes, neighborhoods, schools, and custodial co-parents. **SF)** *Possible* (in ~30% of U.S. stepfamilies). Moving may be sudden and unexpected. It usually causes major concurrent financial, legal, space, privacy, priority, and role, and other changes (losses) and conflicts. This task can recur if co-parents move and/or adults and kids (e.g. teens) clash too much [..Rx/ spl/kid-moves1.htm]. **BF)** *No equivalent task.*

25*) _ Settle legal battles between ex mates, and then _ heal the resulting related guilts, resentments, hurts, disrespects, regrets, and distrusts, over time. **SF)** *Common*. Typical conflict sources are child _ visitations, _ custody, and _ financial support; and _ enforcing or changing legal parenting agreements. Stepparents can add to or withdraw from the turmoil. This task recurs as kids' age, and expenses and co-parents' incomes change. Ex-mate legal battles are *always* symptoms of false-self dominance + ineffective communication skills + (often) blocked grief (Chapter 18). **BF)** *No equivalent task.*

26*) Build stepparent—stepchild _ respect (vs. love) **and _ trust** over time. **SF)** *Required* with each minor and grown child and each stepparent. Long-term success depends on many things, and is not assured. Disrespect and stepfamily unawareness cripples stepparent-stepchild discipline. That promotes divisive loyalty conflicts and relationship triangles, which stress homes and re/marriages. **BF)** *No equivalent task.* Kids may lose respect for, and/or trust in, their bioparents in a low-nurturance home.

27*) Nuclear-family members cope with social biases, misunderstandings, and related isolation. SF) *Unavoidable.* Common biases are *"Stepfamilies are second-best, flawed, abnormal, not as good, and weird."* Step-adults and kids may feel *"We know no other (step)families like ours. We're* alone." High-nurturance stepfamilies learn how to cope with this as they evolve. **BF)** *No equivalent task,* unless mates form a same-gender, bi-racial, and/or mixed religio/ethnic biofamily.

28*) Co-parents _ break their denials of significant childhood nurturance deprivations, and _ steadily pursue personal recovery: **SF)** *Probable.* From 21 years' clinical experience, I estimate that about 80% or more of average divorced and stepfamily co-parents need to do this. *This is probably the single most important factor for long-term re/marriage and stepfamily success.* Recovery from false-self domination is an ongoing adult process. **BF)** *Probable.* From the U.S. first-divorce rate, it appears that over *50% of typical bioparents* need to do this. Most don't know of this task and don't *want* to know. This promotes _ serial divorces, and _ unintentional bequests of psychological wounds to descendents.

Implication: when one or both re/marrying mates has been divorced before and isn't (yet) recovering from inner wounds (Project 1), the odds are very high both will ignore their five hazards [A], and make up to three *wrong* re/marriage choices (*Stepfamily Courtship*).

29*) Co-parents build and use a support network of informed relatives, friends, other co-parents, and professionals to help along the way: **SF)** *More vital*, because of greater stepfamily complexity, tasks, hazards, conflicts, and "alienness." Kin often don't understand typical co-parenting tasks and issues. *Informed* classes and co-parent support groups are rare. **BF)** *Helpful and less vital*, because of the relative simplicity of typical biofamilies. *Effective* community and media co-parenting supports are usually far more available.

30*) Co-parents' _ sort, prioritize, balance, and co-manage all these tasks and normal life activities every day; and _ make enough time to play, relax, and *enjoy* your shared family process enough. **SF)** *Ongoing, and* far *more complex* (Project 12). There are more people, needs, and relationships; and more alien, concurrent tasks to balance. This raises the odds of webs of conflicts, false-self chaos, everyone feeling disoriented and overwhelmed. **BF)** *Ongoing and simpler.* There are fewer adjustment tasks and people to balance, so the odds of mates' feeling overwhelmed are generally lower.

31) Psychological or legal (re)divorce. All extended-family members _ resolve guilts, shames, angers, hurts, regrets, and anxieties, and _ grieve *many* complex losses, for many years. **SF)** *More likely:* over half of U.S. re/married co-parents (and their minor kids) re/divorce within 7-10 years of their commitment ceremony. Unknown millions more elect to avoid legal re/divorce, and live in daily misery or numbness. Minor kids are wounded either way. **BF)** *Less likely:* about 50% of U.S. first-marriage couples and their bio-kids now divorce legally. More divorce psychologically.

If you feel startled, anxious, numb, and/or overwhelmed now, you're *normal!* Recall that one of the five proposed re/ marriage hazards is *unawareness.* How many courting co-parents and lay and professional supporters do you think could spontaneously describe even half of these 31 alien adjustment tasks and how they differ from first-marriage tasks? And there's more: typical multi-home stepfamilies also differ *structurally* from intact biofamilies in ~30 ways: see [..03/compare.htm]. Co-parents' not knowing or ignoring these tasks and differences can hold unrealistic expectations (myths), causing hurt, frustration, disappointment, and conflicts. Stepfamily *awareness* among all your members is vital!

So what do all these adjustment tasks *mean* to your (potential) co-parenting team?

Two Implications

Your unique multi-home stepfamily will encounter some mix of these 31 tasks. Some will be more complex and conflictual than others. One implication is: you co-parents will nurture better if you **evolve a realistic biofamily-merger plan** for tackling all these tasks together, rather than trying to accomplish them reactively, with no plan. Ideally, you caregivers will have begun drafting your plan before any re/weddings. In my experience, that's pretty rare—partly because most co-parents have never seen a task-inventory like this, or the dozen projects they all need to work at [A] for their and their kids' sakes.

"Evolve a realistic merger plan" takes patience, awareness, and *cooperation* on steps like these:

assess each co-parent honestly for false-self dominance, and help each other start any needed personal recoveries (Project 1). False selves usually don't plan well.

assess your adult communication effectiveness, and intentionally learn and apply the seven skills (Project 2). False selves usually don't problem-solve effectively.

acknowledge you all are a multi-home *stepfamily*, and resolve any conflicts over who belongs to it (Project 3).

learn what being a stepfamily *means*, including _ accepting these tasks and structural differences, and _ converting misconceptions into realistic expectations (Project 4 and ..03/sf_means.htm).

draft a family mission or vision statement together, to define what you all are trying to *do* long range (Project 6).

review the teamwork barriers in Part 2, _ draft a plan to reduce them together over time, and _ begin working on it (Project 10); and as you do . . .

evolve a joint strategy to avoid and resolve inevitable merger _ values and _ loyalty conflicts, and _ relationship triangles (Chapter 16). And . . .

have a series of meetings to decide _ what your kids need [F], and which co-parents will fill which needs; _ *what* you all need to merge [..09/merge.htm], _ *how* you're going to merge (e.g. independently or cooperatively), and _ which co-parents are responsible for what (Projects 9 and 10).

Then use all these preparatory steps to . . .

review the tasks above together, and edit them to fit your stepfamily; then _ decide how you all are going to accomplish your set of tasks, and _ resolve any significant disputes or confusions you have as you work at that. And . . .

consult with key relatives and supporters to inform them on your plan, and benefit from their caring, wisdom, and counsel. Finally . . .

adjust your plan if another ex-mate re/weds, and you all need to meld the new partner's multi-generational biofamily into your evolving extended stepfamily.

The point here is: because these new-stepfamily adjustment tasks are numerous, concurrent, complex, and alien, you all will nurture better with a consensual plan to master them together. Your plan will be more effective if it's based on _ a mission statement, and _ your version of the 12 co-parent projects. If this looks like a lot of work—it *is*!

A second implication of these 31 alien adjustment tasks relates to choosing effective human-service professionals. My experience is that very few counselors, clergy, teachers, lawyers, judges, and financial and medical pros have ever seen the key concepts in this book and series. This is true even if *they* are in a stepfamily.

Because of your five stepfamily hazards (can you name them yet?), I suspect your co-parents and kids have a greater need for *informed* professional help than your bio-peers. This is specially true in helping you decide _ whether or not to re/wed; and if you do, _ how to manage the first several merger-adjustment years. If you seek professional clinical, legal, and financial help (e.g. with wills, taxes, and insurance), ask candidates their specific training in stepfamily tasks, structure, and dynamics. If they can't describe "enough" of _ the five hazards, _ these facts [..03/facts.htm], and _ these 31 tasks, *look elsewhere.*

Option: see if any candidate can _ spontaneously name *at least* 15 of the ~60 common stepfamily myths and realities summarized at [http://sfhelp.org/04/myths.htm]. Option: ask if they _ can name many of the typical needs stepkids have [F]. As a paying client, you have a *right* to shop and ask these questions. Your inner and physical kids and descendants need you to!

Individual adjustment needs above may seem trivial. Most of them are concurrent with _ each other, _ your kids' special adjustment needs, and _ your many other responsibilities and daily-life tasks. *Collectively* the alienness and emotional complexity of all these together can feel overwhelming and discouraging during the first several years of your stepfamily's evolution. That's why Project 11 (form and use a support network) and Project 12 (intentionally keep your daily balances) are vital to you all.

Pause and reflect on what you just learned, and what it *means*. Breathe well from your belly. Notice what you feel, and what thought streams your subselves are giving you. Identify the key things you want to remember about this chapter, and any actions you want to take. Does working intentionally to build co-parental teamwork (Part 2) make more long-term sense now?

H) Summary: Communication Basics

This is reprinted from the Project-2 guidebook *Satisfactions* [xlibris.com]. Use it to refresh yourself on the foundations of effective communication _ among your inner family of subselves, and _ with the people who matter the most to you. Use this chapter with Resources [I, J, and K] and this: [..02/evc-quiz.htm].

Options: _ Add notes or hilights to make this digest more useful to you; _ re-read this before or after important communication experiences; and _ give copies of this to key partners [..02/evc-intro.htm], and _ help each other use these basics to get more of your true current needs met together.

Partner below means "current adult or child communication partner." To access referenced Web resources, add the pointers [..**/****.htm] to [http://sfhelp.org/..] to form the full address. See all the Project-2 Web resources at [http://sfhelp.org/02/links02.htm]. Omit the brackets.

Premise: normal human personalities like yours are composed of a group of semi-independent *subselves* or *parts*. At any moment, the dominant subselves cause your and your partner's needs, thoughts, perceptions, and behaviors—i.e. they cause your communication. Your subselves communicate with each other and "you" (your body and conscious mind) all the time, via thoughts, images, memories, hunches, instincts, and "senses."

At any given time, each partner's behavior is determined by who leads their inner family of subselves: their true Self, who is innately skilled at making wise, healthy decisions, or a "false self," which is one or more less-skilled, protective personality parts. For more on this, see *Who's* Really *Running Your Life?* [xlibris.com], or [..pop/assess.htm].

Any perceived behavior *or lack of behavior* of person (or subself) "A" that causes a mental, emotional, and/or spiritual change in person (or subself) "B" is *communication.* People in relationships cannot *not* communicate, because our subselves assume meanings from silences, body language, and absences.

Internal and social communication is the learned skill that adults and kids depend on the most to get daily needs met. When your family members can describe and apply the seven mental/verbal skills that promote effective communication, they're better able to _ fill their daily needs _ in a way that feels good enough, often enough. Their (*your*) life productivity and satisfactions increase significantly.

Needs are emotional/spiritual/physical discomforts. **"Problems" are** *need conflicts. Problem solving* and *conflict resolution* both mean "filling (satisfying) your and my current _ communication and _ other needs (p. 44) well enough."

Six Communication Needs

The **six needs** that kids, adults, and subselves instinctively try to fill by communicating with others are to . . .

Feel *respected* **enough** by _ yourself and _ others involved. This need is present in every solitary or social situation. And we all periodically need to . . .

Give or get information; and/or to . . .

Vent—i.e. to feel empathically _ understood and _ accepted, vs. getting "fixed" or lectured; and/or we need to . . .

Cause or prevent change (feel impactful). *Change* includes increasing or decreasing emotional distance (trust, respect, and intimacy) with your current partner. And we may need to . . .

Create excitement (reduce numbness and boredom), and/ or to . . .

Divert from some discomfort, like avoiding conflict or awareness, or breaking uncomfortable silence.

You and each partner always have two or more of these communication needs at once. The needs flux *fast* during every behavioral interaction ("conversation"), as your inner and outer environments change. Without motivation and *awareness*, people are often unconscious of *what* they need in important communications, specially if governed by a protective false self. Note that each active subself in each communicator has its own mix of these needs—so one part of you may need to vent now, and another part may need to cause change. Such inner need-conflicts cause *unease, ambivalence, doubts,* or *uncertainty.*

Effective Communication

The *effectiveness* of your communication (how often you get your current needs met) can be intentionally improved with practice. **Effective** (vs. *good, open* and *honest*) **communication happens** when each person _ gets enough of their *true*, vs. surface, current needs met (in their opinion); _ in a way that leaves them feeling good enough about _ themselves, _ all others involved, and _ the processes inside and between them.

This two-level definition implies that any two-person communication can have 16 possible outcomes. Only *one* of them is fully effective (win-win) for both people! Do your co-parents have a common definition of *effective communication* yet? If so, do your kids know it?

Effective **communication happens when** all partners' current communication needs match well enough—e.g. I need to vent, and you need to maintain our relationship and get information. When our mix of current needs doesn't match, we have a *communication-need* conflict.

Four Concurrent Messages

We try to fill our communication needs (reduce our discomforts) by decoding up to four messages at once, on each of three "channels":

Message	Communication "Channel"
"Now I think..."	**Verbal**: (words and sounds)
"Now I feel..."	**Paraverbal**: (voice tone + tempo + inflection + volume + accent)
"Now I need..."	**Non-verbal**: (face + body + hands + movement + touch)
"Now I see you as..."	

In most situations, *"Now I see you as . . ."* affects communication success the most. It is often decoded unconsciously, until you become *aware*. These **R(espect) messages have three possible decodings**: *"Right now, I see you as valuing your needs, worth, and dignity . . .*

*. . . more than mine (**you're 1-up / superior**, and I'm 1-down),"* or . . .

*. . . less than mine (**you're 1-down / inferior**, and I'm 1-up),"* or . . .

*. . . equally with mine: **we're '=/='.**"*

Premise: **Communications may be fully effective *only*** when all partners consistently decode clear "=/=" mutual-respect messages from each other. Shame-based (1-down) people often have trouble communicating well, until they evolve _ real Self-respect, and _ empathy for others.

Shame-based (false-self dominated) **people** will often mistake your =/= R-messages for criticisms and discounts, because their ruling subselves feel inferior. You can metatalk

[..02/metatalk.htm] about this together if they're willing, but they have to *want to* raise their own self-respect. Accusing them of such a decoding error will often make communication *worse*.

Face to face, **most of the meaning we decode from our partners comes through our *eyes*;** specially R-messages! Often the least of the meaning we decode comes from our words, but we've been taught to focus on them the most. *Awareness* rebalances that!

Many of our messages are decoded unconsciously: we "leak" our feelings and attitudes. People controlled by a false self often send conflicting messages via different channels: e.g. their words say: *"Good to see you!"* and their body, face, and voice tone imply *"I'm indifferent to you right now."* Such double or mixed messages typically cause confusion, anxiety, and distrust, specially if they're habitual.

Effective communication may (vs. will) happen when all people are undistracted enough. That requires partners' *inner* families to be calm, *aware,* and intentionally focused on a common topic and the mutual communication process.

E(motion) Levels

Kids and adults have a marvelous array of emotions which flux quickly as the environment does. They vary in mix and intensity, and reflect our mosaic of current communication and other needs. *All* **emotions are useful** clues to our needs, vs. being *positive* or *negative*. The way we express or act on our emotions can cause pleasure (need satisfaction) or discomfort (need creation).

Our level of current emotions ranges fluidly between low to high (intense). When a person's E(motion)-level rises, it becomes harder to _ think clearly, and _ listen to others effectively. So any communication situation can be judged to be "low-E" or "high-E," depending on whether one or more people have E-levels "above their ears" at the moment. Effective communication becomes harder to do in high-E situations. So become aware of _ your and _ your partner's E-levels, and choose communication skills to match them (below).

Emotions may cause and/or come from body sensations: pain, arousal, hunger, thirst, cold, cramps, and fatigue. Inner-family and interpersonal conflicts over needs and opinions can become high-E situations. Co-parent teamwork grows if your caregivers agree on what to do with high-E situations. Do you all, yet?

Seven Skills

Seven interrelated communication skills any adult or child can learn and practice to fill their true needs more effectively are . . .

Awareness: *"What's happening now inside me, inside you, between us, and around us?"*

Clear (vs. fuzzy) **thinking:** _ building your vocabulary and _ using clear, appropriate words; and avoiding _ defocusing, _ fuzzy pronouns, and _ "hand-grenade" terms.

Digging down below surface needs to current *true* needs (p. 44), and taking responsibility for filling yours.

Metatalk: talking objectively about *how* we communicate _ now and _ over time.

Empathic listening: sensing and mirroring your partner's _ feelings, _ needs, and _ perceptions without judgement. Empathic listening does not (necessarily) mean *agreeing*!

Assertion: stating respectfully and clearly what you need from others now, and handling reactions calmly; and . . .

Win-win problem solving (need fulfillment), vs. arguing, fighting, and/or avoiding (fleeing).

Each skill is best used in different situations:

Use *awareness* [..02/awareness.htm] all the time.

Use **clear thinking** [..02/fuzzy1-wks.htm], and digging down [..02/dig-down.htm] when you're "significantly" uncomfortable.

Use **metatalk** [..02/metatalk.htm] and the other skills any time you sense that something is blocking effective communication [J].

Use **empathic listening** [..02/listen.htm] _ when your partner can't hear you because they're currently distracted by intense emotions, sensations, and/or needs:—i.e. when their E(motion)-level is "above their ears"; and _ to respond respectfully when your partner resists your assertions as expected.

Use respectful **assertion** [..02/assert.htm] to _ prevent or _ react to conflicts, and to _ give "dodge-proof" praise.

Use **problem solving** [..02/prblmslv.htm] any time you and a partner have significantly conflicting inner-family, communication, and/or other needs. See p. 50.

Use **all seven skills** any time you have an *internal* conflict among two or more of your subselves. See [..01/innerfam1.htm] and [..01/ifs8-innr_cnflct.htm].

Use *awareness* to re-check whether you're using the appropriate skills to match your and your partner's E-level mix:

Use **empathic listening** if your E-level is low, and your partner's is "above their ears."

Use **empathic listening and assertion** if both your E-levels are high. Then use assertion and perhaps metatalk when their E-level is low.

When both your E-levels are "below your ears," use normal conversation, or all seven skills if you have a conflict. Use =/= (mutually-respectful) *awareness* and clear thinking in all situations, regardless of E-level.

See p. 514 for a key to effective =/= assertion, p. 518 for a checklist of common communication blocks, and p. 528 for effective-communication suggestions. Option: take the quiz at [http://sfhelp.org/02/evc-quiz.htm] to assess your or your co-parents' level of communication wisdom.

Find all of these in *Satisfactions* and [..02/links02.htm].

How many of these communication basics do each of your kids know, so far? Modeling and teaching them is one of the most priceless bequests you co-parents can bestow!

Awarenesses . . .

I) Sample: A Personal Bill of Rights

Promote Yourself to Equal!

Premise: for _ effective assertion and problem solving and _ mutually-respectful (=/=) relationships, each person must be clear on, and believe in, their and their partner's *rights* as unique, dignified human beings. Use this sample to form your own declaration of basic rights as a worthy person, and to affirm the equal rights in every other adult and child.

These statements will clarify and remind me of my rights as a unique, normal human being, regardless of age, gender, race, or role. I was not taught some of these as a child, and can strengthen my belief in them today. Reaffirming my rights in uncertain or conflictual situations will free me of old fears and doubts, and help me assert my needs and opinions clearly, firmly, and respectfully. It is healthy for me to honor and respect my own rights and needs as much as I do those of every other adult and child. I *can legitimately proclaim and pursue these rights* without shame, guilt, or fear*, in any way that doesn't interfere with others' equal rights.* These apply to kids and adults:

I have the unarguable right to . . .
1) Feel my emotions. They're a natural part of being me,

and include fear, sadness, anger, shame, uncertainty, confusion, joy, lust, hope, pride, happiness, etc.—even "numbness." All emotions say "I need something now," and are *useful.* No emotions are "negative," no matter what others insist. I'm responsible for deciding _ if and _ how to express or act on my emotions, but *not* for how others react to me.

2) Tell others of my feelings if I choose to, *without* feeling guilty. I am responsible for this choice, but not for their reactions.

3) Say *"No"* **and** *"Yes"* without guilt or shame. I am responsible for *if, how,* and *when* I say these, but not for others' reactions or needs (exception: dependent kids).

4) Choose if, when, and how to meet others' expectations of me. If I choose not to meet them, I need not feel guilty, unless I clearly committed to. I am responsible for such choices.

5) Choose my own friends and acquaintances, and how and when to spend time with them. I may, but don't have to, justify these choices to others.

6) Make my own mistakes, and profit by them if I can.

7) Choose if, when, and how to tell others how their actions are affecting me, and then take responsibility for telling them.

8) Earn and maintain my own self-respect and pride, rather than depending on other people's judgments.

9) Seek and accept or decline **help**, without shame or guilt.

10) Give other adults and kids the responsibility for their own beliefs, needs, actions, feelings, and thoughts, without feeling selfish or uncaring.

11) Seek situations, environments, and relationships that are healthy, growthful, and nurturing for me.

12) Be spontaneous, play, and have fun!

13) Develop and grow at my own pace.

14) Appreciate my own efforts, and fully enjoy my achievements, without guilt, anxiety, or shame.

15) Act to fill my own needs, rather than expecting others to fill them for me as I did as a child.

And I proclaim my personal rights to . . .

16) Periods of rest, refreshment, reflection, and relaxation. These are as productive for me as times of work and action.

17) Choose whom I will trust, when, and with what. Like love, caring, and respect, trust must be *earned*.

18) Take on only as much responsibility as I can handle at any given time, and to tell others if I feel overloaded, without shame or guilt.

19) Nurture, love, and value my self as much as I do others who are special to me. In moderation, non-egotistical *pride* (self-appreciation) is not a sin, and never was.

20) Choose the goals and paths I wish for my life, and to pursue them without guilt, shame, or needing to justify them to others. And I claim the right to . . .

21) Take all the time I need to evaluate and make important life-decisions, even if this stresses others.

22) Care for my body, spirit, and soul lovingly and respectfully, in my own ways.

23) Decide on my own priorities and limits at any given time, and act on them as I see fit.

24) Distinguish between who my family, workmates, and friends say I am (or was) vs. who I *really* am.

And I claim my personal right to . . .

25) Be heard and understood. My thoughts, feelings, wants, opinions, and needs are just as legitimate, worthy, and important as anyone else's.

26) Decide what *perfect* or *excellent* is in any situation, and to choose whether to strive for these or not.

27) Choose how to spend my time, and take responsibility for the results.

28) Tell others respectfully what I expect of them, realizing they may or may not choose to fulfill these expectations. See Chapter 7.

29) Choose how and when to fill my spiritual needs, even if my choices conflict with others' values or wishes. I do not have the right to force my spiritual or religious views or values on other people, nor do I grant them the right to force theirs on me.

30) Heal past personal shamings and wounds, and replace unhealthy inner messages and beliefs I've lived by with more nurturing ones. See Project 1.

31) Listen to and heed my inner voices with interest and respect, and to sort out my true voices from other peoples'.

32) Ask others _ how they feel about me, _ what they think about me, and _ what they need from me. They need not comply.

33) Decide if, when, and how to forgive _ my mistakes, and _ any hurts received from others. I affirm that such forgiveness promotes healing. (See Chapter 11)

34) Work respectfully and peacefully to change laws or rules I feel are unjust or harmful to me and/or others.

Pause, breathe well, and notice what your subselves are thinking and feeling. Consider journaling about these now, and identifying which subselves are saying what.

If you have any ambivalence or anxiety about adopting *and acting firmly on* rights like these, you're probably ruled by a shame-based or fear-based false self. This is also true if you feel that anyone else does not have exactly the same rights and responsibilities as you do. To explore whether a false self rules you or another, use Resource [E] and 11 other self-assessment checklists at [..pop/assess.htm]

To share this Bill of Personal Rights with others, print or email the Web page at [http://sfhelp.org/02/rights.htm].

Options: _ read this out loud, slowly, and notice how you feel; _ use this as a model, and draft your own Bill. It will be more authentic, and therefore more effective for you; _ post a copy of your Bill where you can see it every day; _ review your Bill before important assertions or conflict-resolutions; and _ talk about your and others' personal rights, model them, and invite the kids in your life to evolve *and use* their own Bill of Rights.

Awarenesses . . .

J) Common Communication Blocks

This is excerpted from the Project-2 guidebook *Satisfactions* [xlibris.com]. To share this worksheet, copy or email the Web page at [http://sfhelp.org/02/evc-blox.htm]. *Also see* Resources [E, H, I, and K], [..02/evc-inventory.htm], and [..02/evc-strengths.htm].

Premises

Adults and kids communicate to fill local needs (reduce discomforts). A communication *block* is anything that inhibits one or both people from _ filling their current true needs _ in a way that feels good enough to each person. Most blocks are unconscious and related to false-self dominance, until partners _ put their Selves in charge (Project 1), and _ learn and apply the communication basics and skills [H].

Any perceived behavior that causes a significant emotional, physical, or spiritual effect on another person is *communication*. Each person decides what "significant" is.

Communication aims to fill two to six personal needs in each partner (p. 508). Many combinations of these conflict. First steps: _ get clear on your and your partner's current *communication* (vs. other) needs, and _ value them equally! The need for enough self and mutual respect is constant. Shame-based (wounded) people rarely get enough until in true recovery from false-self dominance.

Effective **communication occurs when** each person _ gets their current communication and other true needs (p. 44) met well enough, _ in a way that promotes self and mutual respect and trust. Anything that hinders this is a communication block.

Communication blocks can occur _ among your inner family of subselves and _ between them and other people's subselves. So ineffective communication can be caused by blocks inside me, inside you, and/or between us.

The learnable skills of *awareness* **and** *metatalk* (p. 512) can help identify such blocks, and the other five relationship skills can resolve them *if* your true Selves are leading your respective inner families.

Suggestions

Before using this inventory . . .

See if your Self is leading your inner family. If you feel some mix of *calm, centered, energized, light, focused, resilient, up, grounded, relaxed, alert, aware, serene, purposeful,* and *clear,* s/he's probably guiding your other subselves.

Check your attitude about you and any partner: if it's "=/ =" (mutually respectful), go ahead. If not, lower your expectations, and look for a false self at work.

If you haven't recently, review _ communication basics [H], and _ your Bill of personal Rights [I].

Use this checklist to help you and your communication partners _ learn and _ fill more of your true needs as teammates, not to blame or fault-fund.

Expect to get the most from this checklist if you partners are fluent with the Project-2 skills of *awareness*, clear thinking, empathic listening, and metatalk. If you identify a communication block, use all seven skills to reduce it *as =/= teammates.* See Resource [K] for ideas.

Note your option to use this checklist to spot and resolve communication blocks between your Self and other subselves. See [..02/fuzzy1-wks.htm].

Consider teaching what you learn from this inventory to any kids in your life, over time.

Pick a recent communication exchange you felt was ineffective, and check whether you feel any of these items was true of _ you, _ your partner, or _ both of you. Option: first learn about *mapping* communication sequences [..02/evc-maps.htm], and then use that tool to help identify situational or recurring blocks . . .

Typical Communication Blocks

me/you

_ _ **1)** Someone gets a verbal or nonverbal **R(espect)-message they decode as "we're not equals** here and now." Such R-messages are usually implied by voice and body dynamics, despite contrary words. They're constantly being decoded by you and each communication partner, usually unconsciously. Communication *works* only when each of you feels _ enough Self respect, and _ gets believable "=/=" (vs. "I'm 1-up" or "I'm 1-down") R-messages from their partners. Dominant false selves usually don't hold genuine =/= attitudes.

_ _ **2) Sender and receiver's communication needs don't match** (p. 508). For example, I want to vent, and you're distracted (can't really listen), or you want to persuade me to do something.

_ _ **3) The sender gives a double message**: their words say one thing, and their face, body, and/or voice imply something else: e.g. *"I'm not angry!"* (said loudly, fists clenched). Common automatic responses to double messages are confusion, frustration, and if they're habitual, growing distrust of the speaker. Double messages are usually caused by the speaker being ruled by two or more subselves who disagree. *Awareness*, clear-thinking, and metatalk skills can help resolve this. See # 10 below.

me/you

_ _ **4) One or both people are distracted** (i.e. can't focus or hear well) by _ physical discomfort (pain, thirst, sleepiness, etc.), _ preoccupation (worry, anxiety, or other strong emotion), and/or _ environmental disturbances (noise, flashing lights, motions, temperature, etc.)—and they're unaware, or try to communicate anyway.

_ _ **5) A "1-up" R(espect)-message is implied by a speaker** who constantly interrupts their partner. This habit signals that the speaker is probably composing their response without *really* hearing their partner. Interruptions can imply *"What I have to say now is more important than your needs or thoughts."* That feels like a discount (insult). Local and habitual discounts *hurt*, and breed anger, resentment, and perhaps withdrawals in the receiver. Frequent interrupting is often unconscious, and will continue unless the receiver asserts to stop it.

_ _ **6) Either sender or receiver make wrong assumptions** about the other's intent, meaning, R-message, emotions, and/or key word/s. This is unconscious or an intentional way of discounting the other: *"I know what you really feel or mean, no matter what you say (or don't say)."* This often evokes resentment, defensiveness, counterattack, and/or withdrawal and denial.

_ _ **7) A common special case of mind-reading happens** when the receiver starts talking before the speaker finishes, because they "know what the speaker is going to say." Even if true, this can feel like a discount. Conversely, the speaker may habitually repeat, ramble, or monologue, and the receiver gets bored. The receiver may use a meta-comment like *"When you string so many ideas and comments together without pausing, I get overwhelmed, and tune out."*

_ _ **8) The sender isn't clear on what s/he needs,** personally, relationally, or from the communication process (see # 2). The receiver will then probably feel uneasy and confused. A related problem is . . .

me/you

_ _ **9) One or both partners unconsciously using fuzzy thinking or terms**, and/or vague or "hand-grenade" words and phrases. The companion block is each person being unaware of these concepts, and their options to use respectful *hearing checks* to confirm that they're decoding the other person's meaning accurately. See [..02/fuzzy1-wks] and [..02/listen.htm].

_ _ **10) Either person may deny or minimize their true feelings** to themselves and/or their partner. The receiver may feel they should be interested (*"Please go on, this is fascinating!"*), when they're really bored or distracted. Even when sent "skillfully," such denials usually cause a double message ("words can lie, and bodies don't"). If habitual, such denials and deceptions breed confusion, and erode trust. Kids are specially quick to sense these "self-lies." See block #3.

_ _ **11) Frequently withholding emotions** from personal (non-business) communications, on purpose or unconsciously, can leave the receiver unsure of the sender's full meaning. The listener may interpret this as *"you don't trust me,"* or *"you're hiding something bad."* Over time, anxiety and distrust usually result, specially if a false self controls the receiver.

The _ receiver may be doing something that makes the sender feel unsafe in disclosing, and _ the sender doesn't confront them on this; or _ the sender may be ruled by a false self, and emotionally numb. This communication block strangles intimacy and effective problem-solving.

_ _ **12) Focusing "too often" on the past or the future** can prevent confronting and resolving problems in the present. A special case is when someone imagines a future event so vividly that they react to their partner in the present as though the imagined event had already occurred (*"I know you'll be late again!"*)

me/you

_ _ **13) Habitually** _ **focusing on yourself, or** _ usually deflecting the focus away from yourself will result at best in unbalanced and "shallow" communication. At worst, the other person may increasingly feel used and discounted, or "disconnected" and resentful, and develop impaired hearing. Awareness and respectful assertion may change this. You can use a flexible "awareness bubble" with metatalk to counter this block. See [..02/a-bubble.htm].

_ _ **14) One or both partners aren't aware of the true needs** (p. 44) under their conflicting surface goals or needs. For example "*I want to talk to you*" (surface need) may really mean "*I need to reassure myself you still care about me because you've seemed distant lately.*" Awareness, clear thinking, patient digging down, assertion, and empathic listening help unearth semi-conscious current true needs. Old "issues" (need-conflicts) keep resurfacing and/or causing strong feelings because the true needs underneath them haven't been clearly acknowledged and filled. See [..02/dig-down.htm].

_ _ **15) Someone sends a paradox.** These are messages that negate themselves, and leave receivers confused and uneasy. "*I insist that you* want *to talk to me!*" and "*Never say 'never'!*" are examples. Demanding something which can only be given spontaneously (like love, trust, or respect) is usually a self-defeating communication. Other examples: "*It's just no use talking about our communication problems!*", and "*I love you so much! You disgust me.*"

_ _ **16) Generalizing** can muffle or distort the current message, and prevent effective problem solving. "*You're always inconsiderate!*" will probably be received differently than "*I'm mad because you're 40 minutes late and I missed my ride!*"

"*You always . . .*" or "*You never . . .*" are deadly because _ they _ imply the receiver is 1-down, and _ invite her or him to feel guilty and defensive about many past events as well as the present one. Normal responses to this block are to flee, tune out, and/or counterattack (vs. listen empathically and problem-solve respectfully).

me/you

__ **17) Preaching, moralizing, or advising** someone with a problem (*"I'm just trying to help!"*) can erode relationships if the "sufferer" just wants to vent (be respectfully heard and accepted). These reactions in the receiver promote dependence, helplessness, and imply *"I'm 1-up: I know how to fix your problem, and you don't."* Unaware males often try to "fix" "upset" females, instead of *listening* empathically.

How common it is for busy parents to "fix" their child's problem before listening carefully, and considering if the best long-range help would be to encourage the child (or anyone) to find their own solution!

__ **18) Sarcastic, critical (vs. affectionate) name-calling** (*labeling*) erodes both the receiver's self-esteem and the odds for cooperative problem solving. *"You're stupid / lazy / spacey / nuts / weird / hopeless / a jerk / spastic"* etc. hurts! The non-verbal version of this block is the withering look that a partner gives, which conveys major disapproval. Do you ever name-call or use such a look? If so, what happens to your self esteem, the receiver's, and your relationship? Who's present needs get met?

__ **19) Physical or emotional withdrawal** is a powerful communication that may imply *"You scare or overwhelm me"* [R(espect)-message: *"I'm 1-down"*], or *"I don't care about you and your needs now: I'm 1-up."* Either way, the abandoned partner will probably feel hurt and frustrated, specially if the withdrawer won't talk about withdrawing (won't metatalk). In resolving this communication block, respectfully explore if the sender is doing something unconsciously that triggers the withdrawal.

__ **20) Making threats or demands vs. requests** often implies *"My current needs outrank yours!"* This usually provokes hurt, resentment, and defiance, and everyone feeling badly about themselves and/or the exchange. The receiver needs to use assertive metatalk when this happens—e.g. (with steady eye contact) *"I feel you're making demands (or threats)* *now. When you do that, I feel resentful, and combative. I need you to make your point another way."*

me/you

_ _ **21) Changing the subject** ("defocusing") repeatedly or suddenly, without checking to see if your partner is done. This can imply that your current needs (and dignity) are superior to your partner's. The partner's responsibility is to _ notice the defocusing and how it feels, and _ be assertive about finishing their first topic, if s/he need to. The implied "I'm 1-up" R-message still arrived . . .

_ _ **22) Hinting, or asking leading (indirect) questions** can be OK, or can imply *"I don't trust one of us to deal squarely with my subject."* Having a hidden agenda often results in sending double messages, which usually leave the receiver feeling confused, suspicious, discounted, and resentful.

_ _ **23) Habitual lack of appropriate eye contact,** speaking hesitantly, and constantly apologizing, all say "I feel 1-down now." This may seem OK if the receiver is comfortable feeling 1-up. Over time, this style promotes loss of respect in both people, which breeds discounting, resentments, poor listening, and ineffective communications.

_ _ **24) Habitual nonstop talking** will probably condition regular listeners that the speaker doesn't care about their needs or feelings. The jabberer's real communication need may be to avoid stressful confrontation, surprises, or intimacy (keep their partner emotionally distant), or to avoid scary thoughts and feelings.

_ _ **25) The receiver may become overwhelmed** ("flooded") with information, ideas, or feelings. If the speaker doesn't pause, or if the receiver doesn't assert and ask them to pause, full hearing (and hence effective communications) will stop. This block often happens when the speaker needs to vent, lecture, or moralize without empathically caring what the listener's current needs are (R-message: "I'm 1-up"). Their "awareness bubble" [..02/a-bubble.htm] excludes their partner.

me/you

_ _ **26) Not *making* enough time to talk** clearly and thoroughly about important or conflictual issues. With lives filled with job, parenting, home upkeep, social, and other personal responsibilities, many couples put personal communications low or last in their day's priorities. *"We just don't have time"* is code for *"Communicating isn't important enough to me / you / us,"* or *"Our re/marital communication is uncomfortable."* Who's responsible in your relationships for *making* enough time to communicate?

_ _ **27) Not checking to see if you and your partner each got your real needs met** in key communication exchanges—specially in major disagreements. Omitting this risks one or both of you wrongly assuming that the other is satisfied. "Unfinished business" will increase. Your trust that communications will fill your true needs will probably shrink too . . .

_ _ **28) Unawareness of gender-priority differences**. Research shows typical males and females differ, often sharply, over which priority to focus on in an interpersonal situation. For example, average "female brains" (See "Brain Sex" on p. 557) focus on relationships, cooperation, social harmony, feelings, and understanding, while typical "male brains" instinctively focus on logic, information, "fixing" things, power, achievement, action, and *succeeding* or *winning*.

These priorities are physiologically based and socially imprinted, vs. being consciously chosen and right or wrong! Ideally, males and females recognize these differences respectfully, and meld them rather than trying to convert each other (*"Why can't a woman be more like a man?"*). Also see [*Satisfactions*], [..02/gender.htm], and Tannen (p. 561).

_ _ **29) Denying that you're doing any of these blocks** without honest self-examination is perhaps the most potent communication block of all. Note the difference between informing your partner of a communication problem (implication: "we're equals here"), vs. *accusing* them of causing a block ("I'm 1-up.")

Suggestion: ask if your partner is open to feedback on their communication habits. Agree that feedback on these blocks doesn't mean *"you're bad,"* or *"I'm right."* Most of us were never taught to use these ideas, so we're *learners* rather than *wrong*! See [..02/evc-feedback.htm].

_ _ **30)** Add your own communication blocks . . .

See Resource [K] for ideas on helping each other reduce blocks like these.

Awarenesses . . .

K) Tips for Effective Communication

Help Each Other Fill Relationship Needs

Use this to augment Chapter 7 and reduce teamwork barriers. Your co-parents can raise your problem-solving effectiveness by _ empowering your true Selves (Project 1), _ expanding your communication skills (Project 2), and _ acquiring accurate stepfamily knowledge and realistic expectations (Projects 3 and 4). The more you progress on these, the more often you and your kids can get your true needs met in satisfying ways. In my experience, adapting versions of the suggestions below as teammates with common goals and priorities steeply raises your odds of shared long-range personal and family satisfactions.

These suggestions augment and underlie all those in the Project-2 guidebook *Satisfactions* [xlibris.com]. There are _ general communication tips below, and _ others for high-E(motion)-level situations like conflicts and crises. *Also see* Resources [H-J and L].

Partner below refers to the person/s or subselves you're currently communicating with.

General Tips

1) Check to see if your true Self is in charge of your inner family in important situations. S/He probably is if you feel a mix of calm, centered, energized, light, focused, resilient, up, grounded, relaxed, alert, aware, serene, purposeful, compassionate, and clear. "Self checks" are vital in important situations because false selves have trouble maintaining the =/= (mutual-respect) attitude which is essential for effective communication. To empower *your* true Self, see Project 1. If your partner seems controlled by a false self, see Chapters 5 and 6.

2) Help each other adopt and keep a long-range outlook. Take your time, and aim for "progress, not perfection." Stay aware of your long-term communication trends, vs. (say) the last three conflicts, like "*Yeah, we definitely interrupt each other less and listen to each better since last summer.*"

3) Evolve shared, clear definitions of . . .

"**a problem.**" In this book and series, inner-family and interpersonal *problems* or *conflicts* are unfilled or conflicting true needs (p. 44).

"*effective* (vs. *open and honest*) communication," (p. 509) and . . .

"*effective* problem-solving" (p. 50).

Use these definitions _ to help assess your status on resolving individual inner and family conflicts, and _ to measure your overall progress with building your seven communication skills together.

4) Periodically review your attitudes about *relationships* and *problems*. Read and discuss Chapters 2 and 3 together, as they apply to your unique multi-home family.

5) Assess your current personal priorities honestly [http:/ /sfhelp.org/08/priority.htm]. Suggestion: usually rank your relationship with your partner second only to your integrity, self respect, recovery, and perhaps your Higher Power. Rank everything else third, including kids' needs, except in emergencies. Paradoxically, this puts your kids first *long term* by protecting all of you from re/divorce.

Stepfamily realities will force you co-parents repeatedly to demonstrate your true personal priorities. If bioparents believe "*My children come first*," or "*I don't have to choose between my mate and kids (or ex mate/s)!*", you risk eventual re/divorce because of inevitable loyalty-conflicts and associated relationship triangles (Chapter 16) *despite* your communication skills.

Also, use your *awareness* skill to note how high each of your co-parents usually ranks *effective communication* in their life priorities. Your actions demonstrate your true ranking. Consider that *communication* (including thinking) is the learned skill you all depend on the most to get your respective current needs met . . .

6) Expect to change some core attitudes (Chapter 3), old habits [J], and maybe basic priorities, to build your communication effectiveness over time. If any of you feels "*They* (your other co-parents) *need to change, more than I do*," _ suspect a false-self is in control, and _ lower your Project-2 expectations. Help each other stay aware of the difference between first-order (superficial) and second-order (core attitude) changes, add these terms to your metatalk vocabulary, and teach them to your kids.

7) Help each other build and keep a teammate (vs. opponent) **mind-set**: share responsibility for helping each other fill your respective true needs well. Develop a mutual awareness "bubble" that consistently encloses your current communication partner/s, vs. one or none of you [..02/a-bubble.htm]. Help each other distinguish between *my* problem (needs), *your* problem, and *our* problem. The latter attitude is a clear sign you've developed a real stepfamily identity (Project 3), and are well along in your complex biofamily merger (Project 9).

8) Periodically assess your communication knowledge with this: [http://sfhelp.org/02/evc-quiz.htm]. The answers are in [H], the guidebook *Satisfactions*, and the Project-2 Web resources at [..02/links02.htm]. Option: tailor the quiz and use it to help your kids learn these vital skills. Also, periodically identify and celebrate each other's communication strengths (including your kids)! See [..02/evc-strengths.htm].

9) Study and practice the seven communication skills together (p. 512). Can each of your co-parents _ name the skills now, and describe _ what they are, and _ when to use each of them? If not, you're probably used to communicating at well below half of your potential effectiveness. You're also missing a vital chance to teach your kids these priceless life-long thinking and communication skills. See the guidebook or [..02/links02.htm].

10) Practice identifying *why* you're communicating in important [high "E(motion)"] situations: i.e. help each other develop your awareness of which of the six universal needs you're each trying to fill (p. 508). Grow the reflex of discerning *"What do I need from my partner now, beyond genuine respect?"* Then practice using your awareness "bubble," metatalk, and empathic listening ("hearing checks") to _ sort out your respective communication needs from other (e.g. relationship or practical) current needs, and _ "dig down" below current surface needs to discern your underlying true needs [..02/dig-down.htm].

11) Practice identifying the R(espect) messages you send and receive, in calm and conflictual situations. *Intentionally choose an =/= (mutual respect) attitude* about each adult and child, despite any dissenting subselves (e.g. your diligent *Inner Critic*). Intentionally promote or demote yourself to *equal*, in terms of human dignity and worth, with all subselves and communication partners. Build a Personal Bill of Rights (p. 514). Carry it with you and *use* it, until _ your Self is solidly in charge, and _ other subselves accept your rights as legitimate, and stop feeling anxious and guilty.

12) Practice identifying where your respective E(motion)-levels are, in general, and in conflicts. That requires you to *want* to be aware of your internal and interpersonal communication processes. When any adult or child is "upset" (inner-family conflict), their E-level is "above their ears," so they can't hear well. That means you and they can't problem solve. **Choose** (or ask for) **empathic listening** [..02/listen.htm] to bring E-levels down so accurate hearing can resume. This works with your Self listening empathically to agitated subselves, too!

13) Practice noticing _ your partner's non-verbal communications, like eye-contact, face and body language, and voice inflections; and notice _ how you decide what these mean—in general, and in conflicts. Work to raise your comfort level and vocabulary in talking about your non-verbals together. Some communication researchers feel they cause most of the meanings we decode from each other's behavior, not our words.

14) Help each other build a metatalk vocabulary [..02/metatalk.htm]. The bigger it is, the more effective you'll be at resolving family communication and relationship problems! See the Glossary in *Satisfactions*.

15) Use *awareness* to practice spotting _ ineffective problem-solving strategies at work, and _ communication blocks occurring within you and with others, *without blame*. Use your metatalk skill to discuss and improve both of these. See [..02/awareness.htm] and Resource [J].

16) Learn the differences in how typical "female brains" and "male brains" prioritize relationships and conflicts. Become aware how these differences regularly manifest in your family (and other) relationships: e.g. he needs to *act*: (to fix her problem); she needs to be *heard empathically* and *accepted* now, not "fixed." Help each other use your complementary gender differences together, rather than competing, judging, or trying to change each other to be more like you. See "Brain Sex" by Moir and Jessel; and "You Just Don't Understand" by Deborah Tannen [N]. I find these more helpful than "Men Are From Mars . . ." by John Gray.

17) Help each other learn how to diagram (map) your present communication sequences and patterns (sequences of sequences over time), specially conflicts and "hot topics." Do this _ when your Self is in charge, _ to understand and problem-solve, not blame. Option: Do this periodically to learn if and how you're communication skills are growing. See *Satisfactions* or [..02/evc-maps.htm].

18) Help each other learn how to give each other effec-

tive feedback when _ your partner's Self is in charge, _ her or his E-level is "below their ears," (9 above), and _ s/he's not distracted. Stay aware of *why* you're offering feedback, specially in high-E situations: who's need are you trying to fill? Stay aware of *how* you're giving it. Grow fluency with assertive "I" messages as an effective way of combining feedback with describing your needs See [..02/evc-feedback.htm] and [..02/I-msg-wks.htm].

19) Identify the un/conscious "rules" [*should (not)s, ought (not)s*, and *must (not)s*] your caregivers used to handle conflict in your childhood homes. Examples: "*Demand, rather than request*;" "*Men can get angry and yell, but women can't*;" and "*It's OK to interrupt each other, except with your boss or people in uniforms*." This can help you avoid unconsciously using ineffective conflict-resolution strategies or the polar opposites ("*I will* never *get angry with my kids!*"). Your caregivers probably never had any Project-2 skill training, and modeled ineffective communication for you.

Reflect on "*How did Mom and Dad (or whoever) try to get their core needs met with each other?*", and "*What did they* do *(vs. 'say') when their needs conflicted or didn't get met well enough?*" Consider using siblings, kin, and your caregivers, if available, as resources. Options: _ Diagram their problem-solving process, and compare it to yours now (17 above); and _ recall your caregivers discussions and fights, and use the communication-blocks worksheet (p. 518) to see if you've adopted any of their blocks. What are your kids learning from *you?*

20) Help each other tailor these communication phrases to fit you, and use them to prevent or resolve family conflicts:
"*What's best for our re/marriage (or relationship) here?*"
"*Right now, I need _____ (specifically) (from you)*"
"*I can't hear you when _____*"
"*We problem-solve better when _____*"
"*I really appreciate it when you _____*"
"*I'm getting distracted by _____. Could we stop, and resume this at (some specific time and place")?*"
"*I'm (not) feeling heard (vs. agreed with) by you now.*"

"I'm sorry (about / because / for) _____"

"So you're feeling _____"

"Yes, I'll _____ (be specific)."

"I (don't) need your help with _____."

"What I see (or feel) about our (conversation) process now is _____"

"I love you (for / because / when . . .)"

"I think we have a values (or concrete, or communication, or loyalty) conflict here"

"Is that a request or a demand?"

"This problem seems too complex. Let's see if we can break it into parts."

"My (your) E(motion)-level is above my (your) ears."

"I'm (not) comfortable with that."

"Whoa—that's a separate problem."

"Does that feel like a true need or a surface need?"

"I feel our communication needs conflict now."

"I feel flooded now. Can you slow down / give me some time to digest?"

"When you keep interrupting me, I feel discounted and irritated (and I need you to stop that)."

"I really need to be quiet now."

"Your hands / face / body / eyes are distracting me."

"I'd feel safer talking to you if _____"

"I lose trust in you (or respect for you) when you _____ (describe a recordable behavior factually)."

"Can you find a different way of making your point?"

"You seem defensive now. Are you feeling attacked / blamed / criticized / judged by me?"

"I notice we're talking a lot about the past, (or the future) instead of focusing on the present (and I need . . .)"

"What does (a child or other family member) need (in this situation)?"

"Let's brainstorm: what are your / my / our options?"

"I really appreciate your following through (with . . .)!"

"When you raise your voice (yell / swear / drone on . . .), I can't hear you / shut off / get anxious / want to leave . . ."

"Who do you feel is responsible for that?"

"I feel put-down / discounted / ignored / disrespected / talked-down to now. (vs. "you're ___ing me"). Alternative: *"I'm getting a 1-down (or 1-up) R-message from you now (and I need _____)."*

"I need a break. Can we stop and resume at (a specified time)?"

"When you _____ (do some recordable behavior), I . . ." _____ *(non-judgmentally describe the specific effect on you)— "and I need (specifically) _____ now."* This is called an **"I" message**. They help assert your needs clearly, and minimize the chance that your partner will feel blamed or attacked, unless their false self rules now.

"Did you get what you needed here?"

"So you need / feel / want _____ ."

"What do you need from me now (specifically)?"

"What are we trying to do right now?" (i.e. vent, problem-solve, create excitement, make noise, avoid silence, exchange information, . . .)

"I feel (attacked / blamed / ignored / discounted / appreciated / heard . . .) right now (and I need _____)."

"I need us to refocus on _____ ."

"I'm getting a 1-up (or 1-down) R(espect) message from you. Will you focus on that with me now?"

"I feel really done with (this issue) now. (Are you?)"

"Thanks for _____ !"

"I need a hearing check from you."

"I need to vent now, and problem-solve later. Can you listen to me now?"

"Do you have time to problem-solve with me now?"

"It would help me if you would _____ ."

"Why do you need that now? / What will happen if you don't get _____ now?"

"No, I'm not able (willing) to do that (now)."

"Who's needs do you feel are more important here?"

"I'm too distracted to problem-solve now. How about (another specific time and place)?"

"I (dis)agree", or "I see it differently," vs. "You're wrong!"

"I'm confused: I'm getting (vs. 'you're giving me') a double message from you." (option: summarize both parts)

"Your anger really scares a part of me, and I shut down."

"When you don't look (or you stare) at me as we talk, I feel uneasy (or _____)."

"I need a hug now," or "Can you just hold me for a while?"

"I really need some alone-time (with you)."

"It's hard for me to believe you right now (because . . .)."

"I need to know how you feel about . . ."

"I can't focus with you now. I'm worried / excited / stressed / confused / guilty about . . ."

"It helps me trust you when you _____ ."

"My false self has taken over. One part of me wants _____, and another part wants _____."

"Am I doing something that makes you feel unsafe (to talk intimately)?"

"I need some feedback from you on _____."

"I think we have a (relationship) triangle going here."

"Feels like we changed topics without finishing."

"That works for me!"

"When you choose to be sarcastic, I _____ ."

"I feel caught in the middle (of a loyalty conflict)."

"This is my *problem, not ours / yours / theirs."*

"What have (you / they / I) lost?" (Chapter 12)

"I think (I / we / you) did really good (conflict resolution) work here!"

"I feel that's a surface need. Let's dig for the true needs underneath it."

"I think we have a loyalty / values / stepfamily identity / membership / communication-need conflict here."

"What part of you (of your inner family) was just speaking?"

"I don't understand _____ ."

Note the themes of these phrases, and invent your own!

21) Help each other stay aware of the vital difference between your communication *topics* (*what* you talk about), and your inner and mutual *processes* (*how* you communicate.) Check to see if your and your partner's current communication needs (p. 508) match or clash. If they clash in significant situations, refocus and use metatalk and the other six skills to resolve that, before continuing.

22) Affirm your communication successes promptly, and learn from your "mistakes" without undue guilt or shame. Follow the wise Zen suggestion to "adopt the mind of a student."

23) Consider developing a set of hand-signals and verbal "trigger" words and phrases: a kind of communication shorthand to simplify your conflict-resolution process, over time. For example, if one of you is feeling flooded (overwhelmed with feelings and/or information), you might put your fingers in your ears, or the edge of your hand under your nose, to symbolize *"Whoa! I need a time-out here."* A circled thumb and forefinger or a thumbs-up gesture can mean *"Right on!"* or *"I feel really well-heard by you now. Thanks!"* Some people are more kinesthetic (action and touch oriented) than others, so these kinds of gestures may or may not fit you. Experiment, and see what helps.

24) Identify communication hero/ines: people whom you see as *effective* communicators. Emulate their values and traits to the extent that's useful, without shaming your own efforts or losing your identity. While building your own communication style and effectiveness, identify what they do or don't do that differs from less effective communicators.

25) Use *awareness* to objectively discern what works (fills your and any partner's true needs), and what doesn't. Value and learn from your "mistakes," minimize self-blame, and keep practicing. *"Progress, not Perfection!"*

26) Help each other keep your perspective: raising your communication effectiveness together is one of 11 concurrent co-parent projects toward building a high family nurturance level and satisfying relationships long term.

Tips for High-E(motion) Situations

27) Make sure your Selves are leading. See Tip # 1.

28) Note without judgment whether your ruling subself **sees this high-E situation as an** *opportunity*, vs. a chore, burden, or menace. The latter suggests that a false self is probably in charge. Encourage yourself and your partner/s to invest time in learning from your (me + you + us) communication *processes*, as well as trying to fill your other needs.

29) Do a "distraction" check. If anyone is physically, emotionally, mentally, or spiritually distracted, use metatalk, assertion, and empathic listening to reduce those before continuing.

30) If E-levels rise as you proceed, **assess if your current communication needs mesh** or conflict (p. 508). If not, switch your focus to correcting that. Also . . .

31) Assess what R(espect)-messages you're exchanging with each other. With *inner* conflicts, do the same with your subselves. If unsure, *ask* your partners or subselves if they're receiving credible "=/=" R-messages, or something else. Option: discern which subselves are sending your R-messages, and watch for opposing ones: a symptom of false-self dominance. If either of you gets other than "=/=", switch your focus to improving that if you can.

32) Do an awareness-bubble check. Are you aware of your partner's current needs, feelings, and inner-process as well as your own? Are they equally aware of yours? If not, use metatalk and problem solving to expand your bubbles to include both of you. When you have trouble with this, check for a covert false self. See [..02/a-bubble.htm].

33) Help each other to do supportive (vs. fault-finding or invading) **"hearing checks."** Practice automatically exchanging empathic listening to grow mutual feelings of being really (nonjudgmentally) *heard*. Note that "listening respectfully and attentively" does not necessarily mean *agreeing*!

34) Help each other use *awareness* **skill to differentiate** between . . .

- *abstract* conflicts (values, opinions, preferences, priorities, and needs);
- *concrete* ("thing") conflicts, like cars, checkbooks, and TVs;
- communication-need conflicts;
- conflicts *inside you* (inner-family disputes), and outside you (interpersonal conflicts); and . . .
- present conflicts, vs. those in the past or future.

Resolving each of these can be significantly different. *Mutual problem-solving is much easier if each partner owns and resolves any major inner-family conflicts first!*

35) Patiently use awareness, dig-down, listening, and metatalk skills to unearth your and your partner's current true (vs. surface) needs (p. 44), and who's responsible for filling them. Break complex problems into small ones. Then prioritize those, and resolve them patiently one or two at a time, as =/ = (mutually respectful) partners, vs. opponents. See p. 50, [..02/ prblmslv.htm] and [..02/win-win.htm].

36) Check for black-white thinking: if you're reducing a complex high-E situation to just two either-or options ("*My way or the highway*"), look for false selves at work. There are *always* more than two options!

37) Consider breaking complex conflicts into three parts: _ your inner-family conflicts, _ your partner's inner conflicts; and _ (interpersonal) conflicts between your respective inner families. Use all seven skills on each of these, internal conflicts first, to help reduce or resolve your major *surface* conflicts, over time.

38) If your communication process feels ineffective, **use** *awareness,* **the communication-block checklist [J], metatalk, and listening** to brainstorm what may be going wrong. Adopt an "our problem" attitude, vs. "my" or "your problem."

39) Use communication-sequence mapping to grow your awareness of what's going on, and how to improve it. Watch for repeating communication sequences (patterns), over time. See *Satisfactions* or [..02/evc-maps.htm].

40) Get quiet, and **decide whether focusing on your "still, small voice"** (your wise or spiritual subself), *and trusting what it says*, would help now. If you can't hear it or trust it, commit to learning which subselves are blocking that.

41) If your high-E partner is a child, note your option to model and teach them these basics, guidelines, and skills, starting with the inner-family concept. These are priceless life-skill gifts! You have the same option with adult partners who's Selves are enabled, and want to learn with you.

42) When you've done all you can with a High-E situation, mentally review or journal what you learned, and what you want to remember. Appreciate yourself and your partner (=/= attitude), even if you disagree with them. If helpful, remind yourself . . .

> *"If I always do what I've always done,*
> *I'll always get what I've always got."*
> -Steve and Carol Lankton

> and . . .

> *"Nothing changes, if nothing (in me) changes."*
> -Anonymous

Notice the themes of these 42 communication skill-builders: Self-leadership, awareness, mutual respect (=/=), knowledge, and teamwork ("*our* problem"). Blend your co-parents' creativities to invent your own communication tips!

Awarenesses . . .

L) How We Handle Loyalty Conflicts

Use This to Explore and Improve, not Blame

Read Chapter 16, and then use this with your other co-parents (and older kids) to apply the ideas there.

A stepfamily *loyalty* or *priority* conflict occurs when an adult or child wants to (or must) please each of two or more important people who disagree on something. A classic example is a bioparent wondering *"Who do I side with: my new (stepparent) mate, or my child?"* Such conflicts are frequent and inevitable in low-nurturance and new divorced families and stepfamilies. No one is wrong or bad when they happen! These conflicts feel different than similar conflicts in biofamilies, because they involve *my* child or *your* child, not *ours*. They also often involve ex mates.

Loyalty conflicts can erupt over many things: clothes, money, pets, chores, language, household rules, privacy, worship, vacations, meals, space, attitudes, holidays, rules, objects, grooming, etc. Any adult or child can feel caught "in the middle," and feel that any choice they make, including choosing not to choose, will upset someone important. Loyalty conflicts usually cause or result from divisive persecutor-victim-rescuer (PVR) "relationship triangles." Co-parent Project 9b in *Build a High-nurturance Stepfamily* (xlibris.com) or [..09/lc-intro.htm] and [..09/triangles.htm] proposes options for resolving these common stressors.

This worksheet aims to _ help you learn something about loyalty conflicts in your multi-home family, _ suggest some choices, and _ to promote discussion and problem-solving among your stepfamily members. Use the worksheet to learn, not to blame someone. Find an undistracted place, fill it out, and ask other family members to do the same. Then discuss your findings as caregiving teammates. If you can't do that yet, refocus on resolving the core barriers on p. 109.

Use Resources [H—K] to augment your findings here.

Name three things that cause repeated loyalty conflicts between three or more members of your stepfamily now:

1)

2)

3)

Pick one of these problems. Name the person who feels stuck "in the middle" between two or more other stepfamily members:

Use your "dig down" skill (Project 2) to identify **what does this "middle" person** *really* **need**? Common possibilities: love, attention, respect, listening, to feel valued, reassurance, safety, strokes, validation, affirmation, information, clarity . . . See p. 44, [http://sfhelp.org/02/dig-down.htm], and [..02/a-bubble.htm].

What does each of the other people involved here *really* need?

_____ needs . . .

_____ needs . . .

And _____ needs . . .

How do these people usually try to resolve their loyalty conflict? Check one or more:

_ 1) They _ ignore or _ postpone acting on the conflict, or _ deny it exists.

_ 2) They hold a group meeting and discuss the problem as _ equals or _ unequals.

_ 3) One or more people _ can't or _ won't say clearly what they need.

_ 4) Some people (who?) don't _ care or _ understand what the others want.

_ 5) Someone orders the other/s to do it their way. (who? _____)

_ 6) The group _ cooperatively brainstorms different solutions, _ tries one or more, and _ the conflict usually gets lastingly resolved.

_ 7) The original problem gets tangled up with others, and gets lost after a while (no lasting solution or decision).

_ 8) Other people are called in to help, fight, or decide. (who? _____)

_ 9) Someone (who?) changes the subject.

_ 10) Those involved _ have "=/=" (mutual respect) attitudes, and _ brainstorm an compromise _ using the seven skills from Project 2.

___ 11) Some people _ blame, _ argue, _ plead, _ yell, _ leave, _ whine, _ cry, _ collapse, _ threaten, _ rage, _ get even, _ numb out, _ pout, and/or . . .
   Who?

_ 12) Other typical outcomes:

_ 13) Everyone, _ no one, or _ _____ usually gets what they or s/he wants here.
   If this situation causes a PVR relationship triangle, who fills each of the three roles?
   Persecutor:
   Victim:
   Rescuer:

- Are the people aware of the triangle? _ Yes _ No _ I'm not sure
- If they are, do they co-operatively try to "unhook" from it? _ Yes _ No _ I'm not sure
- Is each of the people aware of whether their true Self is leading their inner family? (Project 1) _ Yes _ No _ I'm not sure.

When the conflict ends, the "middle" person here probably feels . . .

and the others probably feel . . .

The next time this or a similar loyalty conflict occurs, **the outcome would improve if** (who does what differently—be specific):

Options: Periodically scan Project 9 (p. 433) and use this worksheet to assess your family members' progress in mastering loyalty conflicts in and between your homes. You can also use this worksheet to explore loyalty conflicts and relationship triangles (Chapter 16) among someone's *inner* family of subselves. If anyone feels blamed, anxious, angry, or very guilty after using this worksheet, look for deeper problems.

Awarenesses . . .

M) What's Unique About *Stepparenting*?

40 Environmental Differences

Stepparent and *stepchild* are ancient family roles (sets of responsibilities and related behavioral rules), not *persons*. The goals of typical bioparents and stepparents are usually the same: to guide, teach, nurture, protect, and enjoy dependent kids, and help them achieve productive adult independence [sfhelp.org/10/co-p-goals.htm]. The personal traits that promote satisfaction and success at this complex job are the same for bioparents and stepparents [..10/co-p-traits.htm]. These similarities promote the casual assumption that bioparenting and stepparenting feel pretty much the same.

They usually *don't*, because the environments around bioparent and stepparent roles differ in ~40 concurrent ways. These combine to create important psychological differences and developmental phases between bioparents and their genetic kids, and stepparents and residential or visiting stepkids.

The degree of harmony and teamwork among your three or more co-parents will be affected by _ your unique combination of these differences, and _ how knowledgeable and empathic non-stepparent adults are about the differences and what they *mean* to your adults, kids, and _ your version of the five hazards on p. 428. **This resource chapter summarizes four groups of environmental differences** between the family roles of "stepparent" and "bio(logical) parent": _ societal, _ familial, _ personal, and _ the adult-child relationship.

Even with forewarning (which is rare), the combined impact of these four sets of differences over time can make even well-adjusted stepparents and their partners feel inept, "weird", confused, alone, guilty, unappreciated, misunderstood, frustrated, and self-doubtful. Without experiencing this challenging family role, non-stepparents (including bioparents) often find it hard to empathize with what it *feels* like to be a stepparent. Unless they grew up in a stepfamily, *all* your co-parents, kin, and supporters may find it hard to empathize with the complementary role of *stepchild*, and the daunting alien adjustment needs your stepkids have (p. 464). This lack of empathy, garnished with _ lack of accurate knowledge (Chapter 1) and _ unawareness, promote webs of up to 60 unrealistic (bio-family-based) relationship expectations [..04/myths.htm]. *That,* coupled with _ ineffective communication and _ blocked grief, fosters complex, escalating conflicts and stress in and between stepkids' homes. Result: well over half of the millions of U.S. stepfamilies divorce or live in misery.

Most adults in and around stepfamilies have never seen a version of the four sets of environmental differences you're about to read. Use it to help each other grow empathy and realistic expectations for the people taking on your stepparent and stepchild roles.

Community, Societal, and Media Differences

Community and *society* are composed of (friends + coworkers + neighbors + social service professionals + media + laws and court systems + school systems + clergy and churches) . . .

1) Thanks to medical advances, the bio(logical) family is our society's norm, so **"step-" is second class, unnatural, and abnormal**. A common subliminal belief from folklore is "stepmothers are wicked and evil," and stepkids are pitiful victims.

2) There is **widespread ignorance** of _ the ~60 ways typi-

cal stepfamilies differ from intact biofamilies, and _ these related 40 co-parenting-environment differences.

3) **There are few** *informed* **stepfamily or co-parenting books, classes, counselors**, groups, or other supports available in most U.S. communities.

4) Typical **stepparents have no legal parental status or rights** without adopting their stepchild/ren. If they (and their mate) die without a will, usually the stepparent's estate does not pass to their stepkids.

5) **Mother's and Father's Days** and other holidays usually cause role confusion and stress in new stepfamilies. There are few appropriate greeting cards available for stepparents, stepkids, or step-relatives, which breeds awkwardness, confusion, and stress.

6) **There are few** *realistic* **media portrayals** of stepfamily roles and relationships, so far. This promotes low social empathy with, and major misunderstanding of, how stepparents and stepkids *feel*, and what their unique role-tasks are.

7) **Public media usage of stepfamily labels** and role titles is often in/directly denigrating, implying steppeople are second best, outcast, and abnormal.

Family Membership, Culture, and Structural Differences

8) Most nuclear stepfamilies live in **two or more related co-parenting households**, not just one (p. 84). Harmonizing and stabilizing these homes as everyone ages causes many concurrent tasks that intact biofamilies don't face [G].

9) There are **almost 100 structural kinds of stepfamily**, so it's rare to find one like *ours* or *mine*. This can foster anxiety, uncertainty, alienation, and a sense of isolation in co-parents and stepkids, specially new stepparents.

10) Typical biofamilies have up to 15 "normal" roles (uncle, sister . . .); stepfamilies have **up to 15 alien** *new* **roles and titles** (step-aunt, half brother, custodial ex mate, . . .). Stepfamily members must evolve a stable set of *rules* (how to perform the

role) with each of these, with little social guidance or tradition. They often don't have the awareness or language to do so.

11) Compared to average multi-generational (extended) biofamilies, stepfamilies there are **usually more people and relationships**: often 60 to 100+ members. The number of possible relationships this generates is boggling—e.g. a three-biofamily extended stepfamily with 74 adults and kids can have (74 x 73 ÷ 2) = 2,701 relationships! Typical stepparents and stepkids have many more family members to meet, with whom they usually have no common history, memories, ancestors, customs, or shared experiences.

12) **Family *identity* and *membership*** are often more confusing. Definitions of "who's in our stepfamily?" often conflict between members and related homes [..03/members.htm].

13) **New, unfamiliar family and co-parenting tasks.** Most bioparents in intact first-marriage families have few of the tasks in Resources [F] and [G]. They have much less need for the 12 projects in [A].

14) Stepfamily **finances are more complex** because of _ child support amount, regularity, 'fairness", and allocation conflicts; _ asset titles, _ earning, spending, saving, values and traditions; _ insurance coverages, _ prenuptial agreements, and _ wills and estate plans.

15) **Recent trauma and loss**: most new steppeople have experienced divorce or death, re/marriage, and complex biofamily mergers within the past five to seven years. Each causes major changes and losses that need healthy grieving (Chapter 12 and Project 5).

16) **Less and different love**: stepparents and stepkids, and stepsiblings, often don't grow or feel the same kind of love, loyalty, and bonds that biopeople feel. Relatives of re/marrying adults don't initially, or sometimes ever, *love* each other. There are exceptions.

17) **Higher chance for cultural and/or religious diversity**: re/marrying couples are more likely to have differing faiths and ethnic backgrounds than first-marriage partners. This can promote a range from rich mutual appreciation and experience

to inter-home hostility, conflict, rejections, and cross-generational loyalty conflicts.

18) Typical stepfamilies have **weaker bonding**, loyalty, and multi-home family cohesion than intact biofamilies. That can yield less emotional support and security to typical stepparents and stepkids.

19) **Less household stability**, via child visitations and residence changes. Average co-parenting homes with minor kids have two "states:" kids here, and kids visiting. If both remarried mates have biokids, they can have many different "states" (his kids are visiting, hers are home, . . .)

20) **Initially there are no common family history and memories**; and few or no shared rituals, memories, and traditions. The latter often clash between newly merging households and families, creating webs of values and loyalty conflicts, and relationship triangles. Typical stepmoms are expected by society (and themselves) to automatically know how to manage these confusing events.

21) **My, your, or our home?** Stepparents and their kids may feel like invaders or invadees, depending on who's home they're living in. The least-stress option is usually a home new to everyone, if newlywed co-parents can afford that.

How are you doing with all these stepparent-bioparent environmental differences? Are your eyes glazing over? We're not quite half done! Beside societal, media, and familial environment differences, men and women choosing a stepparent role also experience . . .

Co-parenting *Relationship* Differences

22) **Higher odds of co-parents' childhood emotional neglect**, which means higher odds that all your stepfamily co-parents bear major psychological wounds (p. 448). This has *many* important implications.

23) **More co-parents to coordinate**: stepfamilies usually have three or more harmonize, vs. two in an intact biofamily. This implies higher odds of innerpersonal and interpersonal

child-rearing conflicts among the three or more bioparents and stepparents.

24) **A stepparent is never their partner's first marital and co-parenting partner**, which may reduce feeling special at times—specially if the bioparent makes comparisons. The stepkids, ex mate's relatives, and many household items are constant reminders.

25) **Ages**: co-parents are often seven to 15+ years older at cohabitation than first-time bioparents, so they may have different priorities and attitudes on child conception, work, money, spirituality, etc.

26) **Mistaken expectations**: some or all co-parents can wrongly believe their stepfamily co-parenting will feel and be pretty much like bioparenting. When reality harshly proves that wrong, co-parents and kids usually all feel confused and insecure until they adjust. This usually takes four or more years after re/wedding.

27) **Low or no initial child-care confidence**, specially with teens. Childless stepparents and all other stepfamily adults, stepkids, and any involved professionals, can initially distrust the stepmom's or stepdad's parenting effectiveness. Even if stepparents have kids of their own, their new caregiving role is still alien and very confusing.

28) **More parenting "competition"** – ex-mates can disapprove of stepparents' values and choices, or may compete for "best" parent, and vice versa. Kids can instinctively use this to their advantage.

29) **Different child "ownership"**: yours, mine, (and maybe ours), vs. ours. This usually requires all co-parents to evolve strategies to avoid or resolve webs of stressful loyalty conflicts and relationship triangles (Chapter 16). Relatively few counselors, case workers, and mediators are trained to help effectively with these.

30) **Lower child-behavior tolerances**: stepparents often see their mate (and/or their mate's ex) as too permissive. They may get irritated faster at the stepkids than their own (if any), spe-

cially if the stepfamily is using biofamily expectations. The reverse is also possible.

31) **Greater initial motivation**: previously divorced co-parents can vow never to subject their (or others') kids to family trauma and divorce again.

32) **Higher chance for bioparent quilt**: divorced bioparents, specially if non-custodial, can be Disneyland parents during visitations because of guilt over their kids' losses and pain. Stepparents often grow to resent this, if their stepkids seem to come first too often and their complaints are discounted.

33) **More complex child-conception decisions**: many more people and relationships (including financial) are affected [http://sfhelp.org/Rx/spl/ourschild.htm].

34) **More legal caregiving restrictions** (e.g. parenting agreements) **and court battles** over child custody, support, and visitation. Stepparents often are strongly affected by these, didn't cause them, and have less authority, rank, and legal rights in resolving them. Legal fights between ex mates can erupt for years, polarize all family members, and cast *l-o-n-g* emotional shadows. They *always* indicate false-self dominance. See Chapter 18.

Besides social and media, extended-family, and co-parent-relationship environmental differences, typical stepmoms and stepdads also experience many . . .

Adult-Child Relationship Differences

35) **Stepfamilies typically have more kids than intact biofamilies**, so stepparents and bioparents are "stretched thinner" and often have less time alone. the number of kids in a step-home varies ir/regularly with visitations, requiring extra flexibility among all adults and kids.

36) **Lower (or no) mutual acceptance and tolerances**: stepkids and parents may or may not like each other at first, or ever. Stepkids don't choose, and may not want, their stepparents and/or stepsiblings in their lives. They also may be delighted with them!

37) **Stepparents may be more objective and detached** about their stepkids, so stepkids may confide in empathic stepparents before their bioparents. This may breed jealousies and competitions, or gratitude and bonding.

38) **Alien roles I**: stepparents are confronted with _ disciplining someone else's child/ren "fairly'; _ guiding visitations and holidays; _ grieving; _ resolving stepsib rivalry; _ handling rejections and/or feeling "second best;" and _ cooperating with, or handling criticism from, "the other" bioparent/s. Usually no one is familiar with these.

39) **Alien roles II**: Stepparents and their partners need to understand and guide typical minor stepkids in satisfying up to *30+* adjustment needs that kids in intact biofamilies don't have [F], with little or no training, guidance, and support.

40) **Sexuality**: because stepparent and child (and stepsibs) usually didn't grow up together, **the incest taboo in stepfamilies is weaker;** stepsibs may feel sexual attraction that biosibs don't. Stepkids can feel uncomfortable seeing a bioparent physically affectionate or sexual with a "strange" adult—specially if their other parent seems upset about this. See [..Rx/spsc/lust.htm] and [..Rx/sibs/lust.htm].

41) **Confusing titles and names**: what shall step-adults and kids call each other? This varies by home, situation, and person. There are few social norms. Remarried mates may each have a same-name child (e.g. two Davids), and/or a stepparent and stepchild, a stepchild and ex mate, and/or a new and ex mate may have the same first name. Stepparents and stepkids usually have different last names, unless the stepparent adopts [..Rx/spsc/names.htm]. Some re/married biomoms may have different last names than their biokids.

42) **Full co-parenting responsibility, with less authority**: it takes time for stepparents to *earn* the co-operation and respect of their stepkids as persons and caregivers. Stepchild obedience is often lower than in biohomes, as stepkids test their power and status to see who's in charge of their homes. And . . .

43) **Different physical features**: stepparents and stepkids

don't usually resemble each other, which ranges from a non-problem to some stress for someone.

The bottom line: stepparenting and bioparenting *roles* share common goals: to nurture, protect, and guide each child in the family, and prepare them well for adult independence. The co-parenting *environment* in a typical multi-home stepfamily can differ in over 40 ways from that in an average intact biofamily. Co-parents' knowing and *accepting* these differences can help each other and their kids promote _ realistic role and relationship expectations, and _ build an effective co-parenting team, over time. That raises their stepfamily's nurturance level [D], and lowers the odds of passing on psychological wounds to their descendents. Your intentionally learning about _ these environmental difference and _ what they mean is one way to combat the re/marital hazard of *unawareness*.

To copy or show this resource to other people, see [http://sfhelp.org/10/co-p-dfrnces.htm]. Also see [..03/compare.htm], [..03/similar.htm], and [..04/myths.htm].

Option: give each co-parent and key relative and family supporter a copy of this, and all of you discuss what this means to you and your kids.

Awarenesses . . .

N) Selected Readings

The other books in this Stepfamily inFormation series are:

1) Who's _Really_ Running Your Life?—Free Your Self from Custody, and Protect Your Kids (xlibris.com, 2000). This is the guidebook for co-parent **Project 1**: assessing for significant psychological wounds and healing them, over time. Refer to this book when you see [_Who's_] in these chapters.

2) Satisfactions—7 Relationship Skills You Need to Know (xlibris.com, 2002). This **Project-2 guidebook** will help your co-parents build seven skills to communicate and problem-solve effectively—i.e. to get your and other family members' needs met well enough. When your true Self is guiding your other subselves, these skills also help resolve clashes among your _inner_ family. "[_Sat_]" in prior chapters refers to this guidebook.

3) Stepfamily Courtship—Make Three Right Re/marriage Choices (xlibris.com, 2001). This outlines five epidemic re/marital hazards, and seven projects that courting couples can do together to help choose the _ right _people_ to re/wed, at the _ right _time_, for the _ right _reasons_. These choices are suitors' best protections against future re/divorce. This **Project-7 guide-book** is also useful for re/married mates and first-time suitors. References to this book look like _Stepfamily Courtship_. See the free 8-module course based on this book, at [http://sfhelp.org/07/bhsf/intro.htm].

4) Build a High-nurturance Stepfamily—A Guidebook for Co-parents (xlibris.com, 2001). This outlines five more protective projects for re/married co-parents which augment and overlap six prior projects. The 12 projects in these two books aim to neutralize the five toxic re/marital hazards outlined on p. 428, and promote high-nurturance family relationships. References to this book in the prior pages look like [*Build*].

5) The Re/marriage Book—Master Common Stressors Together (xlibris.com, 2002). This is the guidebook for **Project 8**—nurture your re/marriage amidst *many* other responsibilities and activities. This offers clarity and specific suggestions to reduce 10 common stressors, and nine more common to re/married families. This is significantly different than other marriage books in that it posits five combined re/marital hazards, and includes dealing with psychological wounds, ineffective communication, blocked grief, and stepfamily ignorance.

Future volumes in this series include _ a book focused on stepkids and stepparents, and _ a book for human-service professionals on providing preventive education and effective therapy for courting and re/married co-parent couples, kids, and ex mates.

Many of the ideas and resources in this series are also available at the non-profit *Stepfamily inFormation* educational Web site at **[http://sfhelp.org/]**. All the books above include links to extra resources at this site. See other stepfamily-related titles and resources at [http://sfhelp.org/11/resources.htm].

Other helpful co-parenting titles:

Adult Children Raising Children: Sparing Your Child from Co-Dependency—Without Being Perfect Yourself; by Randy Colton Rolfe (Paperback, February 1990). This is recommended by Sierra-Tucson recovery center, and may be out of print. This is about healthy parenting by wounded parents, not stepfamilies. So is . . .

The ACoA's Guide to Raising Healthy Children—A

parenting handbook for Adult Children of Alcoholics, by Dr. Jim Mastrich and Bill Birnes; Macmillan Publishing Co., New York, NY; 1988. The subtitle should read "A parenting handbook for Grown Wounded Children (GWCs)."

Becoming a Stepfamily: Patterns of Development in Remarried Families; by Patricia L. Papernow; Gestalt Institute of Cleveland; 1998. A somewhat clinical, helpful introduction to how typical stepfamilies evolve, and factors that affect that. Richly illustrated with quotes and vignettes.

Brain Sex—the Real Difference between Men and Women, by Anne Moir and David Jessel; 1993. Doubleday Books, New York, NY. A well-researched, controversial explanation for lay people of why "male brains" and "female brains" work very differently. Very helpful in understanding and accepting (vs. resolving) gender-based communication conflicts. This complements Tannen's book below.

Breaking the Cycle of Addiction—a Parent's Guide to Raising Healthy Kids, by Patricia O'Gorman and Philip Oliver-Diaz; Health Communications, Inc., Deerfield Beach, FL.; 1987. This is specially helpful for wounded co-parents in recovery. It's not about stepfamilies per se.

The Dance of Anger, by Harriet G. Lerner, Ph.D.; 1985. Harper and Rowe, Publishers, Inc., New York, NY. Though slanted toward women, this is a helpful book for anyone wishing to express and use anger constructively.

The Different Drum—Community Making and Peace; by Dr. M. Scott Peck; Touchstone books reprint, 1998. The author of "The Road Less Traveled" shares wisdom from his extensive work at facilitating group (community) development and harmony. Very helpful for harmonizing your *inner* family (Project 1)!

Embracing Each Other—Relationship as Teacher, Healer, & Guide; by Hal Stone, Ph.D., and Sidra Winkelman, Ph.D.; 1989. New World Library, San Rafael, CA. An extension of their first book, examining how the subselves ("inner voices") within partners interact together.

Embracing Your Inner Critic—Turning Self-criticism Into

A Creative Asset, by Hal Stone, Ph.D., and Sidra Stone, Ph.D.; 1993, Harper, San Francisco, CA. Using the ideas in their other books, this suggests how to befriend and convert your *Inner Critic* into a steadfast ally. What a concept!

Games People Play—the Psychology of Human Relationships, by Eric Berne, M.D.; 1996. Ballentine Books, New York, NY. A reissue of the 1964 classic on how we (our false selves) plot covertly to get our true needs met with other people.

The Good Stepmother—a Practical Guide, by Karen Savage and Patricia Adams; Crown Publishers, Inc., New York, NY; 1988. One of many titles for stepmoms. For more, see any of the growing number of Websites for stepmothers [http://sfhelp.org/11/resources.htm].

Growing Up Divorced—Helping Your Child Through The Stages . . . ; by Linda Bird Franke; Linden Press, Simon & Schuster, Inc.; New York, NY; 1983. Timeless.

Healing the Shame That Binds You, by John E. Bradshaw; 1988. Health Communications, Deerfield Beach, FL. The most practical, useful book I've found on identifying and converting shame into self-respect and self-love. Doing this is essential for effective assertion and problem solving. Also see *The Six Pillars* below.

Healthy Parenting—an Empowering Guide for Adult Children, by Janet G. Woititz, Ed. D.; A Fireside / Parkside Recovery Book; Simon & Schuster, New York, NY; 1992. A wise, clear text for co-parents striving to break the Grown Wounded Child psychological bequest. (Not about stepfamilies.)

How It Feels When Parent's Divorce, by Jill Krementz. A poignant glimpse as described by a group of individual girls and boys.

How To Win As A Stepfamily, by Drs. John and Emily Visher; 2nd ed.; Brunner/Mazel, 1991. A classic, from the dedicated co-founders of the Stepfamily Association of America. No focus on personal healing.

If You Could Hear What I Cannot Say—Learning to Communicate With The Ones You Love; by Dr. Nathaniel Branden;

1983. Bantam Books, New York, NY. An insightful paperback and workbook.

The Language of the Heart—the Body's Response to Human Dialog, by James. J. Lynch, 1986. Basic Books, New York, NY. Out of print, and worth searching for.

Living In A Stepfamily Without Getting Stepped On—Helping Your Children Survive the Birth-order Blender; by Dr. Kevin Leman; Thomas Nelson Publishers, Nashville, TN; 1994. Helpful perspective on how kids' and adults' birth-orders can make stepfamily-mergers more challenging.

Making It As a Stepparent—New Roles, New Rules, by Claire Berman; Harper & Row, New York, NY. A classic, updated in 1986. Berman is a former president of the Stepfamily Association of America.

Making Peace in Your Stepfamily—Surviving and Thriving as Parents and Stepparents; by Harold H. Bloomfield, M.D., with Robert B. Kory; Hyperion Books, New York, NY; 1993. Provides many clear, practical suggestions, from a veteran stepfather and clinician.

Money Advice for Your Successful Remarriage—Handling Delicate Financial Issues With Love and Understanding"; by Patricia Schiff Estess; Betterway Publications paperback, 2nd ed.; 1996. Patricia is the remarried founding editor of Sylvia Porter's Personal Finance Magazine, and a Board member of the Stepfamily Association of America.

The New Peoplemaking," by Virginia Satir; Science and Behavior Books, Inc., Palo Alto, CA; 1988. A paperback update of the classic on healthy personal and family relations.

People Skills—How to assert yourself, listen to others, and resolve conflicts; by Robert Bolton, Ph.D.; Prentice-Hall, Inc., Englewood Cliffs, NJ; 1979. Selected by the American Management Association, and totally applicable to couples and families. Bolton outlines five of the seven skills in Project 2, and omits some keys: inner-family harmony, digging down to true problems, awareness bubbles, and R(espect) messages.

Second Chances—Men, Women, & Children a Decade After Divorce; Who Wins, Who Loses, and Why; by Judith S.

Wallerstein and Sandra Blakeslee; Houghton Mifflin Co.; 1996—2nd ed. (follow-on to "Surviving the Breakup" below). This book was controversial because it painted a gloomy picture, from imperfect research. I think it's worth reading, though the authors make little mention of the family trauma that always precedes separation and divorce, or it's early roots.

The 7 Habits of Highly Effective People—Powerful Lessons in Personal Change, by Stephen R. Covey; 1989. Fireside Books, Simon & Schuster; New York, NY. An acclaimed framework for living life effectively. It works—*if* your Self is solidly in charge!

The 7 Habits of Highly Effective Families—Building a Beautiful Family Culture in a Turbulent World, by Steven Covey and Sandra Merrill Covey; Golden Books Co.; 1998. Recommended on the clarity and practicality of Covey's best selling "The 7 Habits of Highly Effective People."

The Six Pillars of Self Esteem, by Dr. Nathaniel Branden; Bantam Books, New York, NY; 1995. A classic on healing old shame, which is vital for building effective assertion skill. *Also see Healing the Shame* and *Who's* Really *Running Your Life?* (above)

Self-Esteem: A Family Affair, by Jean Illsley Clarke (Paperback, 10/88). Ms. Clarke's work is highly regarded by family-health professionals. Applies to all families.

Stepfamily Realities—How to Overcome Difficulties and Have A Happy Family; by Margaret Newman; New Harbinger paperback, 1994. By a veteran Australian stepmother, therapist, and educator, this is one of the two best stepfamily books I have read in 23 years of research. The other is "Becoming a Stepfamily" by Patricia Papernow (above).

Stepfather, by Tony Gorman; Gentle Touch Publishers, Inc.; Boulder, CO. 1985 (2nd Ed.). One of the few books for inquiring stepdads. There are a few Web sites for stepfathers now.

Stepkids: A Survival Guide for Teenagers in Stepfamilies, by Ann Getzoff and Carolyn McClenahan; Walker & Co., New York, NY. 1984. A classic.

The Stepfamily: Living, Loving, and Learning, by Elizabeth Einstein; Macmillan Publishing Co., Inc., New York, NY; 1994. A classic by a devoted stepfamily educator. Includes nothing on healing inner wounds, as the "Adult Child" movement was just starting at this time.

Stepfamilies—Love, Marriage, and Parenting in the First Decade; by James H. Bray, Ph.D., and John Kelly; Broadway Books, New York, NY; 1998. Readable findings on a major multi-year research project.

Surviving the Breakup—How Children and Parents Cope With Divorce, by Judith S. Wallerstein and Joan B. Kelly; Basic Books, Inc., New York, NY; 1982. Useful perspective for understanding and healing prior divorce wounds.

You Just Don't Understand—Women and Men in Conversation; by Deborah Tannen, Ph.D., 1990. Ballentine Books, New York, NY. A readable, practical paperback on the differing communication styles of men and women, by a down-to-earth linguistics professor.

For more recommended titles and stepfamily Web sites, games, and newsletters, see [http://sfhelp.org/11/resources.htm].

Index

P

Q

R